THE ESSENTIAL BOOK THAT FILLS THE GAP BETWEEN CHANCE AND SKILL

John Scarne is universally recognized as the world's leading authority on cards. Not only is he a proven master of every card game, but his writings, lectures, and films on how to spot cheaters have saved countless players from being bilked by the sharks who prey on the unwary.

SCARNE ON CARDS represents the sum total of John Scarne's experience in the card world. In language every layman can understand, it gives the complete rules of card games ranging from poker and blackjack to hearts and cribbage. It clearly describes the various tricks of professional cardsharps and how to foil them. Perhaps most important of all, it sets down the guiding principles and central strategies that can make you a winner at the game of your choice. Signet is proud to publish a paperback edition of this world-famous guide.

♣ ♣ ♣

Scarne
ON CARDS

Revised, Augmented Edition

BY JOHN SCARNE

Illustrations by George Karger

♣ ♣ ♣

A SIGNET BOOK

SIGNET
Published by the Penguin Group
Penguin Books USA Inc., 375 Hudson Street,
New York, New York 10014, U.S.A.
Penguin Books Ltd, 27 Wrights Lane,
London W8 5TZ, England
Penguin Books Australia Ltd, Ringwood,
Victoria, Australia
Penguin Books Canada Ltd, 10 Alcorn Avenue,
Toronto, Ontario, Canada M4V 3B2
Penguin Books (N.Z.) Ltd, 182-190 Wairau Road,
Auckland 10, New Zealand

Penguin Books Ltd, Registered Offices:
Harmondsworth, Middlesex, England

Published by Signet, an imprint of Dutton Signet,
a division of Penguin Books USA Inc.

First Printing, December, 1973
24 23 22 21 20 19

ACKNOWLEDGMENTS

I should like to express here my appreciation for assistance in the preparation of this book to Steffi Storm, Clayton Rawson, Guy Bellubuono, Audley Walsh, Bert and Mac Feinson, Dr. Ben Braude, Matty Sabato, Anna Klunck, George Brown, Red Burnett, Ira Zweifack, William Kelleher, Dr. Alan Barnert, Peter Musto, Frank Moore, George Starke, Howard Wurst, Rufus Steele, Francis Carlyle, Edward Walker, Evelyn and Arthur Martinetti, Charles Feinhals, Bob Esposito, Ben Dalgin, and to W. G. Kessler for the proofreading.

I must also thank the many thousands of World War II servicemen whose questions first indicated to me what it is that people need to know about the games we play.

And for authoritative and uselfish assistance in the formulation of the answers, I must express for all of us my gratitude to the operators of casinos in Nevada—especially Elmer West, manager of the Palace Club in Reno—and throughout the United States; and to many gamblers and one-time card sharpers who, through celebrated in their calling, shall remain anonymous in these pages.

 REGISTERED TRADEMARK—MARCA REGISTRADA

Printed in the United States of America

Contents

INTRODUCTION

to the Revised, Augmented Edition

It is now some 16 years since *Scarne on Cards* was first published. In that time it has gone through nine printings and has provided guidance for many thousands of card players. But with millions of Americans playing cards it was inevitable that, although probabilities and percentages remain the same, there would be some changes in the popularity of the different card games and also some changes in rules. It is because by now these changes are substantial and important that I have prepared a revision of *Scarne on Cards*.

The most important change in rules is in Black Jack, and I have written a whole new section on this popular game. Also Hearts, Cribbage, Kalabrias, and Casino have acquired new fans and new popularity, and therefore I have added full sections on these classic games. I hope that every card player will find in this new, revised edition of my book the guidance he wants on the games of his choice.

JOHN SCARNE

Fairview, N. J., *March, 1965*

A FOREWORD

After the last woman has been sawed in half, after the elephant has been made to disappear, after the last brood of chicks has been made to appear in a spectator's pocket, the magicians will sit around for hours in their magical headquarters and talk about the simplest of all effects.

In the trade it's called the Scarne effect. It's known as in another field the Einstein theory is known.

From an unprepared deck of cards, thoroughly shuffled and cut, John Scarne simply proceeds to cut an ace. That's all there is to it. It is thoroughly undramatic. There's not a gambler, honest or larcenous, that wouldn't give his right arm for mastery of it.

There's a reason. In the late stages of a grueling game, in the small hours of morning or well along toward noon next day, players will be desperately tired enough to risk all they have on cutting a single card. The ability to cut the card he needs would put a man on easy street. Gamblers, knowing this, have tried by mechanical means to imitate the Scarne effect: they crimp their aces, or coat them with floor wax, or resort to the use of strippers. It's risky. It's going to be considerably riskier after this book gets out across the world. They'd much prefer to be able to walk up to a brand-new deck, bore into it with an X-ray eye, put a surgeon's thumb and forefinger on its sides, and produce that earth-shaking ace. But it's quite a problem: it is in capsule form, all the problem there is to magic.

Scarne got to thinking about it. He worked out what he thought might be a solution—or, rather, *the* solution. Here's how he tells it. One night he diffidently dropped the Scarne effect into a program he was giving at a party. He asked for a new deck, shuffled it once or twice, and asked someone to cut a card. The fellow cut a jack.

"Better than average," said Scarne, "much better; but if this was for a thousand dollars it wouldn't beat . . ."

He had cut the deck. He exposed his bottom card. It was the ace of spades.

Two distinguished-looking men in evening dress snapped themselves out of their chairs and converged on him. Scarne was proceeding to finish the little stunt he'd worked up. He was cutting—the ace of hearts, the ace of diamonds, and (you may be sure) the little ace of clubs.

He went on with his act. One of the men in evening dress picked up the deck of cards, examined it minutely, closed his eyes and felt the edges of the cards and then their surface, and finally dropped the pack in his pocket. He glanced at the other man, and almost imperceptibly shook his head negatively.

The show ended. The guests departed—all but two. The second of these waited for Scarne at the door.

"My card," he said. "I'm having a little party at my hotel tomorrow night, Mr. Scarne. I'd like my guests to see your act. *Be there at nine.*"

It meant *command performance.* That was quite a while before Fiorello. The man in evening dress was Arnold Rothstein.

That was a pretty blasé crowd at A.R.'s apartment in the Park Central next evening. These people had seen card tricks from time to time; among them, they'd done most of 'em—for what's known as a pretty penny—in a pinch. They were just barely polite until, along about midnight, the single-minded Rothstein got up and said, "Would you cut for high card with me, John?" Then conversation stopped dead.

A.R. stripped the wrapper off a new deck of cards and handed them to Fats Caldwell, who gave them the gambler's feather-fingered, low-wristed shuffle. George McManus cut the pack, and stepped back. "Yours, Scarne," said Rothstein very quietly. John Scarne riffled the deck once. "Yours, Rothstein," said he.

A.R. cut the ten of hearts.

Scarne squared the deck, cut, and showed his bottom card.

It was the ace of spades.

The silence crashed, longer and more shattering than any applause. Every man in the room had lurched to his feet and moved up around Scarne. McManus picked up the deck, examined it darkly, shuffled, set it down, stood back, and said, "Again."

Scarne did it again. Again a dead silence followed his production of the boss ace. This time Rothstein, looking troubled, himself shuffled, himself commanded: "Again."

Scarne did it again. He could have gone on doing it all night, but he had been hired to work a show, not run a vocational school, and at 1 A.M. he went home, leaving seven urbane men in pious disputation.

Gamblers are, in a queer way, an honorable lot. Those seven could in good conscience watch what it was that Scarne did; they could pool their common knowledge and technique and attempt to duplicate it; but they could not in decency admit before each other that this stranger knew something about their racket which they didn't know. They could offer to buy the effect. They couldn't ask to have it explained. They could simply say, "Again!" Then it was their business to analyze and reconstruct how it was done.

That's where Scarne left them that night. Evidently the process of analysis and reconstruction didn't go too well. Scarne's phone rang next morning. It was Rothstein. "As you might have assumed," he said, "I happen to be giving another party tonight. You're hired again."

As you must have assumed, the same seven men were there, and they went right ahead from where Scarne had left off the night before. McManus cut the cards, stood back, and said, "Again!"

Silently there under the glare of lights John worked . . . and worked. He worked seven nights in a row for Arnold Rothstein at $200 a night— $200 an hour for practicing what he liked to do best—and at last one of A.R.'s men broke.

"All right," he blurted, "that's enough; now, how do you do it?"

Scarne had expected it. "The only possible way," he said. "You notice I always give the deck one riffle myself. When I do it I count the cards so I can see the indices. When the ace falls I just count the number of cards that drop into place on top of it. Then when I cut I count down that number of cards and break the deck there, and of course there's the ace. That must be obvious now, isn't it?"

There was a long silence.

"If that's it," Rothstein said, "it's uncanny."

"You can do it easy, if you practice three or four hours a day, in—hmm—twenty years," said Scarne affably.

"And you're how old?" murmured McManus.

"Nineteen. But," John Scarne added hastily, "I've been practicing ten hours a day."

Look. That night, twenty-two years ago, Scarne could have sold that effect for enough hard cash to put a prudent man into comfortable retirement for the rest of his life expectancy. But there's a stubborn streak of pride in Johnny Scarne, a kind of fierce honesty that maybe even bankers or ministers wouldn't quite understand. He can't be bought. I know people who've tried to buy him. He can't be scared. He broke up a multi-million-dollar gambling racket in the World War II training camps, and made enemies of buzzards as dangerous and crazy as any Hitler, and laughed at their threats.

Scarne uses no apparatus except ten steel-spring fingers and fifty-two playing cards. He moves up close, and instead of distracting your attention with glib business he insists you concentrate. He likes to work right under your nose. You know why, of course. There's the lee-e-etle ace of clubs up your left nostril. . . .

He seems to have started fooling with cards when he was about twelve years old. At an open-air Pinochle party (coupled with clambake) in his native Fairview, N. J., he happened to observe with interest that a well-known pillar of Jersey society who made a habit of winning also made a habit of abstracting certain discards from the table and nipping them under his knee joint. A mellow light burst upon little John. He skittered home, and practiced the knee hold-out, and invented a couple of improvements that would have edified and saddened the pillar of society. By the time he was fourteen years old he couldn't buy his way into a Pinochle game in Fairview. By the time he was fifteen he was haunting the vaudeville houses where the late and great Nate Leipzig played. "But I've been practicing ten hours a day," he told Rothstein, remember? . . .

By the time he was nineteen he was ready. Late one night after a show Nate Leipzig walked up to the desk in his hotel to get his keys. There at the desk a dark young man—looking a little more like Humphrey Bogart than Humphrey Bogart looks—was showing the night clerk a card trick. Leipzig was interested. Scarne had rather thought he would be. Leipzig bent close to watch those sinewy small hands. Scarne liked that. He likes to work under people's noses. You know why.

"Come on up to my room," said Leipzig after an hour of this. The King of Cards was a courtly and generous man. Loudly enough for the night clerk to hear, he added: "I want you to show me some card tricks."

It was Nate Leipzig who, with the endorsement of another Scarne convert, the late Harry Houdini, once put his signature to the statement, "John Scarne is the most expert exponent of wonderful card effects and table work that I have ever seen in my life." Said John Northern Hilliard, manager of Thurston and an authority on magic and its priestcraft:

"A sleight-of-handster when most boys are manipulating marbles, Scarne knows every turn and twist of his craft. He practiced with sedulous perseverance, and the result is a mastery which is unsurpassed."

During World War II at the War Department's solicitation Scarne acted as games and gambling consultant to "Yank," the Army newspaper.

He has been called into consultation as an expert by the Federal Bureau of Investigation, the New York City Police Department, and law-enforcement agencies throughout the country.

John abandoned his own career for the duration, and toured Army and Navy bases lecturing on crooked gambling and teaching G.I.'s how to protect themselves against card and dice cheats.

He was credited by such persons as Admiral Ernest J. King, Navy commander-in-chief, and General H. H. Arnold, the Air Force's commanding officer, with saving servicemen millions of dollars in potential gambling losses. The gambling trade ruefully certifies this estimate.

There is no short cut to card skill. But if you like to play and like to win, if you think no game's worth playing unless it's worth playing well, then I give you into the steady, practiced hands of the— ahem, terrific—citizen who speaks to you out of the pages of this text.

WILLIAM A. CALDWELL

Hackensack, N. J., March, 1949.

Part One

CHAPTER ONE

Introductory

There are four kinds of gamblers at cards:

1. The occasional player, who knows little or nothing about the hard mathematical and psychological facts of the game on which now and then he hazards his money. This player constitutes the vast majority. His losses make cards one of America's big businesses.

2. The card hustler, who knows a little more about the game—any game—than the occasional gambler, and who looks on the latter with elaborate contempt. The hustler makes most or part of his living from the occasional gambler's errors.

3. The professional gambler, who earns his living (or most of it) by operating a card game. Gambler? I don't quite mean that in its dictionary sense. The professional doesn't gamble; he is a businessman who understands his trade, who runs a house for direct levies on the games or for fixed percentages which are his overhead for maintaining a pleasure resort. I have a grudging respect for this professional. He charges what the traffic will stand, but no more; he provides a service; and you can't hold his political acquaintances against him. Since he takes part in a game of chance, he is known as a gambler.

4. The crook, the cheat, whose gamble is not in winning or losing, but rather in getting away with it or getting caught.

To the average card player the man who makes his living by cheating at cards is a sharper, sharp, or shark, but to card hustlers and house men he is known as a *mechanic*. It is a tolerably descriptive word. Card mechanics are the masters of a dull, utterly unglamorous trade; they spend their spare hours at exacting practice; they know no game but their own; they are about as interesting and adventurous as the drunkard who tries to chisel the price of a drink.

There is in cards about the same proportion of honest and dishonest people as there is an any other field. The ratio varies a little from game to game, from state to state, just as it varies in legitimate enterprise. You encounter more sharp practice in war contracts, say, than you do in the personnel office of a theological seminary. Likewise you find that a game which tends to encourage self-policing is less populated by crooks than a game (say, Gin, or Stud Poker) which tends to lull chumps into unwariness.

There aren't many foolproof safeguards against the crook. He may be caught with a bottom-dealt ace in his hand occasionally and be black-listed or beaten up, but this is one of his occupational hazards, and he knows how to deal with it: by moving to the next game. He is least apprehensive about the law. It is all but impossible to convict and jail a crook for cheating at cards.

Sure, occasionally a bamboozled player may stop payment on a check after he has gone home, has tossed through the night, and has realized that he was probably robbed by dirty means. But it doesn't happen often, not often enough to drive the cheat out of business. Most amateur card players get a stealthy masochistic pleasure from paying a debt to a gambling crook—one's honor, you know, and all that.

Is it any wonder that card cheaters stay up nights and pace the daylight streets riddling an angle; that year after year they practice at sleight of hand and distracting illusions; that they invent and have made for them crooked decks, mechanical holdouts, mirror gadgets, and their many other quaint devices? It's no wonder at all. They want your dollar.

In the end, by the way, they get it—one way or another, by fair means or foul. If they weren't getting it, they'd be extinct. And they aren't extinct.

This book is written for Class One, the average citizen, Joe Doakes, who likes to play cards for stakes—small or large. He is the lamb that the other three classes of gamblers are trying to fleece.

When Joe plays with friends he knows well, he has an even chance if his ability at the game is about the same as his friends'. This is the *only time he has an even chance to win.* If he is less expert at the game, he'll have less than an even chance. If he's a better player than his friends, he'll have a better than even chance.

All this is obvious, and naturally we all want to improve our skill at the games we like to play. I have crammed into this book all the cardplaying savvy and skill I have accumulated during many years of association with the country's best gamblers and card players. In fact, this book will improve the chances to win of every card player, even those who play "social games with close friends only."

The only important card game I have not covered in detail is Bridge. I think the game of Bridge is already excellently covered in the existing books on the subject. Nevertheless, Bridge players also will be helped a great deal by the chapters on cheating and cheating methods.

But *nobody plays only with close friends.* Think that over. Let me remind you of what happens. One of your friends brings along a pal, a visiting fireman from Duluth. Of course you'll let him get into the game. Or you're the visiting fireman and your friend takes you along to his game. Or you're on vacation and somebody stirs up a game. You know most of the players pretty well and the others certainly look all right. Why not play? You do, and there's no reason why you shouldn't, except that's how Class Two or perhaps even Class Four may get into your game, if you're not on guard, and you don't know how sharpers and cheats work.

Since as a practical matter you cannot always play with the same people, there is the chance that some time or other there will be a hustler (Class Two) or a cheat (Class Four) in your game. What can you do about it? How can you detect it and avoid being a sucker for him?

Please note the distinction between the cheat who is strictly dishonest and the hustler whose only crimes are not against the law: he plays much better than you and he earns at least part of his living by winning from you.

Human nature makes it difficult to detect the cheats and the hustlers. You hate to think the other fellow is a better player than you. "He's just lucky. All right, he was this time, but he can't be that lucky always. Next time I'll get him!" Unless the other fellow mentioned above is a good close friend, look out for that kind of thinking. The fellow who wins regularly may be a cheat or a hustler.

The ways to beat the cheat are covered in the chapters in Part One. Also, with each game I discuss I describe methods of cheating particularly applicable to that game. The reader's attention is directed particularly to the description of professionals' international signs described in the section on "Cheating at Draw Poker," page 289.

The way to beat the hustler is to choose either of these alternatives: (a) improve your skill to equal or surpass his; or (b) stop playing with him. Many years of observation have convinced me that the second alternative, apparently so simple and easy a solution, is the much more difficult choice to make for the reasons mentioned above. If, in fact, you have chosen the first alternative, I will try to help you all I can, in later chapters.

What about the professional games? What about Class

Three? Well, you know you don't have nearly an even chance. The house percentage will surely beat you if you play long enough, though it's true that in any one session you can come out a winner. Also, the amount of house percentage varies on different bets, in the different games. In the discussions on each game I will give you these percentages and show what the house cut is so that you'll know at least where your best chances are.

I think I know most of this country's big-league blood-suckers. I shan't blow the whistle on any one of them by name. The observation of crooked card players is my business, as the observation of subhuman primates is the anthropologist's, and I'll continue to live and let live. But for what it's worth to you, I'm going to tell you about them. Then I wash my hands of it.

I can't agree with my learned book-writing friends that the discussion of cheating has no legitimate place in the proper study of games. Some of them, being cloistered and naïve, argue that there aren't enough card cheaters at large to warrant exposure of their methods. Some others, not quite so naïve, contend that disclosure of hustlers' and crooks' techniques will nurture a saddening suspicion of innocents. Let us say some opponent fails to offer you the deck for the cut and you draw his attention to the omission; let us say he has a peculiar way of dealing, now with his palm up and now with his palm down and always with impressive effects, and you ask him to avoid this eccentricity. He is offended. A beautiful friendship ends. This, in a world too full of distrust and bitterness, would be a Bad Thing. So say my learned friends.

I cannot subscribe to this rubbish. There is no excuse for illegal play at any money game, just as there is no excuse for illegal practice in any human relationship. If a man isn't prepared to abide by the rules, then innocent as Little Eva or guilty as Satan he deserves the humiliation coming to him. He should obey the law or get out of the game, and let's not have any false consideration of personal friendship obscure the issue. It's a sound maxim: friendship is out the window when the cards are on the table. Moreover, the most honest, ethical, fastidiously high-minded games I've ever seen were games played between top-notch gambling men exhaustively learned in all the mechanics of cheating.

When pros play, they play on the level. Why? Because they play in the atmosphere in which virtuous, virtuoso card-playing can thrive, the atmosphere of total and icy distrust. They cheat not, because they dare not. The game is clean—or else! Relevantly enough, the War Department, which tends to take a rather worldly view of things, allowed me during World War

II to expose in the official Army weekly, *Yank,* the various crooked gambling moves. The Army seemed to agree that the "or else—!" atmosphere was more wholesome than the condition of partial innocence which up to that time had been costing G.I.'s literally *tens of millions of dollars a month.*

CHAPTER TWO

Card Cheats and Their Methods

If all card players knew how to spot a cheat at work there would be no cheats.

There are both amateur and professional cheats. I call the amateur by that name only because he is commonly a back-alley pantaloon and bungler, not because he doesn't cash in on his crookedness.

If all card players could detect a pack of marked cards, then marked cards would become useless and extinct.

The only way in which cheating can be stopped or reduced is by every player learning to defend himself against it.

The only way in which I can conceive of bringing this about is by the exposure of every known cheating method.

I think I know them all. Here we go. In the following material I propose to detail every artifice, gadget, manipulation, distraction, and device used by cheats. If after reading them you still think you are being cheated at cards, let me suggest to you the joys of marbles and hopscotch.

Stacking the Cards

There is the popular delusion that when a deck is stacked, i.e., when certain cards have been put in certain positions in the pack for a crooked purpose, every card is in its special place and the gambler knows exactly where it is.

The sharper does not live who can riffle the pack and retain in his memory the location of every card. Nor does the sharper live who can stack five or more cards for two or more hands—without previous preparation of the pack.

The truth is—and remember it, whether your game is a beery bout of Showdown in a ginmill or the most recondite

Contract Bridge at an uptown club—that a cheater can clean up by knowing simply the location of a very, very few cards. As a matter of fact, knowing—absolutely knowing—the position of just one card of the fifty-two will give the skilled cheater an amazing advantage.

Never overestimate a crook. Don't expect him to work miracles. Just expect him to work, hand in and hand out.

The Pick-up

The pick-up is the sharper's most foolproof way of stacking the cards. It requires no special skill; it rarely fails; it is hard to detect. You're a cheater, and you're playing Poker. The next deal is yours. At the end of the game just concluded five hands were exposed. Examining them not too obviously, you have seen that in each of those hands is one card you'd like to have for yourself in the next deal. Let's say there are four jacks and a deuce, one card in each hand.

So you stack the deck in such a way that you'll now deal those five cards to yourself. Impossible? Why, it's not even improbable. As dealer, you make it your business to pick up the cards on the table. You pick them up a hand at a time, and as you do so you put the card you want at the bottom of each group of five cards. Then you put all five hands together at the top of the deck, and, after some flummery about shuffling and cutting which you take good care to keep from disturbing the position of the top twenty-five cards, you deal. Naturally you get cards Nos. 5, 10, 15, 20, and 25, the four jacks and the deuce you want.

That's darned near all there is to stacking as it's generally practiced. Professionals use it for most of the card games covered in this book.

The Riffle Stack

The riffle stack is one of the most difficult of card-stacking methods, but the cheater who has perfected it is by all means one of the most dangerous of adversaries. If you think you've detected an opponent making one of the moves indicative of this stack, beware—you're up against a practiced, unscrupulous, and perhaps even desperate man, be his game Poker, Bridge, Black Jack, or one of the Rummies.

WHAT'S BEING DONE

The cheater has, say, the four kings at the top of the deck. In the act of riffling (shuffling) he has to cut the cards into two blocks or groups. It is during the shuffle that he interposes cards between the kings so that in dealing—which he will do on the level—he'll get the spaced kings and his opponents will get cards at random. It may take him three or four riffles to count off the cards as he wants them; but, if the riffle is his specialty he can and will do it in a single move. The result he gets is the same as the pick-up's, only it's less likely to be detected.

WHAT TO LOOK FOR

This stack is almost detection-proof, but you do have one way of suspecting it; and, if you can't correct matters by forcing the cheat out of the game, you can protect yourself by forcing yourself out. As a rule cheaters, when shuffling the cards, will riffle the lower half of the deck fast and then slow up when they get near the place where the kings lie. And they must keep their eyes intently on the cards when they're counting them into place. Riffling in this syncopated tempo and a too scrupulous regard for the cards are your danger signals. He may not be a riffle stack expert, but he's acting like one. Look out!

The Overhand Stack

The overhand stack is the stumblebum cheater's best friend. It is used, I've observed, in kibitzing cards from here to Mexico and back the long way, more extensively than perhaps any other stacking device. It doesn't involve as much skill as the riffle stack or as much risk as the pick-up.

The cheater places *on the bottom of the deck* the cards he wants. Then he shuffles the cards, slipping one card off the bottom of the deck and one card off the top at the same time. The shuffle goes from the right hand to the left, and this stack is executed once for each card you want stacked. As your left hand takes the top and bottom cards, you shuffle out of your right hand two cards fewer than the number of players in the game. When the correct number of cards have been stacked, the cheater throws the cards in the left hand on top of the cards in the right, and the deck is ready for the deal as described under the pick-up stack.

False Shuffles

False shuffles are absolutely essential in the arsenal of the accomplished cheater. A man who can false shuffle may look as if he's giving the cards a thorough riffling. He isn't. He's keeping the entire pack or a group of crucial cards in the order in which he picked them up from the table. The most popular and disastrous of these shuffles is the

PULL-THROUGH

This very dazzling and strictly crooked shuffle is executed as follows:

When a hand of cards has been completed, the cheat scoops the tabled cards into his hand, taking most special pains not to disperse the certain melds or discards he wants. These he places at either the top or the bottom of the pack. The device is useful too when a pack has been stacked already and must be shuffled and dealt as is. Now for the pull-through!

The cards are riffled—correctly; no question about that. But watch the dealer in the split second when he has to block together the cards in either hand, assemble the split pack into a single pack. Does he shove them together into a squared-up deck, as he should? No. With a motion probably quicker than the eye, he pulls the cards from one hand *through* the cards from the other, then whips one bunch back on top of the other.

Although the cards have duly clattered against each other and made the noise and appearance of a shuffle, actually they have not changed positions at all. Reassembled, they are in the same position as they had been when the pull-through started. Not a single card has changed position. It only looks as if they have. That's the way it's supposed to look. . . . And you're supposed not to look.

Nullifying the Cut

The most dangerous hazard in the professional career of any card cheat is the cut. Let's glance again at the way you ordinarily cut a pack of cards. The dealer pushes them over toward you and says, "Cut, Mac?" You take a block of cards off the top of the deck and put them on the table, and the dealer completes the cut by putting the bottom block on top of your cut block.

The cheater's assignment is to get the cards back into their pre-cut position swiftly and undetectably.

He does so by *crimping* or *shifting*. Let's study these moves a little more minutely.

CRIMPING

Crimping is used more commonly than *shifting* in Rummy —or any other of the popular card games for that matter— because it is (a) easier (b) almost invulnerable to detection by the untrained or unsuspecting eye.

The crimp left by a good, as it were, cheater, is so very slight that the naked eye can hardly detect it at all (the tactile sense is much more sensitive to this sort of thing), and as a rule the crimp is put in the card only on that edge of the pack that faces the cheater. The idea is that a competent crimp is literally invisible and undetectable to anyone except the cheater himself.

Though this crimp is so fine that it can hardly be seen, it is sufficient to cause the pack to break eight times out of ten exactly where the cheater wants when it's cut by the unwitting stooge. Why? Because the average player generally cuts the cards at about the middle of the squared-up pack, and that's where the cheater put the crimp.

Eight times out of ten, did I say? Well, the earnest professional makes it ten out of ten in any card game involving more than two players; his confederate sits at his right and cuts the cards.

But how is the crimp used? The dealer stacks himself three kings by any of the devices set forth above. He may complete his crooked shuffle with the pull-through; in any event he has his critical cards where he wants them, and he wants them to stay there. But the cards have yet to be cut. And an honest cut would bury those cards in the middle of the deck. So . . .

The sharper gives the pack one more crooked shuffle. As he does so, he gives the top block of cards a fast crimp, then does a quick cut, bringing those cards down to the middle of the deck with a little gap or bevel at their top edge. Now the regular cut is made. The cards break at the crimp. The stacked cards come back on top, and one player at least is happy. Or . . .

The dealer uses the crimp plus sleight of hand to slip the cards back into position after a really honest cut. Here's how. Before the cut, he crimps the top cards. After the cut, he uses the crimp to break the cards where he wants them broken; then he slides his own cards back on top of the deck by sleight of hand.

And that is called

SHIFTING THE CUT

The move, while no particular challenge to the exhibition card manipulator showing off his hobby, is most difficult under pressure at the gambling table. There are many shifts—remember, this is a manipulation restoring the cards to their original position *after* the cut—and there are many shifters surviving in this evil world, but I think I can say without fear of contradiction that the cheater doesn't live who can execute this move undetectably without a *cover-up*.

ONE-HANDED SHIFT

The cards are slightly crimped, just enough to indicate to the cheater's sensitive fingers exactly where to shift the cut. *This move cannot be made without a cover.* Thus the cheater distracts attention by reaching for a cigar or cigarette, sneezing, or, *in extremis,* spilling a drink—while he shifts the cards under his arm with his free hand.

THE TABLE SHIFT

This shift must be done with lightning speed. It is very deceptive when done competently, but it must be done rapidly, in a single sweep of the hand. The block of cards the cheater picked up in his right hand is shifted to the bottom instead of the top of the other block.

THE TWO-HANDED SHIFT

The two-handed shift is a favorite with professional magicians, but it is used by many unpretentious gamblers. The cards having been cut, the cheater demurely puts the lower block on top of the upper, but he doesn't place them there quite squarely; instead, he leaves a step, an infinitesimal terrace, to act as a guide when he picks up the assembled pack. His little finger is inserted at the step, and the shift is executed.

Mechanic's Grip

Almost all *seconds* or *bottom dealers,* as well as what the trade calls *holdout men* (cheaters who palm cards), use the mechanic's grip on a pack of cards. In this grip the index finger is used to square up the pack when a second or bottom card is dealt.

Whenever you see an opponent holding a pack this way, it's time to reach for your hat and remember a date away at the other side of town . . . or to use the Scarne cut (see page 16).

Here's the tip-off. The player who holds a pack of cards, whether in left or in right hand, with three fingers * curled around the long edge of the cards and the index finger at the short upper edge toward you, is a player who probably knows entirely too much about cards. It is not inconceivable that an honest, even innocent, player might hold cards with the mechanic's grip. But it takes a good deal of practice to hold a pack this peculiar way. Don't get excited when you spot the

---

* Some mechanics keep two fingers curled around the long edge of the deck and two around the short upper edge.

lodge grip across the table. Just act cool and friendly, as if you'd found a man practicing at blowing your safe.

Dealing Seconds

Any second dealer of standard model in good repair can and will take the best of honest card players. His name—ordinary gamblers call him a second dealer and specialists of cheating call him a *No. 2 Man*—describes exactly what he does, which is as follows:

The thumb of the left hand, in which the pack is held, pushes the top card forward as if to peel it off and deal it with the right hand.

But the thumb of the right hand darts in and slides out the second card, the No. 2 card, instead.

The left-hand thumb then retracts the top card to square with the pack. It is a split-second co-ordinated act, and when it is done skillfully, even just competently, it cannot be detected.

Some cheats deal seconds with one hand. To do this without being detected, the cheat must turn over the pack while pretending to deal the top card.

But second dealing is impossible and useless *without marked cards*, and herein lies your defense against this line of attack.

If the cards aren't marked the talent isn't worth a plugged nickel—unless the dealer peeks or uses a stacked deck. Dealing seconds is profitable only when the dealer finds a marked card at the top of the pack and wants to by-pass it, saving it for himself or a confederate.

When you suspect this deal, make it your business to examine the cards, not too ostentatiously, for markings.

Bottom Dealer

Bottom dealers, called *base dealers* by crooks, will win your money in a hurry. Even though it takes years to learn the skill, there are entirely too many practitioners floating around.

The bottom dealer saves time because he doesn't have to fuss around stacking the cards. He puts the cards he wants on the bottom of the deck, preferably by some such device as locating them there when picking up the previous deal's melds and wreckage, and he leaves them there through some phony shuffle. Then—it's easier said than done—he deals your cards off the top and his off the bottom. There's a foolproof defense against him. It's the Scarne cut, which loses the carefully iced bottom cards away up in the middle of the pack.

Nearly all bottom dealers use the mechanic's grip on the pack; so you can be suspicious when you lose consistently to a man who holds the deck this day.

Middle Card Dealing

The chances of your colliding with a cheater who can deal cards from the middle of the deck may be calculated roughly at a million to one. To execute this deal smoothly is perhaps the most difficult of all the moves of the modern card cheater. I happen, after twenty-odd years of practice eight hours a day, to be able to deal middles without the move being detected; and so I assume there must be a few others who can do a competent job at it. On this assumption I warn you: when a cheater has mastered middle-dealing he is about as dangerous as a man can get with a deck of cards in his hands. He has by-passed the ticklish business of shifting the cut. Assembling the cards after a hand and leaving the cards he wants at the bottom of the deck, he offers the pack to be cut. It is cut, sure 'nough; but the expert crimps a break where the two blocks of cards are put together again, and proceeds to deal himself from the middle of the deck the card or cards he needs to win.

Check Cop

At the hazard of meddling with a prospering private-enterprise small business, I'd better tell you about this chemical preparation which, smeared on the crook's hand, makes a chip or coin adhere to his palm when he helpfully pushes a pot toward the winner of the hand. "Here you are kid; they're all yours," he says, shoving the winnings across the table; only a dollar's worth of chips or so per shove adhere to his hand when he withdraws it from this amiable gesture. Crooked gambling-supply houses sell for this weird and lucrative specialty a liquid chemical they call *sure cop.* But experienced crooks, always amateurs in the true meaning of the word, make a thing of their own which they call *check cop* by heating a piece of adhesive tape and scraping onto their palm the gummy stickup stuff. It works. Isn't that all that counts?

Some cheats cop chips with sleight of hand while pushing the chips to one side with the hand holding the cards.

Second Dealing Box

The second dealing box is a crooked card box that enables the cheater with minimum chance of detection to deal the second card instead of the top card. It's useful in dozens of card games. These boxes are made by nationally known manufacturers of crooked gambling devices, and sell for what they're worth to the cheater—say, $50 to $150.

Read what one manufacturer has to say about this crude flimflam:

"Our second dealing box is used for various card games. Skeleton type, it is substantially made, with a dull nickel finish which absolutely prevents any flash of the bottom card when dealing. This box bears the most rigid inspection, but at the same time the top card is always under control."

The only thing that is crooked—or has to be crooked—about this box is that it enables the top card to be shifted toward the inside edge of the box, so that the cheat can take the other edge of the second card and deal it. The box is useful only with marked cards, since the point of dealing seconds is to hold back firsts for oneself.

A second dealing box can be spotted instantaneously. Unlike other dealing boxes, whose tops are wide open, the second box has a solid sheet of metal on its top side. Through this sheet is a small hole to enable sliding cards out with the thumb while dealing legitimately—and sliding them back when dealing a second. If you ever get into a game in which the dealing box looks like the one just described, the odds are—let's see, now—twenty-five to one that you're playing with a crook.

Palming

Palming cards, called by cheaters *holding out*, is in all probability the cheating method most commonly practiced and most commonly suspected and detected. Like sex, it can be learned by almost anybody, but doing it well requires some native talent and assiduous practice.

Palming is risky in fast company, but among half-smart card players it can be put to fairly profitable use in almost any kind of game.

It is done as follows:

When the cards are being thrown in for a new deal—it works for any game involving a deal: Poker, Rummy, Black Jack, Pinochle—the cheater secretes the cards he wants in the hollow formed by the palm of his hand. He may hold the hand folded nonchalantly over his arm, or he may conceal the cards under his knee or armpit. The move is normally screened by the cheater's reaching into his shirt pocket for a match or hitching his chair closer to or farther from the table.

Having been dealt his new hand, the cheater substitutes his palmed—or, to be precise about it, armpitted or kneed—cards for an equal number out of the hand, making use of the palm.

Then, biding his time, he gets rid of the cards he's holding out by chucking them back at the end of the deal or palming them into the discards.

DETECTION AND SUSPICION

Keep a respectful eye on the player who keeps his hand rigidly flat with the fingers close together.

False Cuts

False cuts are in order when cheaters move in on card games involving more than two players. The false cut requires a pair of confederates. One deals. The other sits next to him. The latter, when the cards are offered to him, false-cuts. A false cut is one which leaves the deck or a block of cards in the deck in exactly the same position as before the alleged cut.

The false cut can be used in any card game. And it can be worked by a man playing alone without allies—if the other players, going on the assumption he's cutting his deals honestly, don't call for the deck, as is their right, and cut it themselves.

But good use can be made of the false cut on the honest player's deal too. How?

Well, you're honest and awkward. When you shuffle, you fail (a lot of us do fail) to mix thoroughly the cards on the bottom of the pack. The cheater detects something down there he wants. *Or* he glimpses the bottom card during the shuffle, and decides he wants it. *Or* he has just palmed some cards onto the top of the deck, and wants them dealt just so. But the cards must be cut. So, when you hand him the pack for a cut, he employs one of the following most commonly used false cuts:

ONE-CARD FALSE CUT

Very deceiving. The cheater cuts so that only the top card changes position and is sunk in the center of the pack. The rest of the top cards remain as he wants them.

TWO-HANDED FALSE CUT

Although many honest players cut like this, train your re-flexes to beware of the man who makes a series of rapid cuts with both hands, pulling off the top block and putting it on the table, slipping the bottom block on this, then whipping another block out and snapping it on top, etc. This false cut is executed with great snap, and the only way of apprehending it is to watch for a visible step in the deck.

To neutralize this ruse or to avoid any possibility of trouble, ask (as is your right) for the deck and reshuffle it yourself, cut it, then offer it to your opponent for his cut. By that time his dexterity can't make any difference.

Slick Ace Cards

These decks, sold by gambling supply houses for $1.50, allow the user to cut the card desired, usually an ace. To cut an ace, the cheat must give the deck a slight shove. The deck will break at one of the aces. Then he cuts that block at the break and he has an ace as his cut card.

An ordinary deck of playing cards is prepared by waxing the aces, or any cards desired, making them slide easily.

To detect, watch the guy who always shoves the deck before cutting.

Cold Deck

The cold deck is a pack of cards which the cheater stacks with larcenous intent before the game starts, or one which the cheater leaves the game to stack. It is switched into play at the magic moment when there are important stakes to be won.

The cold deck must, of course, be an exact duplicate in color and design of the deck in play. The object of the move, in case there are any men from Mars in the room needing enlightenment, is to insure the crook a killing hand and send the rest of the jolly company home broke.

Among the approved methods of switching them into play:

The prepared deck may be dropped onto the table from under a tray in the act of serving drinks.

A holdout machine may be used, although handling the machine requires some skill. Not many up-to-date crooks use it because of the risk and because of the fact that possession of the gadget is prima facie evidence of absolute guilt. A man using the mechanic's grip or a two-handed cut may be innocent, or can at least raise a persuasive defense; a man caught with a holdout machine can at best try to get out of town in one piece.

The commonest and cleanest cold-deck switch is pure, simple sleight of hand. The sharper slips the cold deck out of his pocket into his lap. Drawing the pack on the table toward him for the deal, he drops it tidily into his lap, in the same motion snapping the cold deck into its place at the table's edge. After the deal the old pack is wrapped in a handkerchief, already spread in the lap, and stuffed away in a pocket. A paroxysm of sneezing, a loud joke with gestures, or a spilled drink will screen the move.

Maximum winnings are obtained by switching the cold deck in the sucker deal. Just as the sucker offers the deck to be cut by the cheater at his right, the cheater 2, at his left, asks the sucker to change a bill. Cheater 1, who has palmed the cold deck in his left hand, covers the deck on the table with a handkerchief, places the cold deck on the table and then pockets the original deck neatly wrapped in his handkerchief. When the sucker turns to pick up the deck for the deal, cheater 1 executes a false cut, putting him at ease. The sucker is now ready to deal himself to the cleaners.

Locater

The locater is a special breed of cheater. I've seen locaters hang around the edge of a banking game for hours without making a play, only to bet the wad and win at just the right instant. Their racket is simplicity itself. It is a matter of keeping track of a single card or group of cards through deal, play, and shuffle; deal, play, and shuffle; over and over. It is not a skill; it's drudgery; but it is particularly profitable in such games as Black Jack, Faro, Chemin de Fer, and Stud Poker. The locater, to repeat, simply gets to know where in the pack his card is; then he bets when that card comes up right for him. The defense against him is to shuffle thoroughly and often, to shuffle the cards face down *on* the table *flat against* the table, and to memorize the following move:

The Scarne Cut

This is a cut which I invented during World War II for the defensive use of men in the armed forces. It will work against any of the ruses set forth above, with the exception of the cold deck switched in after the cut. I'm told by Army officers that this cut alone saved G. I. Joe millions of dollars between 1942 and 1946.

This is how the Scarne cut works:

1. Pull a block of cards out of the center of the pack.
2. Place them on top of the pack.
3. Do it again, and again, and as many more times as you like.
4. Then—and then only—square up the pack, and cut it in the regular manner.

Properly and regularly used, this cut will prevent or neutralize most cold-deck switches (most, not all), stacked cards, the crimp, false shuffles, false cuts, and shifts. At the very least it will give your crooked opponent headaches enough to mini mize his effectiveness. It may frighten him into getting out of the game or, worse, into playing honestly.

Shiners

Shiners are nothing but mirrors, and they make me wonder again why gamblers have to invent mock-fancy synonyms for the crooked tools of their trade. These mirrors, generally very tiny, are built into rings, match boxes, pipes, coins, or anything else that will lie unobtrusively on a card table. A shiner in a pipe bowl, for instance, reflects the top card of a deck being dealt. Antidote: take a good look at any object on the table when you're losing. If you pick up a nickel and see your own face on it . . .

Peeking

One of the cleanest and least detectable ways of reading a top card off the pack is by peeking. Some cheats peek while dealing a player a card, others peek when pretending to look at the face-down card of the hand. Peeking is used in many card games, but is particularly effective in Black Jack and Stud Poker. A good peeker and second dealer is poison to any card game. To detect peeking, suspect a player who continually keeps looking at his face-down card.

PEEKING ON THE DRAW

Spotting the next to the top card of the stock pile by lifting the second card while picking the first card is used by both the bungler and the expert cheat, particularly used in Gin Rummy and other Rummy games, and in Two-Handed Pinochle when drawing from the stock. Keep your eyes on the player who seems to hesitate always when picking from the stock.

The Amateur Cheat

Now, what constitutes a cheater at cards? I myself am sometimes, after all these years and meditations, perplexed about a player: shall he go into my book as a scoundrel or as just a thoroughgoing no-holds-barred good player? I used to play Gin Rummy with an elderly lady, a business acquaintance of mine, who might be characterized as straddling this borderline. She has a habit, after the cards have been cut for her deal, of peeking at the bottom card in squaring the pack. Harmless? Yes. She's looking at a card that will never get into the play of the hand. Harmless? Ye-e-es. But her very knowledge that this card is dead gives her a measurable percentage of advantage over me in planning the play. She has seized relevant evidence that is not available to me.

She is a cheat.

And she is the most dangerous kind of cheat, the amateur kind. For the amateur cheat is generally your friend. You are not going to mistrust him. You are not on your guard. So the amount of money that you lose—you collectively, all you good-natured American suckers—runs into an aggregate millions of dollars.

For every dozen crooked moves made by the agate-eyed professional, the amateur cheat will attempt blandly and brazenly a hundred swindles.

1. The amateur cheat in Gin Rummy will attempt to lay off on a meld a card that doesn't belong in that meld, *or* will discard two cards instead of one, *or* will call his count for the scoresheet as an amount less than it actually is, *or* . . .

2. The amateur Poker cheat will just forget to ante up, and then will swear earnestly that somebody else is shy.

3. The amateur cheat in Pinochle will fabricate five or ten points on the count of the hand. Trapped in a recount—any embarrassment? Not a bit! We're all entitled to a certain percentage of error, aren't we?

4. Finding the dealer panicky or busy, the amateur cheat at Black Jack will call a phony count on his cards, collect his cash, and account the feat an act of skill. Never even pinks his conscience!

I'm going to refer in detail under each game to the more common methods of cheating at that game but let me try to suggest a few general principles.

Never accuse any man, particularly a friend, of cheating. It is highly possible that an honest player may do quite unconsciously some of the things that cheaters do. You have no right, and there is no need, to raise a hue and cry. The application and enforcement, quietly and graciously, of the rules as I've stated them in this book will remedy whatever's wrong or looks wrong. If it doesn't help, you can stop playing then and there, quietly and graciously. No offense, no harm done, to anyone's sensibilities or reputation—or especially to your pocketbook.

Rules are made to be followed—or broken revealingly—by players. A friend told me once: "John, I play with a good friend of mine. He never offers me the cards for the cut. I'm afraid to insist on the cut; he may think I'm accusing him, and I value our good relations. What shall I do?"

I asked him who was the winner between them, and he said his friend was a few hundred dollars ahead.

"I don't know whether your game is lousy or you're being

cheated," I told him. "I've never seen you play. But this I do know: that if you were cutting the cards you would not be suspicious of your friend. That's a lot worse than losing a few dollars."

You must decide such things for yourself. As for me, I play by the rules—I play no more with the old lady who peeks at the bottom card.

CHAPTER THREE

Marked Cards

The mechanical device most widely used by cheats, be they amateurs, semipros, or skilled professionals in any card game, is the use of marked cards:

1. They require no manipulative skill.
2. They are sure-fire money winners.
3. They are all but totally immune from detection by the average easygoing, relaxed, aw-the-hell-with-it card player.

(Not in one case out of a hundred would the novice know how or where to look for markings even if he were handed the deck and told that they were there.)

Markings on a card seldom indicate its suit. It would require too elaborate a code to mark suits as well as values; it would be too confusing to the cheater; so cards as a rule are marked only as to numerical value.

The cheater using "readers" or "paper" knows the rank of every *top card* coming off the deck. He can identify—as to value—every significant card in your hand. Your chances of winning in such a swindle, playing what amounts to an exposed hand, are plainly next to zero.

Marked cards are commonplace because they are easy to get. The catalogues of marked-card merchants are widely distributed—through the United States mails, to be sure—by suppliers of crooked gambling devices; although if you tried to run a raffle for your boys' club Mr. Whiskers would pin your ears back. Crooked gambling machinery's a business too, you know. A cheat may get his toupee knocked off informally for playing with marked cards, but there is no law in these United States that prohibits the marking of cards. So free enterprise, bless it, functioning in due reaction to the law of supply and demand, goes on grinding them out, grinding out crime and misery and maybe even suicide. A pack will cost you $1.50. They sell in the thousands per week.

Though you buy the pack yourself from a retailer you know and trust, it may be marked. On one festive occasion that I remember every pack in Saratoga was crooked. A mob had moved in and switched a case of marked cards in place of a case of cards just shipped by a big and legitimate distributor. The marked cards were duly jobbed and retailed. No matter where a player bought a pack of cards that week, they bore the mob's markings. I have been told, almost reverently, that what happened after that was pretty impressive.

It is a common misconception that cards are marked when printed. They aren't. Reputable manufacturing houses would never consent to such stuff. Nevertheless their cards are used in crooked games—and are marked, like this:

First, the cheat buys an honest deck of standard brand.

Next, he heats the revenue stamp and removes it.

Third, he removes, also under gentle heat, the tissue wrapper of the pack.

Fourth, the cards are marked by hand. (Some plants have as many as fifty girls employed just to mark cards.)

Finally, the marked cards are replaced in the tissue wrapper which is then tidily pasted; the cards are restored to the box, and the revenue stamp is glued back.

Markings on readers or paper are known as *light work* or *strong work*. If a sharper has what he believes to be a smart and alert opponent he will use light work; if he sizes the opponent as a sucker, the strong work goes in. If the cheat is an amateur, strong work is required; if he is a professional, the light will do.

Light work is a finer mark. It imposes more strain on the user. Strong work can be read generally all the way across the table, always up to five or six feet away by anyone with normal eyesight who knows what he's looking for. More ink is used, that's all.

Cards are invariably marked along opposite edges, either horizontally or vertically, so that the cheater can read an exposed edge regardless of the position of the card in the hand.

Regardless of the design of the card and regardless of the cheating system involved, all card marking falls into one of these five kinds of work:

Edge Work

A slight bevel or belly is drawn on the border between the design and the edge of the card. A mark high up indicates an ace. A mark a little lower indicates a king. And so on down.

Line Work

The finest possible lines are worked into the design on the back of the card. The innocent eye can scarcely detect a difference, but the cheat knows in an instant what the card is.

Cut-out

A chemical preparation or a fine knife removes a minute section from the design at the significant place.

Block-out

The same thing—almost. Parts of the design are covered with white ink or the figuration of the design is exaggerated with ink similar to that in which the design is printed. This is especially effective with cards that are calculated to be mark-proof: those that have an all-over design on the back, with no border. An example is the so-called Bee card, the back of which is completely covered with a diamond design. Contrary to popular belief, such cards can be marked easily and effectively by making one of the diamonds smaller or larger than the rest by blocking-out.

So much for cards whose backs bear actual marks. How about marked cards that *are not marked?*

Shading

A section of the back of the card is worked over lightly with a brush, leaving a slight coloration over the identifying part of the design. The ink used is similar in color to the design. Always remarkable in this kind of work is the infinitesimal area spotted and the delicacy of the mark. Yet sharpers can see it across the table.

Trims

This process is used on cards that do have a border between the design and the edge. The border is trimmed—away down on one side for low cards, say, and a little higher for the higher ones (or the other way around). The amount of white space between design and edge is trimmed to less than regulation size, and the amount of the trimming signals whether the card is high or low. Of course, the way to detect a trimmed card is to place it over an honest one. The trim will be smaller.

Sorts

If you want a full-time job for a rainy week-end, or a rainy week, try making up a pack of sorts. When you're done you will think that sorts are so much trouble that nobody would ever bother with them. You will be wrong. One week spent on a pack or so of sorts will guarantee months and months of winnings. Gamblers, many of them, consider it well worth their while. *Sorts are the only marked cards that are not actually doctored,* hence they are the safest of all marked cards. Sorting is based on the one flaw in Bee cards and others with all-over designs. This flaw is the edge. The all-over design does not run off the edge at precisely the same point on every one of such cards. There are bound to be variations along the edges: some designs will go off the edge high on the diamond figure, others close to the bottom, others at varying points midway between. Knowing this, the earnest cheater buys some forty or more identical packs of these foolproof cards. Out of the lot of them he laboriously sorts *one* pack which can be read by the edges. High cards may be those whose diamond design is sliced off high, low cards those sliced off low; or it may be the other way around. Whatever are the markings he decides upon, these cards are easy to read for the man who knows they're crooked and hard to detect for the man who doesn't. All you can do, if you suspect sorts, is to see whether the edges of high cards are all high and the edges of low cards are all low.

Cards with over-all designs can be trimmed to make fake sorts.

How to Detect Marked Cards

To detect marked cards use the Scarne riffle. It is based on the principle of the animated cartoon books with which you played as a kid. Holding the book firmly in one hand, you riffled the pages rapidly with the other thumb. And, as you did, the figures printed on the pages seemed to move. It's the principle on which the motion picture is based.

Try it on any cards which you suspect may be marked by any of the methods set forth above. Hold the cards in the left hand. Pull back the cards with the right hand and riffle them rapidly, keeping your eye on the back of the design. An honest design will stand utterly still. If the cards have been marked, a shifting of lines will appear on the backs. When this occurs, note the exact spot where the shift took place, and compare it with the like spot on other cards.

Pictures

Here's another thing you'll have to remember. Don't play with cards on whose backs are pictures or designs which, when the cards are reversed, will be upside down. A beautiful picture may delight your emotions, but upside down it may signal "High cards!" and right side up "Low!" It seems obvious, but Edgar Allan Poe isn't the only man who knew that the more obvious a device is, the less likely it is to be discovered. If nothing else, card cheats are good psychologists.

Luminous Readers

These are so called because they are marked with an ink invisible to the naked eye and are supposed to be legible only with special glasses or a special visor. Strictly a sucker's item, they are advertised by the manufacturers of crooked gambling supplies as being the last word. When you send your $10 or $15 you receive by express (these boys don't use the United States mail) a red-backed pack of cards that have been gone over very lightly with a green pencil. A large number is made to denote the card's value. Along with this you get a cheap pair of glasses with red-tinted lenses. The theory is that red glasses will cancel out the red design and the green mark will blaze out for you alone.

Professional cheaters wouldn't be caught dead with such junk. But in case you encounter some imbecile who has bought them and is trying to get back the money he paid for them, borrow his glasses or his visor, and look at the cards yourself.

Marking Cards During Play

Cheats are scientists. When they can't work their pre-marked cards into a game—which is what they would much prefer to do—they proceed methodically to mark the cards during the game. This is, to be sure, more dangerous than using cards already marked, but it is not so dangerous as playing with an honest deck.

NAILING

Pressing his thumbnail into the edge of a card, the cheater makes a small identifying mark which can be seen from across the table. He has to put this mark at precisely the same relative position on opposite edges of the card so that, no matter how the card is held, the nailing will appear.

WAVING

In this variety of play-as-you-go card marking the practiced fingers of the gambler skillfully bend the card, over one finger and under the other, leaving an identifying "wave." The position of the wave indicates the value of the card.

(*To detect nailing or waving,* square up the whole pack and look at the edges. The markings will stand out unmistakably.)

DAUBING

The cheater carries in his vest or coat pocket a tube of paste or paint similar in color to the color of the design on the cards in use. Moistening his finger with the color in the act of reaching for a cigarette or match, he presses a tiny spot onto the card at a significant place in the design. The daub is a slight smudge instantly legible to the cheater. Daubing can be detected by the naked eye on deliberate examination.

PEGGING

Another marking method gives signals to the fingers, not the eyes. The sharper appears in the game with a thumb or finger bandage. Generally it is the left thumb, which holds the pack most often. Through this bandage sticks the point of a thumbtack that has been strapped to the thumb under the bandage. With this point the crook pricks the right cards in the right places. In Gin Rummy he will ordinarily prick only the low cards, aces to threes. When, as dealer, he feels a low card on the top of the pack, he deals a second (see page 11) to the other player, and saves the pegged card for himself. To detect pegging run a finger over the backs of the cards. A "peg" will feel like a mountain.

SANDING

Also requires a bandage—for a different purpose. Exposed through the fabric is a slit of the surface of a piece of sandpaper. A card is drawn edgewise across the sandpaper, and the sanded edge becomes white, a glaring clean white. When assembled with the other, dirtied, cards, this sanded card stands out clearly enough to enable rigging the deal. Occasionally, a cheat will merely paste a piece of sandpaper on his finger instead of using the bandage technique.

Belly Strippers

The use of this device is one of the most highly prized—and high-priced—secrets of fast-money winners. Especially useful in two-handed games such as Pinochle and Gin Rummy, it cheats the sucker on his own deal, and accomplishes the swindle by merely cutting the cards.

Once more, give all the credit to the go-getting American businessman. Manufacturers and distributors of marked cards and crooked dice stock this belly-stripper deck as one of their standard items. It sells for $2.

Suppose you want a deck out of which you can strip the four kings. All right. The other forty-eight cards are cut down about a thirty-second of an inch on both long sides. Then their corners are rounded again. They look perfectly innocent, and they are, except in conjunction with the four kings.

But these precious cards are sliced at an angle, so that they have a very slightly protruding belly at the middle of each long edge, and slightly narrower than the other cards on the ends.

Now assemble the deck. In the right hand, tap it upright on the table. Then lift the right hand up and away. Behold! The four kings' bellies have caught against your fingers, and you pull those cards out of the deck. Some crooked gambling supply houses sell concave strippers.

What you do with them now depends on your game and your move. You can deal seconds; you can shuffle them into position to deal yourself a winner; you can deal your opponent two kings and yourself two, and then lure him into a disastrous round of betting. Just knowing where the kings are is all a competent gambler needs to win heavily.

Antidote? Just pick up the cards, square them, and see if any belly strippers come out of the pack. If they do, what's your next move? Don't ask me! But you might try asking for your money back.

As to marked cards I can give you only one over-all tip. To catch "paper" cheaters in any card game, watch the guy who has to keep his eyes glued on the back of your cards, the cards that are being dealt, and, if it's a Rummy game, the top card of the stock. I like an opponent who keeps up a natural healthy interest in the cards, but there's a subtle line of demarcation between a wholesome concern about what's going on and a concern that amounts to cannibalism. I can't tell you at what point an opponent's interest goes morbid. I *can* suggest that, next time his concentration seems to you unwarranted by the current situation at the table, you start taking a scholarly interest in the deck yourself.

And beware of the player who continuously, against all the tables of probability, in defiance of your own instinct for averages, wins and wins and keeps winning. I lay this down as a broad general dictum: *that's not luck.*

CHAPTER FOUR

The Only Player You Can't Beat

I would rather have spared you and myself the writing of this chapter, but we'd better face the facts about playing cards for money. And one of these facts is the cheat you never catch at his work against you, the cheat you never escape, the really international card sharper, that prince of good fellows—yourself.

You'll never be a consistent winner at cards unless you learn the little tricks you play on yourself.

You'll never win unless you devise ways of preventing yourself from working against your own interests.

First, you must learn to shuffle a pack of cards correctly. And acquiring a good new habit must begin with breaking an old bad one. If you've been using the overhand shuffle, which is the very mere matter of sliding cards in blocks of two or three or ten from one hand to the other, mixing them grossly, then you must give up that shuffle immediately. The cards just can't be mixed thoroughly that way. Groups of cards will stick together. Try it right now. Assemble a deck in groups, then give it an overhand shuffle, then take it apart; you find (don't you?) that at least one group remains as you put it together.

Cheaters—and honest, hard-driving card players too—know this about the overhand shuffle, and take advantage of it. Here's how!

In the previous hand someone held four kings. The inexpert dealer picks up the cards, leaving the king meld en bloc, and gives the cards a single overhand shuffle, nonchalantly letting them flop from the upper hand into the lower. The observant opponent, watchful as a cat, notices where the kings lodge in the reassembled pack (that's easy enough!), and gets ready for the kill.

The kings were near the top of the pack in the pickup. The single overhand shuffle puts them close to the bottom. Your opponent cuts the pack a little below its center, say two-thirds of the way down. Now, if the game is two-handed, say, Gin Rummy, ten cards are dealt each player alternately.

Each player gets a pair of kings. The *locater* knows you have a pair. You don't know he has one. It is quite an advantage for him.

Or one of the kings is lost in the shuffle. The locater gets only one king. But he holds it, and your chances of forming a king meld are reduced 50 per cent.

Or you catch three of the kings and the locater gets the fourth; he knows that by holding it he'll be able to lay it off on your meld.

Or the locater catches the three kings and you get the fourth. As a rule you discard it at your first opportunity, giving your opponent a four-card meld.

And the locater's knowing which king you hold will always enable him to avoid discards which would build up a sequence meld in your hand.

There are numerous advantages, then, which you give an opponent when you shuffle incompetently. The only defense is the use of the riffle-shuffle.

And the *riffle-shuffle* also is susceptible to abuse. Some players learn the principle, but then shuffle the cards so carelessly that the bottom four or five cards of the pack go through the shuffle in unchanged order. See—now, with a deck—whether you are one of these soft-touch shufflers. If you are, change your habits immediately, because the locater's accurate knowledge of what those cards are and how they'll fall gives him an insuperable advantage over a long session at any game.

And—again now, with a deck—see whether you are one of the many amateurs who shuffle the cards at such an angle to the horizontal that their opponents can see the cards as they click into position. Always hold the pack close to and flat against the table in shuffling; to correct your angle, practice shuffling in front of a mirror. The mirror will show you everything your opponent can see as you handle the cards. Pretty revealing, isn't it?

How to Shuffle the Cards

At least 50 per cent of amateur card-fanciers make this mistake after a shuffle: they take the pack *up* into their hands to square it before offering it for the cut.

Why, after taking such fastidious pains to conceal that bottom card, must they expose it thus to a hawk-eyed opponent? Because, make no mistake about it, the opponent will take advantage of that card. He'll know where it is after the cut. He can cut the pack in such a way as to force it into the deal (placing it high in the pack) or keeping it out. In either case,

a significant percentage swings in his favor. *Square the cards
flat against the table.*

It must be a matter of record that I'm a card manipulator
by trade. I know how to shuffle, and I'm going to take the liberty of assuming you'd like to be taught by a professional.
Nothing fancy about it; it won't take much time; and, while
I don't guarantee to transform you into a magician, I think
that the next five minutes we spend together will insure you
against ever being embarrassed by shuffling badly.

First, pull about half the cards off the top of the pack with
your right hand, leaving the other half in your left, then putting both halves end to end.

Second, keep your hold on the cards and riffle the halves
together by running your thumbs up the sides of the cards.
Hold the blocks firm by settling the fingers on the opposite
edge of the cards.

Third, after the cards have riffled together, loosen your hold,
and slide them into a single block. *Never take the cards off
the table,* either for the riffle or in the act of squaring the pack.

Fourth, get into the habit of cutting the cards just for insurance at least once during the shuffle by pulling out the bottom half and slapping it onto the top between riffles—good
protection against locaters.

The G.I.'s used to call his the Scarne shuffle. It's foolproof,
crookproof, and tidy as a con man's tuxedo . . . and it'll save
you money if you never play anything but Solitaire. It just
saves wear and tear on a pack of playing cards.

A couple of last warnings against your most insidious
enemy:

You're not playing for paid admissions; so you don't have
to expose yourself to kibitzers. If you can do so without awk-
wardness, try to sit with your back to a wall so as to cut down
your audience. Many a hand is betrayed to an opponent by a
spectator's sigh or chuckle or sharp inhalation of breath or such
a fool crack as: "What a lucky pick!"

Before each game—whether Stud, Draw, Gin, Pinochle, or
any other game—do yourself the justice of counting the cards,
just to be sure the whole pack's there and nothing is missing by
any accident.

And *don't play when you're disturbed.* Most of us are convinced we play a pretty in and-out game; we tend to be
champs one day and chumps the next; and we attribute it all
to the run of the cards.

Mullarkey! Irregularity in quality of play at the amateur
level is strictly a matter of mental attitude.

When you play cards, give the game all you've got, or get

out; not only is that the one way on earth to win at cards; it's the only way you and the rest of the players can get any fun at all out of what ought to be fun.

You can't play a tight hand well if your mind's on that red-head down the street or the horses or your boss's ulcers or your wife's operation. When you don't remember the last upcard your opponent picked and you throw him the like-ranked card which puts him Gin, it's time to push back the chair and say, "Boys, I just remembered I have a previous engagement."

Do as the professionals do. When they make a few bad plays in a row, they just mutter, "That's all for today, gents"; and they mean it. They mean today is, for certain reasons, written off; they mean they'll be back tomorrow, which is another day.

By all means, when you're in this kind of losing streak, don't let yourself get panicky. The more reckless you feel, the more desperate is the necessity that you get away from that table at once. An excited player, a player plunging to recoup losses, is a player at his worst.

Learn to recognize him. That player has been and will again be—unless you learn how to deal with him—your own worst enemy.

And one more thing. The player who resorts to systems is just adding method to his madness—he is systematically insuring his losses. There is no such animal as an unbeatable system. Only the poor chump believes in one.

CHAPTER FIVE

Can Luck Beat Skill?

Whether you'd rather be lucky than skillful or skillful than lucky or just can't make up your mind . . .

You've argued from time to time—haven't you?—the immemorial question: "Can the more skillful player beat the player who is luckier?"

Hundreds of earnest, honest, sincere players have asked me that.

And there's an earnest, honest answer.

But before I write it out let's try to define our terms; let's see what we're talking about.

A *game of skill* i_ a game from which the element of chance has been utterly eliminated. Examples are Chess, Checkers, and four skill games which I invented myself: *Teeko, Follow the Arrow, Scarne's Challenge,* and the game, *Scarne.* If you happen to like skill games, you should like these.

In these games the skilled player will invariably win against an unskilled opponent, and the skilled man's winning percentage will be an exact reflection of the relation between his ability and that of a less skillful opponent.

A *game of chance* is a game from which the element of skill has been utterly eliminated. (Unless you assert that cheating is a form of skill!) Games of chance number thousands. Examples are Roulette, wheels of fortune, and most of the dice games such as Craps.

But hundreds of games played with cards—Gin Rummy, Poker, Pinochle, Bridge, Klob; name your game, mister—combine skill and chance.

Now, what's chance? How does it work?

You'll forgive me if I sound a little pedantic about this. But it brings up a subject which I think should be taught along with the three R's in every elementary school. If it were so taught, gambling would be reduced from a national problem to a sporadic eccentricity, and gambling houses would close. With a very few very dangerous exceptions, the average educated citizen has no knowledge of the subject and no interest in it, and this high-mindedness costs average educated citizens of the United States many millions of dollars a year.

I'm talking about a branch of mathematics called the theory of probability. It is called by gamblers—erroneously—the law of averages.

As far as we're concerned, the theory of probability affords a method of calculating what can be expected to happen in a situation in which some of the factors are not at hand or, being at hand, are too complex to be easily broken down, assimilated, and used.

When you double the insurance on your car you are both gambling and making use of the theory of probability. The whole gigantic life-insurance business is based on the actuarial mortality tables, which are just a list of probabilities. Any business-man drafting a budget or schedule or sales program is applying a theory of probabilities.

The theory holds rigorously true for all card games. Each player, the theory goes, will in the long run be dealt an approximately equal number of good and bad cards, good and bad hands.

"Mullarkey, Scarne," you say, "there are times when for

hours on end I can't get a decent hand dealt me; and even when I draw a fairish hand I can't improve it by drawing cards to it."

You're right. But it's not "mullarkey, Scarne"; it's the theory of probability. Like dice or coins, cards don't and mustn't be expected to behave *exactly* according to the probabilities. But they'll come awfully close.

Toss a coin. It may fall heads up ten times in a row. Then it may fall tails up ten times in a row. And there are gamblers who, after heads have been turned on several successive tosses, will bet heavily that it will be tails up next. They think the odds, the probabilities, favor tails. Likewise most card players operate on the belief that, after they have been dealt four or five successive bad hands, the probabilities abruptly shift to favor their being dealt a good hand. Thereupon they raise the stakes from 1¢ to 2¢ or from $1 to $2 on the next hand, and are shocked and saddened when they lose.

This notion, that luck has a cumulative tendency to change, is known academically as the doctrine of the maturity of chances. Mathematicians have for years referred to it as "the gambler's fallacy." But gamblers—many of them brilliantly educated persons—go right on believing in it and losing their money on it.

The theory of probability is not that a player will be dealt a run of good hands after a run of bad hands. It is that in the long run the cards will be just as good as anybody else's, which is something very different.

"Very well, then," I think you may be saying, "my opponent can indeed be luckier than I am, hand for hand, game for game, night in and night out. Now what?"

You have raised the question: "What is luck?"

Well, my dictionary defines luck as "that which happens to a person as if by chance; a person's apparent tendency to be fortunate or unfortunate."

The key word in that formula is "apparent."

Any card player who really can believe that an opponent is luckier than he just ought to give up the game. He belongs in gypsy shoppes, getting his tea leaves read.

When your Gin Rummy opponent goes down four times in a row, with perhaps only one or two picks, you appear to yourself—*appear*—the unluckiest guy in the world, and as far as you're concerned that closes the subject.

As a matter of fact it is just the threshold of the subject, for the odds have been, are, and will remain exactly even that you will be dealt a hand as good as or better than your opponent's! Over a number of deals sufficient to let the probabilities get their teeth into the statistics, say 10,000 or 100,000 deals, the distribution of the cards will be just about exactly even.

It's true in theory; it's true in the practice of many experimenters; and it's the truth on which gambling-house operators grow rich, since their income is based on the inexorable certainty that the percentages never fail over the long run.

I've seen a rank novice in five games in a row beat a man whom I consider to be one of the ten best Gin players in the country. That was chance, luck, a momentary aberration in the probabilities. They are inevitable in any gambling game. If it weren't for them—and the long-odds winnings they make possible—gambling would be barren of what makes it gambling. Certainly luck operates, to this limited extent, within the theory of probability. All that the theory guarantees is that ultimately each player will have been dealt an approximately equal number of opportunities to win, an approximately equal number of good, bad, and indifferent hands.

Two players, equally skilled, playing Gin Rummy or Poker or Pinochle every night for a year will probably have won and lost an approximately equal number of games.

So much for probability. So much for luck.

You understand me now.

In any game involving skill to any appreciable extent, the more skilled player will outdistance the less skilled in games won, over a long period.

The more pronounced his advantage in skill, the shorter the period required in which the difference will show on the scoresheet.

In the long run, then, the element of chance is canceled out, leveled off, reduced to zero.

I'm not going to try calculating the exact percentage of influence exerted by chance and by skill in any single card game situation, because:

1. Just for instance, there are 15,820,024,220 possible hands in Gim Rummy alone.

2. No two players will play the same kind of game consistently, and the variations in the way a man uses the cards he catches are the crucial variations.

But I can assure you of these things:

In any two-handed game—be it Stud or Draw Poker, Pinochle, Klob, or name your poison—which combines chance and skill, the more skillful player will win in the long run.

Skill is a more powerful factor in Gin Rummy than in the Rummy games involving more than two players, because:

1. The Gin player has only one opponent to study.

2. He gets more picks off the discard pile and the stock.

3. If an opponent errs, it works to a player's immediate advantage, whereas in a five-handed game the odds are three to one that someone else will benefit from the blunder.

Does that settle your argument? Or are you going to keep squandering your money on that fickle, blind, perverse, and cold-bloodedly fair old baggage Lady Luck?

Part Two

CHAPTER SIX

What Is Gin Rummy?

During his visit to the United States in the spring of 1946, Winston Churchill, who has made more history and made more sense than any other man of his generation, veered away from the text of an austere speech at the Waldorf Astoria to talk about cards. He had just been introduced, said the leader of His Majesty's loyal opposition, to "that fascinating game of yours, Gin Rummy." He was a connoisseur of gin and of rum, he added; but hanged if he could detect in the game any traces of either.

"Why," he inquired, "do you people call it Gin Rummy?"

It's a habit of Winston Churchill's. He was making history. He was making sense. It's a good question. It has been asked a million times; it has never been accurately answered; and Gin Rummy has arrived at an estate warranting the dignity of honest research.

There has been preserved in the folklore of cards a weird legend that Gin Rummy and its whole fabulous family are of Spanish origin.

Let's see about that.

Albert Morehead in *The Modern Hoyle* says of *Rum* or *Rummy* that it is derived from a Spanish game called *Con Quien*—with a question mark after it as is the English usage but not before it as is the Spanish—and that the name was corrupted in English-speaking countries to *Coon Can* but was christened *Rum* by the English because they thought it odd. In his *Complete Gin Rummy* Walter L. Richards says that the game, being of Spanish origin, was taken to Mexico, where it was named *Conquian* (this, you are soberly assured, means with whom); and early in the twentieth century it was exported to England, where the name became spelled and pronounced *Coon Can.*

"Coon Can," Mr. Richards says, "made its first appearance

in the United States in Texas, having been brought over the border from Mexico."

It doesn't make sense.

Who brought the game to Mexico? When? Where from? When was it named Conquian? If the game was taken to England in the early 1900's, how long did it take the slow attrition of spoken language to wear it down to Coon Can? But these questions are not crucial. This is: that it was Coon Can that crossed the border from Mexico into Texas.

Come, detectives, they didn't play Coon Can in Mexico; they played Con Quien or Conquian. To consent to Mr. Richards' account it is necessary to assume a cultural phenomenon without a parallel. It is necessary to assume that the Mexicans sent a game of their own with a name of their own abroad, got back and welcomed an alien version of it with an alien name, blithely abandoned their own name for it and universally adopted an unnatural parody of it, and proceeded to propagate the parody into the United States. Folkways aren't like that.

Yet the legend persists, even when the experts don't particularize as disastrously as Richards: *Hoyle's Games*, autograph edition, 1940, calls the game Conquian or With Whom or Coon Can, and says that the game is played with a Spanish pack of forty cards; Albert Ostrow in *The Complete Card Player* says of Coon Can (originally, oh you may be sure, called Conquian): "This is probably the ancestor of all Rummy games. It is Spanish in origin, and is said to have a history dating back at least 400 years." * And whence, then, the legend? Well, it turned up earliest, I think, in the late R. F. Foster's *Complete Hoyle of 1914*:

> The etymology of the game is the Spanish Con Quien (With Whom?) but of the game it stands for, little or nothing is known except that it is a great favorite in Mexico and the Southern States bordering Mexico.

Let's not hold Foster responsible for the later masters' variations on his theme. But let's face the historical fact. If he had taken the trouble, as every philosopher should, to back-track his subject to its prime sources, he should have found Coon Can being played *throughout the South*. And if he had read the 1900 edition of *The American Hoyle* he would have discovered detailed rules for the game Coon Can—and not a blessed word about Con Quien or Spain. And if any of these persons had bothered to reason from the evidence, I think they should have had to see that the American game of Coon

* Said by whom? Herewith I challenge Ostrow to prove all or any part of that statement.

Can was created in the American South under an American
name, that it filtered across the border into Mexico, and that
there it became Con Quien for the blunt homely reason that
that's the Mexican vowel sounds' closest phonetic approxima-
tion of the name.

As for the game's being Spanish because played with a deck
of forty cards, rubbish! Up to seventy-five years go many a
game was played in the United States with decks of various
sizes. The fifty-two-card pack, today's generic pack of cards,
was no standard at all. The 1875 edition of *The American
Hoyle* enumerates rules for many games played with less than
forty cards: Piquet, Escarte, and Euchre (thirty-two cards)
and French Euchre (less than thirty-two cards), and for at
least one played with more than fifty-two, Bezique. The
Bezique is credited in the 1864 *American Hoyle* to a Swedish
schoolmaster named Gustav Flaher, who presented the game
under the name Flahernuble to Charles I of Sweden as an
entry in a contest. It spread, turned up with certain sea changes
in Germany as Binochle, or Penuchle, and appeared at last in
the United States as an American adaptation of a French
adaptation of the Swedish-German game which is now called
Pinochle. It was played with two or three Euchre decks—
sixty-four or ninety-six cards—and the point of this inquiry is
that to attribute a Spanish origin to a game because of the
number of cards in the involved deck is questionable, to say
the least.

Let me try to reconstruct the crime. The first mistake must
have been made by some uncritical writer who heard of a game
they were playing down around the Rio Grande, took a bad
guess and attributed it to the Mexicans, and added another
bad guess to that and tracked it to Spain, all without getting
up from his swivel chair. In sober print such stuff is probably
supposed to have the look of formidable scholarship. Other
scholars either took the first unspoiled error into their systems
intact or magnified it and then incorporated it.

As a matter of fact the only place on earth where the game
is generally played and generally understood is the place where
it was born—Dixie. That it has turned up in Mexico is because
it has followed the American Negro wherever he goes.

That's for Coon Can—and let me tell you now that Coon
Can, for all its relative antiquity, was not the first game to set
the pattern for Gin Rummy.

I have checked back about as far as I think a man can on
the present family of Rummy games. And now, leaving myself
one line of escape: the acknowledged probability that in some
other country there may be obscure records of some game with
some semblance to our Rummy games; after all, the basic

principles of card games are limited, and were explored before America existed—and now I'll go on record with the flat statement that the origin of the Rummy games was Poker, Whiskey Poker, a peculiarly American variant of that game. (Poker is an adaptation of the ancient Persian game, As.)

Here's the tenth (1864) edition of *The American Hoyle*, whose preface page carries the year 1875, on how to play Whiskey Poker:

Five cards are dealt to each player, one at a time, and an extra hand is dealt on the table, called "the widow."

The eldest hand then examines his cards and decides he has a strong hand; he passes. If not, he may take the widow. Each player in rotation has a chance to take the widow.

When a player takes the widow, he must place his discarded hand face up on the table.

And now comes the crucial detail of the play that is responsible for all Rummy games. The discarded hand is face up in the center of the table. And *Hoyle* goes on:

The next player to the left (i.e., from the player who took the widow) selects from it (i.e., the discarded hand) that card which suits him best in making up his hand, and so on around the board, each player discarding a card and picking up another one until someone is satisfied, which he signifies by knocking on the table. If any player knocks before the widow is taken, the widow is turned face up, and each, from him who knocks, has but one draw.

That is the origin of our Rummy games.

Why called Whiskey Poker? Says the 1880 *American Hoyle*:

The game is often played for refreshments.

Most card playing and gambling *circa* 1864 was in saloons, and it was inevitable that this variety of Poker in which the drinks were the prize should bear the name of the drinks. Hundreds of variations followed, and slowly Gin Rummy began to evolve. Here, for example, are the rules for Rum Poker:

Each player was dealt ten cards, and each player drew cards until he had fifteen points or less in his hand. He could then lay down his entire hand, showing the combinations he could meld and counting the pips of the cards that didn't connect with anything. Thus a player held three kings and a run of four cards in sequence, his odd cards being a six, three, and deuce of sundry suits. The deadwood (unmatched cards) counted eleven. All other players laid down their hands now, and the winner collected the difference between his deadwood total and theirs. Sometimes, of course, another player's deadwood was a point or so below the claimant's. The other player got paid.

That's coming pretty close to Rummy. But in the early 1900's along came a third barfly variety of Poker, Gin Poker, and now look at these rules:

A standard pack of fifty-two cards was used. The game was for two players. Game was 100 points. Each player was dealt ten cards, one to each alternately. The twenty-first card was turned face up. Each player could pick off the top card of the discard pile or take a card off the top of the stock, then discard a card. The object of the game was to get sequences of three or more in a suit or three or four of a kind. As soon as deadwood (unmatched cards) totaled ten or less the player could call for a showdown, and had to announce the amount of his deadwood and show his hand, laying the combinations aside. If an opponent had less deadwood than the caller (the present game's "knocker"), he and not the caller got paid. Not only that—he got a 10-point penalty from the caller.

Why was the name of the game (obviously the game of Rummy) changed from Poker to Rummy? Why, by the time it developed along in the first years of this century the Poker family had more variations than any other family of games. Here are just a few, a very few, of the games that bore the name Poker at that period: Draw Poker, Stud Poker, Freezeout, Gin Poker, Jackpot, Rum Poker, Whiskey Poker, Tigers, Table Stakes, Deuces Wild, Blazer, Bluff, Double Up, Mistigris, and Patience Poker. That's what I said: Patience Poker. You've played it often, probably within the last week, always with yourself. More than 100 games of the Patience family are played today. It's Solitaire too, as you'll see if you'll re-examine its basic structure and principles.

Card games are tribes that break off from the main body and drift away into a separate existence of their own, devising their own laws, bearing new generations, hammering out their own morals and language and atmosphere. Rum Poker, in the course of its pilgrimage up through the strata of society, must first have dropped its tawdry family name; and then, I suppose, people fell to calling it by the affectionate diminutive Rummy so as to make it clear that they weren't talking al ut—or playing sweatily for—vulgar booze. And so it bore its young, and it gave them its name, and they prospered, every one. But none has prospered like the variation called Gin Rummy. The essential difference between straight Rummy and Gin is the scoring. And the chief difference in scoring is in the boxes—separate bonuses for each hand won besides the bonuses common to both types (for winning the game, for going Rummy or Gin, etc.). The shutout or schneider bonus is also a factor, but the box bonus is by far the major factor affecting the play.

CHAPTER SEVEN

The Experts Make a Mess of Things

Rummy is played by more people in more ways than any other game.

I've seen thousands of games of Rummy played in the armed forces and by civilians, and not more than half a dozen times have I seen any one game played under like rules.

Why the inconsistency? Why is the Southern game radically different from the Southwestern? Why do Midwesterners play a game just barely comprehensible to a boy from Brooklyn?

Mainly because, like all other card games, Rummy games have had to live their awkward age, to stand their trial, pending the establishment of a standard practice and standard laws universally acceptable.

Some of Rummy's manifest flaws have been eliminated, as have every game's, by the players themselves over the years. Others have been combed out by the experts who have thought and written about the case.

Good men, these experts—but often, in doing away with one flaw, they have introduced others more harmful without knowing they were doing it.

In my opinion there's only one practical way to evolve a set of rules for a game, and that's *the hard way:* playing hundreds and hundreds of games, identifying the bugs as they come up and rewriting the law to account for them, and ascertaining from the best players alive why they use a specific rule or scoring method. A legislator for card games must be an expert on all the rules of all the previous games of the involved family, know what games have stood up through the decades and centuries, and know also every single one of the cheating devices used by sharpers in these games. (Rules must be devised to minimize the possibility of subterfuge and must be made utterly inflexible, though the average player may never understand why he has to do certain things the way he does.)

Here's an example of what I mean about laws. The International Contract Bridge Laws published by the United States Playing Card Company dictate the following procedure for the shuffle, the cut, and the deal:

THE SHUFFLE. Player on dealer's left shuffles the pack for the first deal. During the deal, dealer's partner shuffles the other pack, and places it face down at his right. It remains there until the next dealer takes it for his deal.

THE CUT. Dealer presents the pack to the player on his right, who cuts toward the dealer. Dealer completes the cut.*

That rule has done more harm to Bridge than it is possible to estimate. I'll tell you why, and I may have to call your attention momentarily to the fact that I have some reputation as a card manipulator. Bridge is a game of partners. And in no card game in the world except Bridge does a partner shuffle a pack and then—with the kind assistance of his right-hand opponent—pass the pack to his partner for the cut. True—one of the opponents deals the cards after this pious collaboration, but that does not alter the position of the cards in the deck or the mechanics of what actually happens. Perhaps the experts, who are honorable men, all honorable men, never gave it a thought, but rest assured that the cheaters have, and I can tell you that they have been putting their thoughtfulness to profitable use.

One of the cheaters stacks the cards so that he or his partner will get a good hand—it is a simple manipulation; a couple of high cards per hand above average is a colossal advantage to a skilled player—and then he puts a crimp in the deck which indicates where he wants his partner to cut. After the cards have been cut at the right level, one of the opponents deals the cards: a perfect setup, a million-dollar setup!

I think that experts on any game should know all there is to know about cheating at that game and should assume from the beginning that people are going to play it for money, big money. If they don't write the rules with the crooks in mind, then they make the game a sucker for cheaters, and they kill the game.

Look at what Ely Culbertson says in his *Culbertson System of Playing Gin Rummy* (David McKay Company, 1942, Pages 52–53):

---

* Some Bridge books lay down the rule that the dealer has the right to shuffle the cards before they are cut. I should suggest this slight change in the Bridge laws: *The dealer MUST shuffle the cards before they are cut.*

The official Gin Rummy laws do not require that the cards be cut before they are dealt.

And then:

Many people consider it a waste of time to cut the cards.

As a criticism of one of the practices of a pastime, this seems to me eccentric, but that's not the point; the point is that Mr. Culbertson seems not to think that anybody could or would cheat at Gin Rummy. And of all games Gin Rummy is the easiest at which to cheat—especially without a cut, it is ludicrously simple for any fair-to-middlin' card sharper, of whom there is an abundance on this earth.

It is my sober and reasoned advice that—no matter what the official rules don't require—you not only cut the cards but use the Scarne cut (described on page 16) and that if the hunch seizes you, then you also shuffle the cards for the dealer. I've made it mandatory in my rules to fan the stock in a certain way to prevent any two cards from being picked up and seen at any one turn. The player may say he's sorry and he may even be sorry, but that common error gives him a tremendous advantage in the play. It can happen too with my fan spread, but it will happen less often; and the rules will cover the infraction.

I have also set up certain rules to prevent a variety of cheating which is not only countenanced but encouraged by other card experts. I denounce—and so do other competent players who understand the principles of the game—the following rule:

A player knocking and able to meld all his cards announces Gin and is credited with a 20-point bonus, plus the count of the unmatched cards of his opponent. Only the player knocking may receive the Gin bonus. *The opponent may lay off on Gin.*

This doctrine is endorsed by Culbertson, Ostrow, Morehead, and Richards, and the law is described in *Complete Gin Rummy* as having been accepted by the national laws commission of the American Contract Bridge League. But no expert I have ever encountered, and certainly no gambler with the gambler's unbiased comprehension of the theory of his game, will play in a game which permits a player to lay off cards, to slough off indebtedness, on an enterprising opponent's Gin Rummy.

The case against this safe, cheap, bumbling way of getting rid of cards is twofold:

1. "If you eliminate a player's fear of being caught with a card or group of cards by a Gin-going opponent," said a gambler, "you eliminate the thrill of the game."

2. "What's the use of taking the risk of going Gin," an expert inquired, "if your opponent can toss away the cards you've gambled—successfully—to catch him with?"

Laying off cards after an opponent has gone Rummy is barred in straight, knock, and all other Rummy games. To permit it in Gin Rummy is to corrupt the game.

Here are two other changes on which I am going to have to insist.

1. The expression "undercut" as used by the experts and imposed on the players of the game gripes me. It is a verb supposed to indicate that a player has in his hand fewer points than the knocker. But in the first place it is an inexpressive word, a bad tool for the job. And in the second place it is already committed to another use in cards. As every gambler knows, the word *undercut* means to cut a group of cards from the bottom of the deck and place them on the top of the deck preparatory to the deal.

Gamblers I know use for the Gin Rummy situation the word "klobbed"; and if you're familiar with the game Kalabrias you understand this to mean that the person who knocked has in turn gotten his lumps. (The parallel Klob situation: the player who took the bid made the same points as or fewer points than his opponent, and thus lost the hand.) But even that vigorous idiom is not quite appropriate to Gin Rummy; and so I'm going to dig into the language of the game itself and devise a new term. I'm going to call an undercut an "underknock."

2. Gamblers have already amended *de facto* the old rule that the winner of the previous hand deals the current hand. I'm going to change it *de jure*. My ruling, like the common practice, is that the loser deals.

This change is largely precautionary. A player skilled in manipulating cards is given entirely too much latitude by the old rule. He wins by means of a crooked deal; he gets the pack again for another crooked deal; he wins again; he deals again; he wins . . . it's a little too vicious. The law that the loser shall deal harms no honest man and does safeguard the innocent.

Over the last couple of years most thoughtful Gin players have altered another rule. I wholeheartedly endorse and subscribe to the change. Instead of dealing ten cards to each of the two players and turning the twenty-first card up on the table as the first upcard, they deal ten cards to the dealer and eleven to the nondealer, and there is no upcard; the rest of the pack is squared in the middle of the table as the stock, and the game's first play is a discard by the nondealer.

I think my reasoning will be lucid enough: except in games requiring that a card be faced to establish trumps or indicate the nature of subsequent play, no card should be on the discard pile unless it has been discarded by the deliberate choice of a contestant, not as a matter of blind chance. This rule might well be absorbed into the statutes of other Rummy games, but I'm in no position to insist on it except in the case of Gin, where it is downright crucial to the balance and health of the game.

The question of who profits by the location of the deal has always bought an argument. It will buy a bigger one now, with the nondealer getting eleven cards against the dealer's ten. Two questions will be raised:

1. Isn't there a measurable mathematical advantage in not having to deal, especially under this rule?

2. Doesn't his eleven-card dole actually increase the nondealer's prospects of winning?

Let's take the last question first. Whether the nondealer gets eleven cards in his hand or ten with the right to pick the first upcard makes absolutely no difference to his chances of winning the game. They are the same eleven cards. If in his hand they enable him to knock or go Gin, they would do the same parceled out ten to him and one on the board.

The ten-and-eleven deal doesn't present the nondealer with any advantages, fair or unfair. But it does prevent his being put to severe disadvantages.

Let's set up a case in which a nondealer gets ten cards and picks the upcard. Now . . .

1. His opponent, the dealer, knows and will remember what that card was, and can and will hold up any cards that might form or extend the indicated meld.

2. Or the opponent may hold back a card to lay off on that meld if it materializes.

3. Meanwhile the nondealer must now make his first discard without any idea whatever of the dealer's holdings. That discard is the most difficult play in Gin, and in this circumstance it is utterly blind. (The ten-and-eleven-deal balances the chances for both players.)

4. After the nondealer has discarded, the dealer may either take the discard or pick from the stock.

The evidence persuades me that the game's practicing realists have developed a genuine improvement with the ten-and-eleven deal, and it is herewith incorporated in our jurisprudence.

One more thing about theory before we get down to serious legislation:

The bonus problem pops into my head every time I see a game of Gin Rummy. Some experts, you know, advocate a 20-point bonus for Gin and for an underknock, while others give the two different values, namely 25 points for Gin and 15 points as an underknock bonus.

It seems to me a little chaotic.

It's obvious—see if it isn't—that it is harder to go Gin than it is to score an underknock. Whenever a good reckless player competes with a good cautious player, many more underknocks are scored than Gins.

I've decided, after talking the point over with some of my $1,000-a-game gambler friends, that to maintain equal bonuses for Gin and the underknock would subtly but very thoroughly alter the whole structure of the game.

If you penalize a player 20 points for being underknocked, you effectively compel that player to wait until he has much less than 10 points in his hand before hazarding a knock.

Do you understand what that does to Gin Rummy? Gin is a great game, Gin is Gin, because of the knock feature. Minimize the knock, drive it out of the common play, and you have reduced Gin to straight Rummy.

I have another good reason for allowing only 10 points for an underknock. That is the fact that Gin Rummy is an adaptation of Gin Poker. And in that game for over thirty-five years the underknock penalty, established by trial and error, has been kept at 10 points. To change now, at the whim of rule makers, the value of the game's currency seems to me a disastrous kind of experimentation.

CHAPTER EIGHT

Rules for Gin Rummy

I. Requirements

1. Gin Rummy is strictly a two-handed game.

A. Only two persons may play against each other at a time.

B. Although the game may involve three, four, or more

players, only two of these may be in play against each other simultaneously.

2. A standard pack of fifty-two playing cards is used: from ace to king in the four suits. The ace is the lowest-ranking card, having a value of 1; the king, queen, and jack are valued at 10 points each. All other cards have their numerical face value. The suits have no value.

II. Object of the Game

1. The object of the game is to form matched sets, called *lays* or *melds,* the deduction of which from the hand will bring the value of the unmatched cards to a *total* (called a *count*) of ten or less, at which point the player may knock; * or to meld or lay all the ten cards in matched sets, which is called *Gin.*

A. A matched set may be either a sequence of three or more cards in the same suit—for example, the 5, 6, and 7 of hearts (it is possible to meld the ten cards in a single sequence)—or three or four of a kind; for example, the king of diamonds, king of clubs, and king of spades.

III. Selecting Dealer and Starting Position

1. By mutual consent either player may shuffle the deck of cards.

A. Each player cuts a group of cards from the deck. Player cutting the low facing card deals. In case of tie players cut again.

B. If players want to cut for seat position, player cutting high card takes his choice of seat.

C. The loser of a hand deals the next hand.

IV. The Shuffle and Cut

1. Dealer shuffles the deck. Opponent may call for a shuffle at any time he likes prior to the cut, though dealer retains the privilege of shuffling last.

2. Dealer must offer the deck to opponent for cut. If opponent refuses to cut, dealer must cut his own cards before starting the deal. When cutting, at least five cards must be in each cut portion of deck.

* To knock is nothing more esoteric than to rap on the table with the knuckles.

V. The Deal

1. Dealer deals the opponent eleven cards and himself ten cards, one at a time, alternately, the opponent being dealt the first card off the top of the deck and so on down until the opponent gets the last or twenty-first card.

2. The remainder of the deck, called the *stock*, is placed on the table and is fanned by the dealer.

VI. The Play

1. The nondealer begins the play by discarding one of his eleven cards. That card is called the *upcard*. It is now the dealer's turn to play, and he may elect to pick the *upcard* or to take the top card of the stock. After making his play the dealer must discard one card. Play continues with each player in turn having the option either of picking his opponent's discard (*upcard*) or drawing the top card from the stock. After a player has picked the *upcard* or the top card of the stock and has discarded, his turn of play is completed, and he must wait for the completion of his opponent's play before he can make his next play. The rules in play apply alike to dealer and nondealer, and the play continues thus alternately until a decision or no-game has been attained.

2. If a player has Gin—i.e., if he can meld all ten of his cards—he turns his discard face down on the table, and announces: "Gin!" Then he places all his melds, separate from each other, face up on the table. The opponent then must face all his melds separately on the table, placing his unmatched cards face up to one side.

He then counts the total of his unmatched cards.

3. If a player wants to *knock*, he turns his discard face down on the table and announces: "Knock!" or "Down!" He places his melds face up on the table separate from each other, and places his unmatched cards face up to one side. Then he adds the numerical values of the unmatched cards, and announces the *count*.

VII. When a Player May Knock

When a player holds enough melds to bring the total value of his unmatched cards down to 10 or less he may either knock or, as he elects, continue playing. Should he decide to knock he must first put his discard face down on the discard pile and announce his knock as described above, meld his combinations, and set aside his unmatched cards. After he has announced his *count* his opponent must then expose his hand, and is permitted to discard in any of the following ways:

A. He may place on the table, separate from each other, any melds he holds.

B. He may lay off any cards which can be added to the knocker's melds.

C. He now places on the knocker's unmatched cards an equal value of his own unmatched cards.

D. The knocker now gets credit for the value of unmatched cards still in the possession of his opponent.

This is called a *Box* or *Line*. It is the score of that hand.

VIII. The Underknock

1. Should the opponent have a total of unmatched cards less than the knocker's total or *count* after melding and laying off cards, the opponent wins the box, and is credited, moreover, with the difference in points between the knocker's hand and his own hand, plus a bonus of 10 * points for scoring an underknock.

2. If the knocker and opponent are tied in unmatched cards, the opponent wins the hand and scores a bonus of 10 * points.

IX. To Go Gin

If a knocker lays down his ten cards in melds he has *gone Gin.* In this event his opponent may put down only his own melds, and is not allowed to lay off cards on the knocker's melds. The *Gin* knocker gets credit for all his opponent's unmatched cards plus a 20*-point bonus.

X. No Game

1. Should the hand be played down to the fiftieth card, leaving two cards face down in the stock, the player whose turn it is to draw may pick up the last discard and knock or go Gin, but he cannot pick up either of the last two down cards. Should he fail to knock or go Gin with the upturned card the deal is considered at an end, and a *No Game* is declared. Neither player receives any credits.

2. In either of the following instances the game in play automatically becomes void, regardless of what the scores may be, the moment the discovery is made (though all previous completed games stand and are valid):

* See next page for notes on variations in scoring, XII and XIII.

A. If the deck is found to have less than fifty-two cards.
B. If the deck is found to have more than fifty-two cards.

XI. End of Game

The game ends when one of the players scores 100 points or more.

XII. The Scoring

A. Winner of the game scores the difference between the two totals.
B. An extra 20 points is added to each player's score for each box won.
C. Winner of the game gets a game bonus of 100 points for winning.
D. Variations in Bonus Scoring. Many players use other values for scoring bonuses. A common variant is to allow 25 points for everything (except game)—boxes, Gins, underknocks. I think that's wrong. It's simple, no doubt, but obviously it distorts the balance of the game to reward an underknock as much as Gin. Another common variation is to allow 25 for boxes, 25 for Gin, and 20 for underknock. This is a little more reasonable, but for the reason previously mentioned I don't favor it. The discussions later on covering strategy are based on the scoring I do favor; namely, 10 for underknock, 20 for Gin, 20 for boxes.

XIII. Shutout, Skunked, Schneidered, Blitzed

1. Should a player score 100 points or more before his opponent scores any points at all, winner gets the 100-point game bonus plus a 100-point shutout bonus—plus all other credits.
2. Variations in Scoring. A very popular variation is to double everything for a shutout—point total, box bonuses, game bonus. It's popular because it's exciting, specially thrilling to get that big jackpot when you schneider your opponent. But of course it does throw the game off balance. A whole evening's play may be decided by one lucky shutout game. If you don't mind that sort of thing, go ahead and use this hopped-up scoring system.

XIV. The Score Sheet

The score is added cumulatively. Scores of each successive deal are added to the last previous total and brought down to

a new total. This makes known to both players at all times
what the total score is and how far each is from game.

XV. Unit Scoring

This is a streamlined method of scoring. At the completion
of a game and before the final tally the right-hand digit of each
entry on the score sheet is canceled off.

Thus, you have won a game with the following credits:

22 points' difference in scores.

60 points for boxes.*

100 points for game.

It adds up to 182 points, but in unit scoring you give yourself:

2 points for difference in scores.

6 points for boxes.

10 points for game.

It adds up to 18 points. Some players like this method because it's fast and easy.

XVI. Misdeals

A misdeal is declared, and the dealer of the hand immediately starts a new deal, whenever any of the following im-
proprieties are discovered (there are no penalties for the dealer
or the responsible player):

A. If a card is turned over during the deal.

B. If either player or both players have been dealt an incorrect number of cards.

C. If, during the play of the hand, either player or both
players are found to be holding an incorrect number of
cards.

D. If a player deals out of turn and the error is discovered
before a play has been completed.

E. If a player looks at an opponent's card or cards during
the deal.

F. If a card is found face up in the stock either during the
deal or during the play.

XVII. Discards

1. A card is not discarded until it has been placed on top
of the discard pile. Once it touches the discard pile it completes
a play and cannot be recaptured by the player.

* Note that the box points total almost three times the difference in
score. How this factor affects the play will be discussed later.

2. When a knock or Gin is announced the discarded card must be placed face down on top of the discard pile. But if the player accidentally discards the wrong card when knocking or going Gin, that card may be retrieved and the error corrected without penalty.

3. A player cannot touch or pick a card either from the stock or from the discard pile until his opponent has discarded and completed his play.

4. A player cannot discard a card before taking his pick.

5. A player cannot discard the *upcard* he just picked until his next turn of play.

6. Once a player touches an *upcard* in his turn of play he is compelled to take that card.

7. If at the start of play a player should refuse the first discard (the *upcard*) by stating his decision verbally, he cannot then decide to take it. His refusal to accept it is his final decision on that card.

8. If at the start of the play the nondealer should take the top card of the *stock* without granting the dealer a chance to take or refuse the *upcard*, then that play stands; but in his own turn of play the dealer may now take either one of the two discards or take the top card of the stock.

9. No player is permitted to spread the discards to see what cards have been played.

XVIII. Picking from the Stock Pile

1. Once a player has taken the top card of the *stock* in his correct turn of play he cannot replace it and decide to take the *upcard* instead. And this ruling holds even though the player may not have looked at the card.

2. If a player inadvertently picks off the stock two cards instead of one, or inadvertently sees the face of the card below the one he has just taken, or his opponent has reason to believe that he has seen it, then his opponent may, if he likes, ask to see the face of the card the player has just drawn. If this demand is made the player must comply.

3. If a player plays out of turn, taking the top card of the stock for the second pick in a row, then he must discard the last card picked, and his opponent may now pick either of the two top discards or the top card of the stock.

XIX. False Knocks and Sundry Errors

1. A player who inadvertently knocks with a count of more than 10 points in unmatched cards must place his entire hand face up on the table and continue to play it thus exposed.

2. If while holding a Gin hand a player fails to knock and his opponent thereupon knocks with 10 points or less, the player does not get credit for a Gin hand, but instead gets credit only for an underknock.

3. Once a player has laid down his hand and announced his total and it is entered on the score sheet, he cannot call for rectification of some mistake he has made. An opponent is not required to inform a player that he has committed an error or failed to lay off a card or failed to meld his holding to his best advantage, nor is he required to notify a player that he is calling an incorrect count to his disadvantage.

4. In melding, a player may rearrange his melds in any way he likes, but not

A. If the final count has been entered on the score sheet or
B. If an opponent has laid off one or more cards on the player's melds as first arranged.

XX. For Money Players: One More Rule

It is recommended that two packs of cards, with backs of different colors, be used in the play. While the dealer is shuffling for the deal the nondealer is giving the other pack a preliminary shuffle, after which it is set to one side. *It is shuffled again by the loser of this hand before he deals the next hand.* Reasoning:

A. Many players shuffle so badly that one or more of the melds of the previous hand are undisturbed in the shuffle. Their recurrence in due order in the stock pile makes the game a mere memory test, and a dull one.
B. This rule insures two shuffles for the pack and doubles the troubles of the cheater.
C. Even if neither player shuffles skillfully, it is harder to remember the melds of two hands ago.

And Now Let's Kibitz a Game of Gin Rummy

I think that it may be useful to imagine a reader whose first contact with Gin Rummy has been a perusal of the rules just set forth. He is in a position comparable perhaps to that of a man from Mars who has just read the Ten Commandments, the Constitution of the United States, and a railroad schedule and would like to see what sort of thing they pertain to, what sort of thing they produce. Here, without conflict or comedy, is a step-by-step description of a normal game of Gin Rummy. Pete and Guy, who are our *dramatis personae*, take seats at a table facing each other. Guy has bought a standard fifty-two-card deck of cards, and he shuffles them now, again and again, while Pete with pencil and paper prepares the score sheet.

Guy puts the cards in the center of the table, face down.

"Okay, Pete," he says. "Cut the cards. What shall we play for?"

Pete cuts. Since this is a cut for the deal, Guy does likewise.

"How about a cent a point?" he replies.

"Fine," says Guy. "Make a note of it."

And this is how Pete cuts the cards: He takes a block of them off the top of the faced pack with one hand, holding them squared up and face down. Guy cuts a block from the remaining piece of the deck. Turning their blocks of cards, they expose the bottom card of their cut.

Guy's card is a 5-spot. Pete's a 3-. Pete becomes first dealer.

Now Pete shuffles the whole deck again, and puts the pack on the table face down equidistant between Guy and him, and says, "Cut 'em!" Guy lifts a good-sized block of cards off the top of the deck, puts it on the table face down beside the remainder. Pete picks the remainder up and puts it on top of the cut block, then takes the deck into his left hand, with his fingers squaring the pack so that no card protrudes from its sides. (*Note:* This is an objective report; if you want advice on how to cut cards without inviting larceny, see my chapter on cheats, page 16.)

Pete deals the first card to Guy. If any men from Mars are in the room, what that means is sliding the top card off the deck with the right hand and putting it—or carefully sailing it—face down on the table in front of his opponent. Pete now deals himself the ensuing top card, and so proceeds until he has dealt Guy eleven cards and himself ten, taking pains not to expose the face of any card. (Exposure of a card would constitute a misdeal and compel a reshuffle and a new deal.) The rest of the closed deck goes face down on the table between the two players. It has become the *stock pile* or *stock*.

Each player picks up his cards, gathers them in his left hand, and with his right hand sorts and arranges them. Idiom for this is *setting the hand*. Cards are commonly arranged in legal combinations or potential combinations, say, two or more cards of the same suit in sequence or of the same numerical value.

All set?

It's Guy's turn to play first, and he does so by discarding one of the eleven cards dealt him. It goes face up on the table beside the stock. And it becomes the first *upcard*.

That completes Guy's play. It is Pete's turn. Pete may do one of two things.

1. He may take the top card of the *stock* and then discard a card.

2. He may take the *upcard* and then discard a card.

And so Pete plays, and Guy plays, and the game goes on until Pete decides to *knock*. He forewarns his opponent of this decision by exclaiming "Knock!" or "Down!" or, quite legally: "I'm coming down!"

And this is how he does that:

He puts his current discard *face down* on the discard pile.

He lays his melds *face up* on the table, separate from each other, so that his opponent can read and consent to them.

He lays down too his unmatched cards.

And he declares his *count*, which is the total value of these unmatched cards.

Pete's melds are three kings and the run of the 5, 6, 7, and 8 of hearts.

His unmatched cards are a 3 of hearts, a 2 of diamonds, and an ace of clubs.

His *count*, which he announces aloud, is 6.

So much for Pete's completed play.

Now Guy lays down his melds, sloughs off an odd king on Pete's meld of kings, and puts on the table face up his batch of unmatched cards. The total of these, which *count* he too calls aloud, is 26. And now the total of unmatched cards held by Pete, which was 6, is subtracted from Guy's 26, and the 20-point credit to Pete is entered on the score sheet. The sheet looks like this:

One cent a point

GUY	PETE
—	20

Because Guy lost this box he becomes dealer of the next hand. Now shuffle, cut, deal, and play proceed as before until Guy knocks with 10 points. But this time Pete has a *count* of only 6 points. Thus Pete wins the second box by scoring an underknock, which is worth a bonus of 10 points plus the difference in *count*. And so Pete gets a score sheet credit of 14 points, and the entry is made:

One cent a point

GUY	PETE
—	20
—	34

Loser agan, Guy deals the third hand. Play proceeds. Suddenly Guy calls: "Gin!" And, putting his eleventh card face down on the discard pile, triumphantly he melds his entire hand, all ten cards of it, having no unmatched cards.

Well, Pete has one meld, which he is permitted to lay down. He has besides a card which he could, if he were allowed, lay off on one of Guy's melds. But on a Gin hand laying off cards is not permitted. He cannot lay it off. He does not. His unmatched cards total 65 points.

Guy's credits are for those 65 points plus the Gin bonus, which is 20 points, for a total of 85 points. And this goes into the score sheet, which now looks like this:

One cent a point

GUY	PETE
85	20
—	34

In the next hand, Pete wins by 41 points, which brings his score to 75. In the following hand, Pete also wins, by 40 points, and brings his total score to 115. The score sheet then looks as follows:

One cent a point

	GUY	PETE	
	85	20	
	—	34	
	—	75	
	—	115	
Total	85	115	Pete's score
		−85	Guy's score
Pete wins by		30	

The game is ended. Pete has won. He gets credit for the 30-point difference between his *count* and Guy's *count*, plus a 100-point bonus for winning the game, plus a box bonus of 60 points. (The bonus per box is 20 points. Pete has three boxes more than Guy.) The final score, as duly totaled, looks like this:

Difference in points	30
Game bonus	100
Box bonus	60
Total	190

As agreed—in writing—at the start of the game, Guy owes Pete $1.90.

CHAPTER NINE

Variations of Gin

Gin Rummy for Three Players

Gamblers call this game Round Robin Gin Rummy. The name comes from a horse-racing idiom. Although three players take part, only two are in play against each other simultaneously.

To determine which two shall start, any player, by consent of the others, shuffles and the three cut cards. Low man—that man whose exposed card is of lowest rank—sits out the first hand. The other two play a game of Gin Rummy.

The score of the first hand is credited to the winner, and the loser drops out. The winner proceeds to play the next hand against the third man. (Generally the nonplayer keeps the score.)

So it goes, loser giving way to nonplayer hand by hand, until one of the three scores 100 points or more.

The winner is paid off in the amount of his credit over each opponent. The player with the second highest score collects from low man. A player scoring a shutout can collect his shutout bonus only from the player who scored zero. For example, A scores 110 points; B, 90; and C, none. A gets credit for a shutout over C but not over B. Value of credits and bonuses is the same as in two-handed Gin Rummy. In three-handed Gin Rummy a player may collect from two players, lose to two players, or win from one and lose to one. Sample score sheet:

One cent a point

Guy	Pete	Will
50	30	15
60	60	30
75	90	—
85	—	—
110	—	—

The count credit, plus game and box bonuses brings Guy's total to 310 points, Pete's to 150 points, and Will's to 70 points.

Guy gets $1.60 from Pete and $2.40 from Will. Pete gets $.80 from Will. As it totals out:

Guy wins $4.00.
Pete loses $.80.
Will loses $3.20.

Captains

This is a variation of Gin for three players, borrowed from Backgammon where it is called Chouette or "in the box." A plays the first game as captain against B and C, B playing the first hand and continuing to play as long as he wins. When he loses, C takes his place and continues to play until he loses, when B comes back again, and so on until the game ends. The captain keeps playing to the end of the game, regardless of whether he wins or loses. A single score is kept and totaled at the end of the game. The captain wins or loses the net total from or to each of the opponents.

Then B becomes the captain playing against A and C, and so on. This principle can be extended to five or seven or any other odd number of players as explained under Partnership Gin.

Partnership Gin

This is four-handed Gin Rummy. Two players are teamed against the other two. Two games of two-handed Gin Rummy are played simultaneously and the partners enter their score as one. The players cut for partners, holders of the two highest exposed cards being teamed against the holders of the two lowest. The rules of Gin Rummy apply. The only variation is in the scoring.

Team scores, not players' scores, are entered.

Example: A and B are partners playing against C and D. A, playing the first hand against his opponent C, wins by 28 points. D, playing against B, wins by 20 points. Team A-B wins the box by 8 points. That is the only score entered on the sheet. Mind you, for it is crucial—the score is not entered in Partnership Gin Rummy until both hands have been played, counted, and balanced off against each other.

Here is why:

Score is 85 for A-B and 90 for C-D. Now, A wins the next hand by 41 points for a total of 126, a game-going total. But B may lose his hand by enough points to cancel out his partner's gains and indeed to give the game to C-D.

Game is 125 points.

Game bonus remains 100, shutout bonus 100, and all other scoring is as in two-handed Gin Rummy.

Alternating Partnership Gin: The rules governing Partnership Gin apply, but in this variation teammates compete successively against alternate opponents. Thus (sitting at a square table) A plays against his right-hand opponent of the first game, against his left-hand opponent of the second game, and so on.

Multiple-Partnership Gin Rummy

Team play can be extended beyond four hands. There can be three on a side, four on a side, and I have seen as many as twelve men play in two teams of six each. Game should be increased 25 points for each extra pair. But otherwise the principles of four-handed Partnership Gin prevail. The arrangement of players can be made to suit convenience: either team A on one side of a long table with team B on the opposite side; or in groupings of four, two from each team at each table.

Gin for an Odd Number of Players

An odd number of players may be accommodated also, along the lines of Captains, previously described. For example, let us say there are seven players. They cut for partners. The three highest become the captains; the other four are the opponents. The player who has cut the lowest card is out of the game for the first hand. If his team (the opponents) wins the first hand, he continues to stay out. But when his team loses, he goes into the game in place of his teammate who has lost most points. The captains, playing three against four, play for an extra amount since they will collect from or pay an extra player. Therefore they must decide in advance how they will provide for this: either by dividing it equally among themselves, or by having one or two accept the extra stakes.

COACHING IN PARTNERSHIP OR MULTIPLE-HAND GIN

Gin, as I have said, is essentially a two-handed game and therefore coaching or advising a partner is not permitted. Not only is it against the rules for one partner to advise or consult with another partner as to the wisdom of a play, or the wisdom of going down, but no guiding remarks are permitted, not even a reference to the score, except that it is permissible for a partner who has finished his hand to bring to the attention of a still-playing partner the result of his game. But a partner is not permitted to volunteer information as to the current state of the score. He must not say, "Partner, I lost 47 and that gives our opponents 130 total, so play to save the game." However, if the playing partner says, "How do we stand? What is the total score at the present moment?" the information may be given to him.

LOOKING AT PARTNER'S HAND

When the layout of the game is such that partners sit next to each other, it is perfectly legitimate to look at your partner's hand. In fact, it is wise to do so, and act in accordance with the information thus gained. Whether your partner has a bad hand and is likely to lose or a good hand likely to win should be taken into consideration, especially in relation to the current score.

You are permitted in the play of your own hand to benefit all you can from your observation of your partner's hand. But you must not give him any advantage as a result of your watching his play of his hand. This is specially important in the case of

ERRORS

A basic rule in cards is that the cards stand for themselves. Therefore, if you see an opponent making a miscount—calling a 6, 7, and 4 as 15, for instance—you are privileged to point out the error. You are obligated to do so if your partner makes that error or if the opponent has made a miscount in your favor. Of course, you are also privileged to point out the error when your partner has made a miscount against you.

But if you are watching your partner's hand and see that he is about to make a mistake—going down with more than 10 through miscounting, or calling Gin when he doesn't have Gin —you must not prevent the error. You must not give him any benefit as a result of your watching the hand.

In Spades Double Gin, you should point out that it was a spade hand if that was forgotten by your partner or his opponent or both. You'll want to do that if your partner won the hand and so you're required to do it when your partner loses the hand.

You have no privileges or obligations in the case of a hand laid down *not* to the best advantage. The cards stand for themselves and if the melds, counts, and scoring are correct, that's all there is to it.

In Oklahoma Gin, where the first card turned up determines the maximum number of points for knocking, the Spades Double rule mentioned above applies: a knock above the determined maximum must be pointed out. If the first card was a 6 and your partner goes down with 8, you should refer to the 6 downcard even though both your partner and his opponent have forgotten it.

Hollywood Gin

This form of Gin Rummy got its name from the movie colony that made it popular—in the movie colony. It's not for people like us. I've seen games—yes, witnessed them myself when I was on the West Coast making films and lecturing on crooked gambling—played for $2 and $3 a point. I don't like the ulcers. I have no special yearning for high blood pressure. A tenth of a cent a point will keep me interested and happy.

I know very well one Hollywood Gin player whose losses in the game are out beyond $200,000. Winnings and losses of $5,000 and $10,000 are commonplace. I'm not moralizing. I'm just telling you. If you want to try it at a dollar a point—

Hollywood Gin is played exactly as is Gin Rummy. *The only difference is that in Hollywood three games are played at the same time.*

The scoring is not so complicated as that makes it sound.

1. When a player wins the first hand he scores in Game 1.

2. The second hand he wins is scored under Game 1 and Game 2.

3. The third hand he wins is scored under Game 1, Game 2, and Game 3.

4. Every hand he wins thereafter is scored under all three games.

5. If a player scores 100 or more points under Game 1 and has lesser scores under Game 2 and Game 3, he thereafter enters his scores under Game 2 and Game 3.

6. If a player scores 100 or more points in Game 1 and Game 2, he thereafter enters his scores under Game 3.

7. A game ends when a player has reached 100 or more points in all three games.

Here's how it works; here's a sample game between our wealthy and Gin-whacky old friends A and B:

A wins the first hand by 20 points, and it is entered on the score sheet to his credit under Game 1.

B wins the second hand by 10 points, and this score is entered to his credit under Game 1.

The score sheet looks like this:

		$2 a point			
GAME 1		GAME 2		GAME 3	
A	B	A	B	A	B
20	10				

Now A wins the third hand by 21 points. This being A's second winning hand in this game, the 21 points are entered to his credit under Game 1 and under Game 2.

And A wins the fourth hand by 40 points. So these 40 are entered to his credit under Game 1, Game 2, and Game 3. And the score sheet looks like this:

		$2 a point			
GAME 1		GAME 2		GAME 3	
A	B	A	B	A	B
20	10	21	—	40	—
41	—	61	—		
81					

When A wins the fifth hand by 43 points and the score is entered to his credit under Game 1, Game 2, and Game 3, the score sheet looks like this:

		$2 a point			
GAME 1		GAME 2		GAME 3	
A	B	A	B	A	B
20	10	21	—	40	—
41	—	61	—	83	—
81		104			
124					

By passing 100 points A has won Game 1 and Game 2. In Game 1, A gets the following point credits:

Difference in points   114
Game bonus   100
Box bonus   60
                       Game 1 Total   274

In Game 2, A has scored a schneider, or shutout, and gets the following point credits:

Difference in points   104
Game bonus   100
Shutout bonus   100
Box bonus   60
                       Game 2 Total   364

As the game now continues, A has a total of 638 points to his credit. Scores are, of course, entered under Game 3 only, the contest having evolved into a single game of Gin Rummy.

B wins the third game with an over-all total of 100 points. These 100 are subtracted from A's 638, leaving A with a 3-game total of 538 points. At $2 a point it comes to $1,076, or at a tenth of a cent it is .538¢. One is now ready to start a new game of Hollywood Gin.

See what I mean?

Note: Some Hollywood players indulge in the following extension of the scoring method:

When a player has passed 100 in Game 1 and has scores entered under Game 2 and Game 3, he starts scoring a new series of three games, entering his next score under Game 2 and Game 3 of Series No. 1 and under Game 1 of Series No. 2.

BUT—It is not permissible to start the new series unless both opponents have scores entered under Game 3 of the first series. This is to prevent a player's being shut out in more than three games at a time. You see, of course, that even in Hollywood it would be a little rugged to be collecting shutout bonuses from a man for more than three games at a clip.

A terrific game for fast gamblers; but, come to think of it, not for me even at a tenth of a cent a point.

Round-the-Corner Gin

The rules of Gin Rummy, of which this is a variation, apply in full force with the following exceptions:

1. The ace may be played in either the high or the low sequence of the same suit—hence the name Round-the-Corner. Example sequences: A-2-3; or A-K-Q; or K-A-2. Of course these sequences may be extended.

2. Aces instead of counting 1 point when unmatched count 15 points.

This latter rule makes it harder for a player to hold a count of 10 or less, and cuts down knocks and underknocks.

Since the ace may be used in three sequences, making it easier to go Gin in Round-the-Corner than in Gin Rummy, the 20-point bonus for Gin is reduced to 10 points in Round-the-Corner.

Regardless of the difference in the Gin bonus, the box scores tend to run higher in this variation, because players tend to get caught with high unmatched cards in their hands. They try to organize round-the-corner sequences, which are high-card sequences; and the ace, remember, counts 15 instead of 1.

3. Game is 150 points.

4. Partnership (four-handed) game is 175 points.

5. Team (six-, eight-, or ten-handed or more) game is 200 points.

Streamlined Gin Rummy

Top-notch gamblers seem to like it; a version which saves a lot of bookkeeping.

The game is played exactly as is Gin Rummy—except for the scoring.

Players decide at the start of the game the amount of the stake for winning and the amount each box shall be worth.

(For instance, they may decide to play for $1 a game and 20¢ a box. *Note:* As a rule, boxes are assigned a value one-fifth the value of the game.

In this instance a winner credited with three boxes more than his opponent would collect $1.60.)

Straight Gin Rummy

This version is probably played as much as, if not more than, Gin Rummy itself. Well, it is Gin Rummy itself, but the scoring is drastically simplified. The saving on bookkeeping is the main reason for its popularity. It is played exactly as is Gin Rummy with the following exceptions:

1. The amount of the stake is agreed upon before the start of the game. It is a lump sum, not a multiple of points.

2. The player who first scores 100 or more points is the winner, and is paid the lump amount agreed.

3. The difference in count between winner and loser is irrelevant. Box and game bonuses are not reckoned.

BUT . . .

4. If a player scores a shutout, that winning player is paid double the amount of the agreed stake.

Old-fashioned or Turn-up Gin

In this version of Gin Rummy and all the other versions which follow, the nondealer is dealt *only ten cards* instead of the customary eleven. The twenty-first card dealt is turned face up on the table beside the stock, and is called the *upcard.*

1. The nondealer begins the play by either taking the upcard into his hand or declining it.

2. If he declines it, the dealer in turn has the option of taking it or declining it.

3. If the dealer declines the upcard, the nondealer must take the top card of the stock.

4. After the first card has been picked up by either player, then that player must discard one card from his hand onto the discard pile.

5. Play thereafter continues as in Gin Rummy.

Spades Double Turn-up Gin

If the twenty-first card is a spade, the points won in that hand are doubled. Because of this feature, game is 150 instead of 100.

Oklahoma Gin

In this variation the twenty-first card, which the dealer has faced and made the upcard, determines the maximum number of points in unmatched cards with which a player may knock. For example, if the dealer turns up a 6-spot (suit doesn't matter), then the player who proposes to knock must have in his hand 6 points or less in unmatched cards—as compared with the regulation 10 points or less of Gin Rummy. It is suggested that when playing this game you note on the score sheet, at the moment it is turned, the numerical value of the twenty-first card, the upcard. It avoids debate.

Game is 150 points. Penalty for underknock is 20 points, Gin bonus 25 points, boxes 25 points.

If the upcard is an ace, there is no knock—players must go for Gin. Oklahoma usually incorporates the Spades Double feature. When the upcard is a spade, the count of boxes and bonuses are doubled.

Oklahoma Gin with Extra Bonuses (Kisses)

The same as Oklahoma Gin except that besides the usual bonuses for Gin and underknock, two extra boxes are given for Gin and one extra box is given for underknock. However, in Partnership Gin, only the winning team gets the extra boxes. If A is ginned by X for 37 points but his partner B gins Y for 40 points, AB gets 3 points plus 2 boxes and XY gets nothing. If spades are double, bonus boxes are doubled, 2 for underknock, 4 for Gin. *A Vital Point in Oklahoma Strategy:* The fact that only the team winning the hand can get extra boxes is a crucial factor in the play of the hand. If your partner has been ginned for 67 points and it appears that you can't get it back, even with Gin, don't try for Gin unless the game is involved and then only if you think that going Gin may save the game. Here's why: you can't get extra boxes by going Gin whereas your opponent *can* get extras by ginning you. The odds are far and away against you. On the other hand, if your partner has given you a comfortable lead so that even if you are ginned you will not lose the box, it's worth trying for Gin even with unlikely (but not practically impossible) chances. The odds favor it. You can get extra boxes; your opponent can't.

SCHNEIDER DOUBLES EVERYTHING

Most Oklahoma players and many regular Gin Rummy players double points, game and box bonuses in the case of a shutout or schneider. This is rather high flying and makes for terrific swings, but some like it that way.

Lay-off Gin Rummy

As I've said, I don't recommend this version. I have seen it played a few times, but never by big-money gamblers. In my opinion it is highly unsound to let a player lay off cards on a Gin hand. But in purely encyclopedic interests, here it is:

The game is played exactly like Gin Rummy, with the following exceptions:

1. A player is permitted to lay off cards on Gin.
2. A player who scores an underknock gets a bonus of 15 points instead of the 10-point bonus of Gin Rummy.
3. The Gin bonus is 25 points.
4. And, should a player go Gin by laying off cards, he wins the hand and receives a 30-point bonus plus the difference in points between the players.

Super-Gin

This is Lay-off Gin with two added features:

Gin on Gin. Laying off all unmatched cards on an opponent's Gin to go Gin yourself is worth 50 points.

Eleven-card Gin. Going Gin with all eleven cards matched (not requiring the discard of the eleventh card) is worth 50 points.

CHAPTER TEN

The Play of the Hand at Gin Rummy

Arbitrarily, at the very outset, I can make this promise: no matter how good a Gin player you are, this chapter will improve your game. It is a collection of tips and hints—dark hints, some of them, I'm afraid—that I've gathered over the years from the country's crack players. The analysis, which is the first of its kind ever organized, will center on Gin Rummy, but most of the counsel can be put to profitable use in any game of the Rummy family.

Let me interpolate this right now: I am not going to insist on the fiction that these games are played for pastime only.

They aren't. They are played for money. Card games that lack the gambling element, the profit motive, don't attain mass popularity.

You may not construe it as gambling when you play for small beers, and your wife or mother might be horrified—or tickled—if it were suggested that when she plays for the hand-crocheted quince pot-pie at the Tuesday Afternoon she's gambling. But there it is. It matters not what is the stake. The gambling and the gambling incentive are there, the essence of the thing, and must be taken into consideration.

Why then, luck being canceled out, do some players win more games than others? Why are some gamblers consistent winners over other professional gamblers? Why do some players lose constantly to certain opponents yet win constantly from yet other players? Why are some normally intelligent and diligent persons very, very bad Rummy players? Is it true that good players don't play the same kind of game but have each of them a little special knowledge—their own system—of the play of the cards?

Watching thousands of Rummy players and tens of thousands of Gin games down these last twenty years, I've made it my business to observe the small fleeting mannerisms of winning and losing competitors, to cross-examine hundreds and hundreds of experts, to measure the difference imposed on the play by the stakes of the game, to see not only *that* sober citizens do indeed bet $10,000 on a single game but *how* they bet it.

And so I can tell you this:

Every player who is a consistent winner has little tricks of his own. There are, in the mass, scores of such tricks, developed over the lives of these players by trial and error and by costly experience into a very substantial body of learning. No one player has mastered all of them. Perhaps no one player can. But I'm going to tell you about them.

First, I think we ought to hear to the end the professional gambler who says of a fellow player: "He has no card sense at all!"

What is this card sense? Of what is it made up? Well, its components are not so many. Card sense is knowing what to do and when. At Gin Rummy, shall you go down now or on the next pick; should you take your chance and go for Gin or wait and see if you can't *underknock* your opponent when he goes down; should you break up this pair and try for that sequence; should you throw away this card or will it help your opponent? To be a good card player, to have good card sense, you must have a reason for making any of these decisions. And reasoning is the application of intelligence.

Perhaps it will sound a little too austere to say that card sense requires an understanding that card games are based on mathematics. I won't say that, although the players who appreciate it are the players who win. I'll say instead that card games are based on the fact that in a pack there are fifty-two cards running in sequences of thirteen from ace to king in four suits, clubs, hearts, diamonds, and spades.

You know that. The knowledge is a part of the fiber of most card players. With this vast majority it's a matter of habit.

With a small minority it's a science. Watch them. In the game of Rummy there are ninety-six three-card melds. There are fifty-two melds of three of a kind, i.e., cards of the same rank: three aces, three deuces, and so on. There are forty-four melds of three cards of the same suit in sequence, i.e., 3-4-5 of hearts, 9-10-jack of spades, and the like.

But after you have formed a three-card meld it is twice as hard to extend three of a kind into four of a kind as it is to extend a sequence. For a sequence meld can be extended at either end (except ace-2-3 and jack-queen-king), whereas three of a kind can be bettered only one way. Besides, a sequence meld of four cards can be extended into five, one of five into one of six; and four cards of equal rank have no further possibilities. They're dead.

Let's look further into the mathematics of the game. Take the four aces in your hand. These can be formed into four three-card melds:

1. Aces of spades, hearts, diamonds.
2. Aces of spades, hearts, clubs.
3. Aces of spades, clubs, diamonds.
4. Aces of hearts, clubs, diamonds.

But if one of those aces is dead—discarded or held by an opponent in his hand—the chance of making up a meld of three aces is only 25 per cent of the probability were all four alive.

Not many players drudge it out to this extent, but even the beginner or the hardened muddler practices to a degree what I've been preaching. When he holds a pair of 10's and knows that there are two more 10's in his opponent's hand or in the stock he says that his two 10's are alive—and he is applying mathematics whether he likes it or not.

This must in the Gin Rummy player become automatic: he must be able to visualize all the possible melds in a hand the instant he picks it up. He must memorize and be able to visualize all his possible melds; he must be able to calculate at sight the probabilities for his two of a kind, his two-card sequences; and he must not overlook any melds he may hold. There is a way—a method devised by a famous Gin Rummy player who has won thousands at the game—of cultivating this knack of forming mental pictures and avoiding fatal plays in the early stages of the game.

It is a way of picking up cards which have just been dealt.

This ice-cold splendid gambler never picks up his ten cards all at one time. It is impossible, he says, to impress them on the mind when they confront the eye all in their natural confusion. So he picks them up one at a time, sorting them as he goes, impressing them on his mind and marshaling them for his first play. Moving thus deliberately, he can appraise the odds on every possible combination of his cards; and, at the very least, he has them in orderly array when the time comes for him to make his first draw.

This is his secret. More players make their bad play at the start of the hand than at any other time.

Never forget it: pick up your hand slowly. Arrange it carefully. Think. Think first about your own resources and strategy, then about your opponent's.

The Skill

Gin is a game of deduction and counter-deduction. You must try to figure out what is in your opponent's hand so that (1) you won't give him any useful cards, and (2) you won't be holding cards for an impossible or unlikely meld.

Every upcard your opponent takes and every discard he makes is a clue to what is in his hand and what is not in his hand. And the *cards that are not discarded* are clues also. As the play of the hand progresses, you know more and more about the cards he is holding; and you get this information by what he has shown you in taking certain cards, in discarding certain cards, and in *not* taking or in *not* discarding certain other cards. This is the simple, obvious part of the game. You don't need me to tell you that the discard of a 10 is dangerous if no 10's have shown well along in the play of the hand; or that the discard of the 10 of clubs is safe if the 9 and the jack of clubs and two other 10's have been discarded; or that the 10 of clubs is dangerous if your opponent has taken the 9 of clubs, after two other 9's have been discarded. Those are simple deductions.

But let's examine the case of the 10 of clubs when your opponent has taken the 9 of clubs and no other 9's have shown, nor the 8 or 7 of clubs. Was that 9 for 9's or for a club run? The inexpert player will say to himself, "Can't tell yet so I'll hold on to it," and thereby increase his holding of unmatched cards, and force the discard of some other dangerous card or some other possibly useful card. The expert player approaches the matter in a different way. He says to himself, "This is a high card, quite useless to me. Can I be reasonably safe in discarding it? Could it from a meld of 10's? No two 10's have been discarded. Will this add to opponent's club run or was that 9 of clubs for a meld of 9's? Well, let's see what has happened with the 8's. Opponent took the 8 of diamonds and discarded the 7 of diamonds. Therefore the 8 of diamonds was taken for 8's including probably the 8 of clubs. And so, I'll discard the 10 of clubs. True, opponent may have four 8's with a club run cutting through, but the greater probability by far is that he has 8's and 9's."

In other words, the expert player uses not only direct *positive* evidence but also indirect *probable* evidence, and all the previous play goes into the appraisal of the probability in each case. In this case, the 7 of diamonds discard indicated that the 10 of clubs was a reasonably safe play. That was not the only evidence of course, but taken together with the other evidence, it was the determining factor.

The expert player, then, makes deductions not only from the cards he himself holds, but also from *every* card his opponent has taken or discarded.

However, *counter-deduction* is just as important as deduction. Bear in mind that while you are trying to find out what is in your opponent's hand, he is trying to figure out what is in your hand. You can't help giving him some clues, but you must try to give him as few as possible. Also, in whatever ways possible you should try first to deceive or confuse him by giving him false clues or leading him to make incorrect deductions. I'll go into that further in a moment but I want to point out right here that you must realize that your opponent, if he knows the game, also is engaged in this counter-deduction operation and is trying to deceive you just as hard as you are trying to fool him. If he isn't, you'll have a cinch.

Counter-deduction in Gin is a unique art. Its two major elements are "propaganda" and false-picking (sometimes called "spitballing"). "Conversation" is really the lesser part of propaganda and many experts frown on it. It is more effective actually for amusement and for the relief of the player's nervous tension than for deception. But anyone who is good at "conversation" will affect his opponent's play occasionally by complaining about his hand, by expressing dismay at some difficult discard, by exclaiming with surprise, "That one!" when the opponent takes a discard, by an exclamation of satisfaction when picking a card off the stock, etc. Theoretically, this conversation will cause the opponent to be overoptimistic or unduly scared, to act otherwise than normal wisdom calls for. Feeling safe because he thinks you have a poor hand, he may knock with 7 and be trapped into an underknock. Or, being scared, he may break up the two kings he has been holding and thus either give you the card you want or ruin his own chances for high card melds that are just about due to come in.

The handling of the hand, however, is the better part of "propaganda." What you do with the card you take off the stock is noted carefully by your opponent. If you discard it immediately your opponent knows you haven't improved your hand. I don't say you should never do that. Rather, when you want your opponent to be cautious, when you want him to believe you are in good shape, it's important to do that a few times. Then, when you take a card and put it carefully between two other cards in your hand, he will be certain that you have completed a meld. Conversely, when you want him to be overconfident, be careful when picking a good card to avoid making that evident to your opponent. An occasional shifting of your cards will tend to make him think that you have improved your hand. Dont' shift if you don't want him to know of an improvement. Shift if you want him to believe you have improved.

Every element of your behavior during the play of the hand is a clue to a clever opponent. If you show that you are worried and unhappy about your cards, or, on the other hand, cheerful and confident, your opponent consciously or subconsciously will act accordingly. So remember that your opponent is playing against *you* as well as against your cards. Therefore don't give him any good clues. Either give him false clues or if you think you can do it, play absolutely "dead pan." That's difficult. You must be sure to place each and every card you pick in your hand, deliberate just about the same amount of time for each card and then discard, showing no change of expression throughout the play.

On the other hand, provided your opponent hasn't read this book, you may possibly get clues from the way he handles his cards. Observe his placement of cards for a while. Is he aware of the necessity of concealing the development of his hand?

Let's say he doesn't seem to be. He doesn't shift his cards around, he discards picks immediately, and in general he is playing a straightforward game, unaware of the fact that you are on the *qui vive* for hints and information. Let's act on that. He picks a card, puts it on the left end of his hand and discards the second card from the right end, a king of hearts. It's a fair assumption that the end card on the right is another king or the queen of hearts. Okay, you knock with 9, confident that he has at least a useless king or queen. Were you right? Yes. Then continue to act on this weakness. Were you wrong?

Then study his technique a little more and see if you can find a dependable hole in his play. Feel him out like a quarterback observing and testing an opposing line.

Now let's get back to the start of the game. When arranging cards in your hand, put together:

1. Your melds.

2. Your possible melds; that is, two cards of the same rank or of suit sequence.

3. Your unmatched cards according to suits.

Group your two-way combinations in some way, logical to you, so that they can be recognized easily. If you have the 6 of diamonds, 6 of spades, and 7 of spades, they should go together that way so that if another 6 or an end card of the spade sequence turns up, it will fit tidily into your holding. But—

4. Avoid having a regular high to low order for your ten cards. Don't put your high combinations on one end and your low ones on the other end. Keep combinations together; mix high and low combinations.

After having arranged your cards so as to impress them on your memory, you must now mix them up during play (the same as all expert Bridge players do during the play of the hand). Don't keep your melds or possible melds together, for the simple reason that you may thereby give your opponent the same kind of information that you are attempting to gather from the way he plays and arranges his cards.

Taking or Passing the First Card

Let's say the upcard (assuming you're playing Turn-up Gin) is the 3 of hearts. It does not give you a meld. Does that mean that you should pass it without question? Not at all. It may be worth taking if it helps your hand even though it does not give you a meld. If you reduce your hand by getting rid of a useless high card or if it gives you a likely combination—say you have the 4 of hearts and the 3 of clubs—it may be well worth while because you have the extra advantage of deceiving or puzzling your opponent.

Are you losing a turn, giving up a chance to pick a really helpful card by taking a slightly helpful one? Not at all. You have your choice of passing and not helping your hand at all or helping your hand a little, confusing your opponent a little, and also perhaps depriving him of a chance to improve his hand.

Remember, however, that when your opponent is first, he also may be taking the first card to deceive you.

When to Go Down

There can be no definite instruction at this point without ifs, ands, and buts. All things being equal, it is best to go down as soon as you can. Don't let the extra reward in points, in thrill and in personal satisfaction, trap you into waiting for Gin when your knocking hand is an almost certain winner.

But the major altering factor on this point is the score. Remember that the big reward is the game bonus of 100 points and only slightly less important are the box bonuses of 20 points each. (Box bonuses often amount to more than the game bonus.) Always keep the score in mind, and consider the possibilities and probabilities in the light of the score. This is doubly important in the case of Partnership Gin. If your partner has won 25 points and you can knock even with as much as 10, the thing to do is knock. You can't lose the box even if underknocked (with 10 or 15 points for underknock) and you'll probably win some points. But if you keep playing and are ginned, you can lose 30 points and the box (if the Gin bonus is 20). The same principle applies with a variation of the scoring system.

Get the box. That's worth 20 points and if waiting for Gin puts the box in jeopardy, the odds are almost sure to be against you if you figure that you are staking that 20 points against the possible extra winnings to be gained by going Gin.

On the other hand, if your partner has lost 30 points and you have good possibilities for getting Gin, it is probably worth trying for Gin instead of knocking because then you have the extra reward of the 20 points for the box besides the Gin points to outweigh the possibilities of losing the hand or being ginned. However, if your partner's loss puts the game in danger (your opponent being close to or over 125), then discretion is the better part of valor. Get a few points if you can and save the game.

It may seem elementary to pay attention to the score, but it is amazing how often failure to do so makes the difference between a big winner and a big loser.

This principle applies in even greater degree in Hollywood Gin and in Extra Bonus or Kisses Gin.

You wouldn't give two to one that a tossed coin will come up heads. Then don't give similar wrong odds by holding a knock hand for Gin. Even if your chances of getting Gin are very good, count the stakes first: What is there to gain? What is there to lose? If you stand to lose more than you can gain, you may be giving two to one on heads. If you stand to gain more than you can lose, you may be getting two to one on heads.

In Extra Bonus Partnership Gin, don't try to get Gin (and thereby risk being ginned) when it is hopeless to recoup your partner's loss. If you can't win the boxes for Gin, don't risk losing more boxes. There's no percentage in that.

The Knock-Reserve

Keep a few low cards and try to get three or four that total 10 or less. Then if you get two three-card runs or a three-card and a four-card run, you will be able to knock. In Oklahoma, this factor is even more important. If the knock-point is 2 and you get a deuce or an ace, don't discard it. Save it so that if you fill your other runs you will be able to go down and avoid being frustrated by picking a series of high cards while your opponent is steadily improving his hand.

Holding High Cards or Low Cards

The only thing I can say about this is don't have a set policy on this point. Don't be known as a player who always holds high cards or as one known always to discard high cards. Play your hand for what it's worth. In general, the advantages of high cards—they are most likely to be discarded by your opponent—are matched by their disadvantages: they cost more and they delay your reaching a knock point.

But if you are holding high cards bear in mind

Keeping Under

When your opponent's point total is close to game you must be extra careful about the unmatched card point total in your hand. You must try to "keep under." That means that you must reduce your point total so that, if possible, even if he goes Gin you will still be under. Short of that, try to get your total low enough so that a knock will not win the game for your opponent. I agree that there are times when it is a better bet for reduction to hold those two 10's with the probability of getting the third one, than to discard them in favor of a 5 and a 6. But in most cases, if you are aware of the necessity for reduction, you will be able to discard high cards with safety equal to the discard of low cards. Also there are times when your chances of getting low card melds are just as good as your chances of high card melds.

Just being aware of the necessity of keeping under will improve your winning chances by 25 to 33-1/3 per cent. Except for expert play, my observation is that every third or fourth final hand of a game is lost because of the avoidable failure to keep under.

Tips on Discards

Your first discard is and ought to be the most difficult to decide. You have no idea what your opponent is holding and looking for. The principle being to discard that card least likely to form a meld, you are guided to your judgment by the upcard and the cards you hold.

You are undecided whether to discard this lone king of spades or this lone 10 of spades? Why, it's advisable to throw the king.

And you know why.

Because, of course, there are two ways less to form a meld in a spade sequence using the king than there are using the 10. The only cards with which the king is useful are the jack and the queen. But the 10 will make a meld with the 8 and 9, the 9 and jack, or the jack and queen.

That's the principle. It holds for every successive play in the game.

To a player with a developed card sense, the first few plays at Gin will always seem the most dangerous. After a few plays it is fairly easy for a good Gin player to recognize a live card—one that can be used by his opponent to form a meld—or a dead card. It is deduced by remembering the discards and whatever upcards the opponent has picked, plus watching the shifting array of cards in your hand.

By all means, the more discards you can remember during the play of a box, the better are your chances of winning. Acuteness of this kind of memory must be developed and trained, but one thing the player *must* remember from the very start: that is the upcards, discards, which the opponent has picked up. If he can't do that he can't play Gin; he's playing a game of pure chance, a sort of complicated, bothersome game of showdown.

Throw an opponent two cards in succession that form part of one meld only when you have reason to believe that you can underknock his ensuing knock.

Taking an Upcard That Does Not Help

As for speculation in upcards, that's up to you. Some experts strongly advise against picking up a discard unless it will round out an immediate meld. But I've seen impossible hands pulled out of the fire by just such speculation. I've seen excellent Gin players snatch up a discard for no purpose but to prevent an opponent from knocking: psychological warfare, the war of nerves. I've seen many a speculation end in disaster. It's up to you.

But I don't think that any man is master of the game unless he knows how and when to speculate. It's part of bluffing. It's part of the great game of Gin.

One gambler of my acquaintance invariably picks up any upcard of value of 3 or less. His rationalization of this is that:

1. If he should happen to get caught, his points in unmatched cards would be so low that they would profit his opponent little.

2. And when he knocks with 10 or less—with the aid of his opponent's low discards—he will tend to catch the opponent with higher unmatched cards. A hand deliberately reduced will average lower than a run-of-mill hand with its normal quota of 7's and 10's and honors.

I've watched him play hundreds of games over a period of years, and I've just about come to agree with him that there's an advantage in picking up any card of value of 3 or less—

UNLESS—unless it involves being compelled to discard a live card that may put your opponent Gin.

Since we're speculating about speculation, you'd better hear the other side of the argument. This is the policy of another high-stakes gambler, a consistent winner.

"When I have a hand in which my unmatched cards total 11 or a little more," he told me, "and when I don't think my opponent can knock yet, I'll pick up a live picture-card discard."

That's called a false speculation. "False spec" is the professional idiom.

The arguments in its favor are worth your closest attention.

Suppose you're holding a total of 11 points in unmatched cards—the 5 of clubs, 3 of diamonds, 2 of spades, and ace of hearts. You can't knock. You have to deduce from your opponent's behavior that he can't knock. To knock you must get a card lower than a 5.

Your opponent throws the live king of diamonds. You pick it up.

What do you lose? One pick off the stock.

What do you gain? Well, you have probably convinced your opponent that you have just made a meld in kings or have completed a sequence in diamonds. And now if his hand contained two kings and he broke them up he will suspect you of having a diamond run, while if he is holding the diamond sequence he will be confident that you are playing the kings.

In any event, he will from that point on hold back his high diamonds or his kings. The chance that he will be throwing low cards—cards lower than the 5—is greatly increased. And you are meanwhile taking your usual picks from the stock, minus the one you invested in the bluff.

When you do draw your knock card or your opponent throws it to you, you discard the phony king and you catch him with a handful of high cards that otherwise he would have long since thrown away. And should your ruse fail you lose only 5 points more than you would have lost otherwise.

But it works nine out of ten times. And it is still working when you take a picture card off the discard pile to form a genuine meld. For now your baffled opponent, remembering your false spec, will breezily proceed to throw Gin-going picture cards at you.

Speculate high or speculate low? It's up to you.

Discarding

When possible it is advisable to discard a card of rank equal to one which your opponent has previously discarded. There are only four possible ways in which an equal-rank card can be used against you. Any other card can be used six ways in a meld. That is, unless you're holding stoppers: cards which will prevent a discard from being used in a meld by your opponent.

But when throwing a discard of rank equal to one previously discarded by your opponent bear in mind that this may be precisely what he wanted you to do. He may have thrown the first as what is called a "salesman." He may want your card of equal rank but in a different suit. All players use salesmen from time to time; it is the job of card sense to detect the little fellow and resist his blandishments.

When you decide to break up a pair and the other two cards of the same rank are alive and perhaps in your opponent's hand, don't talk about that. What he doesn't know can't hurt you. And maybe he won't know unless you tell him that all four cards are alive.

Fattening

Sometimes it is wiser to discard a card that you know will add to your opponent's meld than any other card in your hand. If you know he has a four-card run, say 6-7-8-9, a fifth card probably won't help him much and it is extremely unlikely for him to go Gin with two five-card runs. Even if you believe

it is only a three-card run, it may be better to "fatten" him
with a fourth card rather than give him an alternate card which
may give him a new three-card run.

If he has picked the 8 of clubs and you have the jack or
even the 10, don't hold on to it indefinitely without considering
the various possibilities. Did he take it for 8's instead of a club
run? If it is a club run, how far up does it go? Is it possible
that another run has cut it off? He may have the 6-7-8-9 of
clubs *and* two other 9's. He wouldn't take the 10 of clubs if
you threw it, and you wouldn't be able to lay it off if he
knocked.

Furthermore, when you are aiming for an underknock, fattening can be very useful. You can trap your opponent into
going down by giving him that extra card that enables him to
get under 10.

Conversely, be careful when you are being fattened. Will
the extra card force you to discard a dangerous one and break
up a good meld possibility? Is your opponent trying to trap
you into knocking? When he gives you that 10 of clubs, does
he have the jack ready to lay off? What was his purpose?
Think it over. It's important.

Looking at Discards, or, the Magic Eye

Although it is my ruling and the standard practice of the
game that discards cannot be spread and examined, nevertheless experts—gamblers—glean a lot of forgotten lore from the
discard pile.

The discard pile is seldom so perfectly squared up that a
player cannot see a few cards whenever he really wants to.

And the information refreshed in your memory by a glance
may be crucial to the development of the hand.

Before discarding, if you are the least bit doubtful about
the play, go ahead and take a candid peek at the discard pile.
Everyone else in the house is doing it. Don't be a chump.

A crackerjack player put it to me this way:

"Don't try to study the discards. Just try to form them in
your mind into sequences. If you see a 10-jack-king of spades
in the discard pile, you start thinking in terms of queens. All
right; look again. You're looking now for any other queen.
And if you don't see her in the discards, rest assured that the
queens are alive and kicking."

Laying Down Hand When Knocking

Especially when laying down low melds—ace-deuce-3-4 and
the like—there are abundant chances for error. Whenever a

meld can be formed in more than one way, add up the total points of the possible ways and then lay down the meld adding to the highest total.

You have a 2-3-4 of spades and the 2 of hearts and 2 of diamonds. The spade sequence totals 9, the three deuces total 6; so you lay down the sequence.

But caution! If from the play of the hands up to this time you have reason to believe that your opponent can meld a 5 of spades on your sequence, it becomes imperative to break up the sequences and lay off the three deuces. The shifting mathematics of the game must dictate your decision.

Nevertheless, one canon of melding is inflexible. Should you have a four-card sequence and simultaneously three cards of equal rank matching either of the end cards of the sequence, invariably lay down the four of a kind as your meld. Your opponent can't lay off cards on four of a kind. He can lay off at either end of a sequence.

Slicing a Lay-off

Sometimes when knocking, it is worthwhile discarding the top or bottom card of a four- or five-card sequence. Let's say you have picked the 10 of spades after two 10's have been discarded. The king and queen of spades and two other jacks also have been discarded. But you haven't seen the jack of spades. Your opponent is probably holding it for a layoff. You have just picked a third 5 so that discarding a 2, you can go down with a deuce and two aces for 4. Instead, you discard the 10 of spades from the 7-8-9-10 sequence and go down with 6, catching your opponent with a useless jack, perhaps the only unmatched card in his hand. This is a very useful play at times but it must be used with judgment.

The Probabilities

Finally, I advise you to study the mathematics of the game. Here is a table of the chances in Gin. Bear them in mind during the course of play and you'll be sure to come out ahead of the fellow who doesn't know his percentages.

The Mathematics of Gin

It is, I take it, the author's privilege ·to point out—and the player's privilege to ignore—the fact that there are 15,820,-024,220 possible ten-card hands in Gin Rummy. In every game there occurs a certain incidence of useless statistics. I don't expect you to remember how often in how many billion hands

your present holding will occur. I shouldn't be surprised if you
would fail to remember that the chances of the dealer's being
dealt a meld in his first ten cards are about two out of every
five deals—although remembering that will improve your
game. I'm not going to insist that you bear in mind the chances
of the nondealer's being dealt a meld in the first eleven cards
he sees are about one out of two—although noting the subtle
difference in those odds will make you a better player. I'm
not schoolmarm enough to insist that you learn by rote everything I know about every game I know. When you need the
mathematics they'll be here for you. Meanwhile, I shan't impose them on you.

But I think I'm going to have to ask you to pay close attention to what happens when, carelessly or not, you play certain
cards from your hand at Gin.

When you are the nondealer and have been dealt eleven
cards, the chance that your opponent can use in a meld the
first card you discard from your hand . . .

If the discard is a	The odds are approximately
King or ace	1 in 6
Queen or deuce	1 in 5
Any other card	1 in 4.7

(This calculation is based on your opponent's using the card
forthwith in a meld, not on his considering the card as an
improvement of his hand or as reducing his total of unmatched
cards. Nor is the value of the cards in your own hand taken
into consideration. This is a mathematical problem, not a
strategic one.)

It is genuinely important to your play of the cards that you
know and conform your play to the above odds. It is likewise
important that you consider the fact that, holding a split sequence such as the 3 and 5 of spades, you have only one
chance of forming a three-card meld—by drawing the 4 of
spades. It is important that you bear in mind the fact that,
if the king of hearts is dead and you hold the king of spades,
you now have only one way of forming a three-king meld and
only one way of making the king-queen-jack of spades. It is
important that you remember that if the 10 of spades too is
dead, there's no way on earth of your making a four-card
meld with the spade king.

Knowledge of the number of ways a card can be used to
form a three- four- or five-card meld must be a part of every
competent Gin player's equipment.

In Gin the 7 is the most valuable card in the deck as far as
forming melds is concerned—just as the 7 is the crucial point
at Dice because it occurs oftenest. The 7 can be used to

extend melds more than any other card. The 7 can be used in seven different seven-card sequence melds, whereas the most valuable of the twelve other cards can be used only to form six-card sequences.

I don't mean to overload you with mathematics. It would confuse the reader rather than enlighten him if I were to detail the number of ways any card can be used to form sequence melds of six or more cards. I have chosen to restrict the following chart—which should be memorized by every Gin player —to three- four- and five-card melds.

	Number of ways card can be used in a three-card meld.	Number of ways card can be used in a four-card meld.	Number of ways card can be used in a five-card meld.
King or ace	4	2	1
Queen or deuce	5	3	2
Jack or 3	6	4	3
10 or 4	6	5	4
9 or 5	6	5	5
8 or 6	6	5	5
7	6	5	5

The above chart is useful mainly when the player is in the throes of deciding which card to discard. Observe, if you will, that the 5, 6, 7, 8, and 9 are likely to be the most useful to your adversary, the king and ace the least useful. (And observe, too, that the number of ways in which a card can be useful is directly affected by the number of pertinent dead cards known.) The utilitarian disadvantages of the ace, deuce, and 3 are somewhat balanced by the fact that they are low-count cards, useful in knocking.

There are two ways of completing a three-card meld out of a two-card matched combination, whether the meld is to be a sequence or a combination of cards having the same numerical rank. The only exception to this two-way principle is when forming a sequence meld involving the ace or the king. Naturally, the number of ways to complete the meld is reduced by each known dead card. And the split sequence is always the exception. Holding the open-ended sequence of deuce-trey of spades, you can fill either end, you can fill two ways. But if you hold the deuce and 4 of spades, you can form a three-card meld only one way—by drawing the 3 of spades. The point may seem rudimentary. But watch how often thoughtless players will nurse along relatively hopeless split sequences in the delusion that they are handling their cards with uncanny subtlety.

Let's reduce it to a table again.

Ways of Forming a Four-card Meld from a Three-card Meld

	Sequences	Equal rank
Without the king or the ace in the three-card meld	2	1
With the king or the ace in the three-card meld	1	1

Note: Be sure to deduct chances that are killed by dead cards.

CHANCE FOR GIN WITH THREE-CARD MELDS

I.

You have nine ways to go Gin when you hold three three-card sequences which can be switched about to form three three-card melds of the same rank. This holding constitutes your maximum chance of a killing. (Again we except melds involving dead-end aces and kings.)

Example: You hold the 7-8-9 of clubs, 7-8-9 of diamonds, and 7-8-9 of spades. These can be construed and used as three 7's, three 8's, and three 9's. And the player has nine chances of drawing a card to go Gin. (Three 6's, three 10's, one each 7, 8, 9.)

II.

Your minimum chance of going Gin even with three melds in your hand occurs when you're holding three unrelated groups of cards of equal rank or three unrelated sequences, each involving an ace or king.

You're considering whether or not to try for Gin. Now let's compute your chances. And let's assume you have the dream maximum set forth under No. I above. Now, further assuming that none of the 9's has been discarded, here's how to compute your chances of going Gin:

1. Subtract the ten cards you hold from the total in the deck, fifty-two.

2. Subtract the number of discards from this remainder, forty-two.

3. Now divide the remaining total by nine. Your chances of going Gin are one out of the final number you've computed.

4. To determine the average number of picks a player will need to go Gin with a hand composed of three three-card melds, *halve this final answer.*

Example: Let's go back again to the dream hand described above. Six cards have been discarded.

Now subtract from the fifty-two cards in the deck the ten cards in your hand plus the six discarded cards.

This totals thirty-six. Divide that by the nine ways you can go Gin. The answer is four.

In this special circumstance, which is rather special indeed, the player will go Gin on the average with two picks (half of four)—because he has his choice of the upcard (opponent's discard) or the top card of the stock.

The above method of computation is even more valuable on the minimum-chance hands, in which the loss of even one chance for Gin becomes a dominant factor in the development of the play.

IN WHICH WE DENY INFALLIBILITY

To attempt telling the player when to knock or try for Gin when holding a hand that requires only one card for Gin seems to me unsound without knowledge of (a) the cards still alive and (b) the cards one's opponent has taken from the discard pile. As to this play, you must use your own judgment —as, in fact, you must learn to do in any hand at Gin Rummy.

SAUCE FOR THE GOOSE

Card distribution tends to run in patterns at any game. When you draw a good hand on the deal—a hand in which most of the cards are matched or near-matched—the odds favor the probability that your opponent holds at least one meld.

I think you'd better bear this too in mind. Freak distribution in one hand means a freak all the way around any table. When you get a specially promising hand, don't by any means neglect the possibility that your adversary is at least as well off as you are. This is simply a characteristic of cards. It is of no vital importance, once you've absorbed it. Nor need it be of vital importance—now that you've made it a part of your equipment—that the highest count any player can possibly be caught with on one hand is 98 points. That is, you can trap or be trapped with two kings, two queens, two jacks, two 10's, and two 9's not in sequence. Note that I mean the 98 is made up of actual card indices, and does not include Gin or box bonuses.

To go back to the beginning, there are 15,820,024,220 possible hands at Gin Rummy. To discuss any one of them to the exclusion of the rest would be to discuss a thing that—a million chances to one—will never occur in your experience. But there are certain valid general principles. I've tried to cover them, and if you remember nothing else about this chapter, remember this: the next opponent you encounter may know the mathematics of the game better than you. If he does he'll beat you in the long run. It's as simple a matter as that.

OBSERVATION

Maybe the following won't sound cricket. Inquiry: what *is* ethical in cards for cash? One player in the West Coast money crowd likes to arrange to stand behind any potential opponent and size up his style of play. He wants to know whether the man is methodical, whether he speculates rashly or well, whether he tries for a knock hand instead of for Gin, whether he gets nervous under the baleful glare of a fistful of high cards, how he talks when the cards are running with him and when they're against him. Card players, like everyone else, tend to be creatures of habit. They react, often unconsciously but always eloquently, to their circumstances. Is it unethical to study those reactions? I hope not. I've been doing it most of my life. And I'll generalize about what I've seen:

Many players will clam up when they have a bad hand and talk it up when they catch a good one.

The vast majority of players are methodical, no matter how they try to mix up their styles. And method can be observed and learned.

The most dangerous player is the man who has mastered the mathematics of his game, the man who plays what I call the two-way hand: one that will enable you to go Gin with a pick of one or two cards or to knock with a pick of one or two others.

Each hand at Rummy is a new hand. I can't tell you what cards to hold. I can't tell you A-B-C-fashion how to play them. Anything can happen, and you must be prepared to make the best of things as they are.

That takes in a lot of ground, dark and bloody ground, some of it.

It takes in a lot of things, cheats and grifters, some of them.

It's the game. You've got to make the best of it.

CHAPTER ELEVEN

Cheating at Gin Rummy

"Thrice is he armed that has his quarrel just"—
But four times he who gets the blow in fust.
—H. W. Shaw

I should not like to be understood by any means as recommending that you regard all Gin players—or even strangers on Mississippi packets who crisp the waxed tip of their mustaches and ask you if you'd care to engage in a contest of skill—as crooks in being or potential. I like a quiet game myself, and am sometimes allowed to sit in on one at the Chamber of Commerce offices in my home town after the week's work is cleaned up of a Saturday night—as long as I don't get caught dealing. Most card players, by all means the overwhelming majority, are or mean to be honest.

Most citizens are honest too, but we do not think it out of place to maintain police forces and a militia and an F.B.I. Most kids are honest, but we go a little out of our way to teach them ethics and the basic law and the spirit and letter of fair play. Our whole society is built on proper safeguards against the occasional stinker. And I think that a card player's equipment, especially if he plays for cash, must include a working knowledge of how the crook would—and, if he can, will—turn the innocent inside out. I've covered card cheating elsewhere in this book in a broad inclusive way, but there are certain larcenous techniques peculiar to Gin Rummy.

Bottom Stack

After a hand has been played and it becomes the cheater's turn to deal, he will leave on the bottom of the pack as he scoops the cards toward him an entire meld, usually four of a kind. He now gives the pack a riffle shuffle so as not to disturb the bottom four cards.

He cuts about one-third of the pack from the top, putting these cards at the bottom of the pack. And he now offers the pack to be cut. The average player will cut a pack about at the center. And now see what happens. Each of the two players receives two of these four of a kind!

The cheat knows two of the cards in your hand, but you cannot be aware that he has two of the same value. As a rule you will in the later phase of the play discard one of those cards, giving him his meld, or he will throw you one, proceeding to underknock your knock by laying off that fourth card on your meld.

This is one of the most common of all cheating devices and one of the most effective, because it is impossible to accuse any one of resorting to it. An honest player might shuffle the cards in the same way without any intention of burglary.

You can protect yourself against it by shuffling the cards before the dealer shuffles. My rules permit this. You cannot be embarrassed, and neither can your opponent, if you ask for a shuffle whenever you please.

Fifty-One Card Deck

If this one seems amateurish, so it is; but it is one of the commonest and least hazardous of cheating devices. Even when detected it doesn't rowel up suspicion.

When removing the new deck from the box the cheat leaves one card in the box. The cheat knows what card that is.

The advantage appears trivial. Is it? Let's see. Let's suppose that the card left unnoticed in the box is the 8 of diamonds. What can it do for him?

First, he will rarely try to make a meld of 8's, because he knows that the chances are only 25 per cent of normal. Second, he knows—and you don't—that the chance of getting a meld in a sequence involving the 8 of diamonds is zero. There are three such melds: the 6-7-8, the 7-8-9, and the 8-9-10. Plus the three melds of 8's in which the diamond would figure, it totals six dead melds out of a total of 104 melds in the game. It is a terrific advantage.

And there is a further refinement. If, during the play of the hand, you should find the missing card in the box the cheat will proceed to berate you. "Why," he'll say, if he knows his business, "why didn't you take them all out when we started?"—and, having forgotten who *did* take them out, you'll mumble your apologies.

The way to protect yourself against this infantile ruse is to count the cards before starting to play. More candid yet, look in the box.

No Cut

Taking measures, similar to the one described under "Bottom Stack," not to disturb certain cards, players will keep a group of cards at the top of the pack, then shuffle some cards over them, then deal without offering the deck to you for the cut. The effect on the game is the same as the bottom stack's effect.

If you ask for a cut they blandly murmur, "Sorry." If you don't, you're a dead duck.

Some cheats, when the cards have been cut in two but the cut has not yet been completed, will lean back and light a cigarette, then pick up the cards and put them back as they were before. The lapse of time and the intervening stage business may confuse you as to which block really goes on which. If surprised at it they're sorry too. And an innocent really will be sorry. But don't take your eye off your game.

Dealing From the Lower Piece of the Deck

The cheat knows what the top cards are. He shuffles. You cut. Instead of completing the cut, he picks up the lower piece of the deck, deals from it, and then carries out the rest of the cut by putting the remaining cards of the lower piece on the top piece.

It is a casual little informality. Watson could have used it against Holmes.

But after it is over the cheat knows precisely what cards are going to appear, and when, in the stock.

Don't allow any one to deal from half the pack. Insist on the completion of the cut before the deal begins.

Some cheats have a counter for that too, of course. When they carry the bottom piece over onto the top piece in completing the cut, they will not quite square the pack. A tiny step is left, showing them where are the cards they want. Insist that the pack be squared before the deal.

Signaling

He may look like an authentic kibitzer. But when you're playing for money, watch him. Satisfy yourself that no onlooker with access to your hand is signaling. It is often done amateurishly—or expertly. It is easy and deadly effective at Gin Rummy, because all that your opponent needs to know from his confederate is whether you have a high or low count in unmatched cards.

A well-conceived signal system is hard to detect and beat. If you entertain the merest suspicion that signals are being passed, play your next few hands too close to your vest for the kibitzer to see. If your luck unaccountably improves, Q.E.D.

Peeking at Two Cards

This is one of the most flagrant violations in the game and one of the most forgivable. Reaching for his draw from the stock, the cheat affects to fumble, and lifts two cards instead of his one. At a critical stage of the play that glance at your next card is all he needs to know.

To protect players against this violation, whether by design or by accident, I have made it a rule that the stock must be fanned out on the table. This may not eradicate the danger, but it will minimize it. And should the violation occur, the rules provide that the player who has committed it must show his own card just picked to his opponent.

By thus canceling his advantage this will temporarily make an honest man of the cheat.

Recognizable Cards

Some amateur cheats will bend the corner of certain cards so as to be able to spot them in play. Although the card is marked to the equal advantage of both players and thus is not a marked card in the professional sense of the term, it is a cheating device of, by, and for the cheat and against the decent player. *Don't play with an old or defaced pack of playing cards.*

Cheating on the Count

The practitioners of this crude larceny will keep a fair score sheet—until the count gets too close for comfort. Then, knowing that one point is at times the difference between winning and losing a game, with its big-money bonuses, they will miscall their points in unmatched cards and fan them casually before you, holding them in their hands. Then they toss them back into the deck. To prevent this, insist on the rule that unmatched cards be placed face up on the table separate from the melds. And count them yourself.

Also, check the addition of points, not only at the end of the game but also when each hand's score is entered; 87 plus 26 might be entered as 103, but it is 113. And it's so easy to add up a long score and be just an even 100 points out of the way. Added wrong? Oops, sorry.

Shuffling Cards Face Up

Some honest bunglers and many amateur cheats make it a habit to shuffle the cards face up, or to shuffle them edgewise to the table in such a way that their faces can be seen. Maybe it's just a carry-over from Solitaire or some other game in which the shuffle is immaterial. But maybe it's cold-blooded robbery. Demand of any such player that he shuffle the cards properly.

Hiding a Card

This is about as old and fully as sand-lot as baseball's hidden-ball trick. Like the hidden-ball trick, it has a way of working entirely too often. After your opponent has knocked, he lays down his melds, face up, just as the rules provide. His unmatched cards he likewise lays down, face up, right there in front of you.

But under his meld he has concealed an unmatched *high card*.

It works, unless you glance again at his cards and detect the shortage. Always count your opponent's cards to certify that he has exposed ten of them *face up*.

The Counterfeit Meld

Do you examine your opponent's melds closely? If not, you tempt him to slip in the queen of clubs between the king, jack and ten of spades. He'll put them down close together and with a little hocus-pocus about his other cards and "How many did I get you for?" etc., distract your attention and get away with it. How many times have you made a similar error yourself when first glancing at your cards? Watch it.

CHAPTER TWELVE

Other Rummy Games—I

Hundreds of kinds of Rummy, hundreds of different Rummy games, are being played throughout the United States as you read this. They are alike in these two remarkable ways:

1. The basic principles are identical.

2. Except when played by professional gamblers, they have some mathematical defect attributable to incorrect rules.

I have tried in the succeeding collection of laws to eliminate these mathematical flaws as much as I can without changing the structure of the game itself.

Most of the games in this chapter have been neglected by previous authors. To my knowledge they have not appeared in print up to now. I say "most." Some writers have alluded to some of the games, but have given rules either too confusing or too incomplete to be useful to any one trying to learn the game, and never adequate enough to settle controversies that arise in any kind of play.

I find these writers copying from each other. The external evidence suggests broadly that none of them has attempted to play the game for which they undertake to establish rules.

I have played these games. It has taken me years to collect the information about them. Some I picked up during off hours while on lecture tours. Other information I got from service men during the four years I acted as games consultant to the armed forces' *Yank*, the Army weekly, during World War II. I've played these games.

Let me interpolate another word by way of prologue. If you're a student of the game you'll observe that I introduce a few changes of its idiom. These are for the betterment of the game as a whole. For example:

All present-day compilers, copying from the old Hoyles dating back to the first *American Hoyle* of 1845, call the lead-off man, the competitor who makes the first play after the deal, "the Age."

That expression may have been descriptive of something back in the early 1800's, but today it is uncommunicative and useless; try telling your next Rummy player he's the Age, and see. From now on, the man who makes the first play in any Rummy game, the leadoff man, shall be known as the leader. Right?

The top card of the discard pile shall be known as the *upcard*.

An *irregular* pack of cards is:

1. A pack that has more or less cards than are required by the rules of the game being played.

2. A pack that has one or more cards of a design different from the deck's, which cards are not specified as permissible under the rules of the game being played.

A *misdeal* in Rummy, as in all card games, renders the involved deal or hand invalid, and a new hand must be dealt by the same dealer.

An *irregular* hand is one in which:

1. A player has in his hand more or fewer cards than the rules of the game command.

2. A player holds cards foreign to the pack in play.

The other expressions common to Gin Rummy—such as the meld, laying off, underknock, and so forth, have their customary meaning and validity.

One point which I do mean to cover definitely is the location of the deal and the seating of the players. I've seen entirely too many bitter arguments and indeed fist fights over players refusing to deal or to sit at the left of some other player. It's time for a final decision on this critically important aspect of the big-time game, simply because the subject has never been covered before. I'm not exaggerating when I say it's critically important. Why should we tolerate a situation in which Player A can sit all night and throw discards (*upcards*) to Player B just because that's the way they rig the game? If you sit to the left of a skillful player your chances of being thrown a valuable upcard are remote. If you sit to the left of a bad player, his discard errors will immensely improve your chances of winning.

And far too often confederates will sit next to each other and cheat with fantastic success by the primitive means of A's throwing discards that B can use.

I deem it advisable to formulate rules curing this unhealthy situation and obviating argument.

Unless otherwise stipulated under each game, the following general rules apply to all games of Rummy described in this chapter.

General Rules for Rummy Games

SELECTING THE DEALER AND ESTABLISHING
SEATING POSITIONS AT THE TABLE

1. Any player (preferably by mutual consent) shall shuffle the cards. Player to the dealer's right shall cut the cards.

2. Player acting as dealer shall deal one card to each player face up, starting with the player to his left and rotating clockwise.

3. Player dealt lowest-rank card becomes the first dealer, and may select any seat he wants.

4. Player dealt the next lowest card selects any remaining seat; player with third lowest, any remaining seat; etc.

5. In case of ties, each of the tied players shall be dealt another card face up, this to go on until the tie is broken.

6. On completion of each hand, the deal passes to the player to the left of the dealer of that hand.

THE SHUFFLE AND CUT

1. Dealer shuffles the cards. Any player may call for and shuffle the pack any time before the cut, although the dealer has the privilege of shuffling the pack last.

2. Dealer puts the pack of cards face down on the table to his right. The player to his right has first privilege of cutting the cards. If that player refuses to cut, any other player may cut. If all the other players refuse to cut, the dealer *must* cut the cards. He *cannot refuse!* At least five cards must be in each portion of the cut deck.

CHANGING SEATS

Some players like to change seats after a certain time or number of hands, but rarely do players agree on when.

Therefore, let us establish that *at the end of each hour of play* a new deal is in order as prescribed under the rules for "Selecting Dealer and Establishing Seating Positions." This ruling will make for a better all-around game of Rummy.

NO GAME

1. If it is established during or at the completion of a hand that the pack is *irregular*, that hand is void. If any scores have been previously entered toward a game, the entire game of which that hand is a part shall be *void*, and the game is *no game*.

2. If a game is completed and it then is discovered that an irregular pack has been used, that game and all previous games are *valid*.

MISDEALS: YES OR NO?

1. If a dealer or player accidentally turns up a card belonging to another player during the deal, that deal is void, a misdeal is declared, and the same dealer deals again.

2. If the dealer or a player accidentally turns up a card or cards belonging to himself, that deal stands.

3. If a card is found face up in the pack during the deal, there is a misdeal.

4. If a card is found face up in the stock during the play,

5. If one player or more has an irregular hand and it is discovered before the leader has completed his first play, that deal is a misdeal.

6. If *more than one* player has an irregular hand and it is discovered during the play, that hand is a misdeal.

DEAD HAND

If it is discovered that *one* player has an irregular hand during the play (after the leader has completed his first play), that player's hand is *dead*. He must put the cards aside, face down, and be adjudged a loser of that hand.

ON DRAWING FROM THE DISCARD PILE

1. When a play has been made from the discard pile—for instance, if an upcard or group of cards or the entire pile has been picked up as the rules of that game stipulate—and the card or cards have left the table or the top of the discard pile, that play cannot be changed. That play *must* be completed. A player cannot change his mind. He cannot put the card or cards back into the discard.

2. A player cannot discard an *upcard* he has just taken until his next turn of play.

DRAWING FROM THE STOCK

1. If a player picks a card off the stock, it is a play, regardless of whether the player looks at the card's face or not.

2. But if a player merely touches the top card of the stock, he does not have to take that card.

3. If a player in the act of drawing the top card sees any other card in the stock, or any other player has reason to believe that he has done so, then the first player must show his card to the rest of the players.

PLAYING OUT OF TURN

1. If a player takes an upcard or cards from the discard pile out of turn and it is discovered while he still has the card or cards in his hand, he simply puts the card or cards back on the discard.

2. If a player out of turn has taken a card off the stock *and has not looked at it*, he replaces it on top of the stock.

3. If a player has taken a card from the stock *and looked at it*, it is put back on the stock, and the stock is shuffled and cut. There is no penalty.

4. If a player has played out of turn and it is not discovered until after that player has completed his play, the play stands as if it were a proper turn of play, and the player whose turn it was to play *loses that turn*. It is up to the player to protect his own interests at all times.

MISCOUNT

If a player errs in counting his points, he may correct the error—if the correction is made before the next player starts his play.

REARRANGING MELDS

A player may rearrange his melds in any manner he likes, providing he does so before the next player *starts* his play.

ERRORS IN SCORING

If an error has been made in entering or adding scores, it may be corrected, but not if another game has been completed following the hand in which the error was made.

Straight Rummy

One of the most widely played games of the Rummy family; a game at least as widely played as Draw Poker; a favorite with gamblers, cops, athletes, children, ministers, and old ladies; a game in which millions of dollars a year change hands. This is Straight Rummy, one of the humble ancestors of glamorous Gin Rummy.

REQUIREMENTS

1. A standard pack of fifty-two playing cards.
2. From two to six participants.
3. Dealt hands of six or seven cards.

(*Note:* The variation called Seven-card Straight Rummy is favored by expert players, because it affords more latitude for strategy. Six-card Straight Rummy is recommended for two to five players, the most interesting game being constituted of four or five. Six may play, but the element of skill is minimized because the number of draws from stock by each player is reduced. Seven-card Straight is played by two to five players, the ideal game being constituted by four players.)

BEGINNING OF THE GAME

Selection of the dealer, seating positions, changing seats, shuffle, and cut are as provided under "General Rules for Rummy Games," page 89.

OBJECT OF THE GAME

1. To go Rummy by laying down the entire hand at one time in melds of three or four cards of the same rank (kind)

or three or more cards of the same suit in sequence, like the melds in Gin Rummy; or

2. To have the lowest total of points in unmatched cards at the end of the game.

VALUE OF CARDS

For scoring, the ace is low, counting one point; kings, queens, and jacks count 10 points; all other cards have their face value.

THE DEAL

Dealing one card to each player clockwise starting with the player at his left, the dealer gives to each the correct number of cards (six or seven, as agreed). The dealer gets the last card dealt.

(At this point it is the practice of some players to turn the next card face up on the table, making it the first *upcard*. I do not recommend that this card be faced up. It gives the leader an unearned and unfair advantage.)

The rest of the cards, the remainder of the deck, are placed face down on the table, forming the *stock*.

On completion of each hand, the deal passes to the player at the dealer's left.

THE PLAY OF THE HAND

The leader makes the first play by picking the top card of the stock. He then must discard one card. From that point on, each player in his turn of play, which goes clockwise, may take either the upcard or the top card of the stock, discarding one card to complete his play.

Play continues until a player goes Rummy and is declared the winner or until . . .

THE BREAK

Should the players fail to go Rummy and should cards in the stock be reduced to the number of players in the game, we arrive at a phase of the game called the break. The player whose turn it is to pick the top card of the stock is called the breaker.

After the break has begun, a player cannot in his turn pick the top card of the discard pile (upcard) *unless that card can be used in an immediate meld*.

When the cards are *broke* (i.e., when fewer cards remain in the stock than there are players in the game), the player breaking must put down all his melds on the table in separate sets and hold covered in his hand his unmatched cards. The next player does likewise, but may lay off cards if he can on any exposed melds. He also holds covered his unmatched cards. All the players do likewise in rotation.

When the last player has completed his play—

1. He announces the total value of the unmatched cards still in his possession, and shows the cards.

2. Rotating clockwise, each player in turn does the same until all the players have laid their unmatched cards on the table.

3. The player having the lowest score in unmatched cards is the winner.

Players cannot show their unmatched cards until the last play has been completed.

If two or more players have an equal number of points at the end of the game and the breaker is one of those players, the breaker wins. If neither of the tied players is the breaker, the winner is the one closest to the breaker's left.

THE PAY-OFF

1. Should a player be declared the winner after the break, either by having a lower card count or by going Rummy, he receives one unit from each other player.

2. Should a player go Rummy before the break, he receives two units from each player.

3. Should a player (a) go Rummy on his first pick or (b) go Rummy by melding his hand in a sequence of the same suit before the break, he receives four units from each player.

The unit may be any amount agreed upon.

Some players choose to pay off in multiples of the point value of unmatched cards. In such cases the principles enunciated above hold good.* Each player pays the winner on the difference in points between their scores.

VIOLATIONS AND INFRACTIONS

Violations and infractions of the rules are covered on pages 89 to 92.

Bankers' Rummy

The most avaricious dream of any gambler or casino operator is to turn a people's game into a so-called banking game. It took years to develop the game of Indian Craps—which is

---

* When this game is played in clubs or gambling houses, a charge called a *cut* is assessed against and paid by the winner and dropped in a cup on the table, the entirely too familiar kitty. When the game is five-handed and played for 25¢ or 50¢ a game, the cut is commonly a nickel or a dime. In any event, it generally runs to about 5 per cent of the winnings per hand, five cents on the dollar.

what at the end of the nineteenth century they called "craps vulgaris"—into the casino game of Bank Craps. It took years to develop Bankers' Rummy. The game was created by Harry J. Dorey about 1935. Its popularity is greatest in the East, particularly in Northern New Jersey.

REQUIREMENTS

1. This is a regular six-card straight Rummy game. There may be from two to six players, including the banker who is called the book. The game's terminology derives from Craps and the horse race track.

2. The game is played with a standard fifty-two-card pack of playing cards. Two decks are kept on hand to allow change of decks at any player's demand.

3. The operator—another name for the banker or book—sits in the game, and deals the first hand. Deal moves to the left clockwise.

THE PLAY

1. Before any deal, the banker shuffles the deck, then hands it to the dealer to be shuffled again. This is, bluntly, to minimize the chance of cheating. The rules of Straight Rummy (page 93) apply.

2. Before the cards are dealt, players may make two different kinds of bets against the banker:

A. They may bet any amount within the limit on spades. That means they may bet that in the first round of cards dealt the player will hold a space higher in rank than any spade dealt the banker.

Nonplayers around the table, or kibitzers if you insist, can bet on any player's hand against the banker too.

First bet is a free bet. No charge is made against it.

But all bets over $2 after the first deal are taxed.

Any $2 bet by any player is a free bet.

But if a player bets any amount over $2 that his spade will be higher than the banker's, he must pay a 5 per cent charge on the amount over the $2 limit.

For example:

A player decides to bet $10 that he will get a higher spade than the banker in the first six cards dealt. He puts his $10 on the table before him, and throws the banker 40¢ for the privilege of making the bet. The 40¢ is 5 per cent of the amount over the $2 free-bet limit. This is a game with plenty of what the boys call action. That betting charge gives the banker a considerable edge in what is otherwise a nicely balanced game.

The house limit usually runs from 25¢ to $75 on any one player's spade in any one play.

B. A player may bet that he will call correctly the rank and suit of two cards out of the first six dealt him before he picks from the stock or discard pile.

The limit on this bet is from 5¢ to $1 and the bank pays off at seventy for one!

Gamblers call this a combination bet. It gets action, because players like to get their odd nickels, dimes, and quarters into play at these odds.

The banker will generally stipulate that only pairs can be called, because pairs are easier to remember than random cards. It is almost impossible to recall accurately twenty to thirty different combinations; so most players will call two black aces or red aces, black or red kings, the ace and king of spades, or something of that sort. Players get to ride some favorite combination. Bankers get to know them by heart.

The money wagered on combinations is put on the table in front of the spade bets, and the banker usually turns the wagered coin or bill face up to indicate that a red combination was called, tail up to indicate a black combination.

Ordinarily when the play is heavy the banker will keep a lookout standing beside him to prevent players from calling a combination they have drawn instead of one they bet. The lookout can refresh the memory of a green banker or steady the nerves of a confused one.

Often players will bet the *four of a kind*. This bet is called a Round Robin. The player is paid off on the basis of one combination if he catches two aces (for instance), on three combinations if he catches three, on six combinations if he catches all four. "Aces" is used here only as an example. The player may bet any four of a kind. The bet cost him six units, because the cards can fall into six different two-way combinations.

While the banker pays off at 70 to 1 for one combination and while the pay-off is actually 69 to 1, the correct odds are 87.4 to 1 against getting a combination dealt in six cards. It is a pretty substantial percentage margin, but the banker wouldn't be in there without an edge, would he?

VIOLATIONS AND INFRACTIONS

Violations and infractions of the rules are covered on pages 89 to 92.

Knock Rummy

Without doubt the most widely played game of the Rummy family, with the possible exception of Gin Rummy. This form of Straight Rummy is probably responsible for the popularity of all the Rummies. A great game. A big betting game.

REQUIREMENTS

1. A standard pack of fifty-two cards is used.
2. The game is played by two to six players. As in Straight Rummy, six or seven cards are dealt each player. It is generally conceded that the seven-card variety requires more skill.

In seven-card Knock Rummy, a four-handed game is more fun; in six-card Knock, the five-handed game is likely to be found the more interesting.

BEGINNING OF THE GAME

Selection of the dealer and seating positions, and rules for shuffling, cutting, and changing seats are governed by "General Rules for Rummy Games," page 89.

THE DEAL

The dealer deals each player the correct number of cards (six or seven) one at a time clockwise beginning with the player at his left. Dealer gets the last card dealt. *Do not* turn up the next card of the stock as an upcard.

The winner of the hand deals the next hand.

OBJECT OF THE GAME

1. To go Rummy by melding the entire hand at one time in melds of three or four of a kind or three or more in sequences of the same suit; or
2. To knock and terminate the hand at any stage.

VALUE OF THE CARDS

Ace is low, counting 1 point; kings, queens, and jacks count 10 points; all other cards have their face value.

START OF THE PLAY

After each player has been dealt his cards, the leader may elect to *knock*. This he does by rapping his knuckles on the table or just uttering the word "Knock." That means he proposes to end the game then and there.

He must place on the table his melds, if any,* and, separately, his unmatched cards announcing his total of the latter.

Players in rotation from the dealer's left must do likewise.

The player with the lowest total in unmatched cards is the winner.

---

* Please observe that is not necessary to have any melds in the hand as a requisite to knock.

CONTINUATION OF THE PLAY

If the leader does not elect to knock, he must pick a card off the stock and then discard one. Each player to his left in rotation may pick up either the top card of the discard pile or the top card of the stock and then discard one.

A player cannot pick up an upcard and discard it immediately. He must wait until his next turn of play to discard it.

A player cannot knock after he has taken a card from the discard pile or the stock. *If he wants to knock*, he must *decline* to pick a card at his turn of play. Instead, he must knock and expose his hand face up, melds and unmatched cards separately, on the table.

If he picks a card and with that picked card completes a Rummy hand, he then discards one card and lays the hand face up on the table.

But this rule applies only to a Rummy hand.

THE BREAK

No player can knock after the break (see the rule on this under Straight Rummy, page 93). When it is a player's turn to break, he cannot pick the upcard unless he can use it in a meld, and other players are privileged to ask him whether he can so use it. If not, he must not take it, and must pick the top card of the remaining stock. This restriction applies to all players after the break.

There is no laying off of cards on other players' melds in Knock Rummy; each player must hold his own cards in his hand.

Players must discard their highest unmatched card after the break.

When the stock is exhausted, the player with the lowest total of unmatched cards is the winner.

In case of ties the breaker or the player nearest to the breaker's left is the winner.

KNOCKERS AND WINNERS

Even if another player can tie the knocker's count (total of unmatched cards), the knocker is still the winner. If another player or other players have a count lower than the knocker's, the player who has the lowest count wins. In case of ties, the player nearest the knocker's left wins.

THE PAY-OFF

1. The player who wins by a knock is paid one unit by each other player.

2. The knocker who loses to another player having fewer

points in unmatched cards than he (which is an underknock) must pay the underknocker two units. Each of the other players pays the underknocker one unit.

3. When a player knocks and melds *all his cards*, he has gone Rummy, and must be paid three units by each of the other players.

4. If a player goes Rummy without making a pick or by melding his entire hand in a sequence of the same suit before the break, he must be paid six units by each of the other players.

VIOLATIONS AND INFRACTIONS

See pages 89 to 92.

Continental Rummy

Often called Double-deck Rummy, this is the forerunner of the whole family of Rummy games using two packs of cards as one. Called Continental Rummy because it is played throughout the United States, Canada, and Mexico; and it has lately turned up in South America.

REQUIREMENTS

1. Two standard packs of fifty-two playing cards are used as one. The packs may be of the same design or of different design and even color.

2. The game can be played by two to six persons. The four-or five-handed games are best.

BEGINNING OF THE GAME

See the general rules on page 89 on selection of the dealer, seating positions and rules for shuffling, cutting, and changing seats.

THE DEAL

The dealer deals fifteen cards three at a time to each player, starting with the leader (player at the dealer's left) and going clockwise. The rest of the cards are placed face down on the table, forming the stock. On completion of the hand, the deal passes to the player at the dealer's left.

OBJECT OF THE GAME

To go Rummy by melding the entire fifteen cards in matched sets of three or four of a kind or in sequences of three or more in the same suit.

(Sequences of five or six are not uncommon, and sequences have been built up from ace to king in the same suit.)

VALUE OF THE CARDS

The ace is scored low, counting 1 point; kings, queens, and jacks count 10 points each; all other cards have their numerical values.

THE PLAY

1. The first player to the dealer's left picks a card off the stock and discards a card, placing it face up next to the stock. Each player in turn, clockwise, picks the upcard or a card from stock, then discard. This goes on until a player goes Rummy.

2. If the entire stock is exhausted without any player going Rummy, the discards are picked up by the dealer of the hand and reshuffled; then they are cut by the player at the dealer's right, and go back to the center of the table as constituting a new stock. And the play goes on until someone goes Rummy.

3. When a player goes Rummy, he places all his cards face up on the table in melds, separating each from the others so that all hands can certify the Rummy. The rest of the players then lay their own melds, holding their unmatched cards. The scorekeeper, who may be one of the players or a kibitzer, now verifies the count of the player to the left of the winner, and enters this amount as a credit to the winner, at the same time subtracting it from the player's score. This computation is made for each player around the table, going clockwise.

4. A game is four completed deals or hands.

5. Or, arbitrarily, a game can be played to a time limit. Thus we may set a two-hour limit for the game. At the expiration of that time, or at the completion of any hand which reaches beyond the agreed time, the game is over.

THE PAY-OFF

A player's plus points and minus points are canceled against each other, and the pay-off is at so much per point on the remainder. It is not uncommon to pay a prearranged amount to the player with the highest number of points for the game. A cent a point makes for a nice game, in which nobody will lose too much.

SPECIMEN SCORE

The score card at the completion of two hands should look something like the following:

A	B	C	D
+69	−15	−19	−35
+59	+40	−39	−60

Observe that losing and winning points, the plus and minus points, must be exactly equal. In the above score A has gone Rummy on the first hand; B was caught or stuck with 15 points, C with 19, D with 35. In the second game which B won, A was caught for 10 points, C for 20, D for 25. While some players prefer the simplicity of jotting down the scores per game and adding them at the end (see page 49), I keep a cumulative score. This minimizes the possibility of error and trouble, and at the end the penny-a-point pay-off is exactly what the last entry on the sheet shows for each player.

VIOLATIONS AND INFRACTIONS

All violations and infractions are covered under the rules on pages 89 to 92.

CHAPTER THIRTEEN

Other Rummy Games—II

Oklahoma Rummy

A variation of Fortune Rummy. Played for years through-out the Middle West, it is spreading rapidly. Its popularity is probably due to its interesting point-scoring system and its ruling on discards.

REQUIREMENTS

1. Two standard fifty-two-card packs are used, shuffled together and treated as a single deck. Packs of different colors may be used.

2. From two to six persons may play, but the game goes best with four.

3. *The eight deuces are wild.*

OBJECT OF THE GAME

To score 1,000 or more points by laying down melds.

If two or more players score 1,000 or more points, the winner is the player with the highest score.

BEGINNING OF THE GAME

Selection of the dealer and seating positions, shuffling, cutting, and changing seats are covered under the general rules on page 89.

THE DEAL

After the cards have been shuffled and cut, the dealer deals each player thirteen cards one at a time in turn, starting with the player to his left and dealing clockwise. He then turns up the next card, and places it on the table face up. That's the *upcard*. He puts the remaining stack of cards face down beside the upcard. This pile is the stock.

PLAY OF THE HAND

The leader (player to the dealer's left) makes the first play, and the turn to play rotates clockwise.

Each player in his turn may do either of the following:

1. (a) Pick the top card of the stock, (b) then meld if he can and wants to, (c) then discard; or—

2. Pick the upcard (top card of the discard pile)—if he can use that card immediately in a meld.

But note:

If he chooses to pick the upcard, the player must also take into his hand the rest of the cards in the discard pile.

Then he can lay down whatever melds he can and will.

Then he discards a card.

LAYING OFF CARDS

Players may lay off cards only in their proper turn of play *and only on their own melds*.

EXHAUSTED STOCK

If the stock is exhausted without any player having gone Rummy, the discards are managed in the following manner:

1. The upcard stays on the table as the start of the new discard pile.

2. The remaining discards are picked up by the dealer of that hand and shuffled by him, cut by the player to the dealer's right, and put back on the table, constituting a new stock.

3. Play continues from the point where it was interrupted.

If all the cards are exhausted including the discard pile, which rarely happens, and no player has gone Rummy, then each player's unmatched cards are scored against him with a minus sign.

VALUE OF MELDED CARDS

Aces count 15 points each; tens, jacks, queens, and kings, 10 points each with the exception of the queen of spades, which counts 50 points; 3's, 4's, 5's, 6's, 7's, 8's, and 9's count 5 points each.

Deuces count as the card they represent in the laid meld, unless used in a meld as deuces. They then count 25 points each.

For a wild deuce to count as the queen of spades, it must be used to represent the natural queen in a spade meld; for example, a meld consisting of the jack of spades, wild deuce, and king of spades.

The author urges that the above rules be strictly enforced. To let a player meld three deuces and claim credit for three spade queens with a value of 150 points is to corrupt the game. A deuce used naturally in kinds or sequences is worth 25 points, no more.

VALUE OF CARDS IN THE HAND

Cards retained by a player in his hand after an opponent has gone Rummy count the same as when used in a meld—with the exception of the queen of spades.

It counts 100 points.

SCORING

The dealer is the scorekeeper. The player who has gone Rummy is credited with a plus amounting to the points of his melds. Each of the other players is credited with the difference between his meld points and the point value of the cards left in his hand. Melds left in a player's hand are charged against him.

Just to prevent any ambiguity, an example: a player's melds total 70 points. The cards in his hand total 50 points. Under his name on the score sheet is entered a net plus score of 20 points: +20.

Another: a player's melds total 50 points, the cards in his hand total 70; so he is marked for a net minus score of 20 points, or —20.

The player who goes Rummy and wins gets a bonus of 100 points, which is entered to his credit on the score sheet.

WINNER OF THE GAME

The first player to score 1,000 or more points is the winner. If two or more players score 1,000 or more points at the same time, the player with the highest score wins, and takes whatever stakes have been stipulated, say 25¢ or 50¢ a game.

Or the winner may be paid on the basis of the difference in points between his score and the other players'. The rate can be one-tenth of a cent per point—or whatever you think is feasible and fun, not that these two are always synonymous.

Jersey Gin (three-handed)

How often do you wish you could have a three-handed game of Gin, all three persons playing at the same time? Here it is. Frank Moore brought it into my life and yours; he told me that three-handed Gin was being played at several political clubs in Jersey City. I drifted over and investigated it, and found first of all that the game in that form was full of mathematical bugs. I've undertaken to correct these defects, and the result is the following great game, which I've taken the discoverer's liberty of naming Jersey Gin. It's a combination of Gin and Knock Rummy.

REQUIREMENTS

A standard pack of fifty-two playing cards.

SELECTION OF DEALER AND SEATING POSITIONS

Any player shuffles the deck, which is then cut by any other player. Three cards are dealt face up, one to each player. The two players drawing in low cards sit opposite each other. The player drawing the high card chooses his seat; in other words, he decides who he prefers to have throwing to him, or, in other words, which opponent's discards he'd rather play.

Player drawing the high card becomes the first dealer.

VALUE OF THE CARDS

Same as in Gin Rummy: ace, 1 point; picture cards, 10 points; all other cards their face value.

THE DEAL

1. Dealer shuffles the pack, and offers it to the player on his right to be cut; if that player declines to cut, the third player may do so; if he declines, the dealer *must* cut the cards himself before dealing.

2. On the completion of each hand, which is called a box, the deal passes to the player on the previous dealer's left, and continues clockwise.

3. Dealer deals ten cards to each player one at a time clockwise, starting with the player at his left.

4. The rest of the cards are placed in the center of the table face down. They are the stock.

PLAY OF THE HAND

The rules of Gin Rummy govern this game, with the following exceptions:

When a player knocks, the score entered to his credit is the total reached by adding the difference between his score and one opponent's to the difference between his score and the other opponent's.

Whew!

Let's have an example. Only the winner of the box can get any credits in the scoring. Now, A knocks with a count of 5 points. B has a count of 15 after melding and laying off on A's melds. C has a count of 13 after melding and laying off on A's and B's melds.

Now, subtract A's 5 from B's 15. That leaves a difference of 10. Subtract A's 5 from C's 13. The difference is 8. Add up the two differences. A, the knocker, is credited on the score sheet for 18 points.

The counts of B and C have been canceled out in the calculation of the two differences; each gets zero for the box.

Should a player underknock the knocker, that player gets the difference in points between his score and that of the knocker, plus the difference in points between his score and that of the third player, *plus* a 10-point bonus for the underknock.

Should two players score an underknock, only one can be legally declared the underknocker. That one is the player with the lowest point total.

Should two underknockers have the same number of points, the player to the knocker's left is declared the underknocker and winner.

A player going Gin gets the total point difference of both opponents, as described above, *plus* a bonus of 20 points for Gin from each opponent, a total bonus of 40 points.

BREAK

The game does not end in a *no game,* as in Gin Rummy, when the stock gets down to its last three cards. Instead:

Should any player fail to knock or go Gin before only three cards are left in the stock, the player whose turn it is to pick the top card of the stock becomes the breaker. That player *must* pick that top card, *unless* the upcard (top card on the discard pile) can be used in a meld.

After the break, after the stock is reduced to less than three cards, players cannot knock.

The breaker must lay down his melds separately and hold his own unmatched cards in his hand.

The player to the breaker's left must pick a card (top card or upcard) and do likewise—and he may lay off cards on the breaker's melds. The third player also picks a card and must lay down his melds, and may lay off on both other players. If, because of picking an upcard for use in a meld, there remain cards in the stock after that round, the play continues and players may continue laying off on any meld on the table.

Should a player go Gin after the break, the rules of Gin Rummy apply: the hand is completed, and no lay-offs are permitted; but the player does not get a bonus for going Gin; he is credited only for the opponents' unmatched cards.

When the last card of the stock has been picked and the last player has discarded, the player with the lowest count becomes winner of that box, and he is credited with points as set forth for the knocker under "The Scoring," page 48.

If the breaker is one of two players to tie in total of unmatched cards, he is the winner.

If two players other than the breaker tie for low, the player to the breaker's left is the winner of that box. He gets credit for point difference only from the player with the higher total points.

At the break and after the break, a player cannot pick an upcard unless it can be used in a meld.

One Hundred and One Rummy

A Knock Rummy variation interesting enough to be a favorite with professional gamblers throughout the United States.

REQUIREMENTS

1. A standard deck of fifty-two playing cards.
2. From two to six players, four making for the best game.

OBJECT OF THE GAME

This game resembles an elimination tournament. When a player's score reaches 101 or more points, he is barred from further play. One by one the contestants are eliminated until only one is left. The player who hasn't reached 101 wins.

BEGINNING OF THE GAME

Selection of the dealer and seating positions, shuffling, cutting, and changing seats are covered by the general rules on page 89.

PLAY OF THE HAND

Starting with the player at his left and dealing clockwise, the dealer deals each player seven cards one at a time. The remaining cards are put in the center of the table, constituting the stock. The leader makes the first play by picking the top card of the stock, then discarding. Other players, starting with the player at the leader's left, may take the top card of the stock or the upcard, then discarding. This goes on clockwise until a player knocks.

KNOCKING

If a player's score is 91 or fewer points, he may knock with a count of 9 or less points in unmatched cards in his hand.

If his score reads 92, he must have a count of 8 points or fewer to knock.

If his score reads 93, his knocking count must be 7 points or less.

And so on up to 99, when he must have a count of exactly 1 point to knock.

If he has a score of 100 points, he cannot knock at all. *He must go Rummy*.

If a player knocks with more points than this law allows, he is eliminated from the game immediately as his penalty, and the hand is *no game* for the other players.

An underknock does not affect the scoring.

SCORING

When a player goes Rummy he gets a score of zero. All other players must add to their cumulative score their total amount of unmatched cards.

They cannot lay off cards, but can lay down melds.

A knocker must enter his total knocking count on the score sheet.

Scoring and melding for the other players is the same as prescribed for a Rummy.

BUYING INTO THE GAME

This game is generally played for a stipulated amount, say, $1 a game per player, which is put into the kitty beforehand. The winner gets the kitty.

It can grow to a pretty respectable size, that kitty. Because a player can buy his way back into the game after he has scored his fatal 101.

1. It costs an eliminated player $1 to get back into the game. That dollar goes into the kitty.

2. And he must start now with a score equal to the highest surviving player's.

Now, if he should be eliminated a second time, he can still get back into the game. Only this time his re-entry costs him $2. Out again? He can buy back into the proceedings, this time for $4. The cost of returning doubles every time a player does it.

THE BREAK

When the number of cards left in the stock becomes equal to the number of players in the game, that stage of the game is the break. Thereafter the Knock Rummy rules on the break and subsequent play apply in full force (page 97).

When all cards in the stock are exhausted, each player adds his unmatched cards, and the total is entered on the score sheet.

Tonk

Popular with Negroes in the United States and quite a betting game. It combines some interesting features of Knock Rummy and Coon Can.

REQUIREMENTS

A standard fifty-two-card pack and from two to six players, four or five making for the best game.

OBJECT OF THE GAME

To go Tonk by going Rummy or by Tonking (knocking) and having the lowest points in unmatched cards.

BEGINNING OF THE GAME

Selection of the dealer and seating positions, shuffling, cutting, and changing seats are covered by the general rules on page 89.

THE DEAL

After the cards have been shuffled and cut, the dealer, starting with the player at his left and dealing clockwise, deals each player seven cards, one at a time. He then faces up the next card as the first upcard, and puts the rest of the cards face down beside it as the stock.

VALUE OF CARDS

Aces count 1 point; jacks, queens, and kings, 10 points; all other cards their pip or face value.

THE PLAY

After the deal and before the leader makes his play, a player may call "Tonk" if he holds any seven of the following cards:

Tens, jacks, queens, and kings.

He may Tonk whether these cards occur in a spread (meld) or not, and is the winner and collects from each other player whatever stakes have been agreed on.

But if a play *has been made* and a player calls Tonk, this rule does not apply.

If no player calls Tonk, the leader makes the first play. He may either *pluck* (colloquial for "pick" or "take") the upcard or take the top card of the stock. If he plucks the upcard, he cannot place that card in his hand, but must make use of it immediately in a spread (meld) and put that spread on the table. If the card can't be used in an immediate spread he must discard it, and play goes on.

A player may call Tonk any time he thinks he has the low hand, just as in Knock Rummy, *but* if he Tonks and some other player has a lower hand, the Tonker must pay each other player *double* the amount stipulated as stakes.

A player may *hit* (lay off) one card only from his hand at each turn of play, if possible; but when he lays off a card he cannot then discard. He must always have seven cards, no more and no less, either melded before him or in his hand.

BREAKER

No player may Tonk or knock after the break (when the stock has been reduced to one card less than the number of players), but should a player go Tonk (Rummy) after the break, the game is ended and that player is winner. In the absence of a Tonk after the break, the player ending with the lowest total points is the winner. In case of ties, the breaker (player who plucks the first card from the stock when it is reduced to the number of players in the game), or the player nearest to the breaker's left, is the winner.

Coon Can

The only game of the Rummy family played before the turn of the twentieth century that is still popular throughout the country. The reason for its long sovereignty is its provision of reward for fine strategy. It's as generous in this respect as any modern game of the family. The greatest popularity of this game, with its picturesque idiom, is in the South, but whenever Negroes congregate a round of Coon Can is likely to get under way.

REQUIREMENTS

A forty-card deck of playing cards cut down from a standard pack by removing its 8's, 9's, and 10's.

Two players.

PECULIARITIES

The ace counts low, and is used only in melds of three or four aces or in a sequence: ace, 2, 3 of the same suit.

Melds of 6-7-jack or 7-jack-queen of the same suits are legal. The 7 and jack are treated as if they were contiguous values.

OBJECT OF THE GAME

To go Coon Can, which is to lay down your entire hand plus the card which ordinarily would be the discard. The total must be eleven cards. A player may have ten cards melded and discard a card, but—even though he has no cards in his hand—he is not Coon Can, and continues to play. He must have eleven cards in melds on the table in front of him before he can call Coon Can and be the winner.

GLOSSARY

Coon Can is distinguished by (among other things) its own vocabulary, which is characteristically salty and economic in the use of words.

To overlook a play is to *sleep it*.

Laying off a card on a meld is a *hit* (n.) or *to hit* (v.).

A lay or meld of the same rank is a *short spread*.

A lay or meld of three or more cards in sequence of the same suit is a *long spread*.

A draw game is a *tab game*.

To pick or take a card from the stock is to *pluck* it.

To take a card from one lay in order to form another is to *switch*.

A hand you can't go Coon Can with is a *hole*.

SELECTING THE DEALER

Players cut for the deal. Low man deals.

Loser of the previous game deals the next game.

In case of a tab (draw game), player other than the previous dealer deals.

THE SHUFFLE AND CUT

The dealer shuffles the deck. Nondealer may call for a shuffle at any time before the deal starts, though dealer retains the right to shuffle last. After the shuffle, cards are offered to the nondealer for the cut. If he refuses, dealer *must* himself cut before starting the deal.

Dealer deals himself and his opponent ten cards each, one at a time, starting with the opponent. Dealer places the remainder of the cards on the table, forming the stock.

START OF THE PLAY

The nondealer *plucks* the top card of the stock, exposes the card by holding it so that the dealer can see its face, and decides what to do with it. If he decides to take it, he must use it immediately as part of a spread and lay the spread down, or he may discard it.

Mark this well: a plucked card cannot be placed in the player's hand among his other cards. *It must be used as part of a spread or must be discarded.*

The dealer may now either pick up the discarded card (upcard) or pluck the top card of the stock. But if he plucks the upcard he must use it immediately in a spread and put the spread on the board.

The play alternates until the end of the game.

A player may lay off (hit) any number of cards on his own melds. Also he may hit his opponent's melds with *one card* at each turn of play. But when a player hits an opponent's melds, that card is considered his discard. He cannot discard from his hand after a hit. And the player who has been hit cannot pluck a card after the hit but must just discard one card.

This peculiarity of Coon Can, hitting the opponent, leads naturally to another noteworthy feature.

A player will deliberately discard a card which can be used to extend a spread of his opponent's. He calls the opponent's attention to it. The opponent picks it up, adds it to a spread, and then discards.

The purpose of this is to lure an opponent into discarding from his hand. That's called breaking the hand. By getting an adversary to shorten his hand you put him into a *ten-card hole*, which precludes his going Coon Can. A man with a spread ranging from ace to king of the same suit is a man with a ten-card hole on his hands; and since the game requires an eleven-card laydown, including the discard card, that man can't go Coon Can.

A player may lay as many spreads as possible at any turn of play.

Should a player discard a card he can use as a hit, his opponent may call his attention to it and compel him to *hit* it. The attempt to make such a discard is called trying to *sleep* it.

A player having on the table before him a spread of more than three cards may remove or switch one of them to help form another spread—provided the removal doesn't interrupt the sequence of a *long spread*.

Suppose a player has before him a *short spread* consisting of four 5's and has in his hand the 6 and 7 of hearts. He can switch the 5 of hearts from the short spread and meld the 6 and 7 on it, forming a long spread or sequence.

If the upcard plus a switched card, added to any card in his hand, will form a spread, the player is entitled to pluck the top discard, lay his card, and switch the third card.

But bear in mind that whenever a card has been switched from a spread, that spread must still consist of three cards having the same numerical value or at least three cards in sequence of the same suit. Otherwise the switch is barred.

END OF THE GAME

When a player has laid down eleven cards in spreads, he calls Coon Can, and the game ends. He wins.

If the entire stock is exhausted without either player going Coon Can, the game is a *tab*. The amount of the agreed stake is added to the kitty for every tab game until one player wins. He gets the whole kitty.

Combination or Liverpool Rummy

Also played under such names as Deuces Wild Rummy, Progressive, and a variety of others. There are a dozen variations. Some of them are mere confusion. Some of them are intolerably unsound or complicated. I've developed here rules for an eminently playable standard version of an exciting Rummy.

REQUIREMENTS

1. Two standard packs of fifty-two playing cards, shuffled together and used as one. Any packs around the house will do; color and design don't matter.

2. Any number of players from two to eight, although four or five make for the best game.

STIPULATION

Deuces are wild, and count for any rank and suit their holder dictates.

BEGINNING OF THE GAME

Selection of the dealer and seating positions, the shuffle, the cut, and changing seats are governed by the general rules on page 89.

THE DEAL

Starting with the leader and dealing clockwise, the dealer deals each player ten cards one at a time face down. He faces the next card up, and puts the stock beside it in the middle of the table.

OBJECT OF THE GAME

Each game consists of six deals.

It is suggested that the rules on the different hands be copied out and kept handy to avoid what Liverpudlians call a social error, which is playing one's hand by somebody else's rules.

Each deal ends when some player has laid down melds as prescribed by the rules.

We shall call a meld of three or more cards having the same numerical rank a *group*.

We shall call a sequence of three or more cards of the same suit a *sequence*.

A *red sequence* is a sequence of hearts or diamonds.

A *black sequence* is a sequence of spades or clubs.

A *high group* is a meld of three or four or more cards of the same rank having these pip values: 8's, 9's, 10's, jacks, queens, or kings.

A *low group* is such a meld of aces, 3's, 4's, 5's, 6's, or 7's.

Deuces being wild, they may be assigned any rank in any suit.

CHART OF LEGAL PLAYS

For reference at the table, copy out this chart of permissible melds:

FIRST HAND. One high and one low group.
SECOND HAND. One red and one black sequence.
THIRD HAND. One high group and one red sequence.
FOURTH HAND. One low group and one black sequence.
FIFTH HAND. Three sequences.
SIXTH HAND. Three groups.

START OF THE PLAY

Starting with the dealer and playing to the left, clockwise, each player in turn may pick either the upcard or the top card of the stock, then discarding one card.

Before discarding, the player may lay down any meld or group of melds as prescribed by the rule chart for each hand, and he may lay off any cards on his own melds or any other player's.

END OF THE HAND

When a player has laid his melds according to the rules and has no more cards in his hand after discarding, the hand ends.

He may lay off cards on his own or other players' melds, as set forth above, but these are the only conditions under which he can win the hand:

He must have before him the melds prescribed for his hand.

He must get rid of all his cards.

If the stock is exhausted before any player has gone Rummy, the discard pile (except the upcard, which is left on the board as the start of a new discard pile) is shuffled by the dealer of that hand (see page 89), and is thereafter used as the stock in the continuing game.

On a player's going Rummy, he is credited with the total points of all unmelded cards held by the players, that is, held in the others' hands, regardless whether they are groups, sequences, or unmatched cards.

SCORING

Aces, deuces natural, 3's, 4's, 5's, 6's, and 7's count 5 points each; 8's, 9's, 10's, jacks, queens, and kings count 10 points each. On the score sheet the winner's score is marked with a plus sign, and each loser is marked minus the amount with which he was caught. A cumulative score is kept.

END AND PAY-OFF

The game ends when six hands have been completed. Players having minus scores must pay on the table at so much per point, as previously stipulated. Players having plus scores get paid at so much per point.

It is usual to establish a premium for the player with the highest score, payable by each other player. I suggest a 25-cent-per-man premium, and a penny a point seems about right.

Caloochi

A form of Rummy long popular in the Eastern States and now spreading throughout the country.

REQUIREMENTS

Two standard packs of fifty-two cards each and four jokers, shuffled and used as one pack. Jokers are wild.

Two, three, or four players; the game is best suited to four-handed competition.

BEGINNING OF THE GAME

General rules on page 89 govern selection of the dealer and seating positions and changing seats.

SHUFFLE AND CUT

Dealer shuffles cards, then offers pack to player at his right for the cut. That player *must* cut the cards, showing the bottom card of the cut portion of the stock by turning the cut portion face up.

Should the bottom card be a joker, the player cutting the

cards takes it as his first card, and the cut is carried (completed). If it is not a joker, it remains where it is in the pack when the cut is completed. When the cutter takes the joker, the dealer skips that player on the first round in the deal.

Fifteen cards are dealt each player face down one at a time in turn, starting with the player at the dealer's left and going clockwise. The next card is faced up, becoming the upcard. The dealer may take that card if he wants it, discarding one card if he does claim it.

THE PLAY

After the dealer takes the upcard or declines it, play passes to the player at his left, and thereafter clockwise. The dealer cannot take the top card of the stock if he declines the upcard.

Succeeding players may take the top card of the stock, or may take the upcard only if it can be used in a meld immediately.

• A player cannot meld unless the meld totals 51 or more points.

If he takes the top card of the stock he may embody it in his hand and discard one card.

Remember: no meld may be laid unless it counts 51 or more points!

A card laid off on other melds may be counted toward this total, but a player may lay off only when melding himself.

If a player goes Rummy by melding and/or laying off his fifteen cards in the single play, that play is Caloochi, and the player is paid *doubled* stakes by each other player.

If he melds or lays off all his cards *in more than one down*, he is Rummy and wins the game.

Each losing player is penalized 1¢ for each card he still holds in his hand at game's end. With one exception, the cards have this 1¢ value. The exception is the joker. It counts as two cards and 2¢ in penalties.

A player going Caloochi gets doubled stakes from each other player, *plus* the kitty. Generally in a-cent-a-card game, each player antes a nickel for the kitty.

When a joker is one card of a meld and a player holds the natural card for which that joker is stand-in, he can swap his natural card for the joker. Suppose a meld of diamond 8, joker, and diamond 10 are on the board. Suppose you hold the 9 of diamonds. In your turn of play you may exchange the natural 9 for the joker, and use the joker for your own dark purposes.

VALUE OF THE CARDS

All cards bear their pip value except the ace, which counts 11, and the joker, which bears the value indicated by its use in the meld. A meld of three or four jokers gives them an arbitrary value of 15 points each. It had better be added that it is rarely if ever advisable to lay down there or four jokers. There's generally more useful work for them to do.

500 Rummy, Pinochle Rummy

With the exception of Coon Can the oldest Rummy game being played today, and for an excellent reason: that it is a very interesting curio indeed.

REQUIREMENTS

1. A standard pack of fifty-two cards.
2. From two to four players.

BEGINNING OF THE GAME

Selection of dealer and seating positions, the shuffle, the cut, and changing seats are governed by the general rules on page 89.

OBJECT OF THE GAME

To lay down melds totaling 500 or more points. The player so melding ends the game and wins it.

If two or more players meld 500 or more points the *highest* score wins.

HAND

A hand is completed when any player has no more cards in his hand or the cards in the stock are exhausted. Then each player is given credit for all the cards he has melded, and is penalized for the points he still holds in his hand. When one player goes Rummy (or out), each other player is penalized for the count he holds, whether or not they are melds. Ace counts 15 points, except when used with the deuce-trey of the same suit.

THE DEAL

Seven cards are dealt each player in turn one at a time starting with the leader, and rotating clockwise. Then the next card is faced up to begin the discard pile, and the remaining cards are put face down beside it, constituting the stock.

THE PLAY

Starting with the leader and playing in turn clockwise, any player may draw either a card from the top of the stock or as many cards from the discard pile as he pleases; but if he draws from the discard he must use the bottom card drawn immediately as part of a meld. Thus he must have at least two cards of a meld before he draws from the discards.

The cards in the discard pile are fanned out so that the players can see them clearly. In discarding, the card must be placed tidily on the last discard so that all other discards are visible.

In his proper turn of play a player may lay down as many melds as he can and will.

The ace may be laid as either the high or the low card of a sequence: ace-2-3 or queen-king-ace; but it cannot be used *around the corner*, viz., king-ace-deuce.

Cards may be laid off both on the player's own and on opponents' melds. But in laying off on opponents, the player may place in front of himself the laid-off card so that it can be scored for him.

Let me suggest that you'd better watch sequence melds most carefully and stay aware of whether other players' lay-offs have extended sequences on the board. Player No. 1 melds the ace-2-3 of hearts; player No. 2 lays the 4 in front of himself; player No. 3 lays the 5. A little later you find in your hand a 6 of hearts which is doing you no good at all. Glancing around the board, you see the ace-2-3 meld; but if you don't watch the other lay-offs diligently you may discard the 6 instead of laying it off to your profit.

To most experienced Rummy players the following may seem rudimentary, but I'd better point it out to have it on record. When a card can be laid off on either of two melds, the player must specify which meld.

Let's hypothesize that two melds are on the board. One is three treys. The other is the 4-5-6 of diamonds. You hold the 3 of diamonds. Now, melding your 3, you must specify whether it goes on the three of a kind or the sequence. If you meld it on the treys, that meld is dead, and the lower end of the sequence is closed off; no more cards can be melded on it in that direction. But if you meld on the sequence, it remains open to further extension. The point is worth bearing in mind, especially if you have in your hand the diamond ace and suspect some one else might hold the diamond deuce to lay off on the sequence and afford you the chance to down your card.

VALUE OF THE CARDS

The ace counts 15 points—*except* when used in a meld of the ace-2-3 of the same suit, in which case it is valued at 1 point. Jacks, queens, and kings count 10 points each; all other cards, their pip or numerical face value.

END OF THE GAME

It is convenient to keep score cumulatively. *But* some players prefer to run a score sheet for each contestant, entering melds as laid, and some others prefer to add up the totals at the end of each hand.

The game is ended when any player scores 500 or more points. Player with the highest score wins.

Five Hundred is usually played for so much per game or so much per point, the pay-off being based on difference in points.*

STREAMLINED SCORING

This scoring method is suggested for players who like a faster game and abhor bookkeeping. As in Fortune Rummy, count all cards from 2 to 7 as being worth 5 points, all from 8 to king as being worth 10. The ace when laid in a meld with the deuce-trey counts 5 points, otherwise 10.

Michigan Rummy

The game is played exactly as 500 Rummy, with the following exceptions:

1. Each hand is a completed game.
2. Should a player discard a card that can be laid off on a meld, the first player to call stop may use this card, then discard one. The turn of play then reverts back to its proper place.
3. Winner of the game is the first to go Michigan (Rummy).

Mississippi Rummy

The screwiest and most fascinating game of the Rummy family, even if not for professional gamblers, because you can't lose more than $1 in an evening of hammer-and-tongs play. Rules of the game prevent losing more than a sum stipulated before play starts. I know a group of eight women, headed by Mrs. Anna Klunck of Union City, N. J., one of the game's creators, who played Mississippi four hours a day every day through a solid month of vacation last summer. Not one of them lost more than $5 in the month. I strongly recommend this game to women. For some reason which may escape the male of the species, they seem to relish its weird complications.

* Some game experts propose that more than four players can play 500 Rummy by using a double deck. But the game four-handed and up, in my opinion, occasions too much confusion about who has laid off on whose melds. Stick to one deck and four-handed, and let who will commit mayhem.

REQUIREMENTS

Two standard packs of playing cards shuffled and used as one. Color and design don't matter.

From two to eight players, five to eight making for the best game.

ACES AND DEUCES

The deuces are wild, and may be used for any card in any suit.

Aces may be melded only in a group of three or four or in the queen-king-ace sequence. *The ace-2-3 sequence is barred.*

BEGINNING OF THE GAME

Selection of the dealer and seating positions, the shuffle, the cut, and changing seats are governed by the general rules on page 89.

OBJECT OF THE GAME

To score as few points as possible.

Any player scoring 102 points or more is out of the game for its duration. The players being eliminated by this means, the game continues until only one player remains. He—or rather, she—wins and takes the kitty.

SHARING THE WEALTH

Often the kitty is divided between the last two players, who are both declared winners. If, this being the case, any odd cash is left over, it goes into the kitty for the next game.

VALUE OF THE CARDS

In scoring, aces count 15 points; face cards, 10; spot cards, their face value.

STIPULATIONS

Before starting play, it is agreed by open democratic vote what is the maximum amount any player may lose in the course of the evening—say $1.

Commonly a time limit on the play is stipulated. It is entered on a corner of the score sheet.

If chips are available, one of the players is elected cashier, and collects $1 from each player for her supply of chips. After that no player may buy any more chips either from the cashier or from any other player. Should she lose all her chips, she keeps right on playing anyway, as follows:

Should she continue to lose, she owes no penalties to the winners.

But should she resume winning after her losing streak (during which she has not paid penalties), the other players—unless they happen to be broke in turn—must pay her.

Play continues until expiration of the agreed time limit.

THE KITTY

To begin, each player drops in a cup to start the kitty a chip equal in value to a nickel.

Should a player hold ten cards of the same suit, whether or not in sequence, that's a ten-card meld and is called Mississippi, and the melder gets a 20¢ bonus from each other player; *but* she must put 20¢ in the kitty, which goes on growing for the winner.

Should a player go Rummy without picking a card, that's a *dream*, and each other player pays the player 20¢, whereupon she must put 20¢ in the kitty.

Should a player go Rummy, she gets 10¢ from each other player, and must put 10¢ in the kitty.

Should a player score an underknock (having fewer points than the knocker), the knocker must pay the underknocker 20¢ and the underknocker collects 5¢ from each other player. Underknocker then must put 10¢ in the kitty.

Should a player knock with 5 points or fewer, she collects 5¢ from each other player and puts 5¢ in the kitty.

These bonuses have nothing to do with the scoring of the game. They're extras. They are there for the sheer thrill of it.

THE DEAL

The dealer gives herself the first card, then deals to the left, clockwise, one at a time, ten cards to each player except the dealer, who gets eleven cards. The rest of the cards are put face down on the table to constitute the stock.

If the entire stock is exhausted without any player's knocking or going Rummy, the discards are shuffled and cut, the top card is faced up to start the new discard pile, and the rest of the cards become the new stock.

START OF THE PLAY

The dealer makes the first play, discarding one of her eleven cards. Then each player in turn clockwise, starting with the player at the dealer's left, may pick either the upcard or the top card of the stock, discarding one card. This goes on until a player goes Rummy or knocks with less than 5 points in unmatched cards in her hand. To go Rummy a player must lay the whole ten cards in melds, then discard her last card.

With the above stipulated exceptions, the melds in Mississippi are the same as the melds in any other Rummy game.

KNOCK

When a player knocks she must table her melds separately, announce her count, and put her unmatched cards on the table face up so the other players can check them. The count for a knock must be 5 or fewer in unmatched cards.

Players cannot lay off cards after another player has either knocked or gone Rummy. But they may meld their lays after a Rummy or knock, then holding their unmatched cards until the total is entered on the score sheet. Players are scored as being plus the total of their unmatched cards at the rate of 15 for aces, 10 for face cards, and face value for spots.

UNDERKNOCK

When another player has fewer points than a player who has knocked, that's an underknock. There is no extra penalty for the knocker other than the cash penalty stated under "Stipulations" above. Both knocker and underknocker are scored as plus their points in unmatched cards.

BUY

A player eliminated from the game after the second hand may buy herself back into the game. She puts 10¢ in the kitty, and starts again with a score equal to the surviving player with the second lowest score.

COURTESY BUY

If a player has a score of 81 or more, she may make a *courtesy buy*. She puts 10¢ in the kitty, and starts the next hand with a score equal in points to the second lowest score then in the game. A player may make only two courtesy buys per game.

SCORING

A score card like the one shown in Continental Rummy (page 99) is used.

When a player goes Rummy, she gets a minus 10.

When a player knocks and wins, she gets a plus in the number of cards she knocked with.

All other players must add up their unmatched cards, and the total count of each player is entered against her as a plus.

The score is balanced cumulatively and kept running.

Should a player have ten cards in the same suit (Mississippi), she gets a minus of 20 points.

Should a player go Rummy without a pick (the *dream*), she gets a minus of 20 points.

That's Mississippi.

CHAPTER FOURTEEN

Other Rummy Games—III

Fortune Rummy, Deuces Wild

One of the newest and most fascinating games of the Rummy family, played mostly in the Middle West. I happen to think the rules for Fortune and the fun you'll have with it are alone worth the price of this book. Try it as a family game.

REQUIREMENTS

Any two standard packs of fifty-two cards, shuffled and used as one. All eight deuces are wild. Any deuce may be used to represent any card a player likes.

Two to eight players. A four- or five-handed game is most fun.

BEGINNING OF THE GAME

Selection of dealer and seating positions, the shuffle, the cut, and changing seats are governed by the general rules on page 89.

THE DEAL

1. Starting with the leader, the dealer deals eleven cards to each player one at a time clockwise.

2. The next card is faced up on the table as the upcard, and the stock goes face down beside it.

OBJECT OF THE GAME

1. To form melds or lays of three or more cards as in Gin Rummy.

2. And to get the melds down on the board so as to receive credit for them, because.

3. A meld in the hand is a liability; a meld is worth points only when it is down on the table.

4. On the completion of each hand, each player is credited with his total points.

5. Play continues until a player runs up a score of 500 or more points.

6. *Players are credited for the points they have melded.* The scorekeeper subtracts points in the hand from points on the board, and enters the resultant sum against the player's name. If he has more points in his hand unmelded than points on the board melded, he owes his score the difference. If he has not previously scored, the difference goes against his name with a minus before it. If he has a score, the difference is subtracted from it.

VALUE OF CARDS

Kings, queens, jacks, 10's, 9's, and 8's count 10 points; 3's, 4's, 5's, 6's, and 7's count 5 points.

Aces count 10 points when used in a high-sequence meld, to wit, the queen-king-ace.

Used in the low sequence (ace-deuce-trey) or in a meld of three or four aces, each ace counts 5 points.

But an ace in the hand at the conclusion of play, whether unmatched or in an unused meld, counts 10 points against that player.

The queen of spades is the highest-ranking card. It has a value of *50 points* regardless of when or how used.

A wild deuce may be used as a queen of spades, but its value then is 10 points.

DEUCES WILD

An example: You have the queen and 10 of spades and the deuce of clubs. You meld that sequence, and it is worth 70 points, because you are using the wild deuce to represent the jack of spades.

If a deuce is used to represent any card below the 8, it may be counted as only 5 points in a meld.

If a player has a deuce in his hand at the completion of the hand, he is penalized 10 points for it.

THE PLAY

1. The leader may either pick the upcard, in which case he must forthwith lay down a meld including that card;

2. Or take the top card of the stock, after which he may (if he is able) put down any melds he pleases;

3. After either of which he discards one card.

CERTAIN PECULIAR FEATURES

A player may pick the upcard only when he has in hand at least two cards of the meld into which it will go.

The player taking the upcard *must* take the entire discard

pile. But *immediately* he must put down a meld in which the upcard is embodied.

A player may put down as many melds as possible or as he wishes at any play.

After his melds have been laid down, player discards.

A player cannot lay off cards on his opponent's melds, as in other Rummy games; his cards may be laid off only on his own melds.

Discards must always be neatly squared up so that no card below the upcard is visible, and players are not allowed to spread the discards.

If the entire stock is exhausted before any player is clean (Rummy), the discards are *turned over* (with the exception of the upcard, the cards *are not shuffled* but merely turned over), and the game continues with those cards as the new stock.

END OF HAND

The hand ends when any player has melded his entire hand, whereupon the other players, holding cards in their hand whether they are perfected melds or unmatched cards, are penalized for the total number of points they hold.

END OF GAME

When any player (or players) reaches 500 points or more the game ends, and the player with the highest score wins.

In a four-handed game, the two highest players may by previous agreement be declared winners; in a six-handed game, the three highest, etc.

These stipulations must be made before starting the game, and all players must be clearly acquainted with the method to be used in ending the contest.

THE SPEED-UP

Players in a five- six- seven- or eight-handed game who want a faster decision may agree that 300 points is the winning score; or players may decide that three or four hands will constitute a complete game. In this case, the player with the highest score wins, or else (as above) the two highest in a four-handed game, the three highest in a six-handed game, and so on.

Partnership or Persian Rummy

Equally popular under either name as and when applied to it in various parts of the country. One of the few games in the

Rummy family played in partnership; two players team and play against two other partners.

REQUIREMENTS

1. A standard pack of fifty-two playing cards,
2. Plus four jokers, making a fifty-six-card pack.
3. The jokers must be of the same design and color as the pack.

SELECTING PARTNERS AND SEATING POSITIONS

1. The four players seat themselves at any four places around the table; where they sit is for the moment irrelevant.
2. Any player may shuffle the pack and offer the pack to any other player for a cut.
3. When cutting for partners the jokers are excluded from the deck.
4. Each player cuts a group of cards from the pack, immediately exposing to the others the bottom card of his group. Players drawing the two low cards become partners. So do the players drawing the two high cards.
5. If players draw three or four cards of the same rank, a new deal must take place. Upon deciding which two are high and which low, partners seat themselves opposite each other.
6. To avoid controversy as to positions the several partners take, one player for each team cuts the pack and exposes the bottom card of his cut. If it is a black card, partners remain in the positions they have taken. If it is a red card, they must exchange seats.
7. The player who cut low card in the cut for partner positions starts the game by dealing the first hand. From then on the deal moves to the dealer's left, clockwise.

OBJECT OF THE GAME

For a team of two partners to score more points than the other team at the conclusion of three hands or deals.

Points are scored by putting down melds of three or four cards of the same numerical rank or three or more cards in sequences of the same suit, as in Gin Rummy. The ace may be used with two or three other aces, with the king queen of the same suit, or with the deuce-trey of the same suit. It cannot be used in the around the-corner combination of king-ace-deuce.

The jokers are *not* wild. They may be used only in a meld of three or four jokers. They *cannot* be used in a sequence.

Face cards count 10 points; all other cards have their numerical values except the ace. It counts 15 points—except when melded with a deuce-trey, in which case it counts but 1 point.

The joker counts 20 points either in a meld or when caught

in a player's hand, except in case a player melds the four jokers at one time, in which case he is credited with 160 points for them, twice their normal value.

All cards melded four at a time count twice their normal value.

The ace counts 15 points except when laid in a meld with the ace-deuce-trey of the same suit. It then counts but 1.

A player laying down a meld of the three aces would get a point credit of 45 points, and if in a later play he laid the fourth ace on that meld, its points value would become 60 points.

Right?

But if a player melds the four aces at the one time, they score 120 points for the melder.

THE DEAL

Beginning with the player at his left (the leader), the dealer deals each player seven cards one at a time. The twenty-ninth card is faced up, constituting the upcard, and the rest of the cards are turned face down beside it to become the stock.

THE PLAY

Each player in his turn may (a) either take the top card of the stock (b) or take any card of the discard pile—

Provided:

1. That he takes all cards in the discard pile above the card he wants;

2. That he uses this card in a meld immediately with at least two other cards already in his hand.

A player may lay down as many melds as he likes at his turn of play, and may lay off cards on his own melds or his partner's melds, keeping his lay-off cards in front of him.

Then he discards.

END OF THE HAND

1. The deal or hand ends whenever a player melds all his cards, either in proper melds or in lay offs. The player must discard his last card; he cannot meld it.

2. If the stock is exhausted without any player having gone Rummy, the upcard is set aside to start the new discard pile, and the discard pile is turned over to form the new stock. This goes on until some player goes out.

3. When a player goes out, his team goes out.

SCORING

1. At the end of each hand, each player counts the value of the cards he has melded, and subtracts the value of the cards remaining in his hand.

2. Partners consolidate their credits and subtract their consolidated minuses, because partners' scores are entered as one on the score sheet.

3. The player who goes out (Rummy) gets a 25-point bonus.

END OF GAME

The game ends on the completion of three hands. The side having the highest score wins.

BONUSES

The winning side gets credit for the difference between the consolidated team scores.

The winning side gets a game bonus of 100 points.

The game is played for so much per point.

Winning partners divide their winnings evenly.

Canasta

An exotic—and important—new addition to the Rummy family. The card purist can and will find holes in the architecture of this game through which you could drive a wagon—its use of wild cards makes a monkey out of mathematics—but the stark fact remains that when people like a game, as all people seem to like this product of Uruguay as refined in Argentina, that game has something on the ball. In my tests the game (whose name means nothing but "basket," baskets being your melds) turns out (a) to be most fun when four people are playing; (b) to be most enjoyable when the players are mixed partnerships, because girls seem especially to enjoy its weird complexities; (c) like Spanish, to be fairly easy to learn and extremely hard to master. Some further observations: Canasta is certain to become and remain a Pan-American favorite. It will never be a big-money or an infinitely subtle gambling game like Gin Rummy. It is a remarkably pleasant way to pass a friendly evening. It takes exactly one-half hour to learn the game. And the average game takes one and one-half hours to play. Ask me as a card scientist what I think of it, and I'll give you one answer. Ask me as a card player how I like it, and I'll tell you—fine. Let's see.

REQUIREMENTS

1. Four players, two against two, as partners.

2. Two standard packs of fifty-two cards each, shuffled together and used as one, plus four jokers, totaling a hundred and eight cards dealt and played as a single deck. The jokers and the eight deuces are wild. As in Poker, any wild card may be used to represent, in the play, any other card.

Any two (standard Poker) packs you have lying around the house will do for Canasta; the color of the pattern on the back and its design do not matter.

If you don't have four jokers handy, represent them in the Canasta deck with four deuces of the same design as one of the decks, and mark the word "joker" on each added deuce's face.

OBJECT OF THE GAME

For a partnership to score 5,000 or more points before the opposing partnership does so—by laying down melds of three or more cards in the same numerical rank; *sequence melds are not allowed.*

POINT VALUE OF THE CARDS IN SCORING

Jokers	50 points each
Deuces	20 points each
Aces	20 points each
8's, 9's, 10's, jacks, queens, kings	10 points each
4's, 5's, 6's, 7's	5 points each
Black 3's (clubs and spades)	5 points each
Red 3's (diamonds and hearts)	100 points each

(*But,* if a partnership holds four red 3's on the board, their total value becomes 800 points, the fact of their combination giving a value of 200 points to each.)

To receive a plus credit for red 3's, a partnership must have laid down at least one meld. In the event of failure to meld, the red 3's become a penalty against the partnership of 100 points for each red 3, or 800 points if the nonmelding partnership holds four red 3's. (It must be interpolated that the possibility of holding four red 3's without making a meld is most remote.) If upon the completion of the hand a player is caught with a red 3 in the hand, having neglected to put it down, he is penalized 200 points.

NATURAL AND MIXED CANASTAS: WHAT THE TERMS MEAN

This is a *natural Canasta:*

4444444

or

KKKKKKK

or any seven cards of the same rank *regardless of suit.*

Wild cards cannot be used in a natural Canasta. And a natural Canasta has a value of 500 points.

This is a *mixed Canasta:*

6666 plus three wild cards
or
66666 plus two wild cards
or
666666 plus one wild card,
etc.

A mixed Canasta is a combination of seven cards having the same rank, at least four of which must be natural cards and a maximum of three of which may be wild. A mixed Canasta has a value of 300 points.

When a player melds a Canasta—or forms a Canasta by adding to cards melded already on the table—the Canasta is folded together and tagged for identification. When it is a natural Canasta, any natural black card, when possible, is placed on top of it to designate its nature. When it is a mixed Canasta, its identifying top card is a red or a wild card. Once the cards have been folded, the meld is a *closed Canasta*.

In the subsequent play a player may meld (lay off) additional cards on the Canasta. Cards of corresponding rank or wild cards may be added to any Canasta, natural or mixed—*but* adding a wild card to a natural Canasta transforms this Canasta forthwith into a mixed one, with a consequent important alteration in its value. Wild cards *cannot* be added to a mixed Canasta which already embodies three wild cards.

PENALTIES

When a contestant goes Rummy or *out*, any cards still held by *any* player in his hand are totaled and assessed against the player as a penalty. Even when one member of a partnership goes Rummy, the cards left in the other partner's hand are counted against the partnership. And these penalty cards have the same value as they would have if melded, except the red 3's. The penalty for holding a red 3 at the completion of a hand is 200 points; as a penalty card its value is twice its value laid on the board.

SELECTING PARTNERS AND SEATING POSITIONS

1. The four players take places at the four sides of the table..
2. Any player by mutual consent may shuffle the deck, and he then offers the pack to any other player for the cut.
3. From the cut pack each player now cuts a block of cards, turning his block and exposing the bottom card forthwith. Players drawing the two lowest cards become partners, as do players drawing the two highest cards.
If three- or four-way ties occur on the cut for partners, a new deal and cut must take place.

When cutting for partners, the jokers are excluded from the deck.

Partners now seat themselves opposite each other. To avoid any possibility of controversy as to seating position, one player for each team shall cut the deck and expose his card. If it is a black card, partners remain in the seats they have taken. If it is a red card, they must exchange seats.

The player who cuts low card in cutting for the partners' seat positions starts the game by dealing the first hand. Thereafter on the completion of each hand the deal passes to the player at the previous dealer's left, clockwise. On the completion of each game, players may change partners, or may cut for new partnerships and seat positions.

THE SHUFFLE AND CUT

These are governed by "General Rules for Rummy Games," page 89.

THE DEAL

Starting with the player at the dealer's left and dealing clockwise, each player is dealt eleven cards one at a time. The dealer then faces up the 45th card in the center of the table (this card becoming the first upcard). The rest of the deck is placed face down next to the upcard and is now the stock.

If the upcard is a wild card (deuce or Joker) or a red three, the top card of the stock is turned up and placed on top of the first upcard. This procedure is followed until some card other than a wild card or a red three is the upcard.

IMPORTANT RULE AT CANASTA

At a player's proper turn of play should he hold any red 3's, he places them on the table face up as if they were a meld, and for each red three he lays down he picks a card from the stock. If this drawn card is a red 3, that too is laid on the table, and the player draws another card from the stock. This procedure is continued until the player fails to draw a red 3. This rule holds true for each player at each turn of play.

THE ACTUAL PLAY

The player to the dealer's left has the first turn of play. Thereafter the turn of play rotates to the left clockwise from player to player until the completion of the hand.

First player. The player to the dealer's left plays as follows:

1. The player may pick the top card from the stock. He may then meld if he can and wills to do so. Then he must discard one card.

His first meld or melds must total 50 or more points. He

may make up the 50 points by laying as many or as few melds as will suffice.

2. Or the player may pick up the entire discard pile—*if* the upcard can be used with two other natural cards of its numerical rank to form a meld. Again, his meld or melds must total 50 or more points. Before taking the upcard the player must lay down from his hand the cards to be melded with it, and of the discard pile only the upcard can be used to help form the required meld.

After the cards are melded the remainder of the discard pile is incorporated into the player's hand.

The player may now put down any other meld he elects.

Having melded, he must discard one card.

Second player. The rules for the first player, as just stated, govern the play of the second.

Third and fourth players (partners of the first and second). If the partner has not melded cards, the rules as stated above apply to these players. If the partner *has* melded, three new elements come into play:

1. The player may take up the discard pile with only one natural card matching the upcard plus one wild card, instead of needing two matching natural cards.

2. He may take the discard pile when the upcard can be added to his or his partner's meld, except if the discard pile is a prize pile. (See below.)

However, the upcard can never be taken up to be melded with two or more wild cards.

3. Once the partnership has melded 50 or more points for its first meld, a player may meld cards of any value until the score for the partnership reaches 1,500 or more points.

(I say *1,500 or more,* not 1,500 flat, because the scoring doesn't work in convenient round numbers. At one moment a partnership's score may be 1,480; with the next meld, say 60 points, it shoots up to 1,540. To insist on 1,500 in these circumstances would be a pretty feeble legalism.)

Now, after a partnership score has reached 1,500 or more points, the partnership is required to meld at least 90 points in its next succeeding meld or melds. From then on until it reaches a score of 3,000 points *or more* it may make melds of any value. But after the 3,000-or-more level is reached a partnership cannot meld until it is able to put down 120 points in one or more melds.

After that, again melds of any value are in order until a score of 5,000 points is reached. There are no further complications. That's game.

Bonus cards, such as red 3's, cannot be counted in amassing the required 50- 90- or 120-point melds.

In repeated tests with competent friends of Canasta, I've found it uncommonly hard to keep accurate track of the score as it affects these arbitrary melds at the several stages of the game. The attempt to count points on the table to ascertain whether a partnership has reached the 1,500- or 3,000-point level in the last few minutes slows the game, is confusing and inaccurate, and introduces an exasperating element into what is otherwise a wonderfully light-hearted pastime.

Let's take a case in point. A player rummages around and finds he has a count of 1,500. Now it is obligatory that he not meld until he can meld 90 points at a time. A road block has been thrown up against him. While he's struggling to get past it, the opposing partnership goes Rummy. The player's partnership is penalized 300 points for the cards held in hand. So, as a matter of fact, it has only 1,200 points. But for the last part of the game it has had to play under the more exacting conditions that go with having 1,500 points.

If this is not absurd it is at least much too close to being unjust. To correct it I have devised the following rules:

If *after the completion of a hand* a partnership's score totals 1,500 or more points, then the first meld required in the next hand must total at least 90 points.

If *after the completion of a hand* a partnership's score totals 3,000 or more points, the first meld required in the next hand must total at least 120 points.

PRIZE PILE

The discard pile becomes a prize pile when it contains a wild card or a red 3. The prize pile may be taken up only when the player holds two natural cards matching the upcard. It cannot be taken up to lay off the upcard on a meld.

STOP CARD

When the upcard of the discard pile is a wild card or a *black 3* it is a *stop card*, and the next player cannot take the discard pile but must draw from stock.

BLACK THREES

Black 3's can be melded to go Rummy only when a player holds three or more black 3's in his hand.

Black 3's cannot be melded at any other time, and they cannot be melded with wild cards.

EXHAUSTING THE STOCK

If no one goes Rummy and the entire stock pile is exhausted, the player picking the last card from the stock must discard one card. If the upcard of the discard pile can then be laid off on one of the melds of the player whose turn it is or of his partner, then the player must take the entire discard pile and lay off the card. Then he must discard one card.

If the discard pile contains only one card (upcard) and that upcard can be laid off on a meld of the player whose turn it is or of his partner, he must take that card, lay it off, and then discard a card.

This pattern of play continues until the upcard cannot be laid off by the player whose turn it is.

If by this time no one has gone Rummy the game ends, and no one gets the Rummy bonus.

If the last card of the stock pile is a red 3, the hand ends, and the scores are totaled. The player who draws this red 3 does not get credit for it. (This summary end of the hand is because the red 3 cannot be replaced.)

END OF THE GAME

At the end of each hand, new hands are dealt until one partnership reaches a score of 5,000 points. But the partnership reaching the winning score cannot call out; the hand must be completed. If both partnerships have 5,000 or more points, that partnership with the highest score wins. If the teams tie at 5,000 or more points, new hands are played until the tie is broken. There is no game bonus for scoring 5,000 points.

ADDITIONAL RULES, EXPLANATIONS, AND PENALTIES

1. In Canasta the meld or *lay* consists of three or more cards in the same *numerical* rank: three 4's, four 4's, five 4's, six 4's, etc. A meld once laid down cannot be changed.

2. The sequence meld, permitted in most Rummy games, is not a legal meld in Canasta. The 5-6-7 of spades, for instance, is no meld at all in Canasta; the cards have no legal relationship to each other; they cannot be laid.

3. "Laying off" meaning to extend an existent meld, a player may lay off cards on either his own or his partner's melds.

Example: The player or his partner has melded three queens on the table before him. The partner or player has a queen or wild card. He can lay this card on the three melded queens— but, of course, only in his proper turn of play.

4. After a player has drawn a card from the stock he may meld if he wants to and if he has the points required to meld.

5. After a player has drawn the upcard of the discard pile, he *must* meld at least the number of points required at that stage of the game.

6. A player may also meld cards taken in the discard pile

immediately on taking up the discards. But points melded from the discard pile cannot be used to help make up the number of points required with each first meld.

IMPROPER MELDING

If a player melds fewer than the number of points required under the rules for the game at that stage, he may rectify the error if he has additional cards or melds in his hand—enough cards to satisfy or exceed the stipulated necessary amount. If he lacks such satisfying cards, he must discard the exposed cards he has laid on the table, one for each discard, in his proper turn of play. These penalty cards cannot be used in any accounting for scoring purposes. He must continue to discard so until either he or his partner has melded the amount required.

After the player or his partner has melded the amount required, the offending player may pick up any remaining penalty cards in his correct turn of play. He may incorporate them again into his hand, and may meld them if possible in due time.

When an improper meld is made after the upcard has been taken, this card must be returned to the top of the discard pile. And if the discard pile has been taken up, it too must be returned to the table. But the penalty meld may remain on the table, being governed by the above rules.

SEEKING INFORMATION

During the game, any player may ask any other player how many cards he has left in his hand. The other player, whether opponent or partner, is not obliged to answer unless he is reduced to a single card, in which case he *must* answer, "I hold only one."

If, holding but one card, he answers that he holds more than one, on discovery that he has misstated his holding, that player shall be penalized 50 points.

When holding more than one card, it is required of the player to whom the query is put only that he reply, "I hold more than one." This is the minimum legal response. It is perhaps more conducive to affable relations in the play to give an accurately responsive answer; but that is not obligatory.

DISCARDING

After a player has drawn a card and (if he can and will) has melded, he *must* discard one card. If a player goes Rummy he may meld his discard card, and is entitled to the extra points at which it is valued.

HOW TO GO RUMMY

To go Rummy, a player must meld or lay down all the ·cards in his hand, melding or laying them off on his own or his partner's melds—if there are any.

But . . .

A player is not permitted to meld or lay off all his cards without his or his partner's melding to form a Canasta. A player must hold at least one card in his hand if neither he nor his partner has melded or formed a Canasta by laying off cards.

RUMMY BONUS: 100 POINTS

If a player has:

A. Laid down a meld—remembering that red 3's laid on the board are not admissible as a meld—and
B. Then goes Rummy—

he receives a bonus of 100 points, provided his partnership has melded at least one Canasta.

SPECIAL RUMMY BONUS: 200 POINTS

If a player goes Rummy without previously having melded (remember: red 3's on the board are not a meld), he receives a special Rummy bonus of 200 points—provided the Rummy hand contains a Canasta or the player's partner has melded or formed a Canasta.

OPTIONAL RULE: ASKING PERMISSION TO GO RUMMY

Although it is not necessary to ask one's partner's permission to go Rummy, this may be done. This is a useful privilege. If partner A has a lot of points in his hand, it would be unwise to permit B to go Rummy at that time, thereby suffering a considerable deduction for cards held in the hand. The only time a player may apply for permission to go Rummy is *after* drawing a card from stock but before melding or discarding.

In no circumstances may a player ask when taking the discard pile.

SCORING

On completion of each hand the values of melded cards and bonuses of each partnership are added together and entered on the score sheet for the partnership as a unit total.

To minimize the possibility of errors in scoring, the following procedures may be useful.

1. List:

Total value of red 3's.

Value of Canastas.

Bonuses (if any) for Rummy.

The total count of all the cards melded.

2. Add:

These totals together, and mark the total at one side of the score sheet.

3. Deduct from this amount:

The value of cards held by the partners in their hands at the end of play.

Any penalties incurred during the play.

(At the completion of a hand all the cards in a player's holding count against his partnership, whether they are melds or not.)

Each partnership is privileged to check the opponents' count.

The plus and minus scores are canceled against each other. The adjusted score is entered on the sheet as the total for that game.

ADDITIONAL PENALTIES

1. For failing to expose a red 3—200 points.

2. For asking a partner's permission to go Rummy and then being unable to do so—100 points.

3. For seeing more than one card when drawing a card from stock—player must show drawn card to the other players.

Players are not permitted to inform their partners of the value of cards in their hand.

ADDITIONAL IRREGULARITIES

Misdeals and other irregularities are governed by the general rules on pages 89 to 92.

Additional Rule—Minus Score

Upon the completion of the first hand, should a partnership have failed to meld the required minimum of 50 points and finds itself in the minus column, this partnership is only required to meld 15 points for its first meld on the next hand. Upon the completion of a hand if the partnership has attained a scoring in the plus column, the minimum meld of 50 points is required for the first meld of the next hand.

Once a partnership has scored the minimum meld of 50 points, it is not required that it make this meld again even if it were to go into the minus column.

Canasta for Six Players, Partnership Style

Played exactly as is four-handed partnership Canasta, except that there are three players on each side. But in cutting for partnerships and seat positions the rules, otherwise identical to four-handed rules, require that the three highest cards cut determine the partnership.

Canasta for Two, Three, Five, or Six Players

Selection of the dealer and seat positions, rules for shuffling and cutting and changing seats are covered under "General Rules for Rummy Games," page 89.

1. Each contestant plays for himself alone in two- three- and five-handed. Player may lay off cards only on his own melds.

2. If the game is three-handed each player is dealt thirteen cards.

3. If the game is five-handed each player is dealt thirteen cards.

4. If the game is six-handed each player is dealt eleven cards, as in four-handed Canasta. The three high players are partners against the three low players in the cut.

Part Three

CHAPTER FIFTEEN

Black Jack or Twenty-One

It is a matter of record that this game was played more than any other in World War I. My own observation was that it was the World War II armed forces' most popular card game. I don't hold with the sociologists and statisticians who deduce large general conclusions about America from facts about the draftee twelve million, but I think this is a defensible proposition: that among people whose mathematics is bounded on the north by an ability to count to twenty-one and whose finances expendable on gambling range from twenty-five cents to a few bucks, Black Jack is more often played than any other banking game.

Black Jack is played in every horse room from Brooklyn to Seattle, in three out of five saloons, in nine out of ten political clubs. Every casino has at least one Black Jack table. Wherever the proletariat gathers, there you will find cash on the table, two faced-down cards in front of each player, a banker trying to look icily self-assured, and some one shouting: "Hit me again! Oh, damn! I'm over!"

There is almost as dense a scholarly dispute over the game as there is over Coon Can. Italy and France have claimed it as their own, the French alleging a blood relationship with their Baccarat or Chemin de Fer (Shimmy), the Italians insisting that it is a vulgarization of their Seven and a Half. The games are obviously similar structurally. To identify who first played it and when and where is obviously outside the purview of the present work; I should as soon undertake to arbitrate when and where the first blackjack was bounced off the first human skull.

The etymology of the game seems to have escaped the attention of the professors, although it might be a rewarding inquiry. *The American Hoyle* of 1875 calls it Vingt-Un. Foster's *Hoyle* thirty years later in date lists it as Vingt-et-Un

Now see what happens to French in a half century of abrasion in everyday speech. Today a substantial minority of Americans call the game Vanjohn, or Pontoon. From Vingt-et-Un to Pontoon; from Chemin de Fer to Shimmy! A man with a sensitive ear can have a lot of fun at a gambling table and never lose a dime. . . .

Let me stipulate at the outset a distinction which I shall have to emphasize later. There are two kinds of Black Jack:

1. The private, sociable, reasonably equitable game in which every player has a right and chance to become dealer and banker.

2. The professional or casino game in which the house man does all the dealing *and all the banking*.

First let's talk about the private game.

Scarne's Rules for a Private Game of Black Jack

REQUIREMENTS

1. Two to seven players constitute the best game, although
2. Kibitzers may bet on the hand of any player except the dealer.
3. The standard fifty-two-card pack, including joker, is used.

VALUE OF THE CARDS

1. Any ace counts either 1 or 11 according to the discretion of its possessor.
2. Kings, queens, and jacks count 10 each.
3. All other cards count their face value.
4. The joker has no value, and does not enter into the play; it is used only as a locater in the deck.

OBJECT OF THE GAME

To get a higher count (total value of cards in hand) than the dealer up to but not over 21. Should the player draw cards forcing his total over 21, he must immediately pay the dealer-banker, and he sacrifices any chance to beat or tie the dealer. The player may demand and draw any number of cards until he reaches or exceeds a count of 21.

SELECTING THE DEALER

The first dealer shall be selected as follows *and in no other manner:*

1. Any player by mutual consent shall shuffle the deck.
2. Any other player may cut it.
3. By the player acting as dealer pro tem, cards are dealt one each, face up, to each other player.
4. The player dealt the first ace becomes the dealer-banker.

LOSING THE DEAL AND BANK

Ordinarily, I don't think the lawmaker on games should build variations into the basic structure of the game, but for reasons to be stated below Black Jack is an extremely special case. Herewith are specified two rules under which the bank may be lost. Either is legal. I recommend that the second be adopted for the private sociable game. I must emphasize that before play starts all players must be acquainted with the rule under which they are playing.

I

Any player dealt a *natural* (two cards totaling 21) shall become dealer and banker at the completion of that deal. If more than one player is dealt a natural, the player nearest the dealer's left wins the deal. If that player refuses the deal, the player holding a natural nearest to that player's left wins the deal. If all players holding a natural refuse the deal, it remains in possession of the present dealer. Should he refuse to continue dealing, the deal passes to the player at his immediate left. If that player refuses, it passes to his left. If all players refuse it, a new dealer is selected by the means stated above under "Selecting the Dealer."

II

This rule is added to stabilize the situation, too often encountered in Black Jack, in which one player gets the bank for a single deal, then loses it to another player who through sheer luck holds it for eight or ten deals.

1. After the first dealer has been selected by the procedure set forth under "Selecting the Dealer," he shall deal (bank) five complete deals.

2. On completion of these five deals, the deal and bank shall pass to the player at the dealer's left, and, each five deals thereafter, shall move to the left, clockwise.

3. When using this alternate rule, a natural 21 shall not win the bank, although the player drawing it shall still be paid two to one on his bet.

THE BETTING LIMIT

The dealer establishes arbitrarily his own betting limits. For example, he may declare that while he's dealing the bets are 25¢ to $2. He means that the smallest bet that can be put on a hand by any person, player or kibitzer, is 25¢, the largest is $2.

Should a dealer after suffering losses have less money in the bank than the players want to bet, he is privileged to lower his limits. As a result of a winning streak he can increase them.

A dealer deciding he no longer wants the bank is privileged to put the bank and deal up for auction and sell it to the highest bidder. He may auction the deal at any time—provided there are no uncompleted hands on the board.

If the dealer offers the bank at auction and no player bids, it passes to the player at the dealer's left. If he rejects it, the deal passes clockwise around the table until it is accepted or a new deal for selecting the dealer is compelled.

THE SHUFFLE AND CUT

The dealer shuffles the cards and puts them in the center of the table to be cut.

Any player may call for the right to shuffle any time he likes, but the dealer shall have the right to shuffle last.

Any player may cut the cards. If more than one player wants to cut, he or they must be allowed to do so.

After the cut has been completed and the cards are squared, the deck is placed on the upturned joker, which is left resting before the dealer. This faced-up card is used as a locater in the deck.

If a joker isn't handy, the dealer shall remove the top card of the deck, show it to all other players, then put it on the bottom of the deck face up. (This is called *burning a card*.)

PAY-OFFS

All bets are paid off at even money by both dealer and players, *except* when a player is dealt a natural, when he is paid two to one.

BETTING

Before any cards are dealt, each player must put the sum he proposes to bet (within the limit) in front of himself within full view of the dealer.

THE DEAL

To each player, beginning with the player at his left and going clockwise, the dealer gives one card face down, dealing himself last one card face up. Then a second card is dealt each player face up, and a second card is dealt the dealer face down.

(I suggest facing the dealer's first card instead of his second because, by giving the players more time to study the dealer's upcard and possibilities, it tends to speed the game.)

THE PLAY

The dealer now looks at his two cards. If he has caught a natural—that is, a ten or picture card plus an ace, totaling a count of 21—he immediately faces his cards and announces a natural.

The players now announce whether they have a natural. If anyone does, that sets up a stand-off or *push*. The dealer collects the bets of all players not holding a natural. The pay-off is at even money, except in case of a stand-off, in which no bets are paid.

If the dealer hasn't caught a natural, the player to his left plays first. If that player has 21 he calls a natural, and turns over his two cards and puts them on the bottom of the deck face up. If the player's two cards total less than 21, the player can elect within his discretion to *stay* or *get hit*.

If he is satisfied that his count is closer than the dealer's to a total of 21, the player may *stay* by declining another card. He signifies this intention by putting his bet on top of his cards and/or saying, "Good," "I stand," "I have enough."

If he is not satisfied with his count and elects to draw more cards he says, "Hit me!" and the dealer gives him another card face up. The player may draw one or as many more cards as he likes, as long as his count does not exceed 21. When the player is satisfied with his count, he says, "I stay," and puts his bet on his cards.

Should a player draw a card forcing his total count over 21 he must call, "Bust!" and turn over all his cards. The dealer collects the bet, and burns that player's cards face up at the bottom of the deck. And the player is out of competition until a new hand starts.

Play as here described moves around the table to the left, clockwise, a man at a time.

THE DEALER'S PLAY

The dealer plays last. He may, like the players, elect to stay or draw. He turns his down card face up, and announces, "Stay" or "Draw."

If he draws one or more cards and goes over 21, he must pay all players still in the game.

If, staying or drawing, he remains below 21 on completing his play, he collects bets from players who have a lower count than he, and pays all surviving players having a higher count.

When dealer and player have the same count it's a stand-off, and neither wins.

ADDITIONAL RULES

The above rules will suffice for a quiet private game, but there's nothing sacrosanct about them. Players may by agreement incorporate into their private play as many rules as they like out of "Scarne's Rules for Black Jack, Casino Play."

Scarne's Rules for Black Jack, Casino Play *

REQUIREMENTS

1. A regulation Black Jack table with six or seven betting spaces on its layout.

2. A check rack filled with betting chips.

3. Four standard decks of fifty-two cards each, plus two jokers.

4. A miniature transparent Chemin de Fer box, called a *shoe*.

5. A dealer (house man) who deals the game and functions as banker, collecting players' losing bets and paying off players' winning bets.

6. A pit boss, who is a casino inspector and who stands alongside the dealer, observing every action of play. He sees to it that no mistakes are made by the dealer or players. He is in complete charge; he rules on all disagreements and his decisions are final. All players and the dealer must abide by them, provided they are within the laws set down by the casino and in conformity with the regulations set down by the Nevada State Gaming Control Board.

(Of course, there may be variations on the above and sometimes a single deck may be used.)

NUMBER OF PLAYERS

1. The house man, who is the steady dealer and the banker. He never surrenders the deal or bank.

2. One to six or seven active players, each of whom may bet on several hands depending on the betting space available.

3. Any number of outsiders, kibitzers, who may wager on each player's hand. They must not advise the player how to play his hand.

VALUE OF CARDS

The cards have the following values:

1. Aces count either 1 or 11 at the discretion of the player-holder. However, the dealer must value the ace as set down by the casino rules (see the dealer's turn of play, page 145).

2. Kings, queens, and jacks each have a count of 10.

3. All other cards are counted at their face value.

THE OBJECT OF THE GAME

A player tries to obtain a higher total card count than the dealer by reaching 21 or as close to 21 as possible without exceeding that count. If the player's total count exceeds 21, he has busted and must turn his cards face up at once. He has lost his bet, and the dealer immediately scoops it up. The player, at his proper turn of play and at his own discretion, may stand, or draw one or more cards in an attempt to better his count.

THE BETTING LIMITS

The casino sets its own limit, but the minimum and maximum bet must be announced to the players.

The minimum bet in the Las Vegas Strip casinos is always one silver dollar. The maximum limit is $100 in some; in others it is $200, $300, or $500. The operators will often raise the maximum to $1,000 or more at the sight of a high roller.

If you like your Black Jack action small and can't stand the silver-dollar minimum, you can go to the downtown Las Vegas tables, where the minimum may be as little as 10¢. This also holds true in Reno and other Nevada towns.

THE SHUFFLE AND CUT

1. The dealer shuffles the cards and puts the four decks face down in the center of the table alongside a face-up joker.

2. The dealer motions a player to cut. Any player may cut. The player cuts the cards and places the cut portion on top of the faced-up joker.

3. The dealer places the bottom portion of the cut deck on top of the cut portion, squares the deck, and inserts the second joker about thirty cards from the bottom of the four decks. The dealer then places the cards into the box and is ready to deal. When the joker makes its appearance (the joker which has been inserted near the bottom of the four decks), the dealer must begin a new deal repeating the above-described procedure.

BETTING

Before the deal begins, each player must place his bet in cash or chips in the betting space, which is indicated as a rectangle painted on the playing surface directly before him in full view of the dealer.

Strip casino players, especially high rollers, bet as many hands as there are available *holes* (betting spaces). Regulation Black Jack tables bear six or seven betting spaces. When a player plays more than one hand at a time, he must play the hand farthest to his right to completion before being permitted to look at his next hand or hands.

The dealer may check the amount of the player's bet to see that it is not greater than the maximum limit. If a player desires a higher limit, he may ask the pit boss, who will either grant or refuse it.

THE DEAL

After all players' bets are down, the dealer, starting with the player on his extreme left, begins dealing clockwise, giving one card face down to each player and one face up to himself. He next deals each player, including himself, a second card face down.

THE PLAY

If the dealer's face-up card is a 10 count or an ace, he must look at his *hole* (face down) card. If he has a natural 21 (a count of 21 with 2 cards), he must face it and announce, "Twenty-one," or "Black Jack."

Any player with a natural 21 also announces it, and the dealer declares this to be a *stand-off* or *push*. There is no action on this hand, and no pay-off is made.

The dealer wins and collects bets from players not having a natural 21.

When the dealer does not hold a natural 21, the player at his extreme left plays first. If the player holds a natural 21, he announces it and faces his cards so that the dealer can verify the count. The dealer pays off the winning natural at 3 to 2 odds. This means that if the player has bet $2 he collects $5—his own $2 plus an additional $3. The dealer then *burns* (buries) the two played-out cards.

If the player's two cards total less than 21 he may elect:

1. To stay. Either he is satisfied with his count or fears that a third card may make his count go above 21. He says, "Good," or "I have enough," or "I stand"; or he signifies that he is staying simply by sliding his cards under the chips he has bet.

2. To draw a card or cards. When the player is not satisfied with his count, he says, "Hit me," or makes a beckoning motion by closing and opening his hand, or a come-on motion with a finger. The dealer then deals another card off the top of

the deck face up before the player and next to his original two
cards. Although the cards are dealt one at a time, the player
may continue to draw as many as he likes. When he believes
his count the best he can get, he stays. If he draws a card
which puts his count above 21, he must turn his cards up and
announce a bust. The dealer scoops up the player's bet and
cards and burns the cards.

The play moves to the player's left, clockwise, around the
table, until all players have played out their hands.

THE DEALER'S TURN AT PLAY

If all players have busted, the dealer merely places his own
cards face up on the bottom and deals a new hand. If any
active player or players are left, the dealer plays his hand.

1. He turns up his hole card so that all his cards are exposed.
2. If his count is 17, 18, 19, or 20, the dealer must stay.
3. If his count is 16 or less, he must draw a card and continue to draw until his count reaches 17 or more—at which
point he must stay. If the dealer holds a *soft 17*, i.e., a 17
count which includes an ace, he must also stay. This also
applies to a soft 18, 19, or 20.

It is important to note here that the Black Jack dealer has
no choice as to whether he should stay or draw. His decisions
are predetermined and known to the players. Since all the
dealer's cards are exposed at his turn of play, he has no opportunity for any departure from these rules.

The rule requiring the dealer to hit on 16 or less and stay
on 17, 18, 19, 20, and 21 is standard today in all casinos here
and abroad.

FINAL SETTLEMENT

At the end of his play the dealer starts with the first active
player on his extreme right and moves around the table clockwise, paying off players who have a higher count than his with
an amount equal to the bet they placed, and collecting the
placed bets from players showing a lesser count. If player and
dealer have the same count, it is a *stand-off*, or tie, and no one
collects or loses. If the dealer busts, he pays off each surviving
active player with an amount equal to his bet.

SPLITTING PAIRS

Any two cards that are identical except for suit may be
treated as a pair. Also, any two cards each having a value of
10 may be treated as pairs, such as a ten and jack, jack and
queen, queen and king, etc.

A player who receives two cards forming a pair or considered to be a pair on the initial round may, if he chooses, turn

them face up and treat each card as the first card dealt in two separate hands. This is called *splitting pairs*. When pairs are split, the player's original bet is placed on one of these cards and an equal amount must be bet on the other.

The player is then dealt one face-down card on the face-up card on his right, and he must play this hand out. If, in drawing to the first face-up card, he forms a pair again, he may again split pairs, betting an amount equal to his first card on this third hand. He may continue to split any further pairs.

The first hand on the player's extreme right must be played to completion before the adjacent split hand is dealt a second card. Each split hand must be played out in its proper order from the player's right to his left.

When a player splits a pair of aces, he is only permitted to draw one card to each split ace, giving him two cards in all.

If a *paint* (picture card) or ten or ace are part of a split hand and the player makes a two-card count of 21, this is not a natural and the player is paid off at even money.

THE DOUBLE DOWN

After looking at his two face-down cards, the player may elect to double his bet and draw one additional card only. This is known as a *double down*. The player must then double his original bet. He turns his two down cards face up and is dealt a third and final card face down.

INSURANCE BETTING

In many casinos, when the dealer's face-up card is an ace, players may make an insurance bet against losing to the banker's possible natural. The dealer, before looking at his down card, inquires if any player wants insurance. A player who desires insurance places an amount equal to half his present wager on his own hand.

When this bet is made, the dealer looks at his down card. If it is a 10-count, he turns it face up and announces a natural. The insurance better is paid off at the rate of 2 to 1 for every unit wagered. If the dealer's down card is not a 10-count card, the player loses his insurance bet. As a general rule I don't recommend this bet for most players.

CHAPTER SIXTEEN

The Mathematics of Black Jack

The Black Jack Dealer's Exact Percentage Take

Why do you lose at Black Jack? What is your chance to win? What odds are you bucking? What is the bank's favorable advantage, and where does it lie?

Since Black Jack is the only casino banking game that combines both skill and chance, these questions are of primary importance. And yet, although casino Black Jack is second only to Craps in the amount of money wagered annually, very few people, players, game-book authors, even casino employees, know the right answers.

Bridge experts Ely Culbertson, Albert Morehead, and Geoffrey Mott-Smith have admitted they don't know either. In Culbertson's *Card Games, Complete with Official Rules* (Greystone Press, 1952), they say: "In no game that has been played for high stakes has there been less analysis of the science of playing than in Black Jack. The only available guide to strategy is empirical; no one has more than his opinion on which to estimate the advantage of the dealer."

I have questioned hundreds of Black Jack players and haven't found more than one in a hundred who has even the vaguest idea of the odds he is bucking in this game. The great majority simply reply, "I don't know." Since the battle is between player and dealer, the player who goes into the fight knowing nothing about the game beyond the rules is sure to take a beating. Because of the fast action, the smallest percentage against the player becomes a major obstacle to winning. Worse, his unfavorable percentage increases in direct proportion to his ignorance of the game's strategy. In Black Jack it's what you don't know that hurts you the most.

Do you think a pit boss at a top casino would have to know what the bank's edge is? I tried to get an answer out of "Jimmy New Yorker," when he was the colorful pit boss at Mike McLaney's plush Nacional Hotel Casino in Havana. He evaded the question until I pressed him for a direct reply. "Scarne," he said, "no one can figure out the bank's advantage at Black Jack. It's too complicated."

Before we dive into a mathematical analysis of the game, I should tell you just what part of the game it is that gives the bank an advantage. If you ask a dealer what happens to your bet when he and you tie with the same count, his stock answer is: "All ties are a stand-off; no one wins and no one loses." This implies that the dealer doesn't take your bet if you tie. This isn't quite right; in fact it's dead wrong.

True, the dealer doesn't take your bet when you tie on a count of 21 or less, but if his statement that all ties are stand-offs is true, then he should keep his hands off your dough when you tie at 22, 23 or anything above 21. Does he? No, that's not the way Black Jack is played. When a player busts, the dealer doesn't wait to see whether he will also bust and tie at a count above 21. He rakes in the bet and closes that transaction. The player has lost, even though his count may later tie with the dealer's.

This is the crux of the hidden percentage in the bank's favor. This is the real reason why casino operators like Black Jack and why most players lose at the game.

The bank has an advantage in the unspoken and largely unnoticed provision that ties stand off, or push, *provided the count is 21 or less*. Want to prove it? That's easy. Just ask your dealer to play his hand out after you have busted and if he also busts and goes over your count to pay you off. You'll get a fast answer telling you exactly where to go and when.

It is, of course, not feasible to figure the exact percentage against individual players because each man plays differently. Some players will stay on 12, 13, and 14; some will draw on 15 and 16; others stay on 15 or more; and there's always the dub who will draw to an ace and 9.

However, since the dealer has no choice as to whether he stays or draws, because the rules predetermine his action, we can calculate the exact percentage working in his favor. It isn't easy, but it can be done. We know first that the banker's hidden advantage lies in the fact that the player must play first, and if dealer and player both bust at a count above 21 the player loses his bet. If it were not for this (and if, when the dealer's face-up card was dealt face down, the bank paid off a natural at even-money odds, and a player could not split pairs or double down) the game would be an even-up proposition.

There is also another complication. Unlike the bank's percentage at Craps and Roulette, which doesn't vary, the bank's percentage at Black Jack changes considerably during the play. It goes up or down as each card is dealt. The following analysis, therefore, must be based on a full-deck composition. We assume, for purposes of analysis, that all fifty-two cards are present, none having yet been dealt.

Next, we find out how many dealer busts may be expected in the long run. We make use of the standard permutation and combination formulas, plus some straight thinking and simple arithmetic. We calculate how many different ways (using a fifty-two-card deck) the dealer's initial two face-down cards can produce all the possible counts. Like this:

BLACK JACK TABLE I

The 1,326 Two-Card Counts in Black Jack

Count	Number of Ways It Can Be Made	Count	Number of Ways It Can Be Made
21	64	11	64
20	136	10	54
19	80	9	48
18	86	8	38
17	96	7	32
16	86	6	38
15	96	5	32
14	102	4	22
13	112	3	16
12	118	2	6

Total Number of Ways 1,326

We find that the dealer's first two cards can produce the counts from 2 through 21 in 1,326 different ways. Note that the player can count an ace as either 1 or 11, but the dealer must count the ace as 11 in all soft hands with a count of 17 or more; the above table is figured on that premise. We won't try to calculate how many hands out of these 1,326 the dealer will bust, because we'll run into too many fractions. We'll discover what we need to know, however, and avoid most of the fractions, if we multiply 1,326 × 169 to get a common multiple of 224,094. Now suppose your favorite dealer deals this many hands and suppose each combination of two cards appears exactly as often as probability theory predicts it will in the long run.

Two-card counts of 17, 18, 19, 20, and 21 will show up 462 times out of 1,326, which is 462/1326 × 224,094 = 78,078 times. The Black Jack rules demand that the dealer must stay on all these hands, so he cannot bust on any of them.

Two-card counts of 12, 13, 14, 15, and 16 will be held by the dealer 514 times out of 1,326 or 514/1,326 × 224,094 = 86,866. Since the rules demand that the dealer must draw to a count of 16 or less, he will bust 47,456 times and reach 17 to 21 counts 39,410 times out of the initial 86,866 dealt hands.

Two-card counts of 2, 3, 4, 5, 6, 7, 8, 9, 10, and 11 will appear 350 times or $350/1,326 \times 224,094 = 59,150$ times. When the dealer gets any of these counts he must, according to the rules, draw one or more additional cards; he will, therefore, bust 17,018 times and reach a 17 to 21 count 42,132 times out of the initial 59,150 dealt hands.

Now, adding the busts gives a total of 64,474, and adding the non-bust hands gives a total of 159,620. Divide the 64,474 busts into the total 224,094 hands, and we find that the dealer will bust on an average once out of every 3.47 dealt hands, or about 28 out of every 100 dealt hands.

Since the rules of play give the player more freedom in his decisions and since players don't conform to any single strategy (many aren't even consistent, playing one way at one time, another way a few minutes later), how do we arrive at a figure for the number of busts the player may expect? First, we must consider a hypothetical player who is consistent in his play and who follows the same rules as does the dealer. He stays on a count of 17 or over, draws to a count of 16 or less, and cannot split pairs or double down. If we assume this, we can calculate an exact percentage by finding out how many times probability theory says that dealer and player will bust on the same round.

Since we calculated above that the dealer can expect to bust 64,474 times out of 224,094, and since our hypothetical player is playing according to the rules governing the dealer, he will bust the same number of times. We multiply their chances, expressed as fractions like this: $64,474/224,094 \times 64,474/224,094$, for an answer of $4,156,896,676/50,218,120,-836$. Now divide the top figure by the bottom one, and there's the answer: The bank or dealer has a favorable bust percentage of 8.27%.

Out of this 8.27% that the bank collects in hidden percentage, it has to pay off players holding a natural 21 count on their initial two cards at odds of 3 to 2. This occurs, in the long run, once in 21 deals. The bank, therefore, pays out one additional unit as a bonus once every 42 deals, or 2.37%. (The stand-off, which occurs when both dealer and player hold a natural 21, happens once in 441 deals; it affects the percentage figure so very little that we can forget it.)

When you deduct the 2.37% player's advantage from the 8.27% bank advantage, the final favorable percentage for the bank comes to 5.90%. Make a note of that 5.90%. Better yet, memorize it: you now know something about Black Jack that your dealer doesn't know—at least, not until he reads this.

Any questions? Yes, I can hear someone saying, "Wait a minute, Scarne. If the only advantage the bank has is the one it gains when player and dealer both bust, why can't the player turn this bust factor to his advantage? He merely doesn't draw to a count of 12, 13, 14, 15, 16, or more, thus avoiding all bust hands, while the dealer, who must draw on a count of 16 or less, will still bust once out of every 3.47 dealt hands. Brother, I'm heading right now for the nearest Black Jack table!"

Take it from me, the answer to your question is a big NO in capital letters.

Why? Remember that the bank's advantage is based on two factors, not one: the double-bust factor and the fact that the player must play his hand out first. If your strategy consists of avoiding bust hands by not drawing on counts of 12, 13, 14, 15, 16, or more, you'll be fighting an even greater percentage than if you followed the dealer's rule of hitting on 16 or less and standing on 17 or more.

You want proof? Okay, here it is. Let's assume the game is two-handed. Playing are the dealer (who must abide by the casino rules) and one player whose fixed strategy is never to draw to a possible bust hand. The dealer's 224,094 completed hands will be made up of 64,747 bust hands and 159,620 hands with counts of 17, 18, 19, 20, and 21.

The player is also dealt 224,094 hands, but since he refuses to draw on counts of 12, 13, 14, 15, 16, or more, he doesn't bust a single hand. He will, however, get 106,133 hands with counts of 17, 18, 19, 20, and 21, and 117,961 hands with counts of 12, 13, 14, 15, and 16. Since the dealer's lowest count of a completed hand is 17, the player never wins except when the dealer busts by exceeding 21. Since the player will receive 117,961 completed hands with counts from 12 to 16, and the dealer will bust 64,474 hands, we subtract the latter figure from the former and discover that without busting a single hand the player still loses 53,487 more hands than the dealer. In percentage this is 53,487 divided by 224,094, or an edge for the bank of 23.86%.

Again we deduct the 2.37% which the bank pays to holders of a natural 21 and get a final favorable percentage to the bank of 21.49%. I am sure you don't want to buck this percentage instead of the 5.90% we were talking about before you got this bright idea.

And don't go away. There's more you need to know about Black Jack if you are going to play it well. Read the next section to find out how the right strategy can increase your chances of winning.

Strategy for Drawing and Standing

The most important decision the Black Jack player has to make is whether to hit or stand on a count of 12, 13, 14, 15, or 16. This question arises in the long run a little more than once every two hands (to be exact 698 times in every 1,326 hands). In practice it sometimes occurs as often as three or more times during the play of a single hand. Players who do not understand the reasoning that should determine such a vital decision have little or no chance of beating the Black Jack bank in a long session.

The only cut-and-dried procedure of hit-or-stand play that is sound for the player is to hit a count of 11 or less and stand on a count of 17 or more. This will keep most players out of trouble. But the player who doesn't know how to answer the question of whether to hit or stand on a count of 12, 13, 14, 15, or 16 is sure to run into double trouble.

The player who goes against the bank's favorable edge of 21.49% by refusing to draw a card when he has one of these counts for fear of busting his hand is a member in good standing of the Black Jack Chump Society. The lure of Black Jack is its fast action. Wagers are won and lost with the dealing of each new hand, and the pace is so fast and furious that the bank's favorable 21.49% will eat up the amount of the chump player's wager in about five dealt hands. Let me illustrate how this works out in dollars and cents. Assume that you are the chump and have played the dealer single-handed and made a $10 bet on each of 300 dealt hands for a total betting handle of $3,000. The bank has an edge of 21.49%, which means that out of 300 hands it will win 21.49% more hands (approximately 64) than you. The bank would win about 182 hands to your 118. The bank collects, in hidden percentage, .2149 × $3,000 or $644.70. This is what you pay to sit at a Black Jack table for two or three hours of play if you stubbornly refuse to hit a count of 12, 13, 14, 15, or 16.

Suppose you adhere to the dealer's fixed strategy of hitting a count of 16 or less and standing on 17 or more. Here the bank's favorable edge is 5.90%, and on $3,000 worth of your action it would cost you $177.

These figures should make it obvious that both of these hit-or-stand procedures add up to a big percentage charge to the player in the long run.

Since a player's position is weakest when he holds a count of 12 to 16, he should use some strategy that will cut down his losses by helping him to win or draw as many of these hands as possible. He must find a way to cut down the bank's 5.90% edge over the player who adheres to the dealer's fixed strategy. The player can do this by varying his hit-and-stand strategy to fit specific situations. The following three factors, when considered together, will enable him to do that.

1. The knowledge of the dealer's fixed strategy (hit 16 or less; stand on 17 or more) and its possible results on the dealer's completed hand.

2. The sight of the dealer's up card and its mathematical bearing on the dealer's possible two-card count.

3. The knowledge of the mathematical possibilities of the player's own card count when he has a count of 12, 13, 14, 15, or 16.

The hit-or-stand strategy that follows is based on these three factors. Before we suggest any hit-or-stand rules, the player must know what his chances of busting a count of 12, 13, 14, 15, or 16 are, or bettering it by reaching a count of 17 to 21. These chances, in some instances exact, in others approximate, are shown in the following table:

BLACK JACK TABLE II

Player's count with 2 or more cards	Total chances of bettering the count by reaching a count of 17 to 21	Total chances of busting when trying to reach a count of 16 to 21	Chances of busting with a one-card draw
16	20 in 52	32 in 52	32 in 52
15	22 in 52	30 in 52	28 in 52
14	23 in 52	29 in 52	24 in 52
13	25 in 52	27 in 52	20 in 52
12	27 in 52	25 in 52	16 in 52

This table can be very helpful to the player even if he only retains a general idea of his chances of busting on each of these counts. Probability theory says that, in the long run, when the player and dealers are both holding a count of 17 to 21 they are expected to win, lose, or draw an equal number of hands. Therefore, the only losses suffered by the player in the long run under similar conditions will be on the bust hands.

The information in the table above becomes very important when it is combined with a knowledge of the strength of the dealer's up card. We have no sure way (short of cheating) to know the value of the dealer's hole card. But knowing the value of his up card enables us to calculate how many completed hands he will bust and in how many he will reach a count of 17 to 21 in the long run. Then, by considering these results in relation to the possible results of the player's completed hands when holding a count of 12, 13, 14, 15, or 16, we can decide whether it is more advantageous to hit or stand in certain situations.

I am always amused by the Black Jack strategy recommended by bridge experts. Since they all seem to copy from one another, they usually end up with the same wrong answers. For instance, they all state that when the dealer's up card is an ace or ten the player should hit a count of 16 because, they say, the dealer's hand is best when he shows an ace or 10-spot. This may seem like good common sense at first glance but what seems like common sense is noted for supplying wrong answers. This is one of them.

Let's analyze it. Assume that the dealer's up card is an ace and the player's first two dealt cards total 16. Should he draw a card, as the bridge experts recommend, or should he stand?

Whenever the dealer's up card is an ace, he must peek at his face-down hole card to see if it is a 10 count. If it is, he turns it up, and there is no problem; the player has lost the bet then and there. If, however, the dealer fails to turn up a natural (21), we know that he doesn't have a 10 count in the hole, and that his highest possible two-card count is 20 and his lowest 12. We can now calculate the exact number of hands the dealer will bust and the exact number of completed 17-to-21 hands he will hold in the long run.

Since most of our Black Jack calculations are based on a full-deck composition, with the dealer's up card and the player's considered mathematically in the full-deck composition, we will do the same here. To simplify the mathematics, suppose that dealer and players are each dealt 52 hands, that each of the dealer's 52 up cards is an ace, and each of the player's 52 hands has a 16 count. Also suppose that each of the dealer's hole cards and all the remaining cards dealt to both dealer and player fall exactly as probability theory predicts.

Out of 52 dealt hands, the dealer will turn up a natural Black Jack 16 times, bust 11 hands, and reach a count of 17 to 21 on the remaining 25 completed hands.

Because the player holding a 16 count immediately loses the bet each of the 16 times (out of 52 dealt hands) that the dealer holds a natural, these 16 hands cannot be considered. Therefore, a player who stands on a 16 count when the dealer's up card is an ace will collect 11 dealer busts and lose 25 dealer completed hands out of every 36 dealt hands—a net loss to the player of 14 hands. If the player hits the 16 count in each of his 36 dealt hands, then he will bust 22 hands and reach a count of 17 to 21 in the remaining 14 hands. From this player loss of 22 bust hands we must subtract the dealer's busts.

We calculate the number of dealer busts in the player's and dealer's 14 competing hands by multiplying the dealer's bust probability by 14. In this case $11/36 \times 14 = 4\text{-}5/18$ dealer busts. Since the dealer will hold 1-1/2 twenty-one counts

less than the player, he will lose 1-1/2 completed hands out of
his remaining 9-13/18 completed hands. We subtract the
4-5/18 dealer-bust hands and this 1-1/2 completed-hand loss
from the player's bust hands and find that the player hitting a
count of 16 when the dealer shows an ace will suffer a net loss
of 16-4/18 hands out of each 36 dealt hands. And the player
who stands on the 16 count will suffer a loss of only 14 hands.

This proves that, in spite of the advice to the contrary given
by the bridge experts, it is to the player's advantage to stand
rather than hit on a count of 16 when the dealer shows an ace
as his up card.

This example should make it clear to the reader why Black
Jack experts attach so much importance to the dealer's up card.
It should also indicate why the following table based on the
strength of the dealer's up card is of the utmost importance,
especially when it is used in conjunction with Black Jack Table
II. Remember that the table is based on 52 dealt hands, each
possessing the same-valued up card, with the hole card and all
other dealt cards falling exactly as probability theory predicts
they will fall in the long run.

BLACK JACK TABLE III
Completed hands

Dealer's up-card-count for 52 dealt hands	Completed hands with a count of 17 to 21 in 52 dealt hands	Number of dealer's busts in 52 dealt hands
10	40	12
11 (ace)	36	16
9	39	13
8	39	13
7	38	14
6	29	23
5	30	22
4	32	20
3	33	19
2	34	18

The table does not take into consideration the natural
21-count hands the dealer receives because if he turns up a
natural when his up card is a 10 or 11 count, there can be no
hit or stand action for the player.

Taken together, Black Jack Tables II and III are the most
valuable information a Black Jack player can possess.

Note that, since he will bust about 23 hands out of 52 in the
long run, the dealer is in his weakest position when his up card
is a 6-spot.

Since our analysis shows that the player should stand on a 16 count when the dealer's up card is an ace, common sense would seem to indicate that the player should also stand on a 16 count when the dealer's up card is a 7-spot. Again, common sense isn't to be trusted; this is another wrong answer.

Here's the proof. When a player stands on a 16 count and the dealer shows a 7-spot, the dealer will bust 14 hands and complete 38 hands with a count of 17 to 21. Since the player will lose the 38 completed hands and win the 14 dealer busts, he will have a net loss of 24 hands out of 52 dealt hands.

If the player hits his 16 count for each of his 52 dealt hands, he will bust 32 hands and make 20 completed hands equally divided among the counts of 17, 18, 19, 20, and 21. The dealer's 20 opposing hands will comprise approximately 5 busts $(14/52 \times 20 = 5\text{-}5/13)$ and about 15 hands with a count of 17 to 21, about 7 of which possess a count of 17. The dealer loses about 4 and a fraction of his 5 completed hands for a total loss of about 10 of the 20 dealer hands. Subtracting the 10 dealer losses from the player's 32 busts, we find that the player who hits a count of 16 against a dealer's 7-spot up card will have a net loss of 22 hands, 2 hands less than the player who stands on 16.

Therefore it is to a player's advantage to hit 16 when the dealer shows a 7-spot as his up card.

Let us analyze another believe-it-or not factor of Black Jack. The dealer's up card for 52 dealt hands is a 10 count (ten, jack, queen, or king) and the player's count is 16 for the same number of hands. When the dealer's up card is a 10 count the dealer must peek at his hole card to see if it is an ace. If it is, he immediately turns up his natural and collects the player's bet. Since the dealer's hole card will be an ace 4 hands out of 52, that leaves us with 48 hit-or-stand hands. If on these 48 hands the player stands on his 16 count, the dealer will bust 11 times and reach a 17, 18, 19, 20, or 21 count 37 times—a net loss of 26 hands to the player. If the player hits his 16 count in each of his 48 dealt hands, he will bust 30 hands and reach a 17-to-21 count 18 times. Of the dealer's 18 opposing hands the dealer will bust about 4 hands. Subtracting the 4 dealer busts from the 30 player busts, the player has a net loss of 26 hands or hands out of 48. In this case it would seem to make little difference if the player hits or stands on the 16 count, since each action shows a loss of 26 player hands.

But it does make a difference, because the player's 18 hands are equally divided amongst the counts 17, 18, 19, 20, or 21, while 7 of the dealer's completed 14 hands carry a high count of 20 and the remaining 7 are divided among counts of 17, 18, 19, and 21. This means that the dealer will win 3 more completed hands than the player. Adding these 3 additional player losses to the 26 losses he suffered previously, we find that the player who hits 16 against the dealer's 10-count up card will suffer a net loss of 29 hands in 48 dealt hands as compared to the 26 lost hands suffered by the player who refuses to hit.

Therefore it is to the player's advantage to stand on 16 when the dealer shows a 10 count as his up card.

It should now be clear that for each possible up card the dealer shows, there is a certain player's card count on which the player should stand, and up to which he should continue to draw, in order to cut down the bank's favorable percentage.

The hit-and-stand rules which I recommend below will shave the bank's 5.90% edge down to about 3% against the player who follows the same hit-and-stand rules as does the dealer.

1. When the dealer's up card is a 5- or 6-spot, the player should stand on a count of 12 or more.

2. When the dealer's up card is a 2-, 3-, or 4-spot, the player should stand on a count of 13 or more.

3. When the dealer's up card is an ace or 10 count the player should stand on a count of 16 or more.

4. When the dealer's up card is a 7-, 8-, or 9-spot, the player should hit a count of 16 or less.

In order to save space I have not given the mathematical proof for each of the above contingencies. The reader who wants to work it out can do so by using the figures in Black Jack Tables II and III and following the same procedure I used when calculating the strength of the dealer's hand when his up card is an ace, 7, or 10 count, in relation to the strength of the player's hand.

Player's Soft Hand, or Two-Way Count

When a player holds a hand that contains an ace, there are sometimes two possible counts, neither of which exceeds 21. A hand containing an ace and a 6 may have a count or value of either 7 or 17, because an ace can be valued as either 1 or 11. This ambiguous type of hand is known to Black Jack dealers as a *soft count* or a *two-way hand*. Playing it correctly requires special strategic considerations, as follows:

1. When the dealer's up card is an 8, 9, 10, or ace, the player should stand only on a soft 19 or higher.

2. When the dealer's up card is either a 2, 3, 4, 5, 6, or 7 count, the player should stand only on a soft 18 or higher.

Note that the holder of a soft hand should never stand until his total count is at least 18. He should continue to draw to his soft count and stand as indicated above. If, when the player draws one or more cards, his soft count exceeds 21 (this occurs often, since a high soft count is being hit), the player should revert to the standard hit-or-stand strategy, because he no longer holds a soft hand.

Example: The dealer's up card is a 6-spot, the player hits a soft 14 and draws a 9-spot. His total count is now 13. If he counts the ace as 11, he has a count of 23. The hand is no longer soft, so the player reverts to his standard strategy and stands on 13.

Soft hands are advantageous to the player because if he uses the right strategy he gets two chances: he first tries for a high count by hitting a soft count, and if that fails he reverts to the standard hit-and-draw strategy.

Splitting Pairs

Splitting pairs or any two 10-count-valued cards allows the player to make two hands out of his initial two dealt cards. If this situation is handled properly the player can cut down the bank's advantage by about 2%. As before, the important factors which tell the smart player whether or not to split are the sight and value of the dealer's up card and the strength of the player's initial two-card count.

The decision is made this way: Add the values of the two cards of the pair to get the total count and compare this with the total count of each single card. If the single-card count has a better mathematical chance of winning than the two-card count, split them. If the two-card count has the best chance, don't split. The chances are shown in Black Jack Tables II and III.

Here is a specific example showing how the tables are used for this purpose. Suppose the player is dealt a 16 count composed of two 8's, and the dealer's up card is a 6. First refer to Table II in which a 16 count shows 20 completed hands and 32 busts. Then turn to Table III which tells you that when the dealer's up card is a 6 there are 29 completed hands and 23 busts.

Mentally split the 16 count into two single 8's. Table III shows that when the dealer's up card is an 8 there are 39 completed hands and only 13 busts. Since this holds true for each of the player's split 8's, it is obvious that he should split them.

Another bit of strategy when splitting pairs is one I use which I have named the *overlay*. The rule is that it is to the player's advantage to split when his single card has a greater count value than the dealer's up card.

If, after splitting a pair and having drawn one or more cards, the player finds either or both hands have a count of 12, 13, 14, 15, or 16, he should resort to the original hit-and-draw strategy.

Here are my rules for splitting pairs or two ten-valued cards:

1. Never split 4's, 5's, 6's, or 9's.
2. Always split 8's unless the dealer's up card is a 9- or 10-spot.
3. Split 7's when the dealer's card is a 5, 6, or 7.
4. Always split aces even when the casino rules permit only a 1-card draw to a split ace.
· 5. Always split 10-count cards when the dealer's up card is a 5 or 6.

As a matter of fact, I often split ten-valued cards when the dealer's up card is a 10 count. Under most conditions this gives me an advantage of 7-7/13% on each split hand. I don't, however, recommend such a split for the average player.

Here again, remember that these splitting recommendations are based on a full-deck composition of 52 cards.

Doubling Down

The technique of doubling down, like the technique of splitting pairs, deserves close study, because when properly handled it can also cut down the bank's advantage against the player.

As in splitting pairs, there are many times when the initial 2-card count indicates that it is to the player's advantage to double his bet.

This is the only single play at Black Jack which permits him to bet an amount that exceeds the casino's maximum limit. The double-down rules give the player a chance to increase his bet to twice the amount of the bank's maximum limit.

Because most Black Jack players know little or nothing about the mathematics of a double down, their lack of any suitable strategy for using it actually increases the bank's favorable percentage instead of cutting it. Most players double down merely because the dealer asks, "Do you want to double down?"

The art of doubling down at the proper time is an integral part of the best Black Jack strategy and a powerful tool in the hands of an expert.

Since the standard Black Jack rules permit a player to draw only one card to double down a hand, the player should have some good reason to back up his decision as to whether or not to double down. In deciding this question we again have to consider the possible strength of our double-down hand and the value of the dealer's up card. Assume that the player is dealt 52 hands, each of which has a double-down count totaling 11. Then assume that each of the single cards dealt to each 11 count falls just as probability predicts. There will be 20 hands with a count of 12 to 16, and 32 hands with a count of 17 to 21. Note that 16 of these 32 hands are made up of a 21 count. If the dealer shows a 10 count as his up card, turn to Black Jack Table III and note that the possible value of the dealer's exposed 10 count shows 40 hands with a count of 17 to 21, and 12 bust hands.

This shows that the player will gain an advantage of approximately 2 hands in 52 by doubling down on an 11 count when the dealer's up card shows a 10 count. Since the dealer, showing a 10 count, is in his strongest position, the player will gain a still greater advantage doubling down on an 11 count when the dealer's up card is an ace, 9, 8, etc.

This is the best strategy for doubling down:

1. Always double down on a count of 11 no matter what the value of the dealer's up card is.

2. Double down on a count of 10 when the dealer's up card is anything but a 10 count.

3. Double down on a count of 9 when the dealer's up card is a 2, 3, 4, 5, or 6.

4. Double down on a soft 12, 13, 14, 15, 16, or 17 when the dealer's up card is a 6.

The player is in the most advantageous position for a double down when the dealer's up card shows weakness, i.e., any card with a count of from 2 through 6. Proof of this weakness is shown on Black Jack Table III.

CHAPTER SEVENTEEN

Cheating at Black Jack

Cheating at Black Jack is more common than cheating at any other banking card game, because Black Jack is more frequently played than the other members of its family—*and* it's easier to cheat at.

Gambling houses of established reputation fight the cheat as a menace to the business; so the private game is the card crook's paradise—why? Because a new hand is dealt every minute or so; because the action is fast; because the competitors' attention is not on the dealer but on their own cards; because only a few cards, all of them crucial, are dealt at a clip; because all the circumstances combine to make cheating downright easy and steadily profitable.

Most of the methods described under my chapter on professional cheating at cards, such as false cuts, shifts, palming, and second and bottom dealing, are used by cheats at Black Jack. Marked cards and a mastery of their use are, for obvious reasons, a tremendous advantage in a game depending on the cheat's knowledge of whether the next card to be dealt will be low or high.

But there are a few crooked tricks peculiarly suited to this game.

Peeking is an example. Peeking is just exactly what the verb means. The dealer peeks at the top card of the deck, the next card to be dealt. Generally he does so by pretending to examine the card face down before him on the table, since his peeking is facilitated by the fact that in Black Jack the dealer holds the pack in his left hand, moving that hand about all the time in all directions, a superb screen.

To peek at the top card in the pack he sets up some small distraction with his right hand—a gesture or blunder making the players' eyes flicker away for just a split second—and then he brings the pack into his surreptitious vision and bends the top card back so he can see its numeral in its handiest corner.

Peeking leads gently and naturally to dealing seconds, a feat made easier by the Black Jack tradition that the cards are held in the left hand and dealt with an overhand motion. The second dealer peeks, sees a card he wants himself, and proceeds to deal seconds until his own turn comes, whereupon he goes honest for a few split seconds.

Dealers who can't deal seconds—and it is quite a trick—use the services of an anchor man.

Say the dealer has a 16. He peeks at the top card and spots a 10. So he turns his card-handling palm up, a signal to the anchor man on his right which means, "Ask for this card." The anchor man takes it. This goes on until the dealer, peeking, sees the card he wants. Then the deck-holding hand goes over, palm down, the anchor man passes, and the dealer catches the low card he wants.

Stacking, that ancient business of arranging cards as they're picked up, is easy too at Black Jack, in which high and low cards and their sequence are so important. Picking up cards, the dealer arranges them in high-low-high sequence, and keeps them in that order on top of the deck during the shuffle. Then, dealing, he has a pretty good idea what to expect next. The riffle stack, to which your attention is directed (page 6) is a more useful as well as more difficult method of rigging a Black Jack deal. But the riffle stack takes great skill. It involves sliding into the deck a crucial card every fifth or sixth card in the shuffle. This is by all means reserved for the professional working eight hours a day before his mirror; amateurs better keep their clumsy hands off it.

But for gamblers too awkward or dumb to peek or stack or riffle, there are always other ways of establishing in advance what the next card will be. Move the card a bit, and then take the precaution to have on the table before you a mirror—secreted in a pipe or ring or match-box or cigarette pack.

Or maybe "you" is a blunder here, even an insult. Don't you do anything of the kind. Just be suspicious of people who deal in certain curious ways. Be suspicious of mannerisms. Be suspicious of players who drop handkerchiefs and spill drinks and toss you a cigar at a critical moment.

Be suspicious.

Can't cost you anything.

CHAPTER EIGHTEEN

Faro or Farobank

Because of its intricate props and elaborate betting conventions, Faro is no longer widely played, but once—when Mark Twain was roughing it—this was perhaps the most celebrated and popular game in the United States. It may be the oldest banking game in the world, and seems in its relation to Florentini to have been of Italian extraction originally; but it got its vogue and name in the count of Louis XIV. "Faro" is the English version of Pharaon; Louis' royal gamblers called the game Pharaon because one of the honor cards bore the face of an Egyptian Pharaoh. Maybe it doesn't really matter, but the game's language is a matter of legitimate interest; it has given us such ineradicable phrases as "coppering the bet" and "calling the turn"—and will some etymologist tell me why the first card in the box is called Soda and the last Hoc or Hock? Faro was introduced into this country by way of New Orleans, moved up river on the Mississippi steamboats, and spread across country like a prairie fire. Many a plantation, many a slave, many a poke of gold were won and lost on Faro tables. To advertise that a Faro game was available, Western houses used to display a big sign bearing the likeness of a tiger; that's all; that's where the game got its alias, "Bucking the Tiger." It is played today mostly in the liberal, tax-levying Western States; and for the substance of this chapter I am indebted to my good and learned friend Elmer West, manager of the celebrated Palace Club in Reno.

REQUIREMENTS

1. A Faro table, which is a big table covered with green felt on which is painted a layout of thirteen cards, running from ace to king of spades. The spade suit is conventionally used for the layout, but the suit of the cards in actual play has no bearing on the game.

2. A Faro dealing box. This, like all other dealing boxes, is open at the top—so that only one card at a time is available—appearing to be framed by wood on all four sides. The box has a narrow slit at one side through which one card at a time can be slid out. A spring in the bottom of the box holds the deck firmly against the top frame.

3. A device called the casekeeper, which resembles a counting rack, having pictures of the thirteen cards painted across its middle. Running from each card to the outside frame of the rack is a metal spindle. On each spindle are four sliding wooden markers like the big beads on an abacus or a child's toy. Each marker represents one of the four cards of that rank. Their use and usefulness will be developed presently.

4. A rack of chips, generally kept to the right of the dealer, about a foot from his right hand.

5. Markers, used to denote bets—and not be confused with the markers on the casekeeper above. The bet-denoting markers are flat oblong ivory or plastic chips about the size of half a piece of chewing gum.

6. Faro coppers. In the Gold Rush days, pennies were used to *copper* a *lose bet,* but today a black or red hexagonal chip is placed on top of a pile of chips when they are bet that a certain card will lose.

7. Betting chips. Their value runs generally as follows:

WHITE   —Valued from $.25 to $1.00
RED   —Valued at either $ 1.00 or $ 5.00
BLUE   —Valued at either $ 5.00 or $10.00
YELLOW—Valued at either $25.00 or $50.00

Note: Color and value of chips are discretionary with the casino.

8. A standard deck of fifty-two playing cards. The suits have no relative value, the only thing that matters being the rank of the cards.

9. One dealer, who keeps the deal and banks the game; one casekeeper; and one lookout, who manages the markers and sees that bets are paid and collected.

10. As many players as can comfortably sit or stand around a Faro table. About ten is average.

OBJECT OF THE GAME

To win money by betting correctly on the rank of cards as they are dealt from the box and on whether they will be winning or losing cards. *This is strictly a gambling game.* There is very little, if any, latitude for skill and strategy.

THE SHUFFLE AND DEAL

The house banker shuffles the deck, cuts it, and places it in the box face side up. The first card of the deck, exposed in this act, is called the soda card or just *soda,* and is dead as far as betting action is concerned.

After the bets have been placed (see below), the dealer then removes *soda* to the far right of the table, commonly putting it to rest in contact with the rack of chips just off his right hand; and then he removes the next card from the box and puts it immediately next to the box at its right.

This action exposes two new cards.

The card which has been drawn out and put on the table beside the box is the loser card.

The card which remains in the box but is also visible is the winner card.

Now the bets on the two exposed cards are won or lost. And the dealer proceeds to slide the winner card out of the box and discard it on the soda stack.

Thereupon the action is repeated. The next card is put on the loser stack, and the exposed card remaining in the box is the winner.

The entire deck is dealt like that. The card that comes out of the box is the loser, and the exposed card remaining in the box is the winner. All bets remain on the painted layout until a decision is reached through the appearance of the bet card as one of the two dealt cards that have action.

Players may change or remove a bet between actions.

But if a bet remains on the layout, it must win or lose.

Every time the dealer removes two cards from the box it is called a *turn.* The entire deck is dealt—down to the last card—to complete a deal; then after reshuffling the deck, the action starts again. The last card is called the hoc or hock card, and like the soda card it is arbitrarily dead as far as betting action is concerned.

THE CASEKEEPER

As the dealer proceeds to make the turns, the casekeeper with his peculiar gadget keeps a record of each card that has received action and whether it was a winner or a loser.

For instance, if the first 7 dealt is a loser, the first button or marker on the spindle of the 7 is slid down to touch the other end of the frame. Should it be a winner, the marker is moved down the spindle, but not until it touches the frame; a space of about a half-inch is left between frame and marker. If the next 7 is a loser, the next marker is moved down to touch the first. If the next 7 is a winner, the same small space is left between the two. This goes on until all four of that kind are dealt from the box, whereupon all four markers are pushed down together to touch the frame, signifying to the players that there will be no more action on that number in that deal.

From the casekeeper's record the player can tell at all times how many cards are left in the box awaiting their turn, what their denomination is, and whether preceding cards of that rank won or lost. On the basis of this record many players develop and constantly play occult "systems."

CASES

When three cards of a kind have received action, the remaining card bearing that number, the card still in the box, is referred to as cases. The idiom is: "Cases on the King!" Many smart players will bet only the cases on any deal. The reason is that the house does not have any percentage in its favor on this bet, due to the fact that splits cannot occur.

CALLING THE TURN

After twenty-four successive turns of two cards each have been dealt, there remain in the box three cards. This stage of the game is called the *last turn*. (Last card in the box, the hoc or hock card, is dead for betting action.)

When the last turn comes up, the player may either bet any one of the cards as an individual bet or *call the turn*—that is, bet that he can enumerate the next cards dealt in the order of their appearance.

Example: The three cards remaining to be played are a deuce, a jack, and a king. The player may bet that the three will come out as follows:

Deuce first to lose.

King second to win.

Jack to be the hoc card.

Now the dealer pulls out and tables the loser, exposing the winner. But he also moves the winner halfway out of the box, so that the players can see the hoc card at the same time.

A player may call the last turn any way he chooses.

In the instance here cited, the player would say he was calling it deuce-king. On the painted layout before him he would place his bet on the loser card's edge facing his winner card, and would tilt all his wagered chips except the bottom one on the edge of the bottom chip. In this case the player, having perhaps six chips to bet, would place one chip on the edge or corner of the deuce nearest the king and would tilt the other five on that chip so that they would tilt toward the king.

If the player wants to call a last turn on two cards separated on the layout by the third card, he must *tilt his bet* toward the outside edge of the layout, signifying that his call goes around the middle card.

Example: The last turn is comprised of the king, queen, and 8. The player wants to call the turn as king-8; so he must tilt his bet on the outside (lower) edge of the king.

But N.B.: This convention for placing last-turn bets by tilting them on the bottom chip is valid only for a bet of two or more chips, of course. If a player means to bet only one chip, the bet must be placed differently. See "How Bets Are Placed," Example 14, page 171.

LAST-TURN PAY-OFFS

Should the player call the turn correctly, the pay-off is four to one. If he does not call it in exact sequence he loses his bet. There are six ways for the last turn to show up.

Should the last turn include two of a kind in the box, this is called a cat-hop. Obviously it is much easier to call this turn; so the pay-off is two to one. There are three ways for the cat-hop to show up.

Should the last turn be comprised of three of a kind, then players bet on the colors at the same odds as govern a cat-hop.

Example: The last turn has come up with three queens in the box, two red and one black. The players bet on red or black to win or lose.

Bets are placed in front of the dealer and called as to color.

IN CASE OF ERROR

If the casekeeper is wrong as the last turn comes up and does not show there are three cards in the box, then the dealer must check back through the winning and losing discard piles to correct the mistake.

If the dealer has made a mistake and the last turn shows

only two cards instead of three, then the turn is void, and no bets have action.

THE BETTING APPARATUS

The majority of all betting is done with chips of different colors. Most modern houses assign a different color to each player, thus eliminating any possibility of dispute between players as to ownership of a bet. For each color category of chips there is a matching smaller-sized chip, which is placed atop all chips of that color in the rack to designate the price per stack of twenty chips—and, by extension, of course, the price per chip.

Example: The rack of white chips has on top a smaller chip stamped with a numeral 5, signifying the stack is worth $5, the individual chips 25¢ each.

For each color too there is a flat oblong marker which is given to a player if his funds don't allow him to cover all the bets he wants and can't place his remaining money on all his cards. This marker represents the same amount of money he has placed elsewhere on the table, and any action as to either or any of his bets is taken from his actual cash or chips.

Example: The player wants to bet $5 on the king and $5 on the 8, but has only $5 in chips. He places his $5 chips on one card and a *marker* on the other card. Should either of the cards lose, the dealer takes his $5 chips, and the marker becomes void. If a marker is used to signify a bet, there must be a bet of actual chips or cash to match in color elsewhere on the table.

THE LOOKOUT

The lookout man sits to the right of the dealer on a high chair and watches the game. His duties are to see that all bets are paid correctly and that the game proceeds in an orderly way. His job is comparable to that of a floorman in the common casino.

THE ROUTINE PAY-OFF

To place a bet on a card to win, the player puts his money on the table's painted or enameled representation of the card he wants. If the number he bets is the exposed card which remains in the box, he wins the bet. All bets except those on calling the last turn are paid at even money.

THE HOUSE PERCENTAGE

If any turn comes up two of a kind, the turn is called a split, and the house takes half the bet forthwith. The split and the pay-off on calling the last turn are the only percentages in favor of the house. The percentage in favor of the house on splits amounts to approximately 2 per cent. On the last turn, the pay-off is at four to one, the correct odds are five to one, therefore the house gets a favorable percentage on this bet of 16.66 per cent.

BETTING ON THE LOSER

If a player wishes to bet on a card to lose, he still places his money on the layout card of his choice, but must also place on top of his money a small marker, generally black and hexagonal, made for just this purpose. This marker is called a copper. The move is called coppering the bet.

OTHER BETS

As to straight bets on the last turn, the same action applies as during the entire deal. First card out is the loser, second is the winner; and if the bet is made on the card which remains as the hoc card there is no action; the bet is a stand-off.

Another bet may be made: on odd or even. This bet applies to the whole thirteen cards. Only one bet is necessary, and it takes action on every turn. The bet is that the winning (o losing) card will be an even number (or odd: it's your bet). If a split occurs and both winning and losing cards are even or odd, the bet is a stand-off. The money is usually placed in front of the dealer on the table between the represented deuce and the edge of the layout to signify even, behind the five to signify odd.

SYSTEMS

Three main types of systems are played, plus another kind of betting on the high card to win or lose, which is itself in reality a kind of system.

As for this latter first, the player betting the high card puts his money on the proper space on the layout. It signifies that of the two cards in the next turn, the higher-numbered of them will win (or lose, according to the bet placed). In the event of a split, the bet is a stand-off.

The three most common systems may be classified as follows:

Double-out. After the first of a kind has received action, the player bets the other three of the same kind to follow the same pattern of win or lose as the first. *Example:* If the first king dealt is a loser, the player bets the other three too will be losers; and the reverse would prevail if the first king were a winner.

Single-out. After the first card of a kind is played, the player bets the next of that kind to come out the opposite, the third to revert to the first's character, and the fourth to be the same as the second. *Example:* If the first deuce is a winner, the player bets the second deuce to lose, the third to win, and the fourth to lose.

(*Note: Most players bet the above systems on the cases only.*)

Three-one. After the first three of a kind have taken action and if the action was alike, the player bets the last card to be opposite to the first three. *Example:* The first three 8's were winners; so the player bets the last 8 to be a loser.

When a player bets one card to lose and another to win and loses both bets on the same turn, he is said to have been whipsawed.

BETTING MORE THAN ONE CARD

Most players have more than one bet on the layout at the same time; and so there are alternate methods of placing a bet so that one gamble can cover more than one card at a time.

But should any of his designated cards lose, the player loses the entire amount of his bet on the layout, and must cover his remaining bets again if he still wants to pay them.

Example: The player has placed $5 in such a position as to cover the ace-deuce-king. This means he has $5 bet on each of these cards. Now should the ace turn up a loser, the dealer takes the $5, and the player must bet again if he still wants to cover the deuce and king.

But should the turn come up with the ace a loser and the king a winner, then the bet is obviously a stand-off.

HOW BETS ARE PLACED

In the chart on the opposite page the various ways of placing a bet are indicated by the position of the chip on the card. Each bet is numbered. Now for the explanations:

1. Bets the 4 only. This position is used on every card.

2. Bets the 5 and 6. This position may be used between any two cards. Between 6 and 7, and between 8 and 7, the chip would be slightly offcenter from the 7.

3a. Bets the 8 and 5. May be used wherever two cards are diagonal to each other. Cannot be used on a 7. This is called a *heeled* bet. The top chips are tilted on the bottom chip toward the other card included in the bet. This is the usual position for bets of two or more chips. If the player wishes to bet both to lose, he coppers the top chip only. If he wishes to bet one to lose and the other to win, he places the bet as in Example 10. For one chip, see example below:

3b. Bets the 6 and nine. This is the same bet as 3a, except

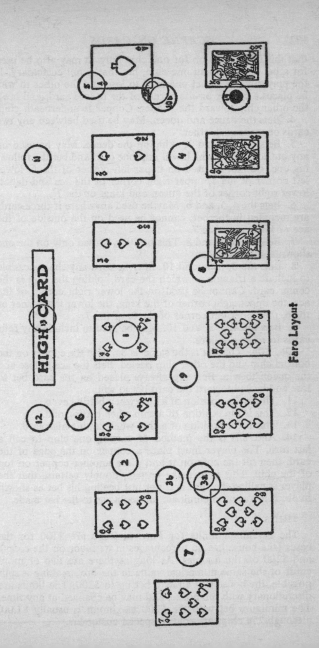

Faro Layout

that this is the position for one chip only. It may also be used for a bet of more than one chip, but that is not customary. If the player wants to bet one card to lose and the other to win, he places a copper on the corner of the to-lose card, and heels the other chip toward the winner. Copper is underneath chip.

4. Bets the deuce and queen. May be used between any two cards opposite each other.

5. Bets the ace and 3, skipping the deuce. May be used on any outside corner which will skip one card and bet the following one. Cannot be used on upper left corner of the 6, lower left corner of the 8, upper right corner of the ace and deuce, lower right corner of the queen and king, or the 7.

6. Bets the 4, 5, and 6. May be used anywhere if three cards are included in the bet; cannot be used on the outside of the ace or king or on the 7.

7. Bets the 6, 7, and 8. This position is used only on the one shown and on no other.

8. Bets the 3, jack, and 10. May be used anywhere possible to include a triangle of which the card holding the chip is the center card. Cannot be used on the lower right corner of the ace, the upper right corner of the king, the lower left corner of the 6, the upper left corner of the 8, or the 7.

9. Bets the 4, 5, 9, and 10. May be used to include any four cards forming a square.

10a, 10b. This bet is the same as 3a, with the copper on the bottom chip and the other chip heeled. Bets the ace to lose and the queen to win. Bets are always placed on the card bet to lose and heeled toward the card bet to win.

11. This is the position of a chip when betting even.

12. This is the position of a chip when betting odd.

13. This is the position of a chip when betting high card.

14. And this is the method of placing one chip to call a last turn. The player must place a copper on the edge of the card, then tilt the chip on it and place another copper on top of the chip. This is to make certain, doubly certain, that the player is calling the turn and not just heeling his bet as shown in 3b. It is meant to eliminate all doubts as to the bet made.

LIMITS

The maximum limits for Faro in Reno are $100 for the cases (the house has no percentages in its favor on the cases) and $200 on the doubles. As long as there are two or more cards of the same numerical value in the box, making a split possible, the house will allow a bet up to $200. The limits are discretionary with the house, and may be changed at any time. The minimum bet with the $200 maximum is usually $1.00, although 25¢ chips are sold to special customers.

Cheating at Faro

Cheating at Faro, in its heyday on the Mississippi packets and in the Gold Rush saloons, was generally by means of a brace box or screw box—a crooked dealing box. Before me as I write stands one of the comparatively crude gadgets. Its operation depends on a tiny button manipulated by a finger of the left hand which narrows or widens the slit through which cards are dealt. Narrow slit, one card; wide slit, two cards. This box requires a pack of crooked cards to be effective, and the most commonly used were called "Sand Tell" cards. The high cards were sanded on the faces, and the low cards on their backs. When both sanded surfaces came flush together they could easily be made to stick together by pressure on the top card. Thus, if a dealer did not want a high card or a low card to appear underneath the top card, he merely pressed on the top card and the screw box permitted him to deal off two cards as one. The sanding was done with sandpaper. Some dealers got the same result by making use of a chemical preparation.

CHAPTER NINETEEN

Stuss, Red Dog and Other Faro Variants

There are a number of gambling games based on the Faro principle, which fundamentally is the matching of card denominations.

Stuss

This is a Faro variant, sometimes called Jewish Faro. It is much more popular than Faro, because it lacks the intricate props, and is much easier for a player to learn to play. Also, gambling houses prefer it to Faro because it has a greater percentage in favor of the bank. The game is played exactly as Faro, with the following exceptions:

1. The thirteen spades on the layout are arranged differently from the Faro layout. For Stuss the cards are arranged in three rows. The top row runs from the king to the eight; in the

second row the seven stands alone; and in the bottom row we have the ace through the six.

2. A Stuss card box is similar to a Faro box except that the former prevents the last four cards from being dealt out. They are held at the bottom of the box, called a pocket, and are out of play.

3. The pack is put into the box face down and dealt from that position.

4. The first card placed face up to the right of the Stuss box is the house card, and if a player has a bet on that card, he loses to the house. However, if the card turned up is not covered by a bet, then the dealer deals the next card, turns it face up and places it to the left of the Stuss box. A bet on this card wins for the player. If there is no bet on either the house or the player card, the next turn or deal of two cards takes place.

5. Also, in Stuss there is no "coppering" of bets as in Faro; in other words, the players cannot bet on any cards to lose. Every bet must be to win.

6. There is no calling the turn on the last four cards left in the box—*no pocket bets are permitted*.

7. After forty-eight cards have been dealt, the Stuss box automatically holds out four cards in the box. Then the dealer takes the four cards out of the box and turns them over. If there are any bets on the layout corresponding to the cards showing on this turnover, all of these bets are won by the house or dealer.

8. *Splits:* In case of splits on ties, where two cards of the same denomination appear on one turn, the house takes the *entire* bet instead of half the bet as in Faro.

9. In some smaller casinos, Stuss is dealt from the hand, entirely eliminating both the Stuss box and the layout.

In some casinos, second bets (a bet on a card after a card of that rank has been dealt) are not permitted. When second bets are not permitted, the house does not pocket the last four cards.

THE-BANK'S PERCENTAGE AT STUSS

The bank enjoys its biggest percentage at Stuss, from the four last cards left in the pocket of the card box, which is calculated as an advantage of 3-11/13 per cent. (Four cards out of a total of fifty-two give a percentage of 7-9/13, but since on average two of these would be house winnings anyway, only half of this percentage—3-11/13 per cent—may be considered extra.)

The bets on splits figure the same as in Faro, approximately 2 per cent. Whereas the house takes the entire bet on splits at Stuss but only half of the bet at Faro, it comes to the same thing because there are no lose bets in Stuss. In Faro, the house takes half of two bets, win or lose. In Stuss, the house takes all of only win bets.

Adding these two figures together, we get a total of approximately 6 per cent in favor of the bank at Stuss.

CHEATING AT STUSS

See "Cheating at Faro." When cards are dealt from the hand, all moves described in the chapters on cheating come into play.

Ziginette

A betting game popular among Americans of Italian extraction and the biggest money card game in Italy. As you read this line hundreds of Ziginette games are going on in smoky little clubrooms throughout the nation; thousands of dollars are changing hands; the yearly turnover is in millions. Although it is a banking game, the house never banks it; it just runs the game, and cuts itself 10 per cent of the dealer's winnings per game.

REQUIREMENTS

1. A forty-card pack—a standard pack from which have been removed the 8's, 9's, and 10's.

2. A metal card box like a Faro box permitting the removal of only one card at a time.

3. A houseman, called the *cutter*, who collects and pays bets for the dealer, as does the croupier in Chemin de Fer, and who extracts the house's cut.

4. A dealer who is the banker, and one or more players, eight constituting the average game.

OBJECT OF THE GAME

For the player to guess which card of his will not be matched before the dealer matches his (the dealer's) card. *To match* means to deal from the box a card of the same denomination as the player's or dealer's card in action. Whenever a card is matched from the box, the player or dealer holding that card loses his bet.

SELECTING THE DEALER

The houseman shuffles the cards, and allows any player to cut them. Squaring the cut, he deals to each player, starting with the player at his left and dealing clockwise, one card at a time face up until a player is dealt an ace. That player becomes the first banker or dealer.

Thereafter on the completion of each deal the bank rotates to the player immediately to the right of the dealer—providing the dealer has matched *his* card. Should the deal run out before the dealer has matched his card, the bank remains in his possession until he does so.

But even though his card has not been matched, the dealer may, if he likes, pass the bank at the completion of a deal; and he may also pass the deal if the table is barren of unsettled bets.

THE BETTING LIMIT

The dealer-banker may establish his own limit, specifying the smallest and largest amount anyone may bet on any card. He may increase or decrease his limits at will. The cutter collects winning bets for the dealer. He pays off his losing bets. If the dealer wins, he must pay the house its cut of 10 per cent of his winnings on that deal.

SHUFFLE AND CUT

The dealer shuffles the cards. Any player may demand the right to shuffle, but dealer may shuffle last. He then puts the cards in the center of the table to be cut by any player who wants to cut them. Then the pack is squared and deposited in the card box face upward. The dealer does this.

THE BETTING

The first two cards are dealt onto the table face up, and any player may lay a bet on either card. The third card, now visible on the top of the boxed deck, is the dealer's card. He does not remove it from the box until bets, if any, are made on the cards on the table.

By putting his money on a faced card, the player bets that this card will not be matched before the dealer's is matched.

Example: Should the first two cards be an ace and a deuce and the dealer's card a 3-spot, the players' bets are laid on the ace and deuce, and then only the dealer takes his 3-spot out of the box. He now puts it under the box, its surface protruding so that perhaps four-fifths of it is visible. If the top card now is another 3-spot, matching the dealer's, he loses; he must pay off the two players who have bet on the table cards; and he loses the bank. If the top card is an ace or deuce the player who has bet on the table ace or deuce loses, and the dealer collects from him.

The same procedure is followed with each fresh card (i.e., a card that has not been matched). When a fresh card appears on top of the pack, it goes onto the table face up, and the players can bet on it.

This goes on until the dealer matches and pays off all remaining bets. Whenever a player matches the dealer wins the bet.

When two cards of the same denomination are dealt in the first three cards it's called a *playette*. Most houses call it *no play*, and the cards are reshuffled and redealt until the first three cards are of different denominations. But some houses insist that when two or three cards of the same denomination appear for the first three cards, they must be doubled or tripled.

Example: If three aces appear on the first three cards, they are put on top of each other representing a single card; the fourth card is placed on the table face up and the fifth card becomes the dealer's card. But before the dealer can lose, he must draw three cards of the same denomination as his card. In other words, a player loses a bet when all four cards of the same denomination are dealt before all four of the dealer's.

If two of the first three cards were of the same denomination, three cards of any denomination would have to be dealt before a decision is effected.

The house assigns a lookout to the game whose job it is to see that no monkey business takes place, that all players who win get their money and all players who lose pay off, and to guard against dead cards getting into the play.

(A dead card is a card that has been matched in that round of play. The holder of that card has already lost a bet on it. Whenever a card has been matched, it and the matching card are picked up by the lookout and put aside, and they—as well as the two remaining cards of that kind—cannot have action again for the remainder of that deal.)

AS TO THE ODDS

Ziginette is dead even; that is, there is no advantage to either player or dealer. Thus in the long run the only consistent winner will be the house, because of its 10 per cent deal cut in the dealer's winnings. After all it's a pretty reasonable price to pay for the privilege of losing your shirt, or am I being cynical?

CHEATING

In cheating at Ziginette a modest skill at stacking, false shuffling, crimping, false cutting, and shifting (see Chapter Two) is useful. But a rather specialized way of breaking a green banker is the use of strippers. Low cards are stripped (see page 24) one way, high cards the opposite way. The cheater cuts the cards for the dealer, and strips out the low cards in the cut and deposits them at the top of the deck. When a low card appears in the early play, he lays a big bet on it; especially if the dealer has a high card. You see, most of the low cards are out of play because they're at the bottom of the box, and the chances are good that the dealer's high card will be matched before the cheater's low card.

Crooked boxes and cards like the screw box and Sand Tell cards of old-fashioned Faro are likewise profitable in Ziginette.

Skin

In my opinion the fastest gambling game played with cards. If you like to bet big and often, this is for you. It seems to be of Negro origin, is played mainly in the South and Middle West, and probably gets its name from its high incidence of bald cheating. However, it is so similar to Ziginette that Skin may merely be short for *zigin* [-ette]. Although it is a banking game, the houses don't bank it; they just run it, and collect a fixed charge.

REQUIREMENTS

1. A deck of cards.
2. A card box.
3. A houseman who acts as lookout and cutter.
4. A banker and two or more players up to six, which is best.

VALUE OF THE CARDS

The cards have no relative value. Neither do the suits.

OBJECT OF THE GAME

To win a bet that the dealer's card or another player's card will be matched before your card. A card is matched when another card of its kind is dealt from the box. *Example:* Your card is the ace of spades. The dealer draws one of the three remaining aces from the deck in the box. Your card has been matched. You lose.

SELECTING THE DEALER

By mutual consent any player may shuffle the pack, then he puts it in the center of the table. Any player may cut. The acting dealer squares the cut, and deals each player including himself one card face up, starting with the player at his left and continuing clockwise until a player is dealt the first ace. That player becomes banker-dealer. When the pack is exhausted on the banker's deal, the bank passes to the player at his right, and so on counterclockwise.

THE SHUFFLE AND CUT

The banker-dealer shuffles. Any player may demand the right to shuffle, but the dealer may shuffle last. The player to his right cuts. If he declines, any other player may cut. The dealer then squares the deck and puts it into the card box *face down*.

THE DEAL AND THE BETTING

The banker slides the top card out of the box and deals it to the player *on his right,* turning the card face up.

1. The player may do one of two things: he may accept that card or refuse it. Some players entertain the belief that certain cards are unlucky for them; others believe certain cards are so lucky they can be taken down to the bank and put up as collateral on a substantial loan. For any reason, a player may decline a card.

2. But if he refuses the first card dealt him, the player is out of the game for that turn of play. He must wait until it comes his turn again to make a bet.

3. Should the first player refuse the card, the right to take it passes to the player at No. 1 player's right, and so on, the right to the card moving counterclockwise around the table.

4. After the first card has been accepted by a player, the dealer now gives himself the second card out of the box.

5. The player now states his bet. He may bet any amount up to the limit, but the dealer is not compelled to accept the entire bet even within the limit; he has the right to reduce the bet to any amount he chooses, and the player must adhere to the dealer's rulings. He cannot withdraw his bet after making it.

6. In accepting the player's bet the dealer puts an amount of money equal to the bet directly on the center of the player's card. The player *covers* the bet by putting his money on the dealer's money.

7. The player is betting the dealer's card will be matched before his own card is matched. Should he bet also against another player, the bet is that the other player's will be matched before his card is. *Example:* The dealer's card is the ace of diamonds, and the player holds the 10 of diamonds. If the next card dealt is one of the other three aces, the dealer has been matched, and loses all the bets on the board. If it is one of the other three 10's, the player has been matched and loses his bet.

8. Should the third card dealt not match either the dealer's or the player's card, it is dealt to the next player whose turn

it is. That player makes a bet in the manner described above against the dealer. *But* he may, if the first player accedes, make a bet against that player—and, in turn, any other. The same rules prevail as between dealer and player.

This goes on until each player has had his turn. Often a player will be betting against every other player in the game plus the dealer. But note that the first bet a player makes *must* be with the dealer. If the player refuses to bet against the dealer he has refused the card, and cannot bet with any other player.

When players bet against each other, the money is stacked to one side to avoid confusion with the dealer's stakes.

The house assigns a lookout to the game whose job it is to see that no monkey business takes place, that all players who win get their money and all players who lose pay off, and to guard against dead cards getting into the play.

(A dead card is a card that has been matched in that round of play. The holder of that card has already lost a bet on it. Whenever a card has been matched, it and the matching card are picked up by the lookout and put aside, and they—as well as the two remaining cards of that kind—cannot have action again for the remainder of that deal.)

A player who has refused a card or lost his bet may, after each other player has had a turn of play, take a *fresh card* (that is, a card which has not been matched), and the betting continues as before. If, with all players holding a card already, a fresh card is dealt, it is placed in the center of the table; and, whenever a player has been matched so that he does not hold a card, he may take any of the fresh cards he wants.

Whenever the dealer's card is matched he must pay off all the players. Should the players have bets riding against each other when the dealer loses his bets, the dealer may (a) complete dealing for the players or (b) take the first fresh card dealt off the pack. Players still in the game are not obliged to bet against the dealer, once the dealer's card has been matched, but may do so if they choose.

AS TO THE ODDS

The game of Skin is *dead even;* that is, dealer and player have exactly equal chances of winning. For that reason—that there is no percentage in the dealer's favor—the house runs the game instead of banking it. In return for supplying a place and the equipment—plus a lookout—it extracts a 25 per cent charge from the player or dealing winning the last bet of the deal. (Variation: Some houses charge a flat 2 per cent on each bet won by a player from the dealer and 2 per cent of the dealer's winnings on any deal—if there are any winnings.)

CHEATING AT SKIN

All the cheater has to know is what that top card will be, and he has the game and all the present cash tucked in his vest pocket.

So watch for: marked cards, second dealing, stacking, fake cuts, cold decks, the second-dealing box, and belly strippers, which are often used to clip the sucker on his own deal.

Spanish Monte

Also called Monte Bank, and played in the United States mostly by persons of Spanish extraction. It is not to be confused with *Three Card Monte*, a notorious confidence game.

REQUIREMENTS

1. A standard deck of fifty-two playing cards.
2. A banker and one or more players. As a rule the admissible maximum is eight.
3. A houseman, called a *cutter*, whose official duty is to pay off and collect for the dealer and whose tacitly agreed function is to see that nobody gets gouged.

OBJECT OF THE GAME

To win a bet that a selected one of four faced-up cards on the table *will* be matched before one of the three other cards. (A card is matched whenever one of the remaining three cards of the same denomination is dealt from the pack.) *Example:* Faced up on the table are the ace, 2, 3, and 4 of clubs. The player puts his bet on the ace, placing his money in such a way that it just touches the deuce as well. He is now betting that one of the three remaining aces will be dealt from the pack before one of the three remaining deuces.

VALUE OF THE CARDS

The cards have no special value relative to each other, and neither do the suits.

SELECTING THE BANKER

By mutual consent any player shuffles the pack, then puts it in the center of the table. Each player cuts a group of cards off the pack. Player cutting the low card is the first dealer and banker. In case of tie for low card, the tied players cut until one is low. On completion of the banker's deal, the deck and the deal pass to the player on the dealer's left, and thereafter rotate to the left, clockwise. The dealer may *pass the bank* (i.e., decline to bank the game) at any time—if there are no unsettled bets on the table. To announce that he means to pass the bank, the dealer utters the word "Aces!"

BETTING LIMIT

The dealer is privileged to establish any betting limit he chooses. He may, if he pleases, lower a player's bet. Or he may without notice increase the limit.

THE SHUFFLE AND CUT

The dealer shuffles the pack. Any player may call for a shuffle before the cut, but the dealer is entitled to shuffle last. After the shuffle the dealer puts the cards before the player at his right to be cut. That player *must* cut, although other players may call for the right to cut before the player to the dealer's right completes his own cut.

START OF THE DEAL

After the cut the banker deals two cards off the *bottom of the deck,* facing up these two cards and putting them in the center of the table two or three inches apart. Then the dealer takes two cards off the top of the deck, and puts them face up two or three inches below the first two cards about the same distance apart, forming a rectangle.

Should the four faced cards comprise two or more cards of the same rank, there is a "no play," and a new deal is in order.

THE BETTING

A player may now bet on any two of the four faced cards, betting that one of them will be matched before the other. For his part, in accepting the bet, naturally the dealer is betting the other will be matched before the one the player has selected. Players may bet any one of the six possible two-card combinations. The cutter keeps track of the players' bets.

The wager is commonly put (in cash) on that card on which the player is betting. (That's why the cards are separated from each other.) As many players may bet on the same combination as the dealer, who is absolute boss of the game, will countenance.

THE PLAY

After the bets have been placed the cutter tells the dealer, "That's all," which formally terminates that phase of the game, and the dealer turns the deck face up in his hand. From now on the cards will be dealt from the pack face up one at a time.

If the top card of the deck matches one of the four faced

cards, either the dealer or a player (or players) wins; and the dealer keeps taking cards off the pack either (a) until all the cards bet on are matched or (b) the cards the players are betting against have been matched. When all bets are won or lost the deal is completed.

Some houses let the dealer place unmatched cards on the board after a card has been matched, as in Skin.

THE PERCENTAGE

If a player wins a bet on the first card dealt from the pack, the house takes a 25 per cent cut from his winnings; but no cut is taken if the dealer wins a bet on the first turn. What house percentage is the player paying under these conditions? Let's see.

After the first four cards have been faced and the money play begins there are forty-eight cards left in the deck, and three of these are *yours*.

The chance that one of these three will be at the bottom of the deck and first dealt is one out of sixteen for a house percentage of .0156. Is that so trivial? Obviously it's advisable to hold the bank under these conditions, since the dealer does not have to pay this percentage when he wins. And since the player's cut is equally divided by the dealer and the house, the dealer-banker's advantage in Spanish Monte is half this or .0078 per cent.

CHEATING

Although some dealers peek, then try to deal two cards as one even with the cards face up, most cheating is done before the cards are faced up in the dealer's hand.

The cheating methods feasible in Spanish Monte—false cutting, stacking, crimping, and the use of strippers—are covered in Chapters Two and Three. In this game, marked cards and second-dealing are useless.

Red Dog

One of the most popular fast-action card games played by servicemen during World War II, surpassed only by Black Jack; an occupational disease with newspapermen; the origin of some great city-room anecdotes and at least one sure-fire short story plot.

REQUIREMENTS FOR PRIVATE RED DOG

1. From two to eight players.
2. A standard pack of fifty-two playing cards.

RANK OF THE CARDS

Exactly as in Poker: deuce (low), 3, 4, 5, 6, 7, 8, 9, 10, jack, queen, king, and ace (high). The suits have no value relative to each other.

OBJECT OF THE GAME

To win by holding in the hand a card of the same suit but higher in rank than the card dealt from the pack on the draw.

SELECTING THE DEALER

By mutual consent any player may shuffle the pack; then he places it in the center of the table. Any player may cut. The acting dealer squares the cut, and deals one card face up to each player including himself, starting with the player at his left and rotating to the left, clockwise. This goes on until an ace is dealt; the player receiving it becomes the dealer.

On completion of each deal the deal rotates to the player at the dealer's *left*, and moves clockwise on the completion of each deal.

THE ANTE

Each player puts in the center of the table a like amount of money, forming a pool called the *pot*.

THE SHUFFLE AND CUT

The dealer shuffles the cards. Any player may call for the right to shuffle, but the dealer shall retain the privilege of shuffling last. The player to the dealer's *right* shall cut, and at least three cards must be left to constitute each cut group of cards. Should the first player to the dealer's right decline the cut, the cards may be cut by any other player.

THE DEAL

After the cards have been cut, the dealer, starting with the player at his left and dealing clockwise, deals each player four cards face down one at a time.

THE BETTING

The player to the dealer's left has the first turn of play, which thereafter moves to the left, clockwise. Any player may bet (a) at least the amount of his ante, (b) the entire amount of the pot, or, (c) any part thereof.

A NOTE AS TO RESPONSIBILITY AT RED DOG

It is up to the dealer to keep track of the bets.

THE DRAW

When a player, having examined his cards most judiciously, has placed his bet—which he does by placing the amount bet, in cash, up close to the pot—the dealer deals the top card off the pack, and turns it face up on the table before the better whose turn of play it is.

Now—

1. If the better holds a card of the same suit as the top card but of higher numerical value or rank, he shows that superior card, and wins the bet; and the dealer removes from the pot for him an amount equivalent to that player's bet.

2. But if he does not hold a higher card of the same suit as the top card he loses the bet, and the dealer sweeps his bet into the pot.

When all players, including the dealer, have had their turn of play, the deal passes to the player at the dealer's left. If any money remains in the pot at that point, there it stays—only now the players ante again to make it bigger.

If the pot gets so big that the players are financially or morally unable to bet it, they may by mutual consent split it among them. Thereupon they ante anew.

VARIATION APPLYING TO THE BANKER

The banker may put any amount of money he pleases into a pot before the deal, and each player in his turn may bet the pot or any part of it. If the pot is exhausted before the deal is completed, the deal passes to the player at the dealer's left.

The players do not ante under this variation.

THE PERCENTAGE AT RED DOG

Because he plays last and gets the last card, the percentage favors the dealer at Red Dog. He has seen several exposed cards played, and this factor is a great advantage. To take a rather extreme example—but an example familiar to every experienced Red Dog fancier—let's say the dealer holds the aces of spades, diamonds, and clubs *plus* the king of hearts. Only one card in the deck can beat him. That card is the ace of hearts. Any other player in the game—say, the first player—knows that his hand is almost certain to win if he bets the pot, though that pot totals the entire United States public debt. But he can't be sure. On the other hand, the dealer having seen a fairly wide assortment of faced cards, plus a few discarded hands, has had a fair chance to see that ace actually exposed and out of the way. He can bet the whole pot with absolute certainty that he can't be beaten.

As mentioned, this is a rather extreme example. But it applies consistently. Holding a hand of jacks, a dealer who has seen a batch of higher court cards exposed can take and win hazards which would be foolhardy for any other player.

STRATEGY AT RED DOG

The only decision you have to make is how much to bet. This depends almost entirely on how good your hand is. Add up the value of the cards in your hand.

Count ace as 14; king as 13; queen, 12; jack, 11; and the spot cards their numerical value, counting only the highest card in any one suit.

If you hold four deuces, your total is 8. With such a hand you cannot win. If you held four aces your count would be 56 and couldn't lose. If your hand adds to 32 you have an even chance of winning. Upon this calculation a player may decide how much he desires to bet.

A VARIATION OF RED DOG

This variation was thought of highly by G.I.'s during World War II. Except for it, all the other rules of the game stand intact as stated.

1. Player cutting high card becomes dealer or banker.
2. Players do not ante; the banker puts into the pot any amount he alone decides.
3. Players may bet the pot or any part thereof.
4. Each player is dealt *three* cards. (Although some dealers allotted four!)
5. If the pot is exhausted, or on completion of three deals, the bank and deal move to the player at the dealer's left.

CHEATING AT RED DOG

Since foreknowledge of the identity of only one card is crucial, cheating is virtually an economic necessity at Red Dog. The game is a favorite of shipboard card sharks, who like to switch in a cold deck on a sucker and take him for the pot—plus. Second dealing and marked cards are an unbeatable combination. See also the cheating methods described in Chapters Two and Three.

CHAPTER TWENTY

Card Craps, Farmer and Other Games

Card Craps

I've never preached a sermon in my life. Any one who squeezes a moral out of this monastically objective report does so without my permission. The creation of Card Craps was the answer to the prayers of gamblers and operators in towns where crapshooting is forbidden by the local police although card games are not molested. This game is crapshooting with playing cards. I know the gamblers who created the game; indeed I was a witness to the first Card Craps game ever operated, in the Horseshoe district of craps-banning Jersey City early in the spring of 1945. At that time the professionals couldn't calculate the correct percentage on the bets they were handling; so they came to me for advice on the odds. I wrote and published a small monograph on the game. It appears to have had some esteem in the trade; at least now, early in 1949, gambling casinos are featuring Card Craps in cities whose local moralities and police will positively not let a low dice game run. Haw!

A NOTE ON THE MATHEMATICS

The present game has been so evolved that if the specified rules, methods of play, and betting odds are scrupulously followed, the right and wrong betters each will have an equal chance of winning. There is one exception: the center bet has a 1.21 per cent advantage for the fader. This is a perceptible improvement on the 1.41 per cent for this bet at craps with dice; the shooter's and the fader's chances at Card Craps are .20 per cent nearer even on this bet. In the long run such a factor, infinitesimal as it may seem on paper, can add up to a good pocketful of cash.

REQUIREMENTS FOR CARD CRAPS

1. A special pack of dice cards consisting of forty-eight cards which are two each in all four suits of the aces, deuces, 3's, 4's, 5's, and 6's. That is, there must be eight each of each denomination. And a complete pack must be used at all times.

187

2. A set of chips or other objects to be used as markers. Each player at the start of the game gets—by buying them, of course—an equal number of markers.

The winner is the player who at the game's end has the most chips.

PLAYERS

Any number may play.

The player who deals the cards is called the shooter.

Any player may, by consent of the others or by any method of choice they elect, start the game by becoming the shooter.

A new player may enter the game any time there is an opening at the table.

The deal moves around the table to the left, clockwise.

SHUFFLE AND CUT

1. The shooter shuffles the pack. Any other player may call for the shuffle at any time before the cards are cut.

2. The shooter has the right to shuffle last.

3. The cards are then offered to the player at the shooter's left to be cut. Any other player may demand and have the right to cut, but the player at the shooter's left retains the right to cut last if he wants to. If he declines to cut then some other player *must*.

THE PLAY OR DEAL

1. The shooter deals off the top of the deck two cards face up on the playing surface, one at a time. And the numerical values of these two cards are added to form a deciding number. (Just as the top-surface numbers on two dice are added.)

2. Any combination of two cards dealt by the shooter shall be called a *throw*.

3. The first throw of the cards starting any new decision shall be called a *come-out*.

4. The two cards of each come-out throw must be returned to the pack for the new deal, regardless of whether the come-out throw is a crap (2, 3, or 12), natural (7 or 11), or point number (4, 5, 6, 8, 9, or 10).

Note: It is critically important that the above rule be faithfully obeyed. Failure to obey it will corrupt the mathematical possibilities and derange the betting odds.

5. If on the first throw the shooter deals a natural 7 or 11, it is a winning decision called a *pass*. If he deals a crap 2, 3, or 12, it is a losing decision called a *miss-out*. If he deals a 4, 5, 6, 8, 9, or 10, then that number becomes the shooter's

point. The two dealt cards are then shuffled back into the pack, which then must be cut, and the shooter continues dealing the cards in pairs until he:

A. throws his point, which is a winning decision (pass);
B. throws a 7, which is a losing decision (miss-out); or
C. exhausts the entire pack without getting a decision; in which case the pack is reshuffled and cut and the shooter continues dealing.

6. When by throwing a 7 the shooter misses out on the point, the cards pass to the player at the shooter's left, and it becomes his turn to shoot.

7. The shooter may, if he likes, pass the cards to the next player on completion of any winning decision, without waiting to miss out on the point.

8. Any player may, if he wishes, refuse to shoot in his turn, and may pass the cards to the player next at his own left.

9. When two decks are available, players may call for and have a change of packs, the exchange taking place immediately before the next succeeding deal.

BETTING

The contribution of markers to a pool by the players shall be called betting.

1. *Right Bet.* A bet that the shooter will pass. (Win either by throwing a natural on the come-out or by throwing a point on the come-out and then repeating the point before throwing a 7.)

2. *Wrong Bet.* A bet that the shooter won't pass.

3. *Center Bet.* Before the come-out the shooter may (but he is not required to) bet that he will pass. Players who cover this bet by betting an equal amount against the shooter *fade* the shooter, and are known as *faders.* Their bets, placed in the center of the playing surface, are *center bets.*

4. *No Bet.* If only a part of the shooter's center bet is covered, he may shoot for that amount; or he may call off the bet by saying, "No bet!"

5. *Side Bet.* Any bet not a center bet is a side bet. The player may make any side bet, including the

6. *Flat Bet.* A side bet made before the come-out that the shooter does pass (win) or doesn't pass (lose). Same as a center bet, except that the shooter is not being faded and the bet is being placed at the side.

7. *Point Bets.* A bet made by a right better, after the shooter has thrown a point on the come-out, that the shooter makes his point is a *right point bet.* A bet by a wrong better that the

shooter misses his point is a *wrong point bet.* The right better takes the odds on that point; the wrong better lays the odds on that point.

8. *Double Hardway.* Making a point the double hardway consists in making any of the even point numbers (4, 6, 8, and 10) with duplicate, or paired, cards; for example, making the point 4 with two deuces of spades, or with any two deuces of the same suit.

THE BETTING ODDS

Odds against passing on the center or flat bet are even money, one to one.

Odds Against Passing on the Points

Point	Correct Odds	Exceptions
4	2 to 1	(Except when thrown the double hardway, in which case the wrong better must pay off at four to one.)
10	Same as on the 4	
5	3 to 2	
9	3 to 2	
6	6 to 5	(Except when thrown the double hardway, in which case the wrong better must pay off at twelve to five.)
8	Same as on the 6	

The double pay-off on the point numbers 4, 6, 8, and 10 when made the double hardway serves to equalize the right and wrong betters' chances of winning a point bet on the even point numbers.

FOR LARGER GROUPS

When a relatively large number of players want to get into the game, I recommend that a deck of seventy-two cards be used. This deck is made up to consist of three each in all four suits of the aces, deuces, 3's, 4's, 5's, and 6's. The odds remain the same as with the forty-eight-card deck except for the pay-off on the double hardway. The point 4 or the point 10 made the double hardway pays off at three to one on point bets in the seventy-two-card deck. The point 6 or the point 8 made the double hardway pays off at nine to five.

THE BOOK AT CARD CRAPS

The *book*, who is a man, not a bound document, works the same at Card Craps as at Bank Craps or Open Craps. That is, he takes win or lose bets, accommodating all comers, and for this banking service he collects a charge called *vigorish*.* Some books charge more than others, but we shall deal here with nation-wide average practice.

Some books charge 5 per cent of the bet; some pick up the vigorish both ways; some pick it up only on right action, and let it ride on wrong action; some charge 3 per cent, and pick it up on right and wrong action alike.

Example, predicated on a book picking up 5 per cent vigorish on the right action and letting it ride on the wrong action:

1. A right better taking $7.50 to $5 on the five would have to pay the book 25¢ for the bet. If he wins he gets $12.50.

2. A wrong better laying the book the correct odds on the five would have to lay $7.75 to the book's $5. If the wrong better wins he gets $12.75.

(If, as some books do, this book were picking up the vigorish on the wrong better too, he would have gotten only $12.50 on winning this bet.)

Following, in tabular form, are the correct percentages against the players for both 5 per cent and 3 per cent charges:

TABLE NO. 1

Correct Vigorish on the Odds Wagers When the Book Picks Up the 5 per cent Charge on Right Action and Lets It Ride on Wrong Action

RIGHT BETTER

Pays 4.761   19/21 per cent   or 25¢ on a $5.25 bet on all points

WRONG BETTER

Pays .813   1/123 per cent   or 4¢ on a $5 bet on 4 or 10
Pays 1.290   10/31 per cent   or 6¢ on a $5 bet on 5 or 9
Pays 1.818   2/11 per cent   or 9¢ on a $5 bet on 6 or 8

But, as I have noted, some books don't give the wrong better such a generous proposition; they pick up the 5 per cent both

---

* For an exhaustive study of vigorish and the many other subtleties of craps and its mathematics and probabilities the reader is referred to my book *Scarne on Dice* (Military Service Publishing Company, Harrisburg, Pa., 1945, $5.00).

ways. Other books pick it up both ways, but charge only 3 per cent—giving the right better a better break. And so . . .

TABLE No. 2

Correct Vigorish When the Book Picks Up the 5 Per Cent Charge Both Ways

RIGHT BETTER

Pays 4.761   19/21 per cent   or 25¢ on a $5.25 bet on all points

WRONG BETTER

Pays 2.439   1/41 per cent   or 12¢ on a $5 bet on 4 or 10
Pays 3.225   25/31 per cent   or 16¢ on a $5 bet on 5 or 9
Pays 4 per cent   or 20¢ on a $5 bet on 6 or 8

TABLE No. 3

Correct Vigorish When the Book Picks Up the 3 Per Cent Charge Both Ways

RIGHT BETTER

Pays 2.912   64/103 per cent   or 15¢ on a $5.25 bet on all points

WRONG BETTER

Pays 1.477   169/203 per cent   or 7¢ on a $5 bet on 4 or 10
Pays 1.960   40/51 per cent   or 10¢ on a $5 bet on 5 or 9
Pays 2.439   1/41 per cent   or 12¢ on a $5 bet on 6 or 8

A WORD OF ADVICE

Any man playing in a private game of Card Craps—that is, a game without benefit of *book*—by accepting the correct odds and shooting no more often than the other players has as healthy a chance of winning as anybody else at the table. Temperament and the degree of understanding of the game's nature will, of course, make some difference; but, granted these are equal, the chances are equal.

But if you play in a book game and consistently bet the book, you must and will go broke eventually. No system, no lucky streak, can beat the percentages.

CHEATING AT CARD CRAPS

Every move in the cheater's repertoire may be—and, you may be sure, will be— used at Card Craps. A few of the more common: marked cards, strippers, seconds, stacking, palming, switching hole cards, and cold-decking.

Put and Take

A fascinating combination of Red Dog and the kind of Put and Take normally played with a spinning top or with dice.

REQUIREMENTS

1. A standard pack of fifty-two playing cards.
2. From two to eight players.

SELECTING THE BANKER

Player cutting high card becomes the banker (dealer). On completion of a deal the bank rotates to the player at the dealer's left.

THE DEAL

The dealer deals each player excluding himself five cards, one at a time starting with the player to his left and rotating clockwise. The dealer then deals himself five cards one at a time face up.

Players holding a card of the same denomination as the dealer deals to himself either put into the pot or take out of the pot a specified number of units, winning or losing according to the fall of the cards.

THE BETTING LIMIT

The value of the betting unit is fixed by mutual consent. Bets consist of from one to sixteen units, as prescribed by the rules of the game.

PUTTING AND TAKING

1. *Putting units into the pot.* The dealer gives himself five cards, as described below, and the players ante into the pot as specified, card by card.

A. The dealer gives himself one card face up on the table. Each player holding a card of the same denomination as that card must put one betting unit into the pot—for each card he has of that rank.
B. The dealer's second card calls for two units from each player for each card he has of that rank.
C. The dealer's third card calls for four units.
D. The fourth requires eight units.
E. The fifth requires sixteen units.

2. *Taking units out of the pot.* The dealer now picks up his

five cards, places them face up on the bottom of the pack, and deals himself, off the top of the pack, five more cards, one at a time.

But this time each player takes on the first card one unit from the pot for each card he holds of the same denomination as the dealer's. And he gets two on the second card, four on the third, eight on the fourth, and sixteen on the fifth.

Any units remaining in the pot at the end of the play go outright to the dealer. If the pot owes any player or players money, the dealer must cover its deficit out of his pocket.

RED AND BLACK VARIATION

Some players have speeded up the game with this variation: Any player holding three or more cards of the same color as the dealer's first card must put one unit into the pot. On the second card the three-card holder's ante is two units; on the third, three; on the fourth, four; and on the fifth, five.

They take out at the same rate on the dealer's second (take) turn of play.

CHEATING AT PUT AND TAKE

See "Cheating at Red Dog" (page 186) and its chapter references.

Farmer

A curiously sophisticated country cousin of Black Jack, commonly supposed to be played by farmers. Rural electrification has done something for American agriculture.

REQUIREMENTS

1. A regular pack of playing cards out of which have been stripped the 8's and all the 6's except the 6 of hearts, making a forty-five-card deck.
2. Two to eight players.

VALUE OF THE CARDS

The cards take the same value and count as the cards at Black Jack, except that aces count for one only.

OBJECT OF THE GAME

To draw cards for a total of 16 or as close to 16 as possible without exceeding 16.

SELECTING THE FARMER

Any player may shuffle. Any player may cut. The acting dealer deals each player one card face up, starting with the player to his left and continuing clockwise. The player to whom the 6 of hearts is first dealt becomes the farmer.

THE ANTE

Each player antes in cash one unit to form a pool known collectively as *the farm*.

THE SHUFFLE AND CUT

The farmer shuffles. While any other player may call for and have the right to shuffle before the cards are cut, the farmer has the right to shuffle last. The deck is then squared and presented to the player at the farmer's right for the cut. He may decline, and any other player may cut the cards; but if all other players decline to cut, it is compulsory that the farmer himself cut.

THE DEAL

Starting with the player at his left and dealing clockwise, the farmer deals each player one card face down, the last card to himself.

THE PLAY

. The player at the farmer's left plays first, and thereafter the turn of play rotates one man at a time clockwise, the farmer playing last. A turn of play consists of a player's drawing at least one card. This is mandatory. The player may draw as many cards as he chooses, as long as his total count does not exceed 16. A player may *stay*—that is, decline to draw more cards—after drawing one or more.

Should a player's count exceed 16, he does not (as in Black Jack) turn up his face-down card and announce that he is over. He merely says, "I stay."

After all players including the farmer have had a turn of play, each player—starting with the one at the farmer's left—face up their down cards, and announce their count.

1. Any player holding a count of 16 wins the farm and becomes the next farmer.

2. If more than one player holds a count of 16 and one of those players has the 6 of hearts he is the winner.

3. If more than one player has a count of 16 without the 6 of hearts, the player having the fewest cards is the winner.

4. Should there be ties and should the farmer be one of the tied players, the farmer is the winner.

5. In case of ties if the farmer is not involved, the tied player first to the farmer's left is the winner. The winner in any case becomes the new farmer or dealer.

6. If no one holds a count of 16 the farm (pool) remains

on the table, and the same farmer deals a new hand; and each of the players must ante again.

PAY-OFF

On completion of each deal, whether or not the farm has been won, each player who has gone over 16 must pay one unit to the farmer who dealt the *bust hand*. Should the farmer bust, he does not have to pay a unit to anyone.

If no one holds a count of 16, the player with a count nearest to 16 gets one unit from each player holding a lesser count—but not from players who have gone over the limit.

In case of ties on counts nearest 16, the tied players divide the paid-off units equally.

CHEATING

The whole family of cheating methods used at Black Jack apply to Farmer. Cheating, like cards, runs in families.

Fifteen

One of the names by which this variation is known, Quince, suggests *Quinze* and a French genealogy. It's also known as Ace Low. Fifteen is Black Jack for two, and all the Black Jack rules apply, with the following particularizations.

1. The count which dealer and nondealer are trying to approach but not exceed is 15.

2. The value of the cards is the same as at Black Jack *except* that the ace counts but one.

3. Before the cards are dealt, dealer and nondealer put up an equal amount in the pool.

4. Now dealer gives his opponent one card face down, then one face down to himself.

5. The nondealer may draw cards (face up) or stay as in Black Jack, but if, drawing, he should *bust* (go over 15), he does not announce that fact; he says simply, "I stay!"

6. Now, as he sees fit, the dealer may either draw cards or stay. In either event, at the completion of his play, both players face their down card, and announce their count.

7. The contestant holding a count of 15, or a count closer than his opponent's to 15 without exceeding 15, collects the bets. If players tie on the same count or both players hold a count of 16 or more, it is a standoff; neither wins nor loses; and bets are carried over to the new deal, when new bets may be laid if it is desired.

8. The loser of a hand deals the next hand.

WHERE THE DEALER'S ADVANTAGE LIES

Although the dealer does not automatically, without himself drawing cards, collect his opponent's bet when the opponent busts at Fifteen, he nevertheless enjoys a tactical advantage in that the nondealer's bust may be clear from his faced-up cards. The dealer, observing that the player *must* have a count of 16 or better, simply stays—stands pat—and wins. Although this situation is uncommon, it occurs often enough to give the dealer an impressive percentage.

CHEATING AT FIFTEEN

See "Cheating at Black Jack," page 161.

Seven and a Half

This is the game Italians say is the forerunner of Black Jack. I've seen it come into rather modest vogue in the last twenty years. Casinos won't run it; it has its public in the little political clubhouses you find in the back streets of every big industrial city with a high concentration of foreign-born people.

REQUIREMENTS

1. A standard pack of cards from which the 8's, 9's, and 10's have been removed, making a forty-card deck.
2. A banker and as many players as can crowd around an ordinary table.
Standers-by may bet on the player's hands.

VALUE OF THE CARDS

The court cards—kings, queens, and jacks—count 1/2. All other cards count their numerical face value: ace, 1; deuce, 2; trey, 3; and so on.
The king of diamonds is designated as the joker, and is wild. A player may assign it any value he pleases from 1/2 to 7.

OBJECT OF THE GAME

To get a card count of 7-1/2 or as close to 7-1/2 as possible without exceeding 7-1/2.

SELECTING THE DEALER

Any player may by mutual consent shuffle the pack. Then he puts it in the center of the table. Any player may cut. The acting dealer squares the cut, and deals to each player including himself, starting with the player at his left and going clockwise, one card face up until the king of diamonds has been dealt. The player receiving it becomes the first dealer and banker.

THE BETTING LIMIT

The dealer may establish for his deal the minimum and maximum bet any player may lay. He may raise or lower his limits as he sees fit.

THE SHUFFLE AND CUT

The dealer shuffles the cards. Any player may call for a shuffle at any time before the cut, but the dealer has the right to shuffle last. He then puts the cards on the table, and any player may cut; if more than one wants to cut, he or they must be allowed to do so.

Note: If, however, the dealer does not like the way in which a cut is made, he may designate a player to make a new cut, and that cut is final.

THE BETTING AND DEAL

Before the deal begins:

1. Each player, announcing the amount orally to the dealer, must place on the table before him the money he proposes to bet;

2. Or, if a player doesn't want to bet on that hand, he must say to the dealer, "Deal me out." He is skipped in the ensuing deal.

Thereupon one card is dealt face down to each player who has placed a bet. The player cannot alter his bet after a card is dealt.

Each round of play requires a new shuffle and new deal.

THE PLAY

The player at the dealer's left has the first turn to play. He may do one of two things, as in Black Jack. He may:

1. *Stay,* which he signifies by saying, "I have enough," or "I pass."

2. *Draw,* in his discretion, one or more cards—provided they and his down card do not add up to a count of 8 or more.

The play moves clockwise around the table. If any player draws one card giving him a total of 7-1/2 he must immediately face his down card and announce his count. This is paid off at premium rates.

THE BUST

Should a player, drawing cards, run his total to 8 or more, he has *busted,* and must forthwith pay the dealer the amount of his bet. The dealer picks up the cards with which the player went bust, and puts them to one side.

All players who have not busted leave their cards in full view of the banker.

THE BANKER'S TURN

The dealer's turn of play comes last. He may, of course, either *stay* or *draw*.

If he draws and busts, he must pay all players surviving in the game an amount equal to their bet, and must pay off at two to one to players holding a count of 7-1/2 with two cards.

If he stays, he collects bets from players having a lower count than he, and pays off players having a higher count. All ties are stand-offs; no one wins or loses.

Note: Although some club games are played in which the dealer arbitrarily wins ties, I do not countenance this rule; it is manifestly unfair to the player, and further reduces his already very meager chance of getting home solvent.

A player holding a two-card 7-1/2 wins the bank on completion of the deal as well as winning his bet at two to one, *but* if the dealer also catches a 7-1/2 with two cards, he retains the bank.

Should more than one player hold a count of 7-1/2 with two cards, the player nearest the dealer's left becomes the next dealer.

A count of 7-1/2 with two cards always beats a 7-1/2 with more than two cards.

THE DEALER'S PERCENTAGE

As at Black Jack, the dealer's advantage at Seven and a Half lies in players' going out of their way to *bust*. The precise percentage in favor of the dealer cannot be accurately computed; there are too many variable factors, including by all means the factor of personal temperament. Some players will *stay* on a count of 3, others will still be in there drawing grandly and confidently on a count of 5. If you want to figure out some reasonably reliable percentages for your own little game, you might try the method of clocking which I set up in the chapter on Black Jack (page 157) and the formula evolved there for reckoning percentages.

SOME ADVICE TO THE BACKWARD

The only way to give yourself anything like an even chance of winning at this game is to bank it whenever you get the chance. Some players have a superstitious reluctance to handle the deck as dealer. That is a sure-fire, never-fail, foolproof way of going broke. The bank is a privilege. Use it.

CHEATING

Because of the fractional values borne by 30 per cent of the cards in this stripped deck, Seven and a Half is peculiarly susceptible to all the tricks of the professional manipulator described in Chapters Two and Three. And the specific methods described in Chapter Seventeen are highly relevant.

CHAPTER TWENTY-ONE

Chemin de Fer and Other Games

Chemin de Fer

Gamblers call it *Shimmy*, it is a variation of the game Baccarat, and it is a rich cousin of Black Jack. Most of this country's rug joints, or fashionable casinos, have a Shimmy table. The game's relative infrequency is due mainly to the size and cost of its equipment. It requires a heavy kidney-shaped table, its surface juicily padded and painted, with built-in money drawer and discard cylinder: price, according to my latest catalogue from a concern in the mid-west, $165. It requires a six-deck dealing box looking like a cranberry scoop that has gone café society: $10 for the American model, $27.50 for the French, in black walnut with chromium-silver finish. The croupier, squatting in the concavity of the kidney table, needs an ebony-finish palette to slide the cash and cards around: five bucks. Chemin de Fer isn't played as much as Black Jack, but its total handle must be pretty close to its tenementward relative's; its bets limits generally run from $20 to $1,000; the Shimmy table is commonly busier even than the crap tables; and late last season I clocked a game in a Southern resort and established that the evening's turnover was $250,000 cash. Shimmy's vocabulary is partly out of Black Jack—"Hit me!"— and partly out of Craps—"fading" a bet. Although it is a banking game, the house doesn't bank it. For a standard cut of 5 per cent out of the banker's winning bets it rents out the equipment and a houseman, the croupier, to run the game for the amateurs of the sport. In return for that 5 per cent the croupier manages the banker's money and pays off and collects bets for him. Chips are very rarely used in Chemin de Fer; so it looks like what it is: the biggest banking card game on earth.

RULES FOR CASINO CHEMIN DE FER

1. Nine players. The banker plays against only one player at a time, but any of the other nine players—plus kibitzers, if they like—may get into the game by laying bets on that one player's hand.

2. A regulation Chemin de Fer table, with a card-mixing discard receiver and a money box to receive the house take.

BANKER

		DRAWS IF DEALING	Does not draw if Dealing		
H A V I N G	3	1, 2, 3, 4, 5, 6, 7, 10	8	9	O P T I O N A L
	4	2, 3, 4, 5, 6, 7	1, 8, 9, 10		
	5	5, 6, 7	1, 2, 3, 8, 9, 10	4	
	6	6, 7	1, 2, 3, 4, 5, 8, 9, 10		

No Mistakes Are Allowed, If Any Are Made It Is Compulsory
For The "Dealer" To Reconstruct The "Coup"

PLAYER

H A V I N G	1 - 2 - 3 - 4 - 10	Draw a Card
	5	Optional
	6 - 7	Stay
	8 - 9	Turn Cards Over

(over)

Because the rules of Chemin de Fer are too many and complicated to remember, each player is supplied with a card describing the players' rules and some of the banker's. A detailed explanation of the rules is appended.

3. A card box, called a *shoe.*

4. Eight standard decks of fifty-two cards each: four red-back decks and four blue-back decks.

(*Note:* In some casinos only six decks are used at a time; in most private games the usage is three decks; but the game can be played with one deck.)

5. A Chemin de Fer palette, a long thin paddle enabling the croupier to transact business at the far reaches of the table without stretching.

OBJECT OF THE GAME

To win money by holding a combination of cards totaling as close as possible to 9, or a number ending in 9. When the total of the cards is a two-digit number, only the latter digit has any value. *Examples:* A count of 17 has a value of 7; a count of 23 has a value of 3; and so forth.

VALUE OF THE CARDS

The ace is the lowest-ranking card, having a value of 1. King, queens, and jacks have a value of 10 each. All other cards have their numerical face value. The suits have no comparative value.

THE SHUFFLE AND CUT

The croupier spreads the eight decks of cards face down on the table. All the players including the croupier are permitted to take a group of cards and shuffle them. Then the croupier collects the cards, and puts them in a series of little stacks. Any player who wants to may cut any one or more of the groups, taking care that the face of no card be exposed. The croupier now assembles all the groups of cards into the shoe, a stack at a time, one atop the other, until all eight packs are in the shoe.

SELECTING THE BANKER

The player first to the croupier's right has the privilege of being first banker (or it is auctioned to the highest bidder). If he declines the bank, the privilege passes to the player to his right, and so on, counterclockwise.

The banker-dealer at Chemin de Fer continues to deal until he misses a pass (loses a bet). When the active player wins a bet, the dealer forthwith passes the shoe to the player to his right. In mid-game as at the start the bank may be declined; then it moves on counterclockwise.

When the cards in the shoe are down to the last three or four, the croupier orders a reshuffle, which is governed by the rules for the original shuffle and cut.

PREPARATIONS FOR THE PLAY

The croupier slides the shoe to the first banker, who places on the table any amount of money within the limits. (This is handled by the croupier.) The banker now removes three cards from the top of the pack, sliding them out of the shoe, and the croupier takes them from him and drops them through a slot in the table into the discard receiver below. He drops all cards into this box as they go out of play. Some manufacturers produce discard boxes which, they say, automatically mix the discards.

THE BETTING

Before any cards are dealt, the players must make their bets. (This is *fading*.) If a player wants to fade the bank for its total worth, he cries, "Banco!" A banco bet has precedence over any other. The player to the right of the dealer has the first privilege of bancoing. If he does not banco, the privilege passes to the next man on the right, and so on around the table. Then, any watcher or kibitzer may cry banco.

If no one bancos, then partial bets are accepted, with the first man on the right putting his bet down for whatever amount he chooses. He places on the table, in front of him, the money he wants to bet. Then the player on his right bets, and so on around the table until the bank is completely faded.

If the bank is not completely faded, the amount left not faded is set aside for the banker. Anyone who bancos, whatever his position around the table, has the right of *banco suivi* (following banco) if he loses. That is, his right to call banco on the next deal has precedence over all others. If more than one person calls banco, the player nearest the dealer starting from the right has precedence even though he may declare banco after another player has done so. This right is known as *banco prime*.

The player who bancos becomes the active player. If no one has bancoed and there are partial bets, the player who has bet the most money is designated by the croupier as the active player.

THE COUP OR PLAY

The banker slides one card out of the shoe and deals it to the active player; then he deals one card to himself, a second card to the player, and finally a second card to himself. These four cards are dealt face down.

THE FIRST TURN OF PLAY

The active player now examines his cards. If they total a count of 8 or 9, he turns them face up on the table. If the count is 8, he calls, "La Petite!" If it is 9, he calls, "La Grande!" The croupier verifies the count. The banker must now turn his two cards face up.

1. If the active player's count is higher than the banker's, the croupier pays off all the winning players. If the active player's count is lower than the banker's, the banker wins, and the croupier collects for him all the bets.

2. If the active player holds a count of less than 8, he says, "Pass," and the banker now examines his own cards. If they total 8 or 9, he turns them face up, and the croupier collects all the bets for him.

3. Should the banker not hold a count of 8 or 9, play reverts to the active player.

4. If the banker's count is the same as the player's count, it is a legal tie, a stand-off, and neither banker nor player wins or loses.

The above four rules apply with equal force to the player's and banker's second turn of play.

ACTIVE PLAYER'S SECOND TURN OF PLAY

1. Should the active player hold a count of 1, 2, 3, 4, or 0, he must draw a card.

2. Should the active player have a count of 5, the draw is optional; he may elect either to *get hit* or to *stay*. This is the only discretionary play the active player may make at Chemin de Fer.

3. Should the active player have a count of 6 or 7, he *must* stay.

BANKER'S SECOND TURN OF PLAY

If the active player *stays* the banker must conform to the following rules:

1. Having a count of 5 or less, he must draw.

2. Having a count of 6 or 7, the banker must stay.

RULES FOR THE BANKER WHEN THE ACTIVE PLAYER

DRAWS A CARD

Banker Holds a Count of 3

1. If the active player in his turn of play has drawn a card valued 1, 2, 3, 4, 5, 6, 7, or 10, the banker must draw.

2. If the active player in his turn of play has drawn an 8, the banker must stay.

3. If the active player in his turn of play has drawn a 9, the banker's play is optional; he may draw or stay at his own discretion.

Banker Holds a Count of 4

1. If the active player fails to draw a card in his turn of play, the banker must draw.

2. If the active player has drawn a card valued 2, 3, 4, 5, 6, or 7, the banker must draw.

3. If the active player in his turn of play has drawn a card valued 1, 8, 9, or 10, the banker must stay.

Banker Holds a Count of 5

1. If the active player did not draw a card in his turn of play, the banker must draw.

2. If the active player in his turn of play has drawn a card valued 5, 6, or 7, the banker must stay.

3. If the active player in his turn of play has drawn a card valued 1, 2, 3, 8, 9, or 10, the banker must stay.

4. If the active player in his turn of play has drawn a 4, the banker's play is optional; he may stay or draw at his discretion.

Banker Holds a Count of 6

1. If the active player in his turn of play fails to draw, the banker must stay.

2. If the active player in his turn of play has drawn a 6 or 7, the banker must draw a card.

3. If the active player in his turn of play has drawn a card valued 1, 2, 3, 4, 5, 8, 9, or 10, the banker must stay.

Banker Holds a Count of 7

Regardless of the active player's draw, the banker must stay.

THE DEALER'S PERCENTAGE AT CHEMIN DE FER
(AND BACCARAT)

The rules governing Chemin de Fer and Baccarat seem unnecessarily complicated, but before we blend our voices in with the Shimmy and Baccarat addicts' immemorial complaint, "Why don't they simplify the laws?" let's re-examine one of the inner secrets of all banking games.

That secret may be stated as follows: Nothing in gambling is unreasonably complicated. If it's complicated, there's a reason. The reason for the strange and apparently unnatural statutes governing the play at Chemin de Fer and Baccarat is that in their complication lies the hidden percentage against the player at the game.

Before giving a mathematical analysis of the game, I would like to point out to the reader that the source of the banker's advantage is the fact that, as in Black Jack, the player must always play first. Although the Baccarat and Chemin de Fer player cannot bust his hand as in Black Jack, he does expose his possible card count to the banker by his decision of play. From there on, the rules of the game do the rest. They are devised so as to give the bank or dealer a percentage edge over the player.

For example, it is the player's second turn of play. He draws a card. This indicates that he holds one of these counts: 1, 2, 3, 4, 5, or 10. His drawn card is face up. We see that it is an 8, and we know his total count now must be 9, 10, 11, 12, 13, or 18.

Now the dealer faces his cards. He has a count of 3. Under the rules, he cannot draw a card. He stays, poor devil, and what happens? It is a 3 to 2 bet in his favor that his low count of 3 will beat whatever count is in the player's hand.

Another example? The player stays. The banker-player holding a count of 5 *must* draw. We know, of course, from the player's staying action that he has a count of 5, 6, or 7. If, on his own turn of play, the banker-player elected to stay, he couldn't possibly win; so the rules compel him to draw a card and give him a possible chance to beat the player.

These are just two of the countless number of situations I had to analyze in order to figure the banker's and player's chances of winning. I did not realize when I started this mathematical analysis that it would take so many weeks of laborious computing. I had to fill sheaves and sheaves of paper with numerous and varied computations in order to obtain the following answers: the chance of winning for the player is 49-33/100% and the chance of winning for the banker-player is 50-67/100%. These percentages apply to the Baccarat rules in use in Nevada casinos and to a similar strategy of play used at Chemin de Fer. The player's disadvantage is the difference of 1-34/100%, which, expressed decimally, is 1.34%.

If the casino did not extract its 5% charge on each of the banker-player's winning bets, the banker-player would naturally have a 1.34% advantage over the other players. Since the banker-player must pay a standard charge of 5% on his winning bets, which occur 50-67/100 times out of every 100 dealt hands in the long run, the 5% casino charge on the banker-player's winnings is actually 2.53%. Subtracting from this the 1.34% advantage the banker-player enjoys over the other players, we find that the banker-player pays the casino 1.19%. The casino enjoys a 1.34% advantage over the player and 1.19% advantage over the banker at both Shimmy and Baccarat, and no matter how you look at it, "If you play, you must pay."

When the casino extracts a 3% charge on the banker-player's winnings, the bank's advantage dwindles to less than 1/5 of 1%—to be exact, .18%. This is the best bet to be found in any casino in the world.

When the casino extracts a 3% charge from the banker-player before the hand is even dealt (win or lose), the banker-player's disadvantage is 1.66%. When the casino charges the banker-player 2-1/2% (win or lose), his disadvantage is 1.16%. The player's disadvantage always remains the same at 1.34% and is not altered by the percentage charge which the casino extracts from the banker-player.

CHEATING AT CHEMIN DE FER

Reputable casinos need not resort to cheating at Chemin de Fer. The management is not itself a participant in the game; it is a beneficiary: there is no economic motive whatever for spoiling the house's reputation. All it wants is a big game, a well-heeled crowd with nothing at all (certainly not suspicion) on its mind, and plenty of action. Its 5 per cent cut in the banker's winnings is not quite as sure a thing as the income of the Internal Revenue Bureau, but 'twill do, 'twill do.

I clocked the house cut in the Chemin de Fer action one night at a Florida casino. It amounted to something in the neighborhood of $10,000. On a risk-capital investment of exactly zero, it seemed a tolerable dividend. Why *would* a casino cheat?

In the private variety of Chemin de Fer, however, there is likely to be little of the above pious atmosphere. Look out for palming, hole-card switching, the cold deck, strippers, and the several methods detailed in Chapters Two and Three.

Slogger (Perhaps from Schlager?)

This simplified and demechanized version of Chemin de Fer appears in print for the first time. The special virtue of Slogger is that it's dead even for banker and player. It might become a serious rival to Black Jack—especially if facts such as these become known, that a labor leader won $60,000 in one brief winter season at a private club in the metropolitan area.

With exceptions, the game is played exactly like Chemin de Fer.

1. The standard fifty-two-card deck is used alone.

2. (Selecting the first banker.) Players may sit anywhere they like. By mutual consent any player may shuffle the cards, any player may cut the cards, and the acting dealer deals each player one card at a time, starting with the player at his left and dealing clockwise until some player is dealt an ace. That player becomes the first banker.

3. (The shuffle and cut.) The banker shuffles. Any player may ask for the right to shuffle at any time, but the banker has the right to shuffle last. After the shuffle, the banker-dealer puts the cards on the table to be cut. Any player may cut. More than one player may cut. If no other player cuts, banker must.

4. Dead cards (cards which have been played) are burned (placed upside down) on the bottom of the pack.

5. When the deck is exhausted or it is a new dealer's turn to bank, a new shuffle must be made.

6. There is no restriction in this game—as there is in Chemin der Fer—on any player drawing a card or staying on any count below 8. This includes the banker. Regardless of his count on the first two cards, the banker or the player may draw or stay at his own discretion.

7. The count of 9 with two cards is called big Slogger, and is immediately turned up by the holder. The same holds true for the count of 8, called little Slogger.

Baccarat

The same as Chemin de Fer except that the house banks the game all the time. The bank does not pass around the table.

Horse Race

Rarely booked by casino management but a favorite with card hustlers who like a muscular percentage on their side. The basic principle of the game has been pirated by some of the big game companies and adapted to board amusements for the general market. Horse fanciers get a special belt out of it, but it is fun for almost anybody . . . provided the stakes aren't allowed to get too big.

REQUIREMENTS

1. A standard pack of fifty-two playing cards.
2. A banker and any number of players.

VALUE OF THE CARDS

Reversing the usual situation, the denomination of the cards has no relative merit at Horse Race; the values depend on suit only.

SELECTING THE DEALER

By mutual consent any player may shuffle the pack, and he puts it on the table to be cut by any other player. The acting dealer then deals each player, starting with the one at his immediate left and going clockwise, one card face up, until a player is dealt an ace; that player becomes the first dealer and banker. Thereafter on the completion of each deal (called a race), the deal and bank pass to the player at the dealer's left.

OBJECT OF THE GAME

To win the race—and you bet on it—by having six cards of your selected suit dealt from the pack before six cards of any other suit.

THE BETTING LIMIT

The banker establishes his own betting limits—the highest and lowest amount of cash any player can lay on the four suits. He may raise or lower the limits if he holds the bank more than one deal.

PREPARATION FOR PLAY

The banker-dealer extracts the four aces from the deck and puts them in front of him side by side in a straight starting line.

SHUFFLE, CUT, AND DEAL

The dealer shuffles the deck. Any player may call for and must be allowed the right to shuffle at any time before the cut, but the dealer retains the privilege of shuffling last. After the shuffle the dealer puts the pack in the center of the table for any player to cut. If the players decline to cut it is mandatory that the dealer do so.

THE DEAL

Now, in a straight line perpendicular to the edge of the table, the banker deals six cards one at a time face up, about an inch apart. The line in which they lie is at right angles to the four lined-up aces, which are below and to one side of the six cards which indicate the distance of the race.

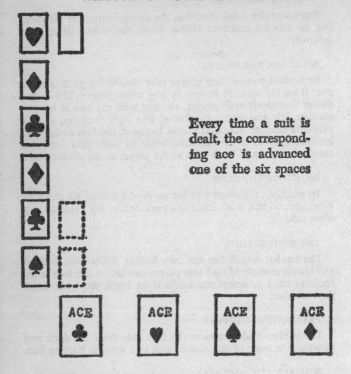

When a card arrives here it is a winner

Every time a suit is dealt, the corresponding ace is advanced one of the six spaces

ACE ♣   ACE ♥   ACE ♠   ACE ♦

THE BETTING

It is up to the banker to declare his own odds depending on the suits of the six track cards—and here is where a little knowledge of arithmetic is handy. *Example:* Suppose the six cards are of one suit, say clubs; now there remain in the pack only six clubs as against twelve cards of each of the other three suits. The six may be three spades and three diamonds—or any of fifteen different combinations. If one suit dominates the six cards the banker may quote five to one on the ace horse of that suit and even money on the other three suits. It is absolutely within the banker's power to fix his own odds, and if any player doesn't like them he just doesn't bet.

Each player's bet is placed below the aces.

A banker may get six cards from another deck to place on the course as guides. Then he transfers four aces from that other deck to the deck in play. He is now dealing from a full fifty-two-card deck, and the odds are corrected to three to one on any suit.

THE PLAY

After the bets have been placed the banker then deals the cards from his hand one at a time face up. The ace of whatever suit he turns up is advanced one card length. When an ace reaches the finish line it wins, and the bets are paid off on that suit at the quoted odds.

CHEATING AT HORSE RACE

Stacking, false cuts, and shifts are especially to be guarded against. See Chapter Two.

Ace-Deuce-Jack

Like Banker and Broker, strictly a game of chance, permitting no exercise of discretion by banker or player. But, because of its technical improvements over its forbear—the old game "You call 'em"—extremely popular with the World War II card hustler and evidently growing in postwar favor.

REQUIREMENTS

1. A standard pack of fifty-two playing cards.

(The only cards having any value are the aces, deuces, and jacks. These twelve are the winning and losing cards. The other forty have no value whatever either as to rank or suit.)

2. A banker and one or more players.

OBJECT OF THE GAME

The banker or the players cut three piles of cards, as in Banker and Broker. The players then place bets that neither an ace, a deuce, nor a jack will appear at the bottom of any pile.

THE LIMIT

The banker establishes betting limits. I should say the average runs from 25¢ and $10 to 50¢ and $25. But the banker is boss.

THE SHUFFLE AND DEAL

The banker shuffles the deck. Any player may call for a shuffle at any time before the cut, but the banker retains the right to shuffle last.

The banker then puts the deck in the center of the table to be cut by any player.

After the cut has been carried the banker removes three cards from the bottom of the deck, and puts them to one side. He must take scrupulous care that those cards are not seen by any player. Those three are dead cards; they cannot enter into the play of the hand.

THE PLAY

The banker now cuts two groups of cards from the squared deck, making in all three piles of cards.

1. Each player may now lay, within the limits, a bet that the bottom card of any of the three piles is not an ace, deuce, or jack.

2. After the bets have been placed the banker proceeds to turn up the piles so that the bottom card of each is exposed.

3. If no ace, deuce, or jack shows as a bottom card of any pile, the bank loses, and must pay off all bets.

4. If the bottom card of any of the three piles does happen to be an ace, deuce, or jack, the bank wins all bets.

No bonuses are paid. Even when more than one winning card turns up, the pay-off is one for one, even.

That's Ace-Deuce-Jack. But . . .

A Note on the Conservatism of the Man-Eating Shark:

As I have suggested in my brief foreword, this game's postwar spread in the United States has been, while steady, more or less unaccountably slow. Professional gamblers, especially of the top rank, have let it severely alone. To me this constitutes adequate evidence that they don't know where the percentage lies. But amateur fanciers of the game keep asking me these three questions:

Is the percentage in favor of the player or the banker?

If it favors the banker, in what degree?

Or is there any way to tell whether this weapon is loaded?

Let me start with a story.

Coming home from a New England show date one night, I was having a 3 A.M. eye-opener of coffee in a midtown restaurant when one of the eastern seaboard's biggest and shrewdest horse bookmakers sat down beside me heavily and announced he'd lost $10,000 that evening banking this game.

"What kind of a limit do you play out there at Fort Knox?" I asked him.

"I'm sane," he said. "This was at a $25 limit."

"Have some scrambled eggs and toast," said I. "And give me the details on this masterpiece. I don't see how you could do it."

It was this way. He was staying at one of the flossier New York hotels, and some gambling friends of his were banking in their room this terrific new game of Ace-Deuce-Jack. He watched for a while. He made some bets, which he lost. Then for a while he banked. The game was as set forth above, only backwards. In standard play the banker wins if certain designated cards show. In this hotel game the players had turned the crucial play backwards. Any player could call out any three cards. The banker exposed the cards at the bottom of his three cut piles. If any of the bottom cards corresponded to the cards called by the player, the player would win his bet. If none appeared, the banker would win.

He quit when he got $10,000 behind.

"Now, Einstein," he said, "why did I lose?"

He lost, I told him, because he had been taking a beating to the tune of 10-1/123 per cent on every bet laid against him. He has the granite countenance of the pro, but his eyes blazed. "What the hell are you talking about?" he snapped. "They were doing the guessing, weren't they?"

And I reflected again that it's a queer thing: most players and at least a majority of professional gamblers persist in the belief that the guy who has to do the guessing automatically has the worst of any gamble.

This disadvantage-of-the-guesser theory originated way back in the dark ages of big-money cards when the players, the rabble, had no clear notion why the operators of games of "chance" almost always made a profit. And there is something about it that sounds so pat, so incontrovertible; it has gained such wide acceptance; it has been challenged so rarely if ever, that even to this day such a man as this—a really brilliant analyst who handles $50,000 a day in horse bets and knows how percentages work—such a man as this still insists that to guess is necessarily to lose.

I handed him a quarter, told him to toss it on the table, and announced that since I was about to guess heads or tails he must lay me six to five I couldn't call the toss.

"Don't be childish," he said. "The odds are even money from now till hell freezes over."

"But I'm doing the guessing, no?" I said, and a light dawned in his eyes.

The outcome of any game depends on its percentages. If the odds are in the guesser's favor, he must win in the long run.

My bookie friend had lost his ten grand because the odds were away over against him instead of in his favor, as he—and, I dare say, you—had supposed.

Figuring percentage and whom it favors is fairly simple if you'll remember your theory of combinations and permutations.

First we must determine how many three-card combinations there are in a fifty-two-card deck. The method is detailed under

"Poker Odds and Probabilities," page 273. Briefly, you set up the following fraction

$$\frac{52 \times 51 \times 50}{3 \times 2 \times 1}$$

and, canceling it out, you get 22,100, which *is* the total of possible three-card combinations in fifty-two cards. But let's simplify the arithmetic and stick to the exact conditions under which this game is played. Let's remove the twelve winning cards from the deck. We now have forty cards, *a deck minus all winning cards,* right? And we want to see how many three-card combinations can be formed in which the ace, deuce, or jack will not appear. We set up this fraction.

$$\frac{40 \times 39 \times 38}{3 \times 2 \times 1}$$

and, canceling, we establish that there are 9,880 possible three-card combinations not containing ace, deuce, or jack.

There's one more step. We subtract as follows:

22,100	(three-card combinations that can be formed with the entire pack)
− 9,880	(three-card combinations that *do not contain* an ace, deuce, or jack)
12,220	(three-card combinations that *do* contain an ace, deuce, or jack)

And now the summing up.

When a man bets that the ace, deuce, or jack will appear in the three-card combination comprised of the three bottom cards of the cut piles in this game, the chances are 12,220 to 9,880 in his favor.

That is, the percentage in his favor is 10-1/123.

In Ace-Deuce-Jack the player loses if those designated cards show in the exposed three-card combination.

The bookie's smart friends had reversed this, so that the bank would lose if any one of three designated cards turned up.

The principle remains as solid as the Rock of Gibraltar: to bet even money that any three-card combination will not contain one of three designated cards is suicidal.

I am definitely against suicide. My advice to the player is to stay away from this game. Nobody on earth, no luck on earth, can beat 10 per cent.

CHEATING AT ACE-DEUCE-JACK

Some hungry carnivores, not satisfied with their 10-1/123 per cent certainty, like to cheat by using belly strippers (see page 24). A crook with only rudimentary skill can always cut a belly-stripper as one of the winning cards. This makes the percentage on the banker's side a flat 100.

Banker and Broker

You win—or lose—in a hurry.

REQUIREMENTS

1. A standard pack of fifty-two playing cards.
2. Two or more players.

RANK OF THE CARDS

Same as in Poker: ace high, king, queen, jack, 10, 9, 8, 7, 6, 5, 4, 3, and deuce low; the suits have no comparative value.

OBJECT OF THE GAME

To win a bet on a card which will turn out to have a higher value than the banker's card.

SELECTING THE BANKER

1. The pack having been shuffled by any player by mutual consent, it is placed on the table, and each player cuts a group of cards and exposes his bottom card. The player with the highest card becomes first banker. In case of tie, tied players cut again—and, if necessary again, etc.

2. When a player has an ace he has bet on, that player becomes the next banker *unless* the banker also has an ace, in which case he retains possession of the bank. If more than one player has an ace, the tied players cut for the bank; highest card cut wins the bank.

THE PLAY

1. The banker establishes minimum and maximum betting limits.

2. He then shuffles the cards. Any other player may claim and have the right to shuffle, but the banker can shuffle last.

3. The banker puts the deck in the center of the table to be cut by any player who wants to cut it.

4. Having squared the cut deck, the banker removes the bottom card, and puts it to one side. (This card is dead, out of play; the move is precautionary, to safeguard against any player's seeing the bottom card.)

5. The banker now cuts the deck into as many groups of cards as there are players in the game, plus one more group, provided the players do not exceed six. If they exceed six, the

banker cuts seven groups of cards regardless. The groups are called *piles*.

6. After the piles are formed the bets are laid.

7. Players may bet on one or more piles, but not the one that is designated the banker's.

8. To make a bet, players put their money on or near the pile they have selected.

9. All bets having been made, the banker turns over his pile so that the bottom card is exposed. The rank of that card is the banker's score. If he turns an ace he collects all bets without turning over the players' cards: in this game the banker wins ties, and the top-ranking ace can't be beaten.

10. If the banker's card is any card other than the ace, he now turns over the first player's pile. Should the exposed card in that pile rank higher than the banker's card, the banker pays off the bet at even money. Should the player's card rank even with or lower than the banker's, the banker wins and collects the bet. So it goes, pile by pile, around the table.

ADVICE TO PLAYERS

Because the bank collects on ties at Banker and Broker, the percentage in its favor is 5-15/17. The player can reduce the odds against him by banking the game at his every opportunity.

CHEATING AT BANKER AND BROKER

If not more prevalent than in any other card game, cheating at Banker and Broker is at least more effective. Up to a few years ago you could see a gang of hustlers working in the gallery on fight nights, clipping suckers with this game. I guess, all things considered, sharks banking this game have rolled more chumps than ever were taken at Three Card Monte or the shell game.

Because with a deck of belly strippers, or humps, a born idiot could win a fortune at this racket. The stripper cards are shaped so that if you cut a stack by taking hold of it at the long sides' middle you can't fail to cut a low card; if you take it at the ends you can't miss cutting a high card. (See "Belly Strippers," page 24.)

As a rule you might suggest that belly strippers are being used when the banker's pile is not cut until last or until after the bets have been laid.

Thirty-Five

This is selected as the best of numerous banking games having this structure. It is a banking but not a house game, and the deal rotates from player to player.

REQUIREMENTS

1. A standard pack of fifty-two playing cards.
2. From two to five players.

VALUE OF THE CARDS

The court cards—kings, queens, and jacks—count 10 points; all other cards have their face value: ace, 1; deuce, 2; and so on.

OBJECT OF THE GAME

To win by having in the hand a card count of 35 or more in one suit. *Example:* Among the cards in his hand the player holds the following clubs: ace, queen, jack, 10, and 5. These cards' value totals 36. The player wins his bet.

SELECTING THE FIRST DEALER

Any player by mutual consent having shuffled the cards and faced the deck down on the table, each player cuts a group of cards, and that player cutting the highest-ranking card becomes first dealer. In case of a tie for high, the tied players cut again, and again, to a decision.

Thereafter the deal passes to the player on the dealer's left, and, on completion of each deal, moves to the left around the table, clockwise.

THE ANTE

Each player antes in the center of the table a sum of money mutually agreed upon, and this becomes the pot.

THE SHUFFLE

The dealer shuffles the cards. Any player may ask for and have the right to shuffle, but the dealer can shuffle last. The player to the dealer's right should cut the cards; but, if he declines, the player to *his* right may cut them. If all other players refuse to cut, the dealer must cut. And the cut must be such that there are at least five cards in each cut group.

THE DEAL

Now to each player including himself the dealer gives one card face down, starting with the player to his left and dealing clockwise. He deals the next card face down in the center of the table. This he repeats, until each player has four cards and there are four cards face down on the table. The latter four cards are called the *buy*. Thereafter each player is dealt a face-down card in turn until all hands have nine cards each; but no more cards are dealt onto the table; and the rest of the cards are set aside. They are dead. They do not enter into the subsequent play.

TAKING THE BUY

The bidding starts now. The player to the dealer's left makes his bid for the buy. The bid may be any part or the whole amount of the pot. The man to the first player's left now has his turn to bid. He may:

1. Decline to make a higher bid than the first player, in which case he passes by throwing his nine cards aside. They're dead.

2. Raise the bid. That's all there is to this: he just bids more money for the buy.

So it goes around the table until one player is identified as the highest bidder. That player discards four cards from his hand, and takes the four cards in the buy.

WHEREUPON THE PAY-OFF

1. If this player holds a card count of 35 or more in one suit, he takes out of the pot an amount of cash equal to his bid.

(*Note:* But if the bid be more than the amount in the pot, he takes the pot only, and there is no assessment to liquidate its deficit against the other players.)

2. Should he hold a count of 34 or less, having lost he must put the amount of his bid into the pot.

3. If a player at the very outset is dealt a count of 35 or more, he announces it then and there, and takes the pot. If more than one player are dealt a count of 35 or more, the tied players divide the pot equally.

The players may at the start of the game establish a maximum tolerable limit on the pot, and if during play the pot is swollen beyond that maximum, it shall be divided equally among all players.

CHEATING AT THIRTY-FIVE

Marked cards may turn up in this game, but it is notable that the markings, to be useful, *must* be both for suit and for denomination. Such paper is harder to read; but the rewards for a man who can determine in advance what cards he will get in the buy are heavy and consistent. More commonly to be encountered (see Chapter Two) are stacking, palming, and false cuts.

Bango

A little like Bingo, a little like the old poker-solitaire game of Lotto, this one has always been an attractive pastime. I've taken some bugs out of the rules to make the game mathematically sound.

REQUIREMENTS

1. Two ordinary fifty-two-card decks having different backs.
2. From two to ten players.

OBJECT OF THE GAME

To go Bango by—in accordance with the rules—turning five face-up cards face down.

SELECTING THE DEALER

By mutual consent any player shuffles one pack of cards, which is cut by any other player. The acting dealer gives each player one card at a time face up, starting with the player at his left and dealing clockwise, until a player is dealt an ace. This player becomes the first dealer; thereafter on completion of each deal the deal passes clockwise, to the player at the dealer's immediate left.

THE ANTE AND DEAL

The dealer and the player at his left each shuffles one pack of cards, and the dealer offers his deck to the player at his right for the cut. (If that player declines to cut, the dealer *must*.) Then to each player the dealer deals five cards one at a time, starting with the man at his left and dealing clockwise. The remainder of the cards are set aside, dead, out of play.

The players turn their five cards face up in front of them.

The dealer takes the pack the player to his left has shuffled, cuts them, and is ready for the play.

PLAY OF THE HAND

Each player antes into the pot an equal amount of cash previously agreed upon.

The dealer turns face up on the table the top card of the deck, orally announcing its numerical value and suit.

Any player having before him a card of the same denomination and suit turns that card face down.

The dealer goes on exposing and announcing cards until some player has turned his five cards face down. That's Bango, the player says so, and he wins the pot.

After a player has declared himself Bango, it is conventional in this game, and no reflection on the player's integrity, for the dealer to examine first the player's cards and then the faced-up stack of dealt cards to certify the correctness of the claim.

CHEATING AT BANGO

Because two decks are used, because they are handled by at least three different players, and because the results are subject to check, cheating at Bango is no pushover. But caution dictates that it be observed that the two players shuffling the decks might be in conspiratorial partnership and would find useful such moves as second dealing, marked cards, stacking, false cuts, and others described in Chapters Two and Three.

The Penny Game

Although this isn't a card game I can't resist the temptation to get it for the first time into print where it belongs, among the banking games. The Penny Game is in some parts of the country called the Tossing Game; it has spread like wildfire since the war; and for reasons I think I understand it seems to exercise a peculiar hypnotic power over professional gamblers.

Although it has been reported inland from time to time, it is played mainly along the waterfront in port cities. Seagoing men, who learned to play it in Australia under the name Two Up, introduced it in the United States. Some highly substantial bookmakers who used to be craps specialists have reconverted to the Penny Game. Theirs is the professional game. There is a private variety, of course, in which some fanciers get together, maybe in the service bar out back, and work their own money against each other without benefit of book or take. The professional game is divided into two kinds.

The first is the *take-off game*, in which the operator takes a cut from the shooter (the player tossing the pennies) when the shooter makes a pass and wins. This is the cut familiar to any craps player.

The second professional variety is the *book game*. Its distinguishing feature is the presence of a bookmaker who accepts bets from players and charges 5 per cent of the bet for his banking services. Believe it or not, this is the more prevalent of the two kinds of play.

The book game has to have the same kind of employees as are needed to run a craps house. To wit:

A cutter, who takes the house charge out of the player's profits for making a winning decision.

The bookmaker, who accepts all bets up to the limit, generally $300, and charges 5 per cent.

Luggers—chauffeurs who drive or direct players to the joint.

Lookouts, who are there to prevent or minimize thievery

among the players and see that the book pays off and collects correct amounts from winners and losers.

The Penny Game gambling house is no rug joint. Generally it is a stripped-down, purely functional, old barn or garage just off some main-traveled highway. It is patronized almost exclusively by professional or habitual—which is not quite the same thing—gamblers. I trust it will offend no district attorneys to say hundreds of thousands of dollars are turned over at this game daily within twenty miles of Metropolitan New York.

REQUIREMENTS

1. Ten or more one-cent pieces, of which two at a time only are in use.
2. A little paddle three inches long and one inch wide.
3. Money.
4. Money.
5. Money.

AS TO PLAYERS

1. Any number may play.
2. The player whose turn it is to play is the *shooter*.
3. The player or players covering the shooter's bet are the *fader* or *faders,* and what they do is *fade* the bet.
4. The players stand forming a circle.
5. By mutual consent or any method in local usage any player may start the game by becoming the first shooter.

THE PLAY

1. The shooter puts any amount he elects in the center of the playing circle, and says, "I shoot X dollars." One or more players fade him by covering part or all of the bet.
2. The shooter selects two pennies from the supply of ten or more, and puts them tail-side up on the little stick or paddle.
3. The shooter tosses the pennies into the air so that they spin to the satisfaction of the observing cutter or operator.
Note well: If they sail or slide or otherwise fail to spin uncontrollably, the cutter calls before they land, "No toss!" This is final. The toss is void. Its result cannot and does not count.

A. If the pennies fall so that the two heads face up, the shooter has won; he has passed, or made a pass.
B. If they fall so that the two tails face up, the shooter has lost (made a miss-out), and the player to his left becomes the next shooter.
C. If the pennies fall so that a head and a tail face up, it is

no decision, and the shooter keeps tossing until he wins or loses.

D. As long as a shooter tosses passes or no decisions, he keeps shooting; when he loses, the stick and the right to shoot move to the player at his immediate left; and the play rotates clockwise.

4. Right and wrong bets are made among the other players. A right bet is that the shooter will toss a pass and win. A wrong bet is that he will toss tails, miss out, and lose.

5. If a shooter or any other player can't get a bet from the rest of the company, they are accommodated by the bookmaker for a 5 per cent commission on the amount they propose to bet. The bookmaker's action is both ways; he will accept right and wrong bets.

6. Most games employing a cutter levy a charge of 25¢ or 50¢ on each pass made by the shooter. The cut comes out of his winnings. The wrong betters are often compelled to pay a cut.

VARIATION OF THE PENNY GAME

To speed the game, some operators and cutters use three pennies for the toss instead of two. This makes every toss a winning or losing decision, since of course at least two heads or two tails must face up on each toss. To avoid ambiguity, let me add that three heads win and three tails lose.

THE FINANCIAL SECTION

1. The game is dead even; there is no mathematical advantage for shooter or fader.

2. But if you like to play the book, you might want to bear in mind that its edge is really 4-16/21 per cent rather than the 5 per cent it charges.

CHEATING

This would seem to be the crookproof gambling game; every move is away out in the open under a strong light, watched by twenty or thirty intelligent and experienced realists. But the assumption that here at last is a game whose only defect is that it's illegal would be a pathetic assumption. Double-headed and double-tailed pennies, which any competent machinist can produce, have been switched into and out of games by gamblers skilled in sleight of hand.

And many a player, once caught in the meshes of this oddly fascinating game, has put in many an hour practicing the control of the tossed pennies. The principle is, of course, merely an extension of the game of mumbly-peg every kid plays in soft earth with a jackknife, a matter of controlling the arc and spin of a thrown object. Some fanatics have actually succeeded in mastering this bizarre skill; they will never make perfect scores, but by passing just a little oftener than average they have a cold lock on the game.

This sets up about the only clue I can give you. When the Penny Game is played on a hard surface, the pennies must bounce after they hit the floor, and then roll and wobble and topple. On this kind of playing surface the controlled toss is utterly useless. For advice:

Don't play on a soft surface like earth, a billiard table, or any padded gambling table.

Don't play unless you can hear those pennies ring when they hit the ground.

If you're losing a little too often to one special player, make it your or the house's business to pick up one of his tosses before he does, and have the pennies examined. A penny with two tails is quite a curio.

Part Four

CHAPTER TWENTY-TWO

Poker—Not According to Hoyle

"How do you play?" they would inquire cautiously, drawing up their chairs in Sitka or Bizerte, Dix or Okinawa or Los Alamos, sizing each other up, trying to guess whether the guy in khaki across the table had been a bank teller or parking-lot attendant or actor or sharecrop farmer. "How," the Second World War's G.I.'s would ask, "do you play Poker?"

And, "According to Hoyle," was the answer—up to the time my articles on Poker began getting published in the Army newspapers.

From then on, Army Poker was played "according to Scarne." If that's my place in history, if all I ever did was make serviceman-Poker go straight, I'll settle for it. "According to Scarne" saved a kid or two a flattened poke and a broken heart. What more could I want?

Ever since Americans decided Poker was their own, their native game, unsuspecting players have believed in Hoyle as the ultimate authority on the play. I'm no iconoclast; I don't believe in making it tough for any man to make a living; but we'd better at the outset face the facts about this venerable myth. You can't play Poker according to Hoyle simply because Hoyle (a) never played Poker, (b) never uttered a ruling on Poker, and (c) never even heard of the game of Poker. Edmund Hoyle was an English barrister who wrote a book on three card games—Piquet, Whist, and Quadrille—the first two of which are now virtual museum curios and the third of which was just recently dropped from the functional game books. Poker was not heard of until years, decades, after Hoyle's death in 1769. But—for reasons which have so far escaped me—it is the custom of modern writers on card games to call their books "Poker According to Hoyle" or "The Up-to-Date Hoyle" or "The Revised Hoyle" or some comparable nonsense. It seems to me about as intelligent as some research engineer's publishing a monograph titled "Fulton on Diesel Engines" or "William the Lion-Hearted on Atomic Energy." With this exception: the writers on Poker who have put on the mantle of Hoyle and handed down their own private prejudices about the game have simply reduced Poker rules to utter confusion. Poker players, confronted by a shelf of Hoyles who don't know what they're talking about, have been compelled to formulate and live by their own regional, village or house rules. It has created a not-too-healthy atmosphere in which to play for money.

The rules set forth in this chapter are not according to Hoyle but *according to Scarne.* They are based on modern conventions and conditions of play. They have been devised for players who understand and love the game. They are based on exhaustive investigation of current practice. They have been tested in casinos and private games throughout the country, and they have stood the test. They are mathematically sound, they recognize the realities of the play, and they are authoritative.

Up to twenty years ago Poker was almost exclusively a man's game. Today as many women play as do men. Or more! In thousands of games any night of any week men and women gamble against each other, with not invariably pleasant results; in the casinos at Reno, man and wife are not permitted to play Poker at the same table.

For what stakes do women play? Same as men: high stakes —and low stakes. It is highly possible, despite the Contract Bridge legend, that Poker is American women's favorite for-money game. Dr. Gallup estimated in a report of the American Institute of Public Opinion that some ten million United States citizens out of an adult population of ninety-four million *consider* Poker their favorite game. G.I. Joe, the greatest germ carrier in history, probably communicated the Poker infection to other millions throughout the world. Poker is about as close to a universal language as there is. But old Hoyle never heard of it.

The first mention of the game—or even the word—Poker has been traced by the author to Jonathan H. Green, a reformed gambler, who in certain writings dated 1834 described the rules for a game then being played on the Mississippi steamboats, and added that this was the first time the rules of the game ever had been published. He called it Poker. And he noted scrupulously that *The American Hoyle* then current neglected entirely to mention the game.

The Poker game Green described was played with twenty cards, the aces, kings, queens, jacks, and 10's; each player was dealt five cards; the maximum number of players was four.

That game did not appear in *The American Hoyle* until thirty or more years later, and then it was not called Poker. The name given it was *Bluff*. Perhaps some players had made this noun of the verb that occurs so often in the play; but it seems more likely that the author of *The American Hoyle* had just failed to do enough leg work on his research job and, like card writers since, invented a name for a game he didn't understand. At least he didn't go on and invent anything more damaging; the rules he laid down were the same rules Green had described in '34. "Bluff" it remained in the book, but the people who played it had their own word for it and stuck to it; and so about forty years later the Hoyles got around to acknowledging that the game was indeed Poker. But it's a funny thing about writers. To this day many a solemn scholar insists on heading his Poker chapter with the word "Bluff" or the mock-learned words "Poker (Bluff)," although no flesh-and-blood player has known the game by that alias in almost a century, if ever.

Some of the features we now regard as peculiar to Poker are unquestionably of French origin, but the game's structure is Iranian. Mr. Shapour Fatemi, a distinguished Persian scholar and statesman, assures me that a game called *As* (from which we get our word "ace") has been played in Iran for at least 2,000 years. Some rather ambiguous historical references suggest it may be 5,000 years old, but I see no necessity for sitting in judgment on that dispute here. At *As* the requirements are as many each of aces, kings, queens, jacks, and 10's as there are players in the game; winning combinations are pairs and such combinations and sequences as form the melds at Rummy; and the characteristic of the game is its tolerance of table talk, bluffing, bargaining, badgering, and general conversational hell.* It does not recognize the straight or the flush, these evidently having been incorporated into the game in its slow European development. If I may indulge in some informed guesswork, I should suppose that Poker's conquest of the civilized world was by way of the Near East into the Mediterranean countries; it turns up very early in Italy under the name Primero; and then across France, into England, and finally with the French settlers at the mouth of the Mississippi, where it took to the packets and the hinterland.

Some of the game's history still colors the terminology of *le Poker Americain* as it is played in France. Three of a kind

* Mr. Bernard Lamb, wartime financial adviser to the Iranian Government on loan from the United States Department of State, tells me of having witnessed games played with gold coins in which one permissible feature was the losers' baldly swiping money off the table in the excitement. The local usage favored the view that if they got away with it they were entitled to it.

is *brelan* still (*brelan* was an early variation of *gilet* or *primero*); four of a kind is *brelan-carré*. The earliest published Poker rules established its French antecedents: it used the Piquet pack; the pack was cut to the left and dealt to the right; certain combinations of cards bore French names (*brelan* and *tricon*). The draw feature of Poker is taken intact from the French game of *Ambigu*. The game *Bouillotte*, which antedated the Revolution, developed such Poker mechanics as the blind, the straddle, the raise, table stakes, the freeze-out, and (back to Iran!) the bluff.

Most common dictionaries and almost all writers on the game say flatly the word *Poker* is the American corruption of *Poque*, the name of a French game of considerable antiquity. To my previous yelps of irritation let me add this: that I can't endorse this kind of breezy scholarship. I never played *Poque*, I have never seen it played, I don't know its structure, and I never encountered any one better informed on the subject than I. The name may be a corruption not of *Poque* but of *Pochspiel*, the name of a very venerable German game in which one element was bluffing—bragging, scaring out the grocery clerks. It may have come from German immigrants' habit of indicating whether they'd pass or open by rapping on the table and saying, "Ich poche!" Somebody has tried to trace Poker to the French *poche* (a pocket). *As*, like Chess and Backgammon, was swapped around between Persia and India for a couple of thousand years, and I've heard Poker traced to the Hindu *pukka*, but the reasoning seems to me shaky. It doesn't matter much. As to the past, any man's guess is as good as mine.

Poker Terms: Their Definition and Modern Usage

The present glossary is designed to define words and phrases extant in the modern vocabulary and play of Poker, not to compile a historical dictionary; to clarify, not to embalm, the game. The pedant will look in vain here for such relics of the 1887 game books as the skip straight, Dutch straight, blaze, little tiger, big tiger, little and big dog, age, and straddle. I gather from certain contemporary writings that some of my colleagues still entertain the delusion that a skip straight (ace-3-5-7-9 not of the same suit) beats two pair and that a blaze (five pictures cards inevitably two pairs) is better than a flush, but as every poker expert if not every Poker player knows, these combinations and their names are obsolete, and have been so for a generation; they may be of some quaint interest to etymologists but they aren't to me. Likewise, I have stricken from this index Poker terms in current use only in provincial

localities and unknown to the mass of players. A Poker vocabulary based on the following list will get you respectful attention in any gambling casino from Maine to Florida, from
New York City to Seattle. I am permitted to say so in behalf
of such Reno clubs as the Palace, Embassy, and Normandie,
and I could say as much of two dozen clubs east of that center
of culture, except that in their states gambling is more or less
prohibited, and identifying them might complicate their management problems.

Active player. A player still in competition for the pot; one
who has not dropped or passed out or folded up by throwing
his hand into the discard pile.

Angling (from the verb angle, or, as in Brooklyn, to yangle).
Proposing to another player an agreement private and outside
the rules; for example, that the pot be split evenly regardless
of which player wins it, or that the players refrain from raising against each other.

Ante (or edge). A stake put into the pot by each player
after seeing his dealt hand but before drawing new cards, or
(in some games) before any cards are dealt; as a verb, to put
one's stake into the pool or pot.

Back to back. In Stud Poker or its variations, cards back
to back are a hole card and first upcard of the same denomination. A *tight,* or conservative, or parsimonious player is a
back to back player.

Bet. An amount of money invested in the pot by a player
in the belief or allegation that his is the best hand in play.

Blind bet. A bet made before the cards are dealt; *to bet
blind,* to make a bet without looking at one's hand after the
deal.

Bluff. To bet an inferior hand with such a show of confidence or cash as to daunt one's opponents and persuade them
that it would be foolhardy to pay for the privilege of seeing
what certainly must be an infinitely superior hand.

Bonus or *royalty.* A sum to be paid by each other player to
any player holding a royal flush, a straight flush, or four of a
kind. Bonus agreements must be made by unanimous consent
at the start of the game.

Buck. To persist in Stud Poker in playing against a hand
whose exposed cards indicate it is the superior hand. To buck
a pair of aces is to play on against a hand among whose exposed cards are two aces when one's own exposed cards are of
lower rank.

Burn or *bury* (a card or cards). To remove one or more
cards from the top of the pack and put them out of play, generally face up, on the bottom of the pack.

By me! A phrase used by Poker players when passing.

Call or *see.* To put into the pot an amount equaling the bet made by an opposing player on the current round of betting: an act compelling that player to show his hand for evaluation and the pay-off.

Check. To signify, as commonly used at Stud and often used at Draw Poker, that the player doesn't want to bet in that turn of play but does propose to remain an active player, reserving the right in his next turn to bet, call, raise, re-raise, or drop out. A player cannot check his bet if a bet has been made earlier in that round.

Cinch hand. A hand which absolutely cannot be beaten (or which the player is convinced cannot be beaten); at Draw Poker, for instance, a royal flush; at Stud Poker, a combination of cards which, regardless of one's opponent's hole card or cards, cannot be beaten by any combination the opponent can organize.

Close to the belly. Conservative; inordinately cautious; a player who will bet only on a cinch hand is playing his cards close to the belly.

Cut. The sum abstracted from the pot to defray the expenses of the game; same as *kitty.* Also the separation of the deck into two or more groups and the re-assembling of the deck in revised order, before the deal. *Cutter.* He who cuts the pot; the operator of the game.

False openers. An example must suffice. If the rules stipulate that a player must hold a pair of jacks or better to open the pot and a player opens with a hand of less than that value, he has opened with false openers.

Foul, irregular, or *dead hand.* A hand that has forfeited all right and chance of winning the pot and must be thrown into the discards; a hand having more or fewer cards than are permitted under the rules of the game.

Four-card straight. A hand consisting of four cards in sequence not of the same suit.

Four-flush. A hand consisting of four cards in the same suit.

Free ride. A round in which no player makes a bet, each therefore getting his next card or cards at no cost.

Front money. A player's winnings.

Hand. The cards dealt to or held by each player at one time in accordance with the laws.

Head to head. Indicating that only two persons are engaged in a card game, one against the other.

High card bet. A bet occasionally made at Stud Poker between players that one's first upcard will be of a denomination higher than the others'.

Hole card. In Stud Poker, a card dealt face down.

Jackpot or *jack pot.* A convention of play under which a player can before the ordinary opening round of betting choose to bet an amount equal to the amount in the pot. Here again I am compelled to protest the laziness or worse of most modern Poker writers. These antiquarians still use the phrase "jackpots" to define a kind of play in which players must hold a pair of jacks or better to open a pot. This use of the word persists in books only, not in human speech and conduct. During my wartime tours and lecture demonstrations I asked hundreds of Poker players, "How do you play jackpots?" and 99 per cent of them replied that in their jackpots you can bet the size of the pot before the opening bet. From now on the phrase "jackpot" means what the vast majority of Poker players intend it to mean.

Kitty. A cup or container kept on the playing table in which a predetermined amount, the *cut,* taken from certain pots (particularly big pots) is deposited to meet the expenses incurred in running the game.

Limit or *stakes.* The minimum and maximum amounts, and intermediate amounts, a player can put into the pot to bet, stay, call, raise, or re-raise. Limits and stakes must be agreed unanimously before the start of play.

Loose player. One who does not fold a dubious hand and wait for a good one but who plays in most of the pots; an unsound and generally heavily losing player.

Misdeal. An illegal deal, after which the cards must forthwith be reshuffled, cut, and dealt again by the same dealer.

Opener. The player who made the first bet of a newly dealt hand and, by placing his bet in the center of the table, opened the pot.

Out of turn. Not in natural or legal sequence, as to bet or to receive a card or cards in some other player's turn of play.

Overs. Money left on the table after a hand by reason of someone's neglecting to take his share or contributing more than his share.

Pass. 1. A term used before the draw at Draw Poker or its variants to indicate that a player will not or cannot open the pot in that turn of play, reserving the right to bet, raise, re-raise, or fold in his next turn.

2. A term used after the draw at Draw or Stud Poker to indicate that the player quits the pot and is folding his hand.

Pat hand. A hand, by definition excellent, to which at Draw Poker a player does not draw cards in an attempt to improve it; the affectation of holding such a hand being useful in *running a bluff.* The phrase is *to stand pat.*

Play or *stay*. Matching whatever bet has been made previously in the round of betting and thus remaining an active player.

Pot. The total in cash or chips bet in the aggregate on any single hand at Poker. It is piled in the center of the table, accumulating as the bets are made, and on decision of the hand is collected by the winner or winners.

Raise. An amount of money put into the pot to equal the previous bet, plus an additional bet.

Re-raise. An amount of money put into the pot to equal the previous bet *and raise*, plus an additional bet.

Round. To deal a round is to deal each player a complete hand; to bet a round is to afford each player in order his choice whether to bet, stay, call, raise, or re-raise.

Sandbagging. Term applied to certain betting techniques: A. When two players who have a third player sandwiched between them keep raising and re-raising with no consideration for the third player. B. When a player checks and then raises after another player has bet. (See "Freezing a Raise," page 238.)

Showdown. The act of decision. After the last bet has been called by all the active players on the final round of betting, each active player, starting with the player who is being called and moving clockwise, announces (at Draw) the rank of his hand or exposes (at Stud) his hole card to the other players.

Shy. Owing a bet or part of a bet to the pot. A player lacking, say, the right change draws out of the pot an amount equal to what he owes the pot, and puts it to one side, saying aloud, "I'm shy so much." He pays the amount immediately after the hand.

Side bet. A bet between players made privately and put aside, separate from the pot.

Sleeper. Money left on the table by a player either in collecting a pot or in making change and picked up by another player.

Spade bet. A bet by two or more players (generally at Draw Poker) as to who will be dealt the highest-ranking spade among his first five cards.

Steal a pot. To win a pot by bluffing or by the failure of another player to press his advantages with a higher-ranking hand.

Under the gun. Sitting immediately to the dealer's left.

Upcard, upcards. A card or cards at Stud Poker dealt face up on the table.

Usual limits (for Stud and its variants). Normally, and popularly, from a 10¢ minimum to a 50¢ maximum, or from

25¢ to $2; although many games are played at higher stakes than these. A player may bet any amount between minimum and maximum, and often, at Stud, it is permitted to bet the maximum only before the last card is dealt and thereafter, not before.

Wild card. A card which, on the player's allegation of its value, may be construed as having any value in the deck. When the joker is added to the deck it is always wild. The deuces are often used wild. A wild card may be used to represent any card or to duplicate any card *already* held by the player dealt the wild card. *Example:* The player holds all four aces plus a wild card. He now counts the wild card as an ace, and he is accounted as holding five aces.

General Rules for Poker

To play the standard games of the Poker family an ordinary fifty-two-card deck is used. In some variations jokers and wild cards are added. And it is not unusual to strip from the deck some low-ranking cards such as deuces and treys.

In Poker each player is on his own; there is no such thing as partnership play in any kind of legitimate game.

THE PACK

The Poker deck consists of four thirteen-card suits: spades, hearts, diamonds, and clubs. The suits have no relative superiority to each other. The ace is the highest-ranking card, and in order of descending value the rest of the cards are the king, queen, jack, 10, 9, 8, 7, 6, 5, 4, 3, and 2 or deuce. But the ace may be used at either end of the suit, as the highest card in a straight or royal flush and as the lowest card in a straight or straight flush. Thus in the straight flush 10-J-Q-K-A the ace is high; in the straight flush A-2-3-4-5 the ace is low.

I recommend the use of two packs of cards having backs of sharply contrasting design or color. This is to enable a change of packs at the request of any player. In two-pack play a contestant can ask for a change at any time, and the change takes place immediately after the showdown of the current hand.

OBJECT OF THE GAME

To win the pool (pot) by holding, at the showdown, a hand of higher rank than that of any other player—as evaluated by the rules of the game being played; or to win by forcing the other players to drop out of the competition. The winner (or winners) collects the pot.

TIED HANDS

When two or more players hold hands of equal rank, they divide the pot equally. If a pot is not equally divisible by the number of winners, the odd sum left after division—breakage, as horse betters call it—goes to the player who was called. In High-Low Poker the indivisible odd amount goes to the player of the high hand.

Standard Rank of Poker Hands With a Fifty-two-Card Deck

It must be specified for clarity's sake that in the following list of Poker hands in ten categories called ranks, any hand listed in a superior rank beats any hand listed in an inferior rank. The royal flush, listed in Rank 1, beats any hand listed in Rank 2. Any hand listed in Rank 6 beats any hand in Rank 7, 8, 9, or 10, and loses to any hand in Rank 5, 4, 3, 2, or 1.

RANK 1 (THE SUPREME RANK)

The Royal Flush: the five highest cards, namely A-K-Q-J-10, of any one of the four suits. The suits have equal rank. Royal flushes tie for winner.

RANK 2

The Straight Flush: any five cards of the same suit in numerical sequence, such as the 10-9-8-7-6 of spades. This flush is called a *ten high*. If there are two or more straight flushes in competition for the pot that one wins whose top card is of the highest denomination; a *ten high* beats a *nine high*, etc.; if two or more players hold a straight flush whose top card is of the same denomination, the hand is a tie.

RANK 3

Four of a Kind: any four cards of the same denomination (A-A-A-A-2). The odd card is irrelevant and does not affect the rank of the hand.

RANK 4

The Full House: three of one kind and two of another (3-3-3-2-2). In evaluating two or more competing full houses, the hand with the highest three-of-a-kind wins, regardless of the rank of the pair. *Example:* A full house including three aces regardless of the pair beats a full house including three kings regardless of the pair.

RANK 5

The Flush: any five cards of the same suit but not in sequence (10-7-5-4-3 of spades). In evaluating two or more
flushes, the winner is determined by the rank of the highest
card in the hand. If the highest cards in contesting hands are
of the same rank, then the next highest cards determine the
winner. And if these are of the same rank, then the winning
hand is determined by the third highest cards. Et cetera! If all
the cards of the players are equal, then the hands are tied.

RANK 6

The Straight: five cards in consecutive sequence but not of
the same suit (3-4-5-6-7). In evaluating more than one straight,
the winner is decided by the rank of his highest card. Straights
of the same denomination are equal, and tie.

RANK 7

Three of a Kind: three cards of the same numerical value
plus two different and irrelevant cards that are not paired
(K-K-K-5-4). In evaluating two or more such hands, the
hand having the highest three-of-a-kind wins regardless of the
value of the unmatched cards.

RANK 8

Two Pairs: two different pairs of cards plus one odd card
(10-10-5-5-4. This example is called *tens up*). In evaluating
two or more two-pair hands, the winner is the player holding
the highest pair. If the highest pairs are tied, the rank of the
second pair in the hands determines the winner; if the second
pairs also are tied, then the higher or highest of the odd cards
determines the winner. If all cards of the competing hands are
of matching value, the hands are tied.

RANK 9

One Pair: two cards of the same denomination plus three
indifferent (unmatched) cards (10-10-9-7-3). In evaluating
two or more hands each including a pair, the player who holds
the highest pair wins. If the pairs are of equal value, the hand
with the highest indifferent card wins. If these are of equal
value, the next card is the determinant, etc. If all the cards in
the competing hands match, the hands tie and the winnings are
divided.

RANK 10

High Card: a hand which contains five indifferent cards not
of the same suit, not in sequence, and falling into none of the

above combinations (A-10-7-5-3 not of the same suit). The example cited would be called an *ace high* hand. If the highest card of two such hands is the same, the next highest card determines the winner; if these tie, the determinant is the next, then the next, etc. If all cards in more than one hand are of matching value, the hands tie, and the pot is divided.

Wild Cards

By mutual prior agreement (and often!) certain cards are designated as being wild. The wild card—as stated above but repeated here to avoid ambiguity—can be used to represent any card of any suit and any denomination, even as a duplicate of a card already held by the player. Here are some wild-card combinations.

1. The joker, which when added to a standard pack makes it a fifty-three-card deck. Often more than one joker is introduced into the play. If no joker is handy, any fifty-third card can be added to the deck, as wild.

2. Deuces wild, the most popular wild cards next to the joker. Any one of the deuces, or the two black deuces, or the two red, or all four deuces may by mutual consent be declared wild.

3. In combination with one or both of the above variations, 3's are occasionally declared wild cards.

4. It is not unusual for players to declare wild the one-eyed jacks, the jacks with mustaches, the black 7's, and/or the profile kings.

For that matter any card or group of cards may be arbitrarily designated as wild.

Rank of Poker Hands With One or More Wild Cards

(In order of their value, Rank 1 being highest and Rank 12 lowest.)
1. Five of a kind, this being the highest-ranking hand.
2. Royal flush.
3. Straight flush.
4. Four of a kind.
5. Full house.
6. Double-ace flush.
7. Flush.
8. Straight.
9. Three of a kind.
10. Two pairs.
11. One pair.

12. High card. (But of course this can occur only when none of the active players has a wild card.)

Rank of Poker Hands in Low Poker

In Low Poker the rank of the hands is just the opposite of the rank in the standard game. *Except* that the ace may be used as high card only, and must not be used to rank as low with a value of 1 unless it is used in the 5-high straight (A-2-3-4-5). Unless otherwise particularized under the rules of the game being played, all Low Poker hands are to be judged by this clause.

The Low Poker hand is evaluated by the rank of its highest card; if there is a tie between highest cards, by the rank of its second card, etc. The value of the lowest card is irrelevant to the hand's value except when on the showdown the four higher cards are exactly matched by another player's. *Example:* A mixed-suit hand such as 9-7-6-5-3, being a nine low, would beat a mixed-suit 10-6-5-4-3, the ten low. The lowest-ranking hand and certain winner at Low Poker is the 7-5-4-3-2 in mixed suits.

Here in categories called ranks, I list the best hands at Low Poker. These are mixed suits, of course. Any hand in a superior rank beats any hand listed below it.

1. 7-5-4-3-2.	6. 8-6-4-3-2.
2. 7-6-4-3-2.	7. 8-6-5-3-2.
3. 7-6-5-3-2.	8. 8-6-5-4-2.
4. 7-6-5-4-2.	9. 8-6-5-4-3.
5. 8-5-4-3-2.	10. 8-7-4-3-2.

Seating Positions

As a rule at the start of the game players may sit wherever they like. A new player may take any vacant seat he chooses unless the game is Dealer's Edge or Ante, in which case he must wait until it becomes his turn to deal before he can have cards.

Just to avoid any possible dispute about seating positions, the start of the game, the seating of new players, and the selection of the dealer, I think it might be well to incorporate the following rules into the game:

SELECTING THE DEALER AND ESTABLISHING SEATING
POSITIONS AT THE TABLE

1. Any player shall by mutual or majority consent shuffle the cards, and the player to his right shall cut the deck.
2. The player acting as dealer shall deal one card to each

player face up, starting with the player at his left, dealing clockwise around the table, and ending with himself.

3. The player dealt the highest card shall become the first dealer and select any seat he wants.

4. The player with the next highest card selects any remaining seat, the player with the third highest any remaining seat, etc.

5. In case of ties, each of the tied players shall be dealt a new card face up until the tie is broken.

6. At the completion of each hand the deal shall pass to the player at the immediate left of the player who dealt that round.

CHANGING POSITIONS AT THE TABLE

At the completion of any hour of play players may demand a new deal for a change in their seating positions. The procedure is the same as in establishing places at the table on the start of a game. The player whose turn it is to deal (1) deals for seating positions and (2) deals the next hand in play.

PREPARATION FOR THE PLAY: THE BANKER AND HIS DUTIES

One of the players is selected by mutual or majority consent to be the banker for that session of play. If cash is to be used in the betting, the banker must make change and see that players bet or ante properly. As a rule it is he who takes the cut out of certain pots (which pots and how much cut are determined by the players) and puts that cash into a kitty— used to buy cards, food, drinks, or to help pay the rent. Under the common usages, all other players help the banker with these chores during the play. If chips are used the banker keeps the supply, sells them to the players, and redeems them to settle accounts at the end of the game.

PROFESSIONAL POKER, OR THE HOUSE GAME

In a house or casino game, the management

1. Supplies all the essentials for Poker playing, namely, the casino, a special kind of Poker table, the chips, the cards, and a lookout man;

2. In return for these goods and services, takes a cut.

The amount of the cut is just exactly what the traffic will bear then and there, in that ward of the city, in that month of the year. Some houses, perhaps a majority, impose a direct charge of 25¢ to 50¢ on the winner of each pot.

VALUE OF THE CHIPS

Nationwide, this is the most common evaluation of Poker chips:

WHITE—One unit.
RED—Five units.
BLUE—Ten units.
YELLOW—Twenty-five units.

The value in cash of the units is entirely up to the players. It may range from 1¢, as in the classic penny-ante game, to $10—or $100.

Optional Rules Better Discussed Before the Start of the Game

1. Before the game starts there must be common agreement on the kind of game to be played. Local conventions on such things as royalties and bonuses must be talked over before the game, and reduced to writing on a pad. These conventions or rulings must be thoroughly understood by all players.

2. Although any player has the right to quit whenever he wants to, a time limit must be decided on before the start of the game.

3. Before play starts, there must be common agreement as to the amount of the *ante* if any, the minimum and maximum amount of money or chips that can be bet at any one time, and the maximum number of *raises* any one player can make at any betting interval. As a rule a limit is rarely put on the number of raises permitted at any betting interval, but see sections on Draw or Stud Poker for details on betting.

FREEZING A RAISE

The following is a rule most Poker players have been seeking for years. The author had something to do with its creation, and has incorporated it into his rules for all Poker games. How often have you been sandwiched between two players who were raising and re-raising each other and raising back with no consideration for you, who had to cough up enough money to match their raises just to stay in till the decision? You made up your mind to stay to the bitter end even if you lost all your money, and there were times when you did exactly that. The author counted thirty raises one night between two players in one round of Draw Poker, and one player who never raised had to match the thirty raises to stay in the pot.

Then and there I decided something must be done to protect a player from being sandbagged between two confederates, two cheaters, or two reckless players with no regard for the other men in the game. Very happily, I give all Poker players a rule that eliminates this hazard from Poker without putting a limit on the number of raises permitted. Here it is— a "freezer."

A *freezer* is a *bet* that can be made only by an active player who is *staying* or *calling* after a *raise* has been re-raised by one or more players.

A player who has raised or re-raised is not permitted to freeze a bet. The only active player who is permitted to bet a *freezer* is a player who has not raised or re-raised in that betting round. A *freezer* only freezes a raise for the betting round taking place.

The amount of the freezer bet must be agreed on by mutual consent before the start of the game, although I would suggest it to be not less than twice the maximum bet and not more than five times the maximum bet. When the non-raiser, in his turn to bet, bets the *freezer* the other players may drop out or stay by putting into the pot the amount of the *freezer* bet.

ROYALTIES OR BONUSES

Some players elect to pay a royalty to any player holding an exceptionally high-ranking hand, such as a royal flush, straight flush, or four of a kind. This is not incorporated in my rules, and is optional with players. I mention it just to make this chapter definite and complete. Royalties and bonuses on a royal flush or any other bonus hand are optional with the players, but as a rule are from three to five times the amount of the maximum permitted bet. Each player, whether active or not, must pay the player holding the bonus hand the amount agreed on at the start of the game.

FIVE-MINUTE TIME PERIOD FOR A PLAY

If an active player is taking too much time to decide how to play his hand, any other active player may call time, and if the hesitant player fails to complete his play within five minutes after time is called, his hand is dead: he is forced to drop out. *Note:* This situation happens often in a high-limit game; the author has seen players take a half hour or more to decide on a play.

THE SHUFFLE

The dealer shuffles the cards. Any player may call for a shuffle at any time before the cut, although the dealer has the privilege of shuffling the cards last.

THE CUT

1. After the cards have been shuffled, the dealer presents the pack to the player at his right to be cut. If he refuses to cut the cards, the player to that player's right has the privilege of cutting, etc. If all other players refuse to cut, the dealer must cut. *It is mandatory.*

2. At least five cards must be in each of the cut packets should a player use a regular cut. Should he desire, a player may use the "Scarne cut" or cut the deck more than once. After the cut, the cut portions must be squared or reunited and dealt as a complete pack. It is not permissible to pick up one cut portion of the pack and start dealing from it. A player can demand to have the cards cut again before a deal has started, but no player has the right to demand a cut after the deal has started, or at any other time.

ASKING FOR A NEW CUT

If a player does not like the way the cards have been cut before the start of the deal, doubting legitimacy of the cut or for any other reason, he may call for another cut; and any other player but the player calling for the new cut may cut the cards.

THE DEAL

The dealer deals one card at a time to each player, starting with the leader (player to the dealer's left) and continuing clockwise until each player in the game has the required number of cards. The cards are dealt face up or face down according to the rules of the game being played.

MISDEAL

In case of a misdeal there must be a new shuffle and cut. The same dealer deals again.

DEALING FROM PART OF THE DECK

A dealer is not permitted to deal from a cut portion of the pack. The cut portions must be united, and the dealer must deal from the entire pack.

CUTTING THE PACK DURING THE DEAL

No player is permitted to cut the cards after the cards have been dealt or the betting has started, unless some overt crookedness has been observed and proved.

CHAPTER TWENTY-THREE

Draw Poker and Its Variations

Draw Poker

Also known as Closed Poker, this is the forerunner of all the other kinds of Poker, including Stud.

REQUIREMENTS

1. A standard pack of fifty-two playing cards (usually at hand are two packs of different backs or colors so a player may call for a change of packs upon completion of any deal).
2. Two to six players make the best game, although up to ten players may play—with the following added rule: Should the pack become exhausted and there are players who still must draw cards to complete their hands the discards are assembled, shuffled and cut, and the draw is continued. But when playing for high stakes, the maximum number of players is six.

THE OBJECT OF THE GAME

For a player at the showdown to hold a higher-ranking hand than any of the other players. The player (or players) having the best hand is declared the winner (or winners), and collects the pot.

PRELIMINARIES BEFORE THE DEAL

All the preparations before the start of the actual play are as described under "General Rules for Poker" (page 232): selecting the banker, his duties, rank of hands, royalties, time limit, betting limits, preparations before play, selecting the dealer and seating positions at the table, irregularities in cutting the cards, the shuffle and cut.

THE ANTE

Two types of antes are used in Draw Poker, as follows:
1. Each player, before the cards are dealt, antes an equal amount into the pot. All players must ante in turn, starting with the player to the dealer's left and rotating clockwise.

2. Dealer's Edge. The player whose turn it is to deal antes an amount into the pot. In *dealer's edge* a new player entering the game must become the dealer immediately on being seated.

OPTIONAL BETTING LIMITS AT DRAW POKER

The most popular betting limits are as follows:

1. Five to 10¢, 10¢ to 25¢, 10¢ to 50¢, 25¢ to $1, 25¢ to $2, etc.

Only two amounts are specified, the minimum and the maximum permitted; which means at a player's turn of play a player must conform with one of the following rules:

A. A player cannot bet an amount less than the minimum limit.
B. A player cannot bet an amount larger than the maximum limit.
C. A player may bet any amount between both limits.
D. The *ante* is usually the amount of the minimum bet.

2. Variation in betting limit: often three figures are mentioned, such as 5¢, 10¢, and 15¢, which indicate the *ante* and *opening* bets are 5¢ and after the draw a bet must be either 10¢ or 15¢. The same holds true for any other three-figure limit, regardless of the amount.

3. Jack Pot. Should all the players pass on the first deal, the amount of the opening bet can be any amount not higher than the amount in the pot, provided the limit bet is less than the amount in the pot before the opening. Thereafter each bet after the draw can also be the amount of the possible *opening bet*. The dealer must announce the Jack Pot limit to the opening player, and that amount cannot be exceeded in betting, except if it be lower than the maximum limit.

4. Pot Limit. Undoubtedly the fastest betting limit of all the limits played today at Poker. A player at his betting turn is permitted to bet any amount up to the total amount in the pot.

5. Table Stakes or Freeze-out. Each player puts up a certain amount of money on the table, but not less than a minimum agreed on beforehand. The maximum amount is often agreed on also, but as a rule it isn't. A player may increase or decrease that amount after the showdown. On any bet a player is permitted to bet any part of the amount or the entire amount any player has on the table. Should a player fail to have as much money as the previous better, he is permitted to play for the pot. (See Tapping Out under "Additional Rules at Draw Poker," page 245.) But, after the tapping-out hand, the player may continue playing by putting more money on the table.

The above variation is not as popular as it used to be about twenty years ago, and "sky's the limit" games have vanished completely in this Poker era.

THE DEAL

Dealing clockwise, starting with the player on the dealer's left, the dealer deals a card to each player until each has five cards. The dealer gets the last card. The remaining cards are put to one side in front of the dealer for future use in drawing.

OPENERS

The player who opens the pot must hold in his hand a pair of jacks or a higher-ranking hand. It is essential for the stability of the game that a player have jacks or better when opening. If this rule is not enforced and a player opens the pot any time he feels like it, one of the greatest factors of skill in the game is automatically eliminated—which depends on knowing that the opener holds at least a pair of jacks.

SPLITTING OPENERS

The player who opened the pot has the right to discard his openers or part of his openers, but he must announce that he is doing so and place his openers or the discarded part of his openers to one side to verify at the showdown the fact that he had them.

PLAYER'S TURN OF PLAY

The leader (player to the dealer's left) has the first privilege of play. After examining his cards and establishing that he holds a pair of jacks or a hand of higher rank, he must do one of two things:

1. He may open by putting a bet into the pot.
2. He may pass, which indicates he does not desire to start the betting.

Should he fail to hold a pair of jacks or a hand of a higher rank, he is compelled to pass. ·

If all the players pass, they must ante again, and the new dealer deals another hand to each player: or, if playing dealer's edge, the new dealer must *ante*.

When a player opens by putting an amount within the limit into the pot, each player in turn can do one of these three things:

1. He máy pass; and, should he pass when the pot has been opened, he merely folds his cards and puts them in the center of the table. This is folding up.
2. Should he decide to *play*, he must put up an amount equal to the bet of the player who opened the pot.
3. If he wants to raise, he merely says, "raise," and puts

into the pot an amount equal to that put into the pot by the opening player, plus an amount for the *raise*.

All the other players may now either play by putting into the pot an amount equal to the total amount of the *raiser* or, should they already have put the opening bet into the pot, they merely put into the pot an amount equal to the raise. Or a player may re-raise by putting into the pot an amount equal to the raiser plus an amount for the re-raiser. Or he may drop out by folding his cards and throwing them into the discard pile on the table. This procedure of dropping out, playing, raising, and re-raising is continued until the players stop raising.

If all the players drop out but one, he wins the pot. Should he be the player who opened the pot, he must show his openers to the rest of the players. If he is not, he does not have to expose his hand.

THE DRAW

When all the players have either *dropped out* or put into the pot an equal amount and there are no uncovered bets in the pot, and when the active players number two or more, these remaining players may, if they desire, draw either one, two, or three cards in an attempt to improve their hands, or stand pat. This procedure is called the draw, and it is played as follows:

The dealer must ask each player (starting with the nearest active player to his left and rotating to the left, clockwise) at his proper turn of play how many cards he wants to draw, if any; this he indicates to the player by saying, "How many?" The player either says he's *standing pat* or tells the dealer how many cards he wants to draw. The dealer must wait until the player discards a like number before dealing the new cards; or he passes the player by should the latter say, *"I stand pat."*

In Draw, every player must take the cards he asked for if the dealer has dealt them off the deck. If too many, player must discard to make a legitimate hand. If too few, he has fouled his hand, as he has fewer than required for a playing hand.

Dealer must take the exact number of cards laid off the deck for himself. Cards once discarded cannot be taken back.

If a player does not get the correct number of cards he asked for, the dealer must rectify the mistake, provided no one at the player's left has drawn cards.

THE BETTING AFTER THE DRAW

The player who opened the pot has the first turn of play after the draw, and the play goes on to each active player, starting with the player to the opener's left and moving clockwise. A turn of play now consists of either checking, betting, calling, dropping out, raising, or re-raising. But a player cannot check at his turn of play after a bet has been made. The play continues around the table until one of the following situations develops:

1. Until a player has made a bet and is not called by any player, in which case he wins the pot and does not have to expose his hand, unless he was the opener. Then he is compelled to show his *openers only*.

2. Until all players have passed; and now the opener must be the first player to expose his hand for the showdown. This is done by announcing the rank of his hand and turning his five cards face up on the table. The same holds for all the remaining players, continuing with the first remaining player to the opener's left and rotating clockwise.

3. Or until an equal amount has been put into the pot by *betting* on the part of two or more active players. In this case the biggest better is being *called*, and he must be the first to announce the rank of his hand and turn it face up on the table for the showdown. The first active player to his left does the same, the showdown rotating clockwise. The player holding the highest-ranking hand as described under "General Rules for Poker" wins the pot. In case of ties, the tied players split the pot equally.

(See rules for "Tied Hands," page 233.)

SHOWDOWN

In Draw Poker the cards in the showdown speak for themselves. If a player calls a lower- or higher-ranking hand than he holds and this error is noticed before the pot has been collected, the error can be rectified. But if it is noticed after the pot has been collected, the error cannot be rectified. The same rule regarding the showdown holds true should all the players pass after the draw.

Additional Rules at Draw Poker

MISDEALS

Whenever a misdeal occurs there must be a new shuffle and cut. The same dealer deals again but should the dealer make two misdeals in a row the deal passes to the player at his left.

MISDEALS—YES OR NO?

1. If one or more cards are exposed in cutting or reuniting the cut packets, there is a misdeal.

2. If the pack has not been offered to the proper player to cut, and the pot has not been opened yet, there is a misdeal.

If the pot has already been opened and the irregularity has not been discovered, the deal stands. There is no misdeal.

3. If the pack has not been cut and the betting has not started, there is a misdeal.

4. If one or more cards are observed face up in the pack before each player has received his five cards or the betting has not yet started, there is a misdeal.

5. If a player's card is exposed by the dealer before the draw, there is a misdeal.

6. If the dealer exposes one or more of his own cards at any time, the deal stands. There is no misdeal.

7. Should a player expose one or more of his own cards at any time, the deal stands. There is no misdeal.

8. If an imperfect pack is being used with fewer cards than the standard pack or duplicate cards and it is discovered before the pot has been collected, there is a misdeal. Play immediately stops when the imperfect pack is discovered, and all the players get back the amounts they put into the pot.

9. If the cards have been improperly dealt—for example, more than one card at a time—or another player has received improper cards and it is noticed before the pot is opened, there is a misdeal.

10. If too few or too many hands have been dealt, there is a misdeal.

11. If too few or too many cards have been dealt to one or more players and it is discovered before the pot is opened, there is a misdeal unless it can be properly corrected before any one player has looked at his hand.

12. If the wrong player is dealing and it is discovered before the pot has been opened, there is a misdeal.

PASSING THE DEAL

A dealer cannot pass his turn to deal unless he is incompetent to deal the cards.

EXPOSED CARDS ON THE DRAW

1. Should a dealer expose one or more of a player's cards on the draw, the player is not permitted to take the exposed cards. They must be put into the center of the table face up, and are out of play. The dealer deals the player whose card has been exposed another card in place of it.

2. Should a player expose one or more of his drawn cards, he must take them.

3. Should a dealer expose one or more cards on his own draw or if they are found face up on the draw, the dealer must take them.

BETTING

A bet once placed in the pot, regardless of whether it's a player's proper turn or not, must stand. It cannot be taken out of the pot.

· If a player should put into the pot an amount less than the amount of the previous better, he must add the required sum so that his bet is equal to the previous bet. Should he fail to do so, his hand is dead, and the amount he bet must remain in the pot.

BETTING OUT OF TURN

The following rules apply to playing, calling, or raising out of turn.

A player making a bet out of turn must leave the bet in the pot. He cannot take it back, and the play reverts to the proper player. When it is the proper turn of the player who bet out of turn he must do one of the following:

1. If no bet has been made by any preceding player, the bet stands as is.

2. If a bet has been made by a previous player smaller than the bet made out of turn, it stands as a raise.

3. If a bet has been made by a previous player equal to the bet out of turn, it stands as a play or call. The player who bet out of turn cannot raise.

4. If a previous bet was raised by another player and the bet is in excess of the amount bet by the out-of-turn player, the out-of-turn player may either drop out of the pot, play or call by equaling the bet made by the previous betters, or re-raise the pot after equaling the raised bet.

VERBAL BETTING

If a player in his turn of play announces he is making a bet, he must abide by the announcement. He cannot increase or decrease the oral bet. Should a player make an announcement at an improper turn of play and has not placed any money into the pot, it should be disregarded and considered a joke or an attempted bluff.

PASSING OR CHECKING OUT OF TURN

If a player passes out of turn before the draw and still holds his cards in his hand, there is no penalty. He just waits for his proper turn of play, but he is not permitted to raise should a preceding player make a bet. The same holds true for passing or checking after the draw, provided no previous bet has been made.

IMPROPER FOLD-UP

If a player decides to drop out of the pot or fold up, he cannot give an indication, verbal or otherwise, until it is his proper turn of play. Strict observance of this rule makes for a better game. But should he fold up out of turn, his hand is dead.

FALSE OPENERS

1. Player opening a pot with false openers forfeits his right to the pot, and his hand is dead. Remaining players in the pot, if any, will play the pot out as though it had been opened legitimately. If no one stays, the opening bet remains in the pot, and a new deal is declared.

2. If opener bets with false openers and his bet is not called, the amount of bet shall be withdrawn, but opening bet remains in the pot.

3. If bet is called, the false opener loses the entire pot to the best legitimate hand.

FOUL OR DEAD HAND

1. If a player holds more or less than five cards on the showdown, that player's hand is declared foul or dead, and he has no interest in the pot. But if the irregularity is discovered after the pot is collected, the hand must stand as legitimate.

2. If a player forgets to draw cards or permits another player to draw cards at his turn of play, he must play his hand as is. If he has discarded and failed to draw, his hand is dead.

TAPPING OUT

When a player has put all his money into the pot and no longer can bet, it is called a *tap-out*. That player is permitted to play for the size of the pot up until the time he now longer has money. If the other players keep betting they put their bets to one side, as the tapping-out player has no legal interest in that side pot. The tapping-out player receives cards until the hand is completed, and should he have the highest-ranking hand on the showdown, he wins only the original pot, not the side pot. That is won by the player having the highest-ranking cards among the remaining betters. Except in table stakes and freeze-out, when a player taps out *and loses,* he is out of the game. He cannot continue playing. However, if he wins on the tap-out and therefore has money, he may continue to play as before.

When tapping out, a player may raise only if he still possesses an amount equal to the maximum limit so that in case of a re-raise he can call the bet. A player cannot tap out with money on the table.

GOING THROUGH THE DISCARDS

In no circumstances is a player permitted to look at the discards before or after the showdown. Nor is a player permitted to look at another player's hand even though he is out of the pot. Looking through the undealt cards is forbidden. The above rules should be strictly enforced.

LOANING MONEY OR CHIPS

Under no circumstances is a player allowed to borrow money or chips from another player during the play. If a player desires to borrow money from another player, it must be done before the cards are dealt. Passing money or chips from one player to another during the play is not permitted.

BETTING FOR ANOTHER PLAYER

Under no circumstances is a player permitted to ante or bet for another player.

ANGLING

Angling is positively prohibited. For example, discussion among two or more players to split the pot regardless of the winner, or to give back part of the money, or ask for a free ride or call, or any violation of the Poker rules is prohibited.

OVERS IN THE POT

No money or chips may be taken out of the pot except when the stakes are cash, under which circumstances a player may take out his proper change after placing a bet at his turn of play. It must be observed by all the players that the proper change is taken.

Should a player ante or put into the pot an amount larger than required and thereafter should another player make a bet, the overage cannot be taken out of the pot.

EXPOSED HANDS ON SHOWDOWN

All players, active or nonactive, are entitled to see all active players' hands on the showdown, provided a bet has been called. Therefore, on the showdown all the players in their proper turn must spread their cards face up on the table.

ILLEGAL CUTTING OF CARDS

Under no circumstances can a player ask to cut the cards after the deal has started. I must stress particularly that cards can be cut at no time except before the start of the deal.

MAN AND WIFE

Most of the outstanding gambling casinos in Reno (such as the Embassy and Normandie) do not permit man and wife to play Draw Poker at the same table, for reasons that should be obvious. This is a sound ruling and therefore I have incorporated it into my rules for Draw Poker. The exception is a low-limit game such as Penny Ante, Five-and-Ten, etc., when the game is played primarily for pastime.

CRITICISM

A player is not permitted under any circumstances to criticize another player's methods. Draw Poker is a game in which each man plays his own hand as he elects. No consideration should be expected by one player from another.

Draw Poker Variations

Countless variations of Draw Poker are played in various parts of the country, and there are numerous house rules which differ in different localities.

The author has selected the most popular variations from this endless group.

Games such as Whiskey Poker, Bluff, Knock Poker, and numerous other obsolete variations of Poker have been omitted because either they have drifted into another family of games or they have been vastly improved and are being played under other names. Inclusion of these games would take the game of Poker back to Jonathan Green's day, namely, 1834.

The player will find most of the rules governing these games covered under "General Rules for Poker" or "Rules for Draw Poker." Any of the cheating methods used at Draw Poker are applicable to its variations, and for pointers in strategy the player may refer to the chapter "Pointers on Draw Poker."

L-BALL OR LOW BALL

This fine variation of Draw Poker is played principally in the West and Middle West. It is not being played in the East simply because all previous game-book compilers have omitted it completely. It is much more strategic than Draw Poker. The author highly recommends this game to the player who considers Draw Poker too slow, who likes to speed a Draw Poker game, especially when four or fewer players are engaged and it is difficult to get a pair of jacks or better as openers.

Lowball is played exactly as is Draw Poker. If, however, openers do not happen to be dealt and every one has passed, the game is continued on the basis of the *low hand wins*, and the first player to the left of the dealer has the option of opening or passing and each player has a turn in the same rotating order as the previously played Draw Poker hand. Should all players pass, a new deal is dealt as in Draw Poker, and the game continues as described above.

RANK OF HANDS AT LOWBALL

In Lowball a hand such as 1-2-3-4-5 not in the same suit is an unbeatable hand, and is commonly called a *bicycle*. Aces are counted as low, and straights do not count. All other hands are rated as usual. See ranks under "General Rules for Poker."

And if you still desire to further speed up the game of Lowball, do what the casinos in Nevada do; add the joker, and make it wild. Your Draw Poker hands will rank in the following sequence. No change in Lowball hands. Draw Poker hands: five of a kind, royal flush, straight flush, four of a kind, full house, double ace flush, flush, straight, three of a kind, two pairs, one pair.

STRATEGY AT LOWBALL

The player should realize that when playing Lowball, a pair, particularly a high pair (from 9 up), is almost worthless.

It is foolish to play a hand after an opening bet on the strength of having three low cards with the hope of getting two low cards on the draw. This is one of the most foolish draws at Lowball. Players do not seem to realize that the probability of drawing two low cards is almost as remote as the probability of filling a three-card straight at Draw Poker. And if you draw two low cards, you have the possibility of pairing your other three low cards; and you now hold a pair or probably two pairs.

So, as an over-all tip, the best hand at Lowball is a good pat hand, but you don't always get good pat hands; therefore I suggest you draw only one card to a four-card no-pair at this unique game.

Hands such as 6-high are equal to a straight flush in Draw Poker, and a 7-high is equal to four of a kind. These hands usually will win the pot.

STRAIGHT DRAW POKER

This is the forerunner of Draw Poker, but most of the present game writers still believe it is played more than Draw Poker, because they usually lead off their Poker chapters with this game. Rarely do I see this game played in my travels through the country; therefore I merely include it as a variation of Draw Poker.

The game is played exactly as is Draw Poker, with the following two exceptions:

1. A player may open the pot on any hand he desires.
2. A player, should he desire, may draw up to five cards on the draw.

DRAW POKER—WITH A ONE-, TWO-, THREE-, FOUR-, OR FIVE-CARD BUY OR DRAW

The game is played exactly as is the standard game of Draw Poker. All the rules that apply to the standard game apply to this variant, with the following exception: that a player is permitted to draw one, two, three, four, or five cards on the draw.

DRAW POKER—BLIND OPENERS

If you think Draw Poker is too slow, then this is your game—that is, if you can get enough players who feel as you do.

All the rules that apply to standard Draw Poker apply to this game, with the following exception: that you can open the pot on the blind; that is, you do not have to hold jacks or better to open. Or, if you like, the leader must open the pot regardless of the value of his hand.

DRAW POKER—DEUCES WILD

This variant of Draw Poker is played exactly as is Draw Poker, and all the rules that apply to Draw Poker apply to Deuces Wild; with the following exception: that a deuce may be counted as any card a player desires to call it. It may even be counted as a duplicate of a card already held by a player. Therefore the highest-ranking hand a player can hold is five aces.

A player should take extreme care in calling the rank of his hand, because the *rank* called must stand, contrary to the practice in Draw Poker, where the cards speak for themselves. Take for example, a hand like this: 2 of clubs, 2 of diamonds, 2 of spades, 6 of hearts, and 10 of hearts. The average player very often calls four 10's instead of a 10-high straight flush. Deuces and natural cards have the same value. Rank of hands in Deuces Wild is described under Wild Cards, page 235, under "General Rules for Poker."

DRAW POKER ENGLISH VARIANT

The English version of Draw Poker is played exactly as is Draw Poker, with this exception: that the *leader* is permitted to draw up to four cards, whereas all other players are permitted to draw up to three cards only.

DRAW POKER—JOKER WILD

When one or more jokers are added to a standard pack of fifty-two cards the game is called Joker Wild. The amount of skill required in playing Joker Wild is reduced immeasurably, more and more with the addition of each extra joker. The more jokers added, the less strategy to the game. Rank of hands is described under "General Rules for Poker," Wild Cards, page 235.

DRAW POKER BLIND BETTING

This variant of Draw Poker is recommended to the boys who like fast and furious action. The game is played exactly as is Draw Poker, with the following exceptions:

1. No players ante into the pot.
2. The players are not permitted to pick up their cards and look at them.
3. The leader must make the first blind bet, without looking at his hand.
4. The players in proper rotation, as in Draw Poker, may either drop out, stay, raise, or re-raise.
5. After the blind betting has ended and two or more active players remain in the pot, the active players are permitted to look at their cards.
6. The privilege of playing first goes to the player to the left of the player who made the last blind raise.
7. If no player raised blind, the privilege passes to the player to the dealer's left.
8. The betting now proceeds as in Draw Poker, except that a player is not permitted to pass or check. He must either drop out, call the bet, play or stay by putting into the pot an amount equal to the better's raise, or re-raise.

PROGRESSIVE DRAW POKER

In this variation of Draw Poker, all the rules that apply to Draw Poker are binding, with the following additional rules:

Should all the players pass (not open the pot) on the first deal, the requirement for openers on the second deal becomes a pair of queens or better. If the pot is not opened on the second deal, a pair of kings or better is required as openers for the third deal, and a pair of aces or better for the fourth deal.

The requirements for the fifth deal are kings or better; for the sixth, queens; and for the seventh, jacks; and then back up to aces and back to jacks.

Once the pot has been opened by a player, the game reverts back to Draw Poker, jacks or better as openers, etc.

DRAW POKER HIGH SPADE BET

A side bet between two or more players that one will hold a higher-ranking spade card than any of the other players in his first five cards dealt. Players announce the approximate value of their hand to each—for example, a player says, "I have a low spade." The other player says, "I have a high spade," then shows it to all the players betting on spades. The reason for this is not to expose too many cards. Although spades is a popular bet at Draw Poker, it often exposes a hand of a player, and gives other players, not betting on spades, a slight advantage in the game.

SHOWDOWN STRAIGHT POKER

In this variation of Draw Poker, the only betting is done before the cards are dealt, as if anteing into the pot. Then five cards are dealt each player, one at a time face up, starting with the leader and rotating to the left clockwise. The player holding the highest hand wins the pot. All other rules are identical to those for Draw Poker.

SPIT IN THE OCEAN

There are numerous variations of this variation, which are themselves always being changed by one player or another. The author has seen at least twenty-five different variations played throughout the country. I include only the most popular versions of the game.

In Spit in the Ocean itself, each player is dealt four cards instead of the usual five as in Draw Poker. After each has received his four cards, the next card is turned face up on the table. After a betting round, the players draw cards same as in Draw Poker. Each of the players must consider the *upturned card* his own fifth card. The player to the dealer's left must open the pot regardless of the value of his hand.

On the showdown each player must hold only four cards in his hand, and is compelled to include the upturned card on the table as his fifth card.

PIG IN THE POKE

A variation of Spit in the Ocean is to call a wild card any of the three other cards of the same denomination as the upturned card, but not to call wild the upturned card in the center of the table.

And another variation is to call the upturned card in the center of the table wild—plus the three cards of the same denomination.

X MARKS THE SPOT

A variation of Spit in the Ocean: Four cards are dealt to each player as in Draw Poker. After the dealer receives his fourth card, he now deals five cards face down in the center of the table in the form of an X.

After the players look at their four cards, the dealer turns face up one of the cards in the center of the table, and a betting round takes place. Each outside card of the X is turned face up singly, and a betting round takes place. The center card of the X is turned up last, and is considered wild, and the three cards of the same denomination are also considered wild.

The player may select the best five cards out of the nine for his hand. A variation is to use the three cards in either line of the X. Therefore the best five cards out of seven may be used as a Poker hand.

TWIN BEDS

Another variation of Spit in the Ocean: Each player is dealt four cards as in Draw Poker. After the dealer has received his fourth card, two rows of five cards each are dealt face down on the table. The betting round takes place, and the dealer turns up one card from each row. Another betting round, and another card is turned up from each row. Continue betting and turning a card from each row until the last card in each row has been turned face up and the betting round has been completed.

The last card to be turned up from each row is wild, and so are the three cards of the same denomination as the wild card in each row. The player may use up to five cards from either row to complete his hand, but he cannot use cards from both rows to help his hand.

STORMY WEATHER

This version of Spit in the Ocean is a variation of Draw Poker with extra draws. Each player is dealt four cards, singly, face down, as in Draw Poker: only, after the dealer has received his second card, he deals a card face down in the center of the table, another card onto the center of the table after receiving his third card, and a third card face down in the center of the table after dealing himself the fourth and last card of the deal.

The betting round and the drawing of cards is as in Draw Poker, except that a player may open the pot on any hand he desires (jacks or better are not required), and a player may draw up to four cards if he desires. If all the players pass, a new hand is dealt, and all the players ante again, as in Draw Poker.

If the pot is opened and the active players have completed their draw, there is no betting at this time; instead:

The dealer now turns up the first card dealt of the three cards in the center of the table, and a betting round begins, the opener making the first bet. When all bets have been met, the dealer turns up the second card dealt in the center of the table, and another betting round ensues, with the opener having the first turn. The same holds with the facing up of the third card in the center of the table.

On the showdown, a player is permitted to make use of his fifth card of any one of the three cards turned up in the center of the table. Player must indicate verbally, at his proper turn of play, which of the three upturned cards in the center of the table he is using for his fifth card. No mistakes may be rectified after his proper turn of play has passed.

CINCINNATI OR LAME BRAIN

A variation of Spit in the Ocean: In this game, five cards are dealt each player and five cards are dealt face down in the center of the table. The dealer, after dealing himself a card on each round, deals one face down in the center of the table. There is no draw in this game as in Draw Poker. After each player has looked at his five cards, the dealer turns face up the first card dealt in the center of the table. The betting now starts. The player to the dealer's left has the first turn of play. Betting and the rotation of play are as in Draw Poker.

On completion of the betting round, the dealer turns face up the second card dealt in the center of the table, and another betting round takes place. This procedure is followed until the five cards in the center of the table are face up and five betting rounds have taken place. On the showdown, a player may make use of any or all the five cards shown face up in the center of the table. In other words, he selects the best hand of five cards out of a total of ten—five in his hand and five face up in the center of the table.

LAME BRAIN PETE

In this variation of Cincinnati or Lame Brain, the lowest-ranking card in the center of the table and the three cards of of the same denomination are wild.

HIGH-LOW POKER

The game is played exactly as Draw Poker, except:

1. That a player can open on any hand. (Jacks or better are not required to open the pot.)

2. In the showdown the pot is divided between the holder of the highest-ranking hand and the holder of the lowest-ranking hand. See "General Rules for Poker" for rank of low hands.

LAME BRAIN HIGH AND LOW

Played exactly as is Cincinnati or Lame Brain, with the added feature of High and Low. In this game of High-Low, it is not uncommon for a player to win both the high and the low, nor is it uncommon to find two players tying for high or low.

DOUBLE-BARREL SHOTGUN

Also known as Texas Tech. The game is played High and Low. Each player is dealt five cards, as in Draw Poker. There is no opening or drawing card. The leader turns up one card, and each active player in his proper turn of play, as in Draw Poker, does likewise. A round of betting takes place. The leader turns up a second card, each active player does the same, then there is a second betting round. This procedure is followed until the five cards have been turned face up. There are four rounds of betting.

SHOTGUN

Played the same as Draw Poker, except that any hand may open the pot, and each player is dealt only three cards on the first round and must draw two cards on the draw. Betting is exactly as described under Draw Poker.

HURRICANE

A variation of Draw Poker on a reduced scale. Each player is dealt two cards, singly, as in Draw Poker. On the draw a player must do one of the following:

1. Stand pat.
2. Draw one or two cards. The highest-ranking hand in this game is a pair of aces.

MONTY

Played exactly as is Hurricane, plus this: the deuces are wild, and the game is played as is High-Low.

CHAPTER TWENTY-FOUR

Stud Poker and Its Variations

Stud Poker

Stud Poker, also known as Open Poker, is the fastest gambling game in the Poker family. Rich and poor play it for cash ranging from penny ante to table stakes in thousands.

Stud Poker allows for more strategy than Draw Poker, and has four betting rounds, whereas Draw Poker has only two betting rounds.

In Stud Poker the average rank of the winning hands is lower than in Draw Poker, since in Stud the maximum number of cards anyone is dealt is five.

PRELIMINARIES BEFORE THE DEAL

All the preliminaries before the actual play are as described under the "General Rules for Poker," such as the pack of cards, rank of cards, rank of hands, betting limit, time limit, royalties, preparations for play, selecting the dealer and establishing seating positions at the table, the shuffle and cut, and irregularities in cutting the cards. The number of players at five-card Stud may range from two to ten. The better Poker players like best a game with eight, nine, or ten players, on the theory that this allows more latitude for strategy.

OPTIONAL BETTING LIMITS AT STUD POKER

There are numerous types of betting limits at Stud Poker, from among which the author has selected the most popular and most commonly used. Whatever the limits, the minimum and the maximum must be specified before the start of the game.

Betting Variation I

1. Players do not ante, nor does the dealer edge.
2. A minimum amount and a maximum amount are specified before the start of the game: for example, a penny and two, 5 and 10, 5¢ to 25¢, 50¢ to $1, 25¢ to $2, or any two specified amounts.

258

A player may bet the minimum, the maximum, or any amount between limits at his turn.

Betting Variation II

In this betting variation only two different amounts may legally be wagered, no amount between limits. For example, 10¢ and 20¢ means a player cannot bet 15¢, which would be between limits. Other limits: 5¢ and 10¢, 25¢ and 50¢, $1 and $2.

The maximum amount may be bet only on the following conditions:

1. If a player holds an open pair or better.
2. On the betting round prior to a player's being dealt his fifth or last card, and on the final betting round before the showdown.

Betting Variation III

Often *three* figures are mentioned in the limits—such as 5¢, 10¢, and 25¢—meaning the player is permitted to bet the minimum amount or up to the second amount until the third and fourth betting round or until an open pair shows. Then he is permitted to bet up to the maximum.

Dealer's Edge (Variation IV)

Before the deal starts the dealer edges into the pot an amount agreed upon, usually equal to the amount of the minimum limit.

Player's Ante (Variation V)

Each player antes into the pot an amount equal to the minimum bet, or a larger amount agreed upon by mutual consent.

JACK POT

The following additional betting feature may be added to any of the above variations except Variations IV and V. When the opening better fails to have an active opponent on his first bet—that is, all the players have dropped out—the next deal is called a Jack Pot. All the players must ante into the pot an amount equal to the bet made by the *lone active player* in the previous hand. After all the players have anted and a new hand is dealt, the opening better (in Jack Pots high or low card can check on the opening bet or thereafter as governed by the Stud Poker rules) is permitted to bet an amount equal to the total amount anted into the pot. In other words, if that amount is in excess of the maximum limit, the new maximum limit for that Jack Pot is the amount anted into the pot before the opening bet is made.

TABLE STAKES OR FREEZE-OUT

Each player puts up on the table a certain amount of money, but not less than a minimum amount agreed upon beforehand. The maximum amount is often agreed on also, but as a rule it is not. Upon the completion of each showdown, a player is permitted to increase or decrease the amount on the table and on any bet a player is permitted to bet any amount or the entire amount that a player has on the table—excepting that a player may continue playing by putting more money on the table.

Should a player fail to have as much money as the previous better, he is permitted to play for the pot. (See Tapping Out under "Additional Rules at Stud Poker," page 266.)

The above variation is not as popular as it was twenty years ago.

POT LIMIT

Undoubtedly the fastest betting limit of all the limits played today at poker:

A player in his betting turn may bet any amount up to the total amount in the pot.

THE BEGINNING OF THE DEAL

The dealer deals each player face down one card (which is known as the hole card), starting with the player to the dealer's left and rotating clockwise, dealing the last card to himself (the dealer), then one card face up to each player in the same order. Then he places the pack face down on the table in front of himself so that the cards are handy for the following part of the deal. The hole card is very carefully protected by each player to keep it hidden from his opponents. The hole card is the only card in Stud Poker that is unknown to the other players, and on the rank of this card depends the betting and the outcome of the hand.

Each card that is face up on the table shall be known as an *upcard*, after the expression I coined for Rummy games.

FIRST ROUND OF BETTING

The players having carefully examined their hole cards, the player holding the highest-ranking upcard must make the opening bet (first bet). It may be a specified amount agreed on or any amount within the limit. (Some players, to speed the betting, rule that the lowest ranking card must make the opening bet.) Should two or more players hold matching high-ranking or low-ranking cards (whichever rule is adopted), the player nearest to the dealer's left must make the opening bet. Thereafter each player in turn, starting with the player to the better's left and rotating clockwise, must make one of the following plays:

1. He may fold up or drop out, which means he does not want to continue playing his hand. This is indicated by his saying, "Out," and putting his two cards on the discard pile on the table.

2. Or he accepts the bet, and says, "I'll play," or "Stay," and puts into the pot an amount of money equal to the opening better's.

3. Or he *raises the pot,* and this is done by putting into the pot an amount of money equal to the previous better's plus an additional amount within the limit.

4. Or he *re-raises* (if a previous player has raised) by putting into the pot an amount equal to the raiser's plus an additional amount. Any active player can re-raise the re-raiser by putting into the pot an amount equal to the re-raiser's plus an additional amount, etc. Each player in proper turn must follow this procedure until:

A. Only one player remains in the game; he wins the pot. Should all the other players drop out and only one player remains, he does not have to expose his hole card.

B. Or until two or more players have put an equal amount of money into the pot, which means the opening bet, raise, or re-raise if any has been *met* by all the active players.

If two or more active players are still in the game and all bets have been met by these players, the dealer continues the deal by dealing each player one card (their third card) face up in the same rotation as before, except that from now until each active player has been dealt a complete hand, or if only one player is active, the cards must be dealt in the following manner: The dealer cannot pick up the remaining stock, but must leave the stock resting on the table. Dealing must be done with one hand, picking one card at a time off the top of the stock.

This rule is highly recommended to minimize dealer mistakes and to help eliminate cheating on the deal. This method of dealing is used in most of the high-stake games the author has witnessed.

SECOND ROUND OF BETTING

The player holding the highest ranking hand with the two upcards has the option of making the first play, which consists of:

1. *Dropping out* of the pot; and this he signifies by saying, "Out," and throwing his hand face down into the discard pile.

2. *Checking,* which he signifies by saying, "Check"—which means he desires to play but does not desire to make a bet at present.

3. *Betting,* which he signifies by putting an amount of money into the pot, within the limit.

If the player who has the option of betting does not bet, the turn to check, bet, or drop out passes to the player on his left. This procedure continues until all players have had their turn of play.

Should all the players *fail to bet* and there are two or more remaining players in the game, which means they have *checked,* the dealer deals each player one card (his fourth card) face up in the same rotation as before.

But should a player make a bet, each player in turn starting with the player to that player's left must:

1. *Play* or *stay,* by putting into the pot an amount equal to the previous better's.

2. *Drop, fold up,* or *go out,* by throwing the three cards he is holding face down into the discard pile.

3. *Raise,* by putting into the pot an amount equal to the previous better's plus an additional amount within the limit.

4. *Re-raise,* provided a previous player has raised. This is done by putting into the pot an amount to equal the raiser's plus an additional amount. Any active player can re-raise the re-raiser by putting into the pot an amount equal to the re-raiser's plus an additional amount, etc.

A player cannot check after a bet has been made. Any player who had previously checked must abide by the above four rules.

This procedure is followed until only one player is left in the game and he wins the pot, or two or more active players remain in the game and all bets have been met by the remaining players.

The dealer then deals each player another card face up in the proper rotation for a total of three upcards plus a hole card, and the third round of betting takes place under the same rules as for the second round.

On completion of that betting round, if there are still active players, the dealer deals each player one upcard in proper turn for a total of five cards to each player.

FOURTH AND FINAL ROUND OF BETTING

This is the final round of betting. The same rules govern this play as are stipulated for the second round of betting, except that a play hand is now called a *call hand.* If at any time before the hand is called only one player remains in the game, he wins the pot and does not have to expose his hole card. The only time the players must expose their hole cards is when a call is made after each player has been dealt five cards.

A *call* is similar to a *play* or *stay* in Round 2, only it completes the hand.

The dealer must call attention to, by announcing orally, the highest-ranking hand at each turn of play. Should any player hold a hand comprised of a pair or better, he must call it so that all players can hear. He must also call possible flushes or straights, and must announce the last round of cards being dealt.

SHOWDOWN

When the final betting round is over, all active players, starting with the player who is being called and rotating to the left clockwise, must turn their hole card face up on the table for all the players to see. The player holding the highest-ranking hand wins the pot. For further rules on tied hands see page 232 under "General Rules for Poker."

On completion of each showdown the game continues in the same manner with a new deal.

Additional Rules at Stud Poker

MISDEALS

Whenever a misdeal occurs there must be a new shuffle and cut. The same dealer deals again. Should the same dealer make a second misdeal, the deal passes to the player to the dealer's left.

MISDEALS—YES OR NO?

1. If one or more cards are exposed in cutting or reuniting the cut packets, there is a misdeal.

2. If the pack has not been offered to the proper player to cut and the betting has not started, there is a misdeal.

3. If the pack has not been cut and the betting has not started, there is a misdeal.

4. If one or more cards are observed face up in the pack and the betting has not started, there is a misdeal.

5. If the dealer exposes his own or a player's hole card while dealing it, or a card is found face up while dealing a player a hole card, there is a misdeal.

6. If a player exposes his hole card after it is dealt face down, it is *not a misdeal*. Nor can a player call for a face-down card to be his new hole card. He must face down the exposed card, and it continues to be his hole card. A player must protect his hole card at all times.

7. If an imperfect pack is found being used containing fewer cards than the standard pack or duplicate cards, the play must stop immediately on its discovery, and the players take out of the pot the money they put into it. If it is discovered after a pot has been collected, the previous hands stand, and are legitimate.

8. If any player has been dealt out, or an extra hand has been dealt in, there is a misdeal.

9. If a player (or players) has been dealt too many or too few cards before the betting has started, there is a misdeal.

10. If the dealer has dealt a player a hole card out of turn and that player has looked at it, there is a misdeal.

PASSING THE DEAL

A dealer cannot pass his deal in his turn to deal unless incompetent to deal the cards.

DEAD HANDS

If a player holds too few or too many cards during the betting interval or at the showdown, his hand is foul or dead. But should this be discovered after that player has collected the pot, it stands as a legitimate hand.

ON BEING DEALT AN EXPOSED CARD

If a card is found face up in the pack and the betting has started, the player must take that card in his turn of play, except if it is the first card to be dealt of a new round. That card is immediately *burned* (put to the bottom of the pack, *out of play*), and after the betting has been completed on that round, the dealer must burn enough other cards from the top of the pack so that the total number of burned cards equals the active number of players in the game.

DEALING IN MORE OR FEWER PLAYERS

If a dealer deals a player out or deals an extra hand in, and it is discovered before the players have looked at their hole cards, and if the error can be corrected so that each player receives his proper cards (by shifting a card from one player to another and placing the extra card or cards back on top of the pack or dealing one or more cards from the pack *without any of the cards being exposed to any player*), there is not a misdeal.

EXPOSING THE FIRST CARD OF A ROUND

If the dealer exposes the top card of the pack before the betting has been completed on the previous round, he leaves the card face up on the pack until the betting on that round is completed. After the betting has been completed on that round, the dealer must burn or bury from the top of the pack as many cards (including the exposed card) as there are active players left in the game. Under no conditions are the players permitted to look at the burned cards. Thereafter, the play continues according to the rules.

IMPROPER DEALING

A dealer is not permitted to deal the first card face up and the second card face down. The first card must be dealt face down, becoming the player's hole card.

PROTECTING A HOLE CARD

A player must protect his hole card at all times. Protecting a hole card is to permit no other player to know its identity, regardless of whether the player is active or dead.

A player is not permitted at any time to turn up his hole card and call for his next card face down.

A player, when folding up, is not permitted to expose his hole card to any of the players or to mention its identity.

CHECKING ON THE LAST ROUND

If a player checks on the last round, all other players in order to check too must be able to beat the checking player's four open cards. Otherwise a check is not permitted. For example, a player who has checked has a pair of open aces. The next and following players *cannot check* unless they can beat the open pair, although they may bet if the situation permits. This rule is incorporated to protect a player's hand against another player who calls an impossible hand, although there is no penalty that could be imposed on a player for failure to comply.

BETTING OUT OF TURN

The following rules apply to staying, calling, or raising out of turn. A player making a bet out of turn must leave the bet in the pot. He cannot take it back, and the play reverts to the proper player. When it is the proper turn of the player who bet out of turn, he must do one of the following:

1. If no bet has been made by any preceding player, the bet stands as is.

2. If a bet has been made by a previous player smaller than the bet made out of turn, it stands as a raise.

3. If a bet has been made by a previous player equal to the bet out of turn, it stands as a stay or call. The player who bet out of turn cannot raise.

4. If a previous bet was raised by another player and the bet is in excess of the amount bet by the out-of-turn player, the out-of-turn player may drop out of the pot, stay or call by equaling the bet made by the previous betters, or re-raise the pot after equaling the bet.

VERBAL BETTING

If a player in his turn of play announces orally that he is making a bet, he must abide by the announcement. He cannot increase or decrease the bet. Should a player make an announcement not in his proper turn of play and has not placed any money in the pot, it should be disregarded and considered a joke or an attempted bluff.

TAPPING OUT

If a player has put all his money into the pot and no longer can bet, it is called a tap-out—when that player is permitted to play for the size of the pot up to the time he no longer has money. If the other players keep betting they put their bets to one side, as the tapping-out player has no interest in that side pot. The tapping-out player receives cards until the hand is completed, and should he have the highest-ranking hand on the showdown, he wins only the pot, not the side pot; that is won by the player having the highest-ranking cards among the remaining betters. A player is permitted only one tap-out during a Poker session.

A player when tapping out can raise only if he still has an amount equal to the maximum limit, so in case of a re-raise he can call the bet. A player cannot tap out with money on the table.

IMPROPER FOLD-UP

If a player decides to drop out of the pot or fold up, he cannot give an indication, verbal or otherwise, until it is his proper turn of play. Strict observance of this rule will make for a better game. Should he fold up out of turn his hand is dead.

DEALER ERRS IN CALLING HIGHEST OPEN HAND

When the dealer errs in calling the highest open hand and as a result the wrong player bets (if it is discovered before the betting is completed on that round), the dealer must correct the play by giving back out of the pot the money that was improperly bet. This is the only time a player is permitted to take money out of the pot.

GOING THROUGH THE DISCARDS

In no circumstances is a player permitted to look at the discards either before or after the showdown. Nor is a nonactive player permitted to look at an active player's hole card before or after the showdown, unless a bet has been called and the player is compelled to expose his hole card.

LOOKING AT UNDEALT CARDS

Looking at the top card or any of the undealt cards while a hand is in progress, regardless of whether the player is out of that pot, is not permitted.

LENDING MONEY OR CHIPS

Under no circumstances is a player allowed to borrow money or chips from another player during the play. If a player desires to borrow money from another player, it must be done before the cards are dealt. Passing money or chips from one player to another during the play is not permitted.

BETTING FOR ANOTHER PLAYER

Under no circumstances is a player permitted to bet for another player.

ANGLING

Angling is positively prohibited—for example, discussion among two or more players about splitting the pot regardless of the winner or giving back part of the money, asking for a free ride or call, or any conspiracy toward violation of the Poker rules.

OVERS IN THE POT

No money or chips may be taken out of the pot except that a player may take out his proper change after placing a bet in his turn of play (it must be observed by all the players that the proper change is taken), or as specified under the infraction when the dealer errs. Should a player put into the pot a larger amount than required and should another player make a bet, change may not be taken out of the pot.

EXPOSED HANDS ON SHOWDOWN

All players active or nonactive are entitled to see all active players' hole cards on the showdown, provided a bet has been called.

ILLEGAL CUTTING OF CARDS

Under no circumstances may a player ask to cut the cards after a bet has been made. I must stress particularly that cards cannot be cut *after* the deal has started or for that matter at any other time except *before* the start of the deal.

MAN AND WIFE

Most of the Reno casinos forbid man and wife to play Stud Poker at the same table. This is a sound ruling, and I incorporate it into my rules. The exception is when they play in a small-limit game primarily for pastime.

CRITICISM

A player is not permitted in any circumstances to criticize another player's methods. Stud Poker is a game in which each player plays his own hand at his own risk as he desires. No consideration should be expected by one player from another.

Stud Poker Variations

In the following selections of the most popular variations of Stud Poker the rules are those that apply to Stud Poker itself unless otherwise specified. Most of the cheating methods used in Stud are used also in most of its variations. Tips on how to improve your game are contained in the chapter "Strategy at Poker."

STUD POKER DEUCES WILD

Played exactly as is Stud Poker, except that the deuces are wild, and that on the showdown, cards do not speak for themselves; player must announce the value of his hand in his proper turn of play. Announcement cannot be changed after a player's turn of play has passed on the showdown. Often a joker is added as an extra wild card.

LOW HAND STUD

Played like Stud Poker, with the following exceptions:
1. The lowest-ranking hand wins the pot.
2. The player with the lowest-ranking card or cards showing has the option of making the first bet in each round of betting.

SIX-CARD STUD

Played exactly as is Stud Poker, with the following additional rules:

1. A player is dealt his sixth card face down to give him two hole cards.

2. The best five cards out of six may be used to form a poker hand.

SEVEN-CARD STUD POKER

A variation of Stud also known in the Western part of the country as Seven-Toed Pete. Played exactly as is Stud Poker, with the following exceptions and additional rules.

THE DEAL

Each player is dealt two hole cards singly in proper rotation, as described under dealing in "General Rules for Poker." The third card is dealt face up for each player, then a round of betting takes place, as in Stud Poker. The fourth card is dealt face up to each active player, and another round of betting takes place. The fifth and sixth cards are dealt face up to each active player; a betting round takes place after the fifth card has been dealt, another betting round after the sixth card has been dealt. The seventh card is now dealt face down, giving each active player his third hole card, and the last betting round takes place. On the showdown, each player selects for his hand the best five cards of his seven. One should be especially cautious in sorting a five-card hand from the seven cards dealt.

SEVEN-CARD STUD, LOW HOLE CARD WILD

Played exactly as is Seven-card Stud, except that a player can call his lowest-ranking hole card wild. Cards of a similar denomination are wild only for the holder.

In another variation any one of the hole cards is called wild.

SEVEN-CARD STUD, DEUCES WILD PLUS THE JOKER

Played exactly as is Seven-card Stud, except that a joker is added as a wild card and the deuces are wild. In this variation of Stud, cards shown do not speak; player must call or announce his hand. Once called, hand must stand; it cannot be changed.

BASEBALL POKER

A variation of Seven-card Stud, with the following additional rules.

1. All players must ante before cards are dealt.

2. All 9's are wild.

3. All 3's are wild.

4. Whenever a 3 is dealt, all players must ante again or drop out.

5. Any 4 dealt face up entitles the holder to receive his next card face down, excepting when it is the sixth card dealt. Then a player must receive his last card face up.

6. Best hand, if you can conceive it, wins.

Another variation of this game is:

1. Same.

2. Same.

3. A 3 dealt face up and your hand is dead; a 3 dealt face down is a wild card.

4. Same as 5.

General Rules for High-Low Poker

High-Low Poker has been gaining popularity in the last few years. Perhaps the most popular of the High-Low games is Seven-card High-Low Stud, which had a vogue with G.I.'s in World War II.

Most of the rules that apply to Draw or Stud Poker apply to the High-Low variations, with the following additional rules.

OBJECT OF THE GAME

For a player at the showdown to hold a higher- or a lower-ranking hand—or both at the same time—than any other active player. (Holding both is possible in games of High-Low where the player has more than five cards to select from on the showdown.)

WINNERS ON SHOWDOWN

When playing High-Low, regardless of the variation, the player holding the highest-ranking hand, provided he has declared for high, and the player holding the lowest-ranking hand, provided he has declared for low, share the pot equally. In High-Low poker with five cards, the cards speak for themselves on the showdown, as is described under the Draw or Stud Poker rules as given under the caption "Showdown." (See pages 245 and 263.)

But when wild cards are used or the game permits a player to select a five-card hand from among six or more cards, then the player must state the value of his hand. If a player declares his hand incorrectly and the pot has not yet been collected, he may correct the error; but if the pot has been collected the error must stand.

The rank of Low Poker is inverse to the standard rank of a

high hand. If the hand contains less than a pair, its determinant is its highest-ranking card; if two players are tied as to highest-ranking card, the next highest-ranking card decides the winner, etc. See rank of Poker hands in Low Poker for further details (page 236) under "General Rules for Poker."

ANNOUNCING HIGH OR LOW OR BOTH

ON THE SHOWDOWN

There is only one sound method of announcing high or low or both high and low before the showdown, although all other game-book experts give you several methods.

Here is the only method the author recommends:

Prior to the last bets being made before the showdown, each player must covertly take a chip without letting any of the other players see its color and place it in his left hand. Should he decide to go for low, he places a white chip in his hand. Should he decide on high, he places a red chip in his hand. Should he decide on high and low, he places a white and red chip in his hand.

Now, when all the active players have their hands above the table, the dealer starts by asking the player who made the highest bet (the player who is being called) to place his chip or chips on the table in front of his hand. In turn each active player (moving clockwise from the front) does this. After all active players have declared for high or low or both by this show of chips, the showdown takes place.

If players are playing for cash and chips are not available, a nickel can represent a low hand, a dime a high hand.

FAULTY ANNOUNCEMENTS

Following are two methods of declaring high or low which the author does not recommend:

Variation I (not recommended)

The player who is being *called* must expose his hand and make his announcement at the same time. Each active player to that player's left, rotating clockwise, does the same.

This method of declaring one's intentions has a mathematical flaw, which may best be shown in the following example.

A, B, and C are the only active players to remain in the game prior to the showdown. All bets have been met, and A is being *called*. A announces for high, and exposes his hand on the showdown. B sees A's hand and announces accordingly. If A has a visibly better hand, B can decide to announce for low, exposing his hand on the showdown. Player C has the

advantage of seeing both A's and B's hand; should he hold a
higher hand than A, he can announce high; should he hold a
lower hand than B, he can announce low. In some variations
of High-Low it is possible for C after seeing A's and B's hand
to win both ends of the pot by announcing high and low on the
showdown.

The author does not agree that maneuvering for position in
calling should be classified as Poker skill.

Variation II (*not recommended*)

The first active player to the dealer's left after all bets have
been met, prior to the showdown, makes his announcement
for high or low or both. Each active player to this player's left,
rotating clockwise, does the same. After all active players have
made their announcement, the showdown takes place.

Note the mathematical flaw in this common ruling. Three
active players are left prior to the showdown, and all betting
has ceased. A is the player to the dealer's left, B is to A's left,
and C is to B's left. A calls high, B calls high. C cannot lose
by calling low, even before the showdown.

ADDITIONAL RULES FOR HIGH-LOW POKER

1. If the pot cannot be divided equally by the high and low
hand, the indivisible amount goes to the high hand.

2. If two or more players are tied for low, half the pot is
equally divided among the winners tied for low. The other
half of the pot goes to the winner with the high hand. If there
is an indivisible amount left over, the high hand gets it.

ADDITIONAL RULES ON ANNOUNCING HIGH OR LOW

OR BOTH

1. When a player announces for low, he no longer has any
interest in high.

2. When a player announces for high, he no longer has any
interest in low.

3. When a player announces high-low both, he must win
both high and low to collect the pot. Should he announce high-
low and win only one half of his claim, he forfeits all rights to
the pot.

BETTING

If the game is a variation of Draw Poker, the betting rules
are similar to those for Draw; if a variation of Stud Poker, they
are similar to Stud Poker's rules unless otherwise specified for
the particular game.

SEVEN-CARD STUD HIGH-LOW

The game is played just as is Seven-card Stud, except that the highest- and lowest-ranking hands split the pot equally. See "General Rules for High-Low Poker."

DEALER'S CHOICE

A favorite with G.I.'s during World War II; and the particular reason for its popularity was the fact that G.I.'s hailing from one part of the country were accustomed to their locally favorite game, while others from a different part had their own favorite parish game. To make everybody happy (although in the general rejoicing most of the skill characteristic of Poker was usually lost), Dealer's Choice was the remedy.

Dealer's Choice is exactly what the name implies. When it is your turn to deal, you have the privilege of naming the game to be played, and often a little lesson in teaching your version of the game is necessary. As dealer you may deal any game you know how to play—Stud, Draw, Seven-card Stud, Low Ball, Spit in the Ocean, High-Low—or any other.

CHAPTER TWENTY-FIVE

Poker Odds and Probabilities

GENERAL AND PERCENTAGE

The relative value of Poker hands was not just conjured up by some rulemaker or arbitrarily assigned by the first primitive Poker players. It was instead determined by counting the exact number of possible five-card Poker hands in a fifty-two-card pack. The counting was under a mathematical formula based on the theory and doctrine of permutations and combinations, a formula used for calculating probabilities.

Making use of it, the exact total of possible five-card Poker hands was determined; this total was divided into groups or ranks—such as a pair, two pair, three of a kind, a straight, etc. These ranks were then arranged in relative value according to the frequency of their occurrence.

There are 2,598,960 possible Poker hands in a fifty two-card pack. This is the number of groups of five into which fifty-two different cards can be arranged, and is equal to the product of 52 × 51 × 50 × 49 × 48 = 311,875,200 divided by the product of 5 × 4 × 3 × 2 × 1 = 120, producing a final total of 2,598,960. A simplified method of calculation is to set up the permutations and arrangements as fractions and cancel them out:

$$\frac{52 \times 51 \times 50 \times 49 \times 48}{5 \times 4 \times 3 \times 2 \times 1} = 2,598,960$$

The above method of calculation, plus clear thinking and a knowledge of elementary arithmetic, determines the occurrence frequency of different five-card Poker hands.

ROYAL FLUSHES

There is only one royal flush in each suit; there are four suits, for a total of four royal flushes.

STRAIGHT FLUSHES

To calculate the number of straight flushes, first find the number of straight flushes in one suit. Let us take spades. Starting from the bottom and working up we get nine straight flushes in spades: The ace, 2, 3, 4, 5, the 2, 3, 4, 5, 6, the 3, 4, 5, 6, 7, and so on. Since we have nine straight flushes in each suit, we get a total of thirty-six straight flushes for the four suits.

FOUR OF A KIND

Though there are only thirteen four-of-a-kind combinations (one for each denomination), there are 624 Poker hands containing four of a kind. With each of the thirteen combinations, the fifth card could be any one of the other forty-eight cards. Therefore, we must multiply thirteen by forty-eight to get the total possible hands containing the thirteen four-of-a-kind combinations.

FULL HOUSES

To calculate the number of possible full houses is easy— when you know how. Let's take three deuces as a starting point. There are four possible combinations of three deuces, since we are are making use of only three deuces out of the four. But we have thirteen different denominations from ace to king, and each of these has four possible combinations, for a total of fifty-two possible three-card combinations. Now we must find the possible number of pairs to be matched with the three of a kind. Suppose we start with a pair of fours. The fours can be paired six ways. The same holds true for all the other denominations. But we cannot use the deuces; those have already been used to form the three of a kind. That leaves us with twelve different denominations. Multiplying, we get a total of seventy-two possible pairs to hold with our three deuces. To get the total number of full houses we multiply the fifty-two possible three of a kind by the seventy-two possible pairs, and get a total of 3,744 full houses.

FLUSHES

To find the number of possible flushes we first must find the number of five-card arrangements that can be formed with thirteen cards of the same suit. This we cancel out as follows:

$$\frac{13 \times 12 \times 11 \times 10 \times 9}{5 \times 4 \times 3 \times 2 \times 1} = 1287 \text{ total}$$

But this total also includes one royal flush and nine straight flushes. Subtracting 10 from 1,287, we get 1,277 flushes in one suit. But we have four suits—hearts, clubs, spades, and diamonds—therefore we multiply the 1,277 by 4, and get a total of 5,108 flushes.

STRAIGHTS

A simple method to calculate the number of possible straights is to start from the bottom and work up. For example, we use four aces, four deuces, four 3's, four 4's, and four 5's. Multiplying $4 \times 4 \times 4 \times 4 \times 4$, we get 1,024 straights 5-high. We get a like number headed by each of the following high cards: 6, 7, 8, 9, 10, J, Q, K, and ace. Adding, we get a total of 10,240, from which we must discount four royal flushes and thirty-six straight flushes, leaving us a total of 10,200 straights.

THREE OF A KIND

We have already calculated the number of hands containing three of a kind at fifty-two (see Full Houses). But the two remaining cards in the hand must be odd cards. To prevent including the chances of making four of a kind or a full house when computing the chances solely for three of a kind, we must calculate that the first odd card must be one of forty-eight cards and the second odd card must be one of forty four. Our complete figure is obtained thus:

$$\frac{52 \times 48 \times 44}{2 \times 1} = 54,912, \text{ the number of hands con} \\ \text{taining three of a kind.}$$

TWO PAIRS

We already have calculated the possible number of pairs with each denomination as six (see Full Houses). Multiplying six by thirteen denominations, we get a total of seventy-eight possible pairs. A player may hold any one of these seventy-eight pairs plus another pair—but not of the same denomination—which total we arrive at by multiplying the twelve denominations by the six possible ways a pair can be in each denomination, for a total of seventy-two pairs.

Now, find the number of ways two pairs can be arranged, making use of the fifth, odd card; and our total figure is obtained thus:

$$\frac{78 \times 72 \times 44}{2 \times 1} = 123,552$$

ONE PAIR

The total number of possible pairs is seventy-eight, as already calculated; therefore the player can hold any one of seventy-eight pairs. But with this pair he must also hold three odd cards. Our total figure is obtained thus:

$$\frac{78 \times 48 \times 44 \times 40}{3 \times 2 \times 1} = 1,098,240$$

NO PAIRS

To obtain the total number of hands containing less than one pair, merely add all the hands containing a pair or better, and subtract that total from the total possible five-card hands, which we have already calculated at 2,598,960. It gives us a total of 1,302,540.

To ascertain the chances of being dealt any one of the above-ranking hands *pat* (in the first five cards dealt), divide the final total into 2,598,960, which again is the number of possible five-card Poker hands in a fifty-two card deck. For example, if you want to find your chances of getting a flush dealt pat you divide 5,108 (total number of flushes in a fifty two-card pack) into 2,598,960, and the result is 509.80. Our chance of drawing a pat flush is one in 509.80.

The chances of being dealt any certain pat hand are the same, regardless of the number of players in the game. The same holds true in drawing cards to improve your hand.

The 2,598,960 possible five-card Poker hands are divided as follows:

Rank of the hand	Possible number of each
Royal Flush	4
Straight Flush	36
Four of a Kind	624
Full House	3,744
Flush	5,108
Straight	10,200
Three of a Kind	54,912
Two Pairs	123,552
One Pair	1,098,240
No-pair hand	1,302,540
TOTAL	2,598,960

Note: Although there are actually only thirteen four-of a kind from ace to king, the figure of 624 as shown above gives you the total of probabilities caused by holding one of the other forty-eight cards to make a five-card Poker hand.

The 1,302,540 possible five-card no pair hands are divided as follows:

Rank of the hand	Possible number of each
Ace High	502,860
King High	335,580
Queen High	213,180
Jack High	127,500
Ten High	70,380
Nine High	34,680
Eight High	14,280
Seven High	4,080
TOTAL	1,302,540

The lowest ranking five-card Poker hand is comprised of the 7, 5, 4, 3, 2 in various suits. The above chart is particularly instructive to players who play High-Low variants of Poker.

In recent years numerous Poker tables have been printed purporting to give the correct odds and probabilities on being dealt a certain valuable hand in one's first five cards. The authors of these tables harp on the same theme, about as follows.

Almost a century ago one of the Hoyle revisions on Poker carried the first Poker chart, which embodied many mistakes because of errors in computation. Since Hoyle is now in the public domain, the authors or publishers of Poker tables have copied the Hoyle tables without checking them for mistakes. The mistakes are repeated, but you are soberly informed that the tables were checked and double-checked for accuracy, and then the authors conclude by publishing their own Poker tables—which usually contain one or more errors; and the rest of their figures are never exact but always approximate.

Here are the exact chances and probabilities of drawing various Poker hands in the first five cards dealt.

CHANCES OF HOLDING VARIOUS POKER HANDS IN THE FIRST FIVE CARDS DEALT

Rank of hand	Probability	Chance
Royal Flush	.0000015	1 in 649,740
Straight Flush	.0000138	1 in 72,193.33
Four of a Kind	.00024	1 in 4,165
Full House	.00144	1 in 694.16
Flush	.00196	1 in 508.80
Straight	.00392	1 in 254.8
Three of a Kind	.0211	1 in 47.32
Two pairs	.0475	1 in 21.03
One pair	.422	1 in 2.36
No-pair hand	.501	1 in 1.99

Note: The last decimal point has been dropped from all the above figures excepting figures 4,165 and 649,740.

In computing the probability of being dealt any of the above hands, the reader must bear in mind that when the probability is 0, the event is impossible. When it is 1, the event is certain. All other probabilities are expressed in decimals falling between these two numbers. When the probability is .50 we say the chances are even or half and half. The probability of being dealt one pair in the first five cards is .442, which indicates that the chances of being dealt a pair with the first five cards dealt are less than half. But being dealt a no-pair hand is .501, almost even.

CHANCES OF HOLDING A FOUR-CARD FLUSH OR A FOUR-CARD STRAIGHT WITH THE FIRST FIVE CARDS DEALT

Rank of hand	Chance
Four-card flush	1 in 23
Any four-card straight	1 in 5.9
Four-card straight open at one end	1 in 115
Four-card straight open at both ends.........	1 in 28
Four-card straight open inside	1 in 8

How to Use Preceding Poker Tables

The preceding Poker tables are not intended to be an aid to better Poker playing but are published, *first*, to prove the relative value of Poker hands; *second*, to settle disputes that arise regarding the probabilities or chances of drawing certain valuable hands in the first five cards dealt. . . .

And *last*, as a guide in setting the proper odds on certain unusual Poker bets! For example, in the New England States, it is common for the bookmaker to lay 15 to 1 that a single player is not dealt a four-card flush in his first five cards. And the bookmakers get plenty of action. Why? Because the players have no idea of the correct odds. By glancing at the chart you will observe that the correct odds are 22 to 1; the bookmaker has 30-10/23 per cent in his favor when laying odds of 15 to 1 on a four-flush.

Another example of the usefulness of these Poker charts was unfolded to me at one of my recent lectures when a member of the audience asked me if this were a fair bet: laying odds of 2 to 1 to any single player that he would not hold a pair or better in his first five cards dealt. When I informed him that the odds were approximately even for either player and that he was taking a beating of 33-1/3 per cent, he was surprised. Both these problems and countless others like them can easily be answered by referring to the preceding tables.

CHANCES OF HOLDING VARIOUS POKER HANDS IN THE FIRST FIVE CARDS DEALT WHEN THE JOKER IS ADDED MAKING A FIFTY-THREE-CARD PACK

Rank of hand	Number of each	Chance
Five of a kind	13	1 in 220,745
Royal Flush	24	1 in 119,570.2
Straight Flush	216	1 in 13,285.5
Four of a kind	3,120	1 in 919.7
Full House	6,552	1 in 437.9
Flush	7,768	1 in 369.3
Straight	20,532	1 in 139.7
Three of a Kind	137,280	1 in 20.9
Two Pairs	123,552	1 in 23.2
One pair	1,268,088	1 in 2.26
No-pair hand	1,302,540	1 in 2.20
Total hands	2,869,685	

Note: The last decimal point has been dropped from all the figures under "Chance" except the figure 220,745.

The author brings to the attention of the reader a very unusual mathematical situation which arises in Joker Wild regarding the relative value of three of a kind and two pair. Studying the above chart closely, the reader will observe that the chances of drawing three of a kind are one in 137,280 and the chances of drawing two pair are one in 123,552. Since there are more chances of drawing three of a kind than two pair, two pair should be of a higher rank and beat three of a kind.

This peculiar situation is caused by the fact that there are 82,368 possible five-card Poker hands that contain a pair plus a joker. When a player holds one of these 82,368 hands he values his hand at three of a kind, making the joker count the same denomination as the pair he is holding. But should we permit the two pair to become a higher-ranking hand than three of a kind, we would accomplish nothing, because the player holding one of the 82,368 possible Poker hands containing a pair plus the joker would use the joker to form another pair with the highest-ranking odd card and would value his hand at two pairs. This would bring the total number of two pair in a pack of fifty-three cards to 205,920 and the possible number of three of a kind to 54,912. Under these conditions, considering the relative value of both hands, three of a kind must remain of higher value than two pair.

There are two solutions to this baffling little puzzle, which I give you in case among my readers there will be a few players who may want to play a mathematically sound game. As for my incorporating either of the two following rules in my laws for Joker Wild, I say no, because I have come to learn that you cannot change habits that easily. Anyway, here are the two rules, which will mathematically permit three of a kind to retain its higher value in relation to two pair.

1. If a player possesses a hand containing a pair plus the joker, the joker cannot be considered wild, and therefore carries no value whatever; and the joker must be considered an odd card.

2. If a player possesses a hand comprised of paired aces, kings, queens, jacks, 10's, 9's, or 8's plus the joker, he is permitted to rank his hand as three of a kind. Should he possess a pair ranking lower than 8's plus the joker, he cannot value his hand at more than two pair.

Bucking a 5 Per Cent Cut in a House Game

I don't care if you are the best Stud player in the country; if you play in a house game with rank suckers and the house takes a cut of 5 per cent of the pot from a winner, you must go broke if you play often enough.

Contrary to the operator's claim that the charge is 5 per cent, it is much greater, and at times it amounts to 10 per cent. Poker is one of the very few games where the house takes a cut not only on the player's winnings, but also on the winning player's money.

For example:

Four Stud players play an entire hand to the showdown, the pot totals $20, and the house takes a 5 per cent cut of $1. The winner of the pot has paid a cut of 5 per cent on his own $5, the money he had to gamble to win. Therefore, the house is actually taking a cut of 6-2/3 per cent on that player's winnings.

Suppose two players play a hand to the showdown. The pot totals $20. The cut amounts to $1, same as in the four-handed game. In this case the house is extracting a 10 per cent cut.

In order to have a nucleus of hard fact to work with, I clocked thirty different Stud games for a period of one month. The betting limit in these games ranged from $2 to $5. After these clockings were averaged, I got the following approximate answers:

1. That it takes about one and one-half minutes to play an average hand.
2. That in a fast Stud game, approximately forty hands are dealt out per hour.
3. That the average pot contains about $10 on the showdown (using the two above betting limits in my clockings).

To prove how strong this 5 per cent cut is over a Poker session, let us take a six-handed game. The limit is $2; the average hand will take one and one-half minutes to play; we have played forty hands in an hour's play.

The average pot contains $10, the operator takes a cut (charge) of 5 per cent totaling 50¢ on the average pot for a total of $20 per hour. The game lasts six hours, giving the operator a $120 cut for the six hours.

Let us assume that each player entered the game with $30 and luck, or the law of averages equalized itself for each player. The total money all the players possessed at the start of the game was $180. The total cut is $120. Now there is only $60 left in the game; or each player has paid 66-2/3 per cent of his original amount, meaning that he has paid a cut of $20 out of his original $30, leaving him $10.

Should that game last eight hours, which plenty of Stud

games do, and should only two players be left (meaning that the rest have gone broke), these players have only $20 between them—the operator has taken a charge of $160 out of the original $180. In other words, the house's cut amounted to 88-8/9 per cent of the total amount during the night! Believe it or not, there are millions of Stud players who try to win under these conditions. Just imagine if you play Stud two or three nights or so a week—what percentage you pay the operator!

There are numerous operators who are not satisfied with the 5 per cent and who often steal an extra amount from the pot. This is usually done when making change or taking out the cut, and the active player who wins the pot is so happy to win that he seldom notices the operator has taken the cut not to mention the extra amount.

It is difficult to see the logic of the operators of Poker games. If they lowered their cut to 2 or 3 per cent they would have a Poker game going most of the time. But as it is, they break most of the players in a few weeks, then wonder why they no longer have a game.

Many Poker players who stay away for a while try to figure out why they went broke. Often they think they were cheated. Maybe they were; as a rule that 5 per cent did the trick. But they eventually come back again trying to buck the impossible.

If you play in such a game, can read the above analysis, and still think you can beat that game, don't read any further, brother, because it won't do you any good.

The next thing a player should learn is to protect his money against cheaters. If you can't do that you'd better stop playing Poker right now. Take time out now to read about cheating at Draw or Stud Poker and the chapter on gamblers and cheats. Spend a little time learning to protect your money against card cheaters. One second of sleep in a fast Poker game might break you for that session and plenty of others. Among other things, it will pay to keep your eye on the discards. Often a player who is not a skilled cheater will reach for a valuable card of use in his hand. When you catch him, he is kidding; when you don't, he takes your money.

CHAPTER TWENTY-SIX

Cheating at Poker

Cheating at Draw Poker

It is much easier for the sharp to cheat at Draw Poker than at Stud for the relatively simple reason that the player at Draw can hold his cards closed in his hand while the hand at Stud remains in full view of the other players on the table before him at all times.

All of the methods (see Chapters Two and Three) of sharpshooters' handling cards crookedly are applicable to Draw Poker. Marked cards give the cheater an insuperable advantage; and there's nothing the merely skilled player can do that will bring him up even with such mechanical devices as bottom and second dealing, palming, false cuts, stacking on the pick-up, the pull-through, and shifting the cut. . . .

But sharpers have found that the most consistently profitable way to cheat at Draw Poker is to work in a team with a confederate or confederates. Example: Seated next to each other, one sharp stacks the pack, then offers it to his confederate for the cut; the confederate does cut, but either he uses a *false cut* or he cuts into a *crimp* put in the deck by the dealer-stacker.

Sharpers don't have to sit next to each other. They can operate at any distance.

Let's say you're in a Poker game. You're no cheat. A good-natured stranger sits down to play. Across from this stranger sits another player who looks like a pretty good guy and who spends his time chatting with you about the Series, maybe. You don't suspect them; how could they be confederates? They never even glance at each other, much less speak to each other.

But, brother, as of right now they've got you boxed; they have already used time-honored, sure-fire methods of reaching an understanding and working together against you. That understanding is based on the gambler's sign language, practically as old as cards and understood by card sharps all over the world. If there's any international language, that is it.

Matter of fact, these signals are known to the sharps as the *international signs.*

Watch these players! When a man casually puts his open hand across his chest or flat on the table in front of him, that open palm is the first word in the crooks' dictionary. Whether this man means it that way or not, he is giving a sign which is interpreted by sharps from New Orleans to Singapore as: "I'm a professional crook. Is everything at this table all right? Does anybody want to team with me?"

And now watch. There are two replies to this opening gambit. The real pro can signal:

With the open hand on chest or table: "Right. I'm a sharper too. We're teammates, and I'll see you later about the split. Let's go!"

But with a clenched fist: "I'm a crook all right, but I happen to work alone. I'm too damn good for the likes of you gangsters. Keep your hands off and your trap shut!"

The first signal implies all the rest. Even the latter sign-off doesn't preclude further signals throughout the play. Using their wordless language, sharpers who never saw each other before can table-talk throughout a game as eloquently as if they were allowed to use an intercom telephone across the board to each other.

Here are some common manual signals:

I need a king: dealt cards held well back in the palm of the hand with the index finger on the edge of the design. (To indicate an ace, the index finger on the edge of the card; the position of the finger, whether toward the top edge or the lower margin of the card, indicates specific rank of card held or card wanted.)

I need a 3: cards held by the lower tip.

I have two of a kind: second-from-left card nervously pulled out of hand and jogged up and down.

I have a spade, a heart, etc.: jogging the first-at-left card in hand indicates a crucial club holding; the second, a diamond; the third, a heart; the fourth, a spade.

I have two pair: two fingers extended from the closed fist on lap or table.

Raise now, partner!: This signal is given by putting down the clenched fist on the table and raising the thumb. (These signals, whether with card or thumb or finger, are for split seconds only.)

The spread: But maybe now I'd better go into detail.

Let's say a guy named Joe, crook No. 1, holds three kings in a Poker hand. The pot is big and growing bigger. Joe wants to win, and is sure that four kings (if he had 'em) would take the pot. So he signals to crook No. 2, name of Harry, asking

(index finger on edge of design) if he has a king. Harry signals yes.

Now all the boys have to do is get that king from Harry's
hand to Joe's—across the table. They resort to the *spread*.

First step in the spread is for Joe to get rid of a card. Natu-
·rally this is not one of his three kings but one of the two
worthless cards in his hand. He uses sleight of hand to duck
this card into his pocket or he may put it under his armpit or
knee angle. Or, if he's near the discard pile, he then and there
can dispose of the card by putting it into the dirt, which is
what gamblers call the discard pile. First he palms the card.
Then, in a seemingly harmless gesture, he reaches over and nervously pushes the discards a little to one side, as though they
annoyed him. But what he really does is to furtively drop his
unwanted card on top of the discard pile.

Now he has only four cards in his hand. Joe keeps raising.
He keeps getting raised back, and at last he is called. He has to
show his hand—that four-card hand. "Four kings!" he announces confidently, smacking his cards down as a unit, one
squarely on top of the other, so that only the top card shows.

This is the moment Harry, across the table, has been awaiting. Since Joe signaled, he has had his king palmed neatly in
his right hand (the face of the card toward the palm). Now,
before anyone else can reach over to spread Joe's hand, Harry
does it. And as he sweeps his hand over the cards to spread
them, he slips in his king to make the fifth—and winning—
card.

The spread shows how neatly gamblers work together and
what skill they have used to perfect their teamwork. To catch
a team or teams of crooks working together, watch for signals
such·as those required for the spread. Sharpers always try to
work sitting opposite one another. They never look each other
squarely in the face, but keep their eyes glued on each other's
hands.

So keep your eye peeled for that slanting professional look.
But when the sharper at Draw Poker does not have a confederate to work with, then the sharp has to work lone hand,
and his best bet is the hold-out, called H-O by the wise players.

You've guessed it: H-O means the sharper slips the good
card or cards out of a succession of bad hands. These stolen
cards he secretes about his person until the right cards are
dealt him. Then he switches the hold-outs back again to make
a winning hand.

Naturally, the main job then is to get rid of the extra cards,
once the hold-outs are switched back into the hand.

Say the gambler has been holding out three aces. He is
dealt a fourth ace, and his big moment has come. Quickly he

pivots the three holdouts from under his knee and into his hand. Now he holds four aces, all right. But he also has eight cards—an embarrassing number to be caught with in a Poker game.

This fellow does with his three hot cards just what our friend Joe did with his one. He goes into the dirt. If he sits near the discards he goes in right away. If he doesn't, he uses the old H-O for the extra ones until the discards work around near him. Then he quickly pivots them into his palm and into the dirt.

But let's take a sharper who is an expert and appreciates the finer points of cheating. He doesn't like to be bothered with holding extra cards in his hand or with waiting for the discards or with any more H-O's than are strictly necessary.

What does he do then? He tops the pack.

Here is what that means. For simplicity, let's say this sharper too has held out three aces. These he pivots back into the game when a fourth ace is dealt him. But instead of slipping the hold-outs in with his other cards, he keeps them palmed. Then, when the time comes, he discards his three worthless cards and asks for three more.

Now he goes into action. Before the dealer has time to pick up the pack, the sharper finds some pretext to touch it. If possible he brushes it nervously aside; or he may reach over and pretend to tap the pack for good luck. Whatever the pretext, what he really does is slip the three aces on the top of the pack—so that the unsuspecting dealer deals the sharper the same three aces the sharper has been holding out!

Hard, yes! But it's done all the time by experts.

Best way of detecting the kind of cheating described here is to watch the players. Look out for the nervous guy who is always shifting around, touching cards, ears, tie, and so on. Chances are his motions include a few signals.

What the man who frequently hitches his chair up to the table. He's possibly holding out in the crook of his knee. Watch especially for hold-outs in high spades. It's easy to hold out a single card, and an ace of spades is all you need to win many hands.

By the same token, the fellow who reaches into his vest pocket for matches or digs into this pocket for a handkerchief may be holding out under the arm or in a pocket.

The man who holds out in his pocket may even be holding out a whole cold deck, which he switches in at the right moment. And don't think the deal is necessarily honest just because you are dealing: that's a favorite trick for building up false self-confidence. You may be dealing a cold deck, already stacked against you.

Watch the man who loses as well as the one who wins. The loser may be a confederate who will receive his split afterward. He signals too.

Always keep your eyes open for any funny business. If you see something suspicious, pull out of the game. If you don't see anything, keep watching anyway.

When working ocean liners, sharps usually work in teams of four. Their specialty is *cold-decking the sucker*. They don't bother with seconds, bottoms, spreads, or any of the other cheating metohds I have previously explained; they have to score a big touch (touch is an amount won by cheating) to defray their expenses.

It is done like this. The four sharpers pick their intended victim, play on the square for a couple of days, then have a cold deck ready for the moment when the sucker agrees to play pot limit on the suggestion of one of the sharps. He never realizes that a game where each player antes $1 he is to lose $20,000 or $30,000 on one hand—and on probably not more than six raises in all.

The cold-decking is done on the sucker's deal in the following manner:

The sucker agrees to play pot limit. It is his deal. He shuffles the pack, and places it to his right to be cut. A slight hesitation arises when the player to the sucker's left requests the sucker to change a bill. During this brief interval the sharper to the sucker's right has switched in a cold deck.

When the sucker turns to pick up the deck to deal, the sharper to his right executes a false cut to put the sucker at ease that the cards have been cut. The sucker deals the cards, and when he picks up his hand and examines the cards, he is speechless because he has dealt himself a straight flush (king high in hearts)—and only one hand, a royal flush, can beat it.

The player to the sucker's left holds the ace, king, and queen of spades plus two low cards. The next two players usually hold three of a kind, and one of them opens the pot. After the pot is opened the draw takes place, and the player to the sucker's left draws the jack and 10 of spades for a royal flush. The other cheats also draw cards. The sucker stands pat with his straight flush.

Then the sandbagging begins, one confederate betting the entire pot, another doing the same. After this has gone on for about six raises, I.O.U.'s and checks come into play. The sucker will usually bet very big because he rarely if ever suspects cheating while he is dealing. Millions of dollars have been won by sharps with cold decks.

Just to prove to the reader that it is possible for a sucker caught by one of these card mobs to lose $30,000 in one pot when playing pot limit—naturally with the use ·of the cold deck—I give you the following example:

Suppose four card cheaters plus a sucker are playing pot limit. The ante is $1. Each of the five players antes $1 for a total pot of $5 before the cards are dealt. The cheater to the sucker's left we will call Pete, the cheater to Pete's left is Joe. The other two players' names are irrelevant. The sucker will be known as —Mr. Sucker.

The pot is opened by Pete for $5. All the players stay, and each puts $5 into the pot, making a total of $30 in the pot. The draw now takes place. After the draw Pete bets the pot limit, which is $30, making a total of $60 in the pot. Joe calls Pete's $30 bet, and raises it $5, making a total of $95 in the pot. The other two cheaters drop out. Mr. Sucker calls the raise by putting $35 into the pot. The pot now holds $130. Pete calls Joe's $5 raise, and re-raises the pot limit, which is $135. The total amount in the pot is now $270. Joe calls Pete's $135 bet, making the pot limit $405, and raises this amount. The total amount in the pot is now $810. Mr. Sucker calls the two raises by putting in $540 for a total of $1,350 in the pot. Pete calls Joe's raise of $405, and raises the pot limit, which is now $1,755, making a total of $3,510. Joe calls the $1,755 bet, making the pot limit $5,265, and raises the pot limit, making a total of $10,530 in the pot. It will cost Mr. Sucker $7,020 to call Pete's and Joe's raises. Should Pete not raise and should he just call Joe's raise of $5,265, the total amount in the pot would be $22,815. The total amount lost by Mr. Sucker is $7,601, and that was with only five raises. Should Pete desire to make another raise of pot limit, it would cost Mr. Sucker $22,815 more to call the hand. So a player must not only watch the dealer to prevent himself from being cheated, but must also keep his eyes on his own deck while he is offering the pack to be cut.

You can't be too careful in Poker when playing for pot limit or any big stakes.

Cheating at Stud Poker

All the crooked moves in the cheat's armory, such as stacking, crimping, shifting, false cuts, and bottom dealing are put to good use by the sharp; but one of the sure-fire gimmicks for the sharp at Stud is the second deal. A sharper with a marked deck and a good second has broken many a Stud player. And, when marked cards weren't in use, the *peek*, as described under ."Cheating at Black Jack," is commonly used.

Sandbagging is used as often by confederates at Stud

Poker, as in Draw Poker. Signaling is commonly used at Stud between two confederates, but the signaling is usually done by making use of the hole card and the first upturned card.

If the upturned card is placed tidily on the hole card so as to cover the hole card completely, it usually indicates that the upturned card is paired with the hole card. If the upturned card almost covers the hole card but permits a quarter of an inch of the hole card to be seen, it represents an ace, etc.

The international signs are used.

Hole-card switching, although dangerous and requiring considerable skill, is to be guarded against at Stud. A high card is held out and switched for the hole card when desired, by palming.

Marked cards are more commonly used at Stud than at Draw Poker; and in two-handed games strippers are the favorite of the unskilled card cheater.

Strippers are used by cheats when playing two-handed Poker, either Stud or Draw. The three aces are usually stripped. The cheat when cutting the cards for his opponent in a two-handed game strips the three aces to the top. Opponent deals the cheater a pair of aces back up at Stud and to himself an ace in the hole. To detect strippers, see page 24.

PLAYERS WHO STEAL FROM THE POT

Always watch a player when he is putting money into the pot or taking change out of it. Some players have a cold-blooded habit of putting up less than they are supposed to; others do it unintentionally. These little swindles add up to large amounts during an entire Poker session. Make sure players don't steal from the pot. It may be the pot you will win—which brings to my mind a player who used some "check cop" on his hand and when helping a winning player pull in his pot would steal a chip from the pot. He entered the game with ten chips, lost a pot which cost him four chips, quit the game, and cashed in eleven chips (by stealing a chip out of five different pots). This player won money without winning a pot, had even lost one instead. Learn to protect your money.

CHAPTER TWENTY-SEVEN

Strategy at Poker

How to Win at Poker

To play winning Poker, the most important thing to remember is to *be alert*. Every little movement has a meaning all its own. Every draw, every card shown has a vital bearing on your possibilities of winning the pot. Therefore you must watch every player in the game to see that you are not being cheated or chiseled; you must watch every active player so that you can gauge the strength of his hand, so that you can judge his reactions to a raise or re-raise, to a draw of two cards or three cards, etc. In Stud especially you must observe each card carefully to see what it does not only to your own chances for improving your hand, but also what it does to improve or spoil the chances of each and every other player as well as the player who received the card. Finally, you have to watch yourself, to see that you don't betray your hand, to see that you don't give clues to your opponents. Yes, you have to be alert.

And you *can't* be alert if you're overtired or mentally disturbed by something either in the game or apart from the game. And you can't be alert if you're drunk or have been or are drinking excessively. Don't play Poker for sizable stakes if you've had a tough day at the office, if you're worried about business or about Junior's behavior, or if you've had a few too many Martinis. And do not drink intoxicating liquor while playing—not if you want to win.

You must be keen at all times, to size up all situations. If you do that, you have a good chance of winning, even if you are just an average player. For there will always be one or more players who, because of fatigue, irritation, recklessness, or fuzziness, will play badly and give you the edge.

If it's for fun, and the stakes are unimportant, and you don't care whether or not you win, do what you like. But if you want to win, remember the first rule is—you must be on your toes, you must be alert all the time.

Whether the game be Stud or Draw Poker, seven-card or five-card, deuces wild or nothing wild, there are three important rules of play to remember. If you remember these rules, it is almost impossible for you to lose in an evening of Poker unless you are playing with a group of experts who also know them. If you play Poker regularly with the same group of players and find that there are a few people who win consistently while the rest of you lose, leaving the possibility of dishonesty aside, it is because these players are aware of these rules and play according to them.

The first rule is: *When you have nothing, get out.* More money is lost by the Stud Poker player who goes in with two indifferent cards and drops out later, or by the Draw Poker player who stays with a low pair and folds after the draw, than is ever lost by having three kings beaten by three aces. The player who has the patience to stay out of pot after pot, sometimes for hours if necessary, is the player who, in the long run, will win.

The second rule is: *When you're beaten, get out.* You may have a pair of queens back to back in a Stud game, a high hand, good enough to win ninety-nine pots out of a hundred. But if on the next card one of your opponents should show a pair of kings or aces, in most cases the smart play is to *drop out at once.* You may improve your hand, but the chances are you won't. And even if you should improve, your opponent may improve also, and his pair was better than yours to begin with. Except for going in on nothing, more money is lost by trying to beat a big pair with a small one than anything else in Poker.

The third rule is: *When you have the best hand, make them pay.* If *you* have the pair of aces back to back, make it as expensive as possible for the man with the pair of queens to play. It is true that every once in a while he will outdraw you, but you will beat him much more often, and you can afford his occasional victory.

There are many fine points to the game of Poker, but if you get nothing out of this section of the book but these three rules, you will be a consistent money winner against most players.

The following tips, hints, bits of strategy, and warnings if added to the above, studied seriously and applied faithfully, must make almost any sane man a winner at Poker.

The author has selected for discussion only the traits possessed by gamblers who make their living or a part of it from some sort of Poker. We may call them Poker hustlers. Some of these warnings to the reader were inserted after watching numerous Poker games in which cheaters operated.

If the player suspects some of the tips given are too severe —such as "Never give a Poker player a break even if he is your best friend"—he may merely declare his attitude at the start of the game by saying, "Boys, if you get them, bet them up, because that is what I am going to do." If you fail to bet a cinch hand for all it's worth when you hold one, you will rarely if ever be a good Poker player. The best gamblers have a slogan which goes as follows: "You must pay to look."

Poker is a money game, not just a pleasant way to spend an evening. If you want to play cards for recreation, there are many games more interesting than Poker. If you take the gambling spirit out of Poker, the game is an awful bore.

To become a winner the Poker player must give himself all the advantages possible. If he has skill and is bucking a cheater, it will all be in vain. The same holds if he is paying too exorbitant a charge for the privilege of playing Poker.

For example: If you play Poker in a gambling house, be it the smoke-filled back room of a cigar store or a rug joint where the house furnishes refreshments, the Poker player must pay a charge for this privilege of playing. But the charge must be fair.

There are certain charges extracted by operators from a pot, charges that make it impossible for a player to win any money over a period of time. This charge is so great that both good and bad Poker players must go broke. Are you one of those players bucking a 5 per cent cut, be the game Draw Poker, Lowball, Seven-card High-Low, Stud Poker, or any of the Poker variations? If so, read the breakdown (see page 280) for Stud Poker, and remember the same holds true for any Poker game.

Do's and Don'ts

Insist on players' putting the proper amount in the pot at all times. Many card hustlers have a decided edge by playing shy and forgetting to make good. Nickels and dimes stolen in this fashion amount to dollars at the end of a Poker session. Don't you be a sucker for a card hustler. Make him put up always.

The next thing a Poker player should do is to learn the correct rules of the game so that in case of an argument he may protect his money. Often a bad decision against a player has broken him for the evening. If you know the rules, no smart-aleck will be able to cheat you of a pot by a bad decision. Learning the rules of Poker is easy enough; read them in this book. A player familiar with the rules enjoys a considerable advantage over one who is not.

If you are a neophyte Poker player, don't get into a game

in which the boys are old hands. Experience is a big factor in Poker; it is very hard to overcome with mere talent. If you are lucky in a game with such players, you win little; if unlucky, you lose heavily. Try to find a game where the players are no better than you.

Before entering a Poker game, ascertain the minimum and maximum limits, whether the game is being played with a freezer (see "General Rules for Poker," page 238), or whether the number of raises is limited or unrestricted. You must be able to answer these questions to determine whether you have enough money on your person to sit in the game. There is no law at Poker to prohibit a player from sitting in a $5 limit game with $10, but you must realize that you will probably lose your $10 on the first pot and get plenty of criticism from the other players. Only rarely will you be lucky from the start and win many times the $10 invested.

The smart Poker player has a couple of hundred dollars as a cushion in a $5 limit game. The same ratio would hold true for smaller or larger limits. For example, a player should figure his cushion at $40 for a $1 limit; at least $20 for a 50¢ limit; etc.

The smart Poker player reasons in this fashion:

His skill will win for him over several hours of play (the author agrees with this); therefore, if he lacks sufficient money to overcome a streak of bad luck which may occur in the first few hands, he has, for that evening, lost any opportunity of putting his ability to work.

Before sitting down to a Poker game with a group of strangers, it is suggested that you observe the game for at least an hour, studying the characteristics of the players. See who plays the cards loose and who plays tight. When you do join in, play a conservative game at first because you may be in a steer game (crooked game). If you are dealt an exceptional hand in a strange game, don't bet everything you have with you. Be satisfied with small winnings on the hand; if it is a steer game, your losses will be small, and perhaps the cheaters will consider you too wise to be taken in.

Do not lend money to another player in a Poker game. The money you lend will often help break you. And, as a rule, it is an even bet you will never get it back. Gambling debts aren't paid back as often as legitimate debts.

If you desire to improve your Poker game, play as often as you can because skill develops with experience. But don't play in a big-limit game during the learning period.

Poker furnishes one of the best illustrations of the law of chance. As a matter of fact, the game is pure chance until a player has looked at the cards dealt him first (the cards received before the first betting round has begun).

From then on until the showdown, the law of chance receives serious competition from the element of skill. Skill may be broken down into three components:

1. Knowledge of mathematics.
2. Money management.
3. Psychology (judgment of other players' traits).

To what extent a player makes use of these will determine his Poker ability.

It is almost impossible to teach one to become a good Poker player by setting a standard pattern, because all players have different traits. Some are *nervous,* and crave to be in every pot; others like to *raise* just for the thrill of the game; others are very *conservative;* others have no *courage* (afraid to bet up their cards at the proper time).

The author, unlike other game writers, does not believe that sample problems with the writer's solution will lead to better Poker playing. Assuming that such problems are solved correctly and that the player has memorized each problem with its solution, he would grow old waiting for one of these sample hands to develop in an actual Poker game. The chances would be one in millions. And if by some miracle this did occur and the player remembered the solution exactly, what chance is there that the other players would have the same Poker characteristics and the same amounts of money as the illustration specified? It is obvious that any attempt to memorize the play of sample hands is foolish.

But there are certain fundamental rules that a player must follow to give himself a better chance to win. Let us get back to one of our requirements, knowledge of mathematics, which means merely making use of common arithmetic plus a little patience to guide your Poker playing.

A player must remember that in a Poker game the average becomes less valuable with the addition of more players.

For example: A pair of jacks in a two-handed game is worth holding, whereas in a seven-handed game it is a very weak hand. A Poker player will better his game immediately if he remembers this.

Next, a player must have some knowledge as to the chances of bettering certain hands.

Study some of the Poker charts in this book. Don't try to memorize them; merely absorb the general implications. Some of the best Poker players just play a tight game, knowing nothing of specific probabilities but unconsciously applying the general principles.

Keep a poker face. Don't complain when losing or show elation when winning. The emotional aftermath will prohibit clear thinking and proper evaluation of your hand. Don't indulge in unnecessary conversation. Keeping a poker face means keeping the same disposition at all times. Such restraints are very difficult to acquire overnight, but they are essential requirements of a good Poker player. Not only will you play your best game, but your opponents will not be able to figure your hand so easily.

Forget friendship. Upon entering a Poker game, leave friendship behind. If you hold a "cinch hand" at Stud and you allow your friend to see your hole card without putting in the last bet to call your hand, I can assure you that you will not be a winner. Poker is a game for blood. If you want to play a good game, you must forget friendship and bet your hand for what it is worth. Top money winners do. You must. Trust no one at Poker.

Psychology. A good Poker player must be a good psychologist. During a big money game, every type of human emotion comes into play. I used to play Stud with a player who, whenever he was dealer and had a pair back to back, would invariably fail to deal himself an upcard until his attention was called to it. This player was concentrating so much on his pair that he didn't realize he would better the pair by drawing.

Another player with whom I played Draw Poker would always ask the others, "Whose play is it?" When he asked this question I knew he had openers or a four-card flush. At least I knew he was going to play, because when he had a poor hand he would keep quiet and put his cards down before him. These are little mannerisms, if observed by the smart Poker player, that will help him win because he will know what to do at the proper time.

Study the Playing Mannerisms or Styles of Your Opponents

As a rule, players follow the same pattern of play without realizing it. Some are loose players, some play tight or close to the vest. Knowing the characteristics of your opponents may save you much or even win pots. For example, I know a player who never tried to steal or bluff a pot in twenty years of Poker playing, and I also know another player who tries to steal almost every other pot he is in. This knowledge has directed my play with these two players. In every group you will find players with similar idiosyncrasies. Study your opponents' play. It will pay off. Whenever you get an opportunity to watch the mannerisms of players in a game before you sit down, do so. You can learn much more about technique by watching than by playing.

Study particularly the playing mannerisms and techniques of winning players. They must have something on the ball (if they aren't cheaters) to win most of the time.

When you hold a good hand, don't be too anxious to put your money into the pot until it is your proper turn, don't even have your bet ready. Untoward eagerness will inform an opponent, before he need know, that you intend to play. Most beginners or poor Poker players are very anxious to bet on a good hand and conversely, when holding a weak hand, to turn down their cards before their turn of play.

Don't try to win a small pot with a big bet. Example: A player makes a 25¢ bet at Stud Poker, holding the high card; another player raises the bet $2 for a total of $2.25 in the pot. The player with the high hand drops out; the player who raised wins the 25¢ with a lower hand than the player who dropped out had. That is not considered a bluff. Such a player may win a few quarters, but he will eventually lose many times more on one hand when he raises that $2 and finds that his opponent has that high pair backed up. In short, don't try to win those small amounts with a big bet. It doesn't pay off.

Don't attempt to bluff a pot when four or five players are still in the game, or keep raising before you have your full hand, with the thought in mind that you are going to win with a bluff. The legends of money won by bluffing at Poker are greatly exaggerated. Seldom do good Poker players attempt a bluff, because as a rule they are not in the pot at the showdown with a weak hand. The best time a bluff may be attempted is when one or two players are in the pot—and they are heavy losers. If they are heavy winners, don't attempt to bluff, because, ninety-nine to one, you will be called. Don't try to bluff on a beginning player, because as a rule he will call. The really good Poker player can be bluffed more easily than the beginner.

The only time the bluff is an important factor in a Poker game is when playing table stakes, where a player may bet $100 on a bluff hand to win a $10 pot. But when a pot totals $50 and the limit is $2 and you were not the opener or high hand, you will be called at least twenty-four times to one.

Never attempt a bluff at Stud unless you have a little something in your hand. When playing Draw Poker you must start the bluff by raising before the draw to attempt to impress on the other players that you have a strong hand.

Should you get caught bluffing twice, it's about time for you to stop for that evening. It is too costly to attempt bluffing after being burned once or twice. Not ever to attempt to bluff, however, would mean a considerable loss of call money on the showdown, once you became known as a player who never bluffs. The other players would hesitate to call you, when you do bet.

It is good practice not to show a hand after a successful bluff, unless you do not intend to bluff for the remainder of the Poker session. And if a player does not call on the showdown, bluff or no bluff, don't show your hand. This merely serves to give the other players more information concerning your playing methods. Conversely, a player should at times call a hand even if he knows he is going to lose, just to gather information concerning his opponent's methods.

Good memory is a valuable asset in Poker. If you play Draw or any variation, practice remembering the number of cards each player draws; that information is vital to you. Memory serves also in Stud. For example, several players may turn down their hands after the third-card draw, and those cards may include three kings. Now if you draw a king for your fourth card in a no-pair hand and the king is your high card and another player has queens, you might—if you don't remember that three kings were dead—gamble on drawing a king because the pot is big. You gamble on an impossibility. Observation will save your money.

Strategy at Draw Poker

With all of the above hints and warnings pretty well absorbed, the Draw Poker player might like some advice on when to play or drop out. Read on!

The pot has been opened, and you would like to have some nucleus of fact to guide your play. Well, common arithmetic plus a little patience will do the trick. If you fail to hold a pair or better or a four-card straight or flush, the answer is, drop out without any hesitation—for the simple reason that your chances of drawing a better hand than the opener and the other players is remote. To draw to improve a hand, you must have something to draw to. Drawing to a three-card flush or straight is throwing money away. The chances of making a flush by drawing two cards are approximately one in twenty-four. The chances of filling a straight when holding ace, deuce and 3 are approximately one in sixty-eight. Sure, you also have a chance of two pair or three of a kind, but you must bear in mind that the other players—especially the *opener*—have one of those hands or better already, plus the chance of improvement.

It is permissible to draw to any pair above a 10, provided

the opening bet is reasonable, because the chances of improvement are approximately one in three and a half, which means the improvement may be to any one of the following: two pairs, three of a kind, full house, or four of a kind; and one of these hands may win the pot.

WHEN TO OPEN

A player should always open the pot when he has an opportunity to do so, regardless of the value of his hand. Should the player hold *jacks* and be *under the gun* (immediately to dealer's left), it is suggested to hold a kicker and make your opening bet rather stiff. This play is made in an attempt to drive out any hand that may be of a higher value.

Some players hesitate at opening the pot with a pair of jacks and then play with the jacks should another player open the pot. This is very bad logic and poor Poker playing. At other times a cautious opener will unhesitatingly play with a small pair. The author is of the opinion, after watching hundreds of Poker games, that it is *unsound* to draw to a low pair if the opening bet is higher than the minimum bet.

Players have often asked me, does it pay to hold a kicker with one pair? My answer is, yes and no. True, by holding a kicker your chances of improving the hand are lessened. The exact chances of improving a pair with a kicker are 1 in 3.86, whereas the chances of improving a pair (without kicker) are 1 in 3.48. But the player holding a kicker has added a certain deceptive value to his hand. Your judgment must decide if it is worth holding. Your decision must be made after analyzing both the players' characteristic methods and the number of cards each player has drawn before your turn to draw.

Here is a hint on whether to stay in with a four-card flush, which the author has found sound both in theory and in actual play. Calculate the amount of money in the pot and recall the chances of drawing the fifth card to make the flush. The chances of drawing one card to make a flush are 1 in 5.2. Therefore the pot should contain at least five times the amount it will cost you to draw a card. In other words, if the opening bet was $1, there must be at least $5 in the pot before it is worth your risk in paying $1 to draw a card in an attempt to make a flush.

"But," you ask, "should I make the flush, it may not win; therefore shouldn't the pot make me better odds?" The answer is no, for as a rule there isn't too much money in the pot before the draw; and, second, a flush will win many more times for a player than it will lose.

Whether to raise and bluff in Draw Poker is determined by

the situation involved. A player must take into consideration
the temperament of the players with whom he is competing,
the amount of money in the pot, the number of cards drawn,
and the relative value of the player's own hand. All these factors are learned over years of Poker playing, and so is the
faculty of evaluating them correctly. It isn't necessary to do
these things perfectly to win money at Poker. All you must do
is to play a better game than your opponents. If you can't do
that with the information contained in this book, I suggest
you look for a Poker game with younger and greener players.

Study the Poker Table

The Poker table on page 300 is intended as an aid to better
Draw Poker playing. A player who has a fair idea of the
chances of improving his hand in Draw will have a great advantage over the player who does not have the vaguest idea.
It is suggested that a player try especially to memorize the
exact chances of bettering certain hands, such as a pair, four-
card straight, and four-card flush.

Strategy at Stud Poker

The better Poker player prefers five-card Stud to any other
game in the Poker family. They shun such games as Draw
Poker, Spit in the Ocean, Twin Beds, or any of the variations
wherein wild cards are used. Stud Poker permits a player to
use much more strategy than any of the variations. When wild
cards are added, the element of skill is greatly diminished, and
the element of chance is greatly increased.

The best game of Stud—looking at it from a smart gambler's
viewpoint is without an *ante* or *dealer's edge,* but if the dealer
does edge, the amount must be comparatively small. For example, in a $2-limit game, the dealer edges 25¢. The reason
is that the gambler likes to have some information to guide
himself before betting. Gamblers don't like to put money into
the pot without seeing at least part of their hand, therefore
the first two cards dealt in Stud (the hole card and the first
upcard) are the cards that are valued by the gambler, and
determine the betting.

Getting back to the reader (whom we might as well call the
player), let us assume he has been dealt a hole card and his
first upcard. This is the most important period in any Stud
game. The player must decide the value of those two cards,
which is done by considering the value both of his two cards
and the value of every other player's upcard. To give you a

general rule to cover this situation is impossible; so instead I am going to discuss what one of the smartest gamblers in the business does under any conditions.

Chances of Improving a Draw Poker Hand of Five Cards with the Draw

Cards held after discarding	Number of Cards drawn	Improved five-card hand after draw	Chances of improvement
One pair	3	any improved hand	1 in 3.48
One pair	3	two pairs	1 in 6.25
One pair	3	three of a kind	1 in 8.7
One pair	3	full house	1 in 98
One pair	3	four of a kind	1 in 360
One pair plus a kicker	2	any improved hand	1 in 3.86
	2	two pairs	1 in 5.9
	2	three of a kind	1 in 12.9
	2	full house	1 in 120
	2	four of a kind	1 in 1,081
Two pairs	1	full house	1 in 11.75
Three of a kind	2	any improved hand	1 in 9.6
	2	full house	1 in 16.4
	2	four of a kind	1 in 23.5
Three of a kind plus a kicker	1	any improved hand	1 in 11.8
		full house	1 in 15.7
		four of a kind	1 in 47
Four-card straight open at both ends	1	straight	1 in 5.9
Four-card straight open in the middle or at one end	1	straight	1 in 11.8
Four-card flush	1	flush	1 in 5.2
Three-card flush	2	flush	1 in 24
Four-card straight flush open in the middle	1	straight flush	1 in 47
Four-card straight flush open on both ends	1	straight flush	1 in 23.5
Four-card royal flush	1	royal flush	1 in 47
Three-card royal flush	2	royal flush	1 in 1,081

First, if his hole card is lower than a 10-spot, he folds up (provided he does not hold a pair back to back), regardless of the value of his upcard. If it is an ace or a high card and he is compelled to make the opening bet, he bets the minimum amount permitted.

The player must bear in mind that the chances of being dealt a pair or better in five cards are approximately one in two. Therefore, if three or four players remain until the showdown, almost invariably the winning hand will hold a pair or better. With this thought in mind, the smart gambler, failing to hold a pair, always has to have a higher-ranking card in the hole than any other player's upcard. He bases his calculations on the theory that if he holds two cards lower than the upcard of one or more players and he has the possibility of pairing one of his low cards, each of his opponents also has the same possibility. And, if he or one of his opponents each pairs a card, his hand is valueless, because his opponent paired a higher card. This gambler uses sound judgment.

So much for the first two cards. Now the first betting round has ended, and each player has received his second upcard.

This gambler, should he see any other player's two upcards paired, and if he fails to hold a pair, will at his proper turn of play fold up. His theory, which is sound, is *"Never play a hand at the start which you know is lower than your opponents'."* In other words don't chase a pair or a higher hand when the pot is small; because if you did play for the third upcard, you might be tempted to chase your money which you have in the pot, and that is not good Poker playing.

The substance of the above boils down to this: you must play them tight, at least up until you receive your third upcard.

Let us get back to the hole card and the first upcard. When your hole card has a ranking value of jack or better and your upcard is a 10 or lower, it is worth a reasonable bet. That is, provided a jack is not showing as one of your opponent's upcards. Should this be the case, fold up at your turn, because your chances of pairing that jack have been reduced 33-1/3 per cent.

The player must always bear in mind that an upcard paired has much less value than a hole card paired; and the smart player will consider playing the hand in an attempt to pair his hole card rather than an open card or upcard.

It is also advisable for a player to know that the chances of pairing a hole card with a second upcard (provided no player holds a card of the same denomination as his upcard) are deduced by checking the number of upcards. Example: The game is seven-handed; a player sees seven upcards, none of which can pair up his hole card. The computation is as follows: The player's chances of being dealt a card to pair his hole card are 3 in 44, or 13-2/3 to 1 against pairing his hole card. And the chances of pairing either his hole card or his upcard, provided the upcards showing are not of the same denomination, are exactly 7 to 1 against. So if the pot holds eight or more times the amount it will cost you to put in and draw that second upcard, it is worth the gamble. If the pot has much less, it is not worth the risk.

One thing a player must not be afraid to do is to fold up. Sure, you like action; that is why you play Stud. But I still have to find the Stud player who enjoys losing money. And if you are afraid to fold up, and crave action when your hand doesn't merit your playing, you must eventually lose.

A player must also realize that should he fold up his first two or three cards, he will lose little or nothing, because rarely is the big betting under way at this part of the game. As a rule, a player holding a big pair back to back won't raise at that time for fear of causing the other players to fold up. And a player holding a weak hand doesn't raise, because he is trying to better his hand with the second upcard.

Should a player raise before drawing his second upcard, his opponents must analyze the player who made the raise as well as the upcard he is holding. Is he a winner up to this time? If he is, the chances are better than even that he is bluffing; a big winning player frequently seems to go on a betting spree. Or is he a heavy loser? If he is, maybe he is trying to steal the pot or might be trying to change his streak of bad luck. If you hold a good hand at this time, it is advisable to play for that second upcard.

Whenever a player has his hole card paired with one of his two upcards and another player has an open pair showing of a lower rank than the first player, it is worth a raise for two reasons: a) to attempt to drive out the other players and possibly the holder of the pair; b) the holder of the lower hand must intimate the value of his hand by either dropping or raising. But the main reason is to get the most money possible into the pot with the fewest players.

One of the most stupid plays at Stud is to play for a flush when holding only three cards of a flush. The chances of making it by drawing two cards depends on the number of cards of the same suit in the upcards. For example, with three cards of the same suit showing in the other players' upcards, the chances against making the flush are approximately twenty-four to one.

When you are in a pot and have drawn your third upcard, with one more to go—should a player have you beaten with his upcards and if the pot is not especially big, fold up. But should the pot be extra big and a merely reasonable amount be required of you to bet to receive that last card, and if you believe your chances of winning that hand are good should you draw a certain card (and the card is still alive), then by all means play.

If you do not hold a cinch hand and are in doubt about your holding the winning hand, a check is the proper play. You must think about trying to save money on an uncertain hand, and by checking you won't play into a trap and give your opponent a chance to raise should *he* hold a cinch hand.

After you have received your last card at Stud, odds should no longer be considered. By this time you know whether you have a cinch hand or not. If you have a cinch hand, bet the limit; don't check, hoping that your opponent will bet and you can raise him. If he has a raise in mind the chances are that he will raise anyway should you bet. If not, he probably will check also, and you are out money.

Never give an opponent an opportunity to see your hole card free when holding a cinch hand.

Strategy at Seven-Card Stud

Most of the tips covered under "How to Win at Poker," plus many of the tips given under Five-card Stud apply to Seven-card Stud, in addition to the following:

This concerns the betting by a player after he receives his first three cards (two down cards plus an upcard). It is more important to have three good cards at the start in Seven-card Stud than it is in Five-card Stud. But it is a strange belief among Stud players, even the good ones, that they should enter the first betting round with a lower-ranking hand than they would in Five-card Stud.

The Stud player's course of action should be simple. He can see three-sevenths of a complete hand before he bets a cent. If he fails to hold a three-card straight, a three-card flush, three of a kind, a pair, or at the least two high cards such as ace and king, he must fold without putting a bet into the pot.

Strategy at High-Low Seven-Card Stud

By far the soundest method of play at High Low Seven-card Stud is to play for low with the first three cards dealt. Because if you start with low cards, you have a chance to wind up with a straight or possibly a flush or a straight flush which will win high for you, while at the same time your low cards may give you low hand and you may win the entire pot.

Playing for high at the start, you may win high, but it is practically a foregone conclusion that you will never win low also.

You may ask, "If most players play for low, isn't it a good

idea for me to play for high?" If you are playing for low and a high card hits your hand, which automatically eliminates your chances for a possible straight or flush, you drop out. But when you're playing for high and hold a fairly high pair, you usually play right through.

In brief, a player who insists on starting out with a high hand must lose in the long run.

Strategy at Low Poker

(*Not to be confused with Lowball. For strategy at Low-ball, see page 250.*)

Most of the tips covered under "How to Win at Poker" apply to Low Poker, plus most of the tips covered under the mother game, be it Draw or Stud. But, a specific bit of information on Low Poker:

When playing a Draw variant, it is advisable to play your hand pat, or rarely if ever to indulge in more than a one-card draw. To warrant drawing two cards in Low Poker the pot must be an extra big one, and the amount of money required to draw those two cards must be reasonable.

In Low Poker Stud variation, the player should play a tight game. The hole and upcard cannot be higher than 7. Play the game tight, and you will be a winner in the long run.

Strategy in Wild Games

Most of the tips covered under "How to Win at Poker" and the mother games go out the window when more than one card is wild in the game.

If only the joker is wild, the rules are followed except in valuing a player's hand. Here a player must use caution by attributing a little higher value than usual to his opponent's hand.

Wild-card games with more than one joker, or variations that are not standard—such as Spit in the Ocean, Twin Beds, etc.—are not discussed in terms of strategy, because of the greater amount of chance that takes effect in these games compared with the other games analyzed.

CHAPTER TWENTY-EIGHT

The Dealer Who Moves Without Getting Up

The managers of Poker casinos tend to regard Homo Americanensis' favorite pastime as a bit of a bore. Let us be frank. They are right. Unless your money is at stake, nothing on earth could be more tedious; and the less your monetary interest, the less your absorption in the contest. So the casinos I haunt—they aren't as far from New York as some district attorneys would like you to think—have stimulated their sympathetic concern with what goes on in the premises by increasing their cut (the dab of money taken from each pot as a charge for the use of the house and its services) through the employment of a professional dealer. This nimble-fingered shark's services are a substitute for letting each player fumble with the cards in his regular turn of play.

Two professionals are assigned to each Poker game in the house. Sharing the assignment enables a change of dealers whenever a player demands the change, which is his privilege, and allows dealers to rest and breathe between sessions. It's pretty hard work—fast, exacting; the sort of thing that leads to nervous tension and coronary thrombosis. Most casinos fix a five and a half-hour time limit on Poker games. Each dealer is paid something like $15 a night, and works about half of the five and a half-hour session. Nine or ten out of every dozen games he deals will be a variety of Stud.

It's pretty thoughtful of the house to provide de-luxe dealing service at a cost to itself of $30 a night, isn't it? Indeed it is. The house is being pretty thoughtful of its own interests. A pro dealer can increase the number of hands played per hour to something like fifty, last time I clocked. By chanting incessantly, in a nettlesome drone, "If you don't bet you can't win!" he solicits plays from men who would normally fold promptly. The amounts in the pots increase. The house cut leaps. At $30 it is a spectacular bargain for the management.

Besides the professional's skill in card handling there is another reason why his presence at the table results in more and bigger pots. It is he, not some fumbling bank vice-president or gasoline-station owner, who handles the players' money. When he's at the table and you win a pot you don't even have to reach across the table to haul in the boodle. The dealer hands you the winnings, fastidiously counted, neatly stacked.

In spite of these mechanical advantages, players have for years objected duly to letting a pro deal the cards. The complaint was in the realm of spiritual—you might, and probably do, call it a matter of superstition. If you caught the seat to the immediate left of the pro—the leader's seat—you always got the first card dealt in the hand. If you were in No. 2 seat you always got the No. 2 cards. No matter what the laws of probability insist, you insisted that if the house dealer would go away and shoot himself and let the players deal their cards in order, your luck would improve.

To the scientific mind it sounds frivolous, but a man persuaded that the mechanics of the game are against him makes a bad customer; and so a casino operator whom I shall call Ducky—since that's the name he's known by throughout the East—devised a method of meeting and silencing those complaints.

I encountered it the other night. I think it will be news to the rest of the country.

This was the problem:

To develop a method of dealing by which each player would get his correct turn at cutting the cards, by which each would in turn be the first player to get cards, by which the deal would move clockwise around the table—but which would maintain the speed and precision which only a pro can bring to a game.

How would you solve it?

On that recent night when I walked into Ducky's, I was after grassroots statistics on a fine point in Pinochle. The game I was watching went a little leisurely. I glanced around the room. Over yonder was a Stud Poker game. A pro was dealing and banking with the pro's ice-cold accuracy, droning his ancient motto, forking the money to and fro with automaton precision—and nobody looked unhappy. If you've been around casinos you know that's news. I drifted over.

The deal was rotating around the table. The customers were satisfied with their seat positions. They were cutting in order. They were, vicariously, dealing in order. I'd never seen it before. Decided yet how you'd solve the problem?

FIRST HAND OF THE GAME

The pro dealer is representing the first player to his left as dealer.

In full view of the other players he puts on the table in front of that first player, the *leader,* a copper penny.

He shuffles the cards, and puts the deck to be cut before the first player to his right.

Then he deals, exactly as specified under the rules for Stud, starting with the *second* player to his left—the leader, with respect to the player whom he represents in the deal. He deals no cards to himself. He's not a player. He just works there.

SECOND AND SUCCEEDING HANDS OF THE DEAL

As in normal Stud, social Stud, the deal rotates clockwise around the table. As in normal Stud, the player to the leader's left becomes the next dealer—but the pro dealer does the work.

1. So the pro pushes the penny over in front of the second player to his left, indicating there's where the deal is.

2. After shuffling, he puts the pack in front of the player to the second player's right—i.e., the player to the dealer's left— to be cut.

3. Now, starting with the player who with respect to the nominal dealer is leader—that is, the player third from the pro dealer's left—the pro deals the cards.

So it goes. The penny moves hand by hand around the table, locating the deal, the cut, the first man to get cards on that deal.

Could anything be simpler? Why didn't you think of that?

Part Five

CHAPTER TWENTY-NINE

Pinochle—General Rules

Some General Considerations on the Nature of the Game

Generally speaking—although, if you've followed me this far, you know I don't generally speak generally—Pinochle is perhaps more interesting to more people than is any other single card game.

Bridge has had more devotees. According to a poll by the American Institute of Public Opinion in December, 1947, some twelve million of the fifty-two and a half million Americans who then played cards regularly preferred Bridge as against the ten and a half million whose No. 1 game was Pinochle. Even then, Pinochle ran Bridge a very close race for top honors. And since then Gin Rummy has cut deeply into the ranks of the Bridge players.

The elements that make any card game great are present in every respect in Pinochle. They may be stated in the form of a question: Does the game involve enough science—that is, does it sufficiently challenge our intelligence, our subtlety, our alertness—to hold the interest of the serious student of cards? Does it appeal to our gambling instincts: that is, does it hold out hope to the underdog; does it avoid lapsing into an arid measurement of the superior craftsman's experience and skill? Pinochle passes the test. Like either of the Bridges it repays delicacy in teamwork and skill in the play; like Poker, it repays daring in the bidding and imagination in gambling for the draw. It can be played for fun or a fortune, and it still commands your devotion. That's the test.

Item: No matter how expert the player may be, there will always arise a new problem to tax his ingenuity.

Item: There is no such thing as *the* correct play. Rarely will two different players, conceded they are of the same intellectual and technical level, play the same complex hand quite the same way.

Item: There are more second guesses and vain regrets at Pinochle than at any other card game, including Contract Bridge.

Item: A general knowledge of the mathematical probabilities, for knowing how the opposing cards lie, is essential to playing Pinochle well. (See page 357.)

Item: To be an expert at this game a player must have good memory, good rough-and-ready mathematical ability, and icy precision in evaluating a hand in the bidding or before the start of play.

Lacking these faculties, it is most unlikely you will ever attain real expertness at Pinochle. That doesn't mean you won't enjoy it. According to Dr. Gallup, here's how card players voted on their favorite game in 1946, when seventy-three million card decks were sold and people were just settling down to enjoy themselves in peacetime leisure:

	Bridge	Poker	Pinochle	Others
By sex				
Men	14%	27%	21%	38%
Women	30	9	16	45
By education				
College	45	17	12	26
High school	22	18	20	40
Grammar school	9	19	22	50
By age				
21 to 29	14	22	21	43
30 to 49	22	19	18	41
50 and over	26	13	18	43

All the games of the big Pinochle family are played with the same deck of cards (although in some variations two or three decks are shuffled together and used as one); but there are significant differences among the important varieties.

Two-handed Pinochle affords the widest latitude for scientific play of any game in the family, and I might as well put into the record my personal opinion that properly played, no game puts a higher premium on skill and subtlety.

Three-handed Auction Pinochle with a Widow is the biggest betting game in the family—and, perhaps for this reason, the most popular in the United States right now.

But here's a prediction.

In just a little while (see page 384) I'm going to describe to you, for the first time in print, a game called Radio Pinochle. I herewith predict that this newcomer among Pinochle games will in short order become one of the most popular of all partnership games.

To write these chapters on Pinochle I've put in literally years of leg work. Every sentence I've put on paper has been subjected to the test of play. I want American card players to regard what I say as absolutely authoritative. . . .

I should like to be remembered as the card expert who didn't have a theory about the history of the game.

Tracing Pinochle to its roots through prime sources would be a lifetime job for the most astute researcher on earth. I haven't a lifetime to give to such barren work as this. And I'm not the most astute researcher; I'm just astute enough to know that the history of a card game is not important enough to warrant risking one's reputation on a resonant bluff.

Take your choice. P. Hal Sims, writing in his book *Pinochle Pointers* (1935), says, "Pinochle was invented by the Germans, and as the Germans lean strongly towards the mathematical feature in games, that aspect has been introduced in Pinochle, making the game highly scientific." As against this *post-hoc*, or racist, theory, consider the opinion of R. F. Foster in *How to Win at Pinochle*, 1941: "Pinochle is generally spoken of as a German game, but its origin is Swiss, it being almost unknown in Germany." Some writers have traced the game's name to the same root as our word "binoculars"; a little shakily they say it has something to do with raillery at the table when somebody overlooking a meld is advised to put on his glasses; but the more these writers examine their theory, the worse it gets. The B in "binocle" is changed to our P by the Potash-and-Perlmutter dialect of nineteenth century German immigrants; the H of our "pinochle" is introduced either by sheer accident and is left there by sheer lethargy, or gets into the word by reason of a typographical error, thereupon consented to, endorsed, and adopted by ten million Americans.

This is really quite silly. So, in my opinion, is some writers' laborious effort to trace the game's name to some illiterate German's mispronunciation of the French word *binage*, the name in French of the meld of the spade queen and diamond jack. So is the effort to trace it to the Latin *bis* (twice) and *oculus* (eye). So is the effort to trace it to the German *bis* (until) plus *knochle* (knuckle), referring to an old habit of rapping the table, as in Gin Rummy, to end a game. I do not by any means agree with Henry Ford that history is bunk, but having examined a sad lot of it in preparing this text, I am reluctantly persuaded that a lot of bunk is history; and I'm not going to add to it. Pinochle's origin as a word is lost in the mists of antiquity; it grew up in the vernacular speech; it is a corruption of some other word; this is all we can really know, and it is all we have to know just now. For some centuries now, men gathered in places that smelled of beer and tobacco have enjoyed the pleasure of rearing back in a chair and slamming a winning card down on the table. That was Pinochle. Why they called it that is, in my opinion, not quite so provocative a study as why it is that people play the game with this peculiar vehemence. What is the history of the table-splintering, thumb-fracturing tradition? Why does it occur in practically no other card game? Aha!

I am disposed to agree with Foster that Pinochle is in fact an improved form of Bezique, a descendant of Cinq Cents (or Five Hundred), itself a descendant of an ancient game called Mariage. In Mariage (c. 1700), two players melded from hands dealt out of a thirty-two-card pack. But this game was dull and limited; it gave way to something called Brusquembille, which in turn was supplanted by Briscan and Brisque. With all these the same thing was wrong: there weren't enough cards. You wouldn't have been interested.

Let's finish this off. I'm stringing along with the 1864 *American Hoyle*. Our story is that Bezique was *invented*—just as I've invented *Scarne's Challenge* and *Teeko* and *Follow the Arrow*—by a Swedish schoolmaster named Gustav Flaher, who presented the game under the name Flahernuble to Charles I of Sweden as an entry in a contest. It spread, turned up with certain sea changes in Germany as Binochle or Penuchle, and appeared at last in the United States as an American adaptation of a French adaptation of the Swedish-German game which is now called Pinochle. It was played with two or three Euchre decks—sixty-four or ninety-six cards. Let's get on with the game.

Scarne's General Rules for Pinochle

For most games of the Pinochle family the standard Pinochle deck is used. In some variants of the game two or even three Pinochle decks are shuffled together and used as one.

The Pinochle deck is composed of forty-eight cards—two cards in the four familiar suits (hearts, diamonds, spades, and clubs) in each of the following denominations:

Ace, king, queen, jack, 9, 10.

If no packaged Pinochle deck is at hand, players can make up their own deck by stripping all cards below the 9-spot from two standard fifty-two-card packs (Poker cards) and combining the remainder into a deck consisting of eight aces (two of each suit), eight kings (two of each suit), eight queens (ditto), eight jacks (ditto), eight 10's (ditto), and eight 9's (also ditto).

Better combine two decks having identical patterns on the back.

RANK OF CARDS AND SUITS

The cards at Pinochle rank in the following order:
Ace (highest ranking)
10
King
Queen
Jack
9 (lowest ranking).

Except as to the suit designated as trump, the suits have identical value. When a suit is designated as trump (either by the turn of a card or by bidder's choice), that suit outranks the three others.

A card of the trump suit wins over a card of any other suit regardless of face value. *Example:* If clubs are trump, the 9 of clubs (that suit's lowest-ranking card) wins over the ace of hearts (that suit's highest-ranking).

When two cards of the same suit and rank are played, the first played has precedence: it is construed as having the higher rank.

OBJECT OF THE GAME

1. To score the points necessary to win the game (usually 1,000 points is game) by adding together the value of one's *melded* cards and the value of the cards taken by winning tricks. In some variations each hand is a separate game.

2. If the bidder in a version involving bidding, to score the number of points one has bid.

STANDARD VALUES OF MELDED CARDS

Irrespective of what brand of Pinochle you play, the following score values for melds are standard in the United States. Only the names commonly used throughout the country are used; expressions of merely local meaning, signifying nothing anywhere else, are not liable to general discussion.

1. Ace, 10, king, queen, jack of trump, commonly called a *flush,* a *run,* a *yard and a half,* or a *royal sequence. Scoring value 150 points.*

2. Nine of trump, which herein will be called the *deece* (after American usage) rather than the affected and confusing *dix* of some outdated game books. *Scoring value 10 points.*

3. King and queen of trump, commonly called the *marriage in trump* or the *royal marriage. Scoring value 40 points.*

4. King and queen of any suit, not trump, generally called a *marriage* or *common marriage*. *Scoring value 20 points*.

5. Queen of spades and jack of diamonds, called *Pinochle*. *Scoring value 40 points*.

6. Four aces of different suits, called *a hundred aces*. *Scoring value 100 points*.

7. Four kings of different suits, called *80 kings*. *Scoring value 80 points*.

8. Four queens of different suits, called *60 queens*. *Scoring value 60 points*.

9. Four jacks of different suits, called *40 jacks*. *Scoring value 40 points*.

10. King and queen of each suit, commonly called a *roundhouse*, a *round trip*, or *around the world*. *Scoring value 240 points*.

If a player holds duplicates of the above melds, each meld itself has the value set forth above.

THE RULES FOR MELDING

1. Melds may be laid down (melded) at one time only; that is, before the start of play—in all Pinochle games except two-handed Pinochle.

2. To score his melds, a player must win at least one trick with his playing hand. Failure to win a trick loses for that player all the cards he melds in that hand.

3. When playing a partnership game, each partner must meld for himself. But in a partnership game only one of the players need win a trick in order to score the melds of both partners.

A player cannot meld a flush (royal sequence) and claim credit for a marriage in trump to boot. He can have a credit of 150 points for the flush only; the marriage does not count. Nor can a player use a party of one marriage to help form another marriage.

Example: A player melds the marriage of the king and queen of hearts, and retains in his hand the other king of hearts. Now he cannot meld the second king with the queen already melded; to meld another marriage he must have the other queen of the suit. The rule holds for all marriages, including the marriage in trump; and marriages once melded cannot be altered.

Now, three queens of suits other than hearts *can* be added to a melded queen of hearts to make up a meld of 60 queens. Or three kings of suits other than hearts *can* be added to the heart king in the example cited above to make a meld of 80 kings. And the ace, 10, jack of hearts can be added to the heart marriage, for a flush meld, provided hearts are trumps.

But if a player holds four kings and four queens of different suits, he might better meld a *roundhouse* and get his credit for 240 points at the one time.

If a player melds Pinochle (the queen of spades and the jack of diamonds), he may use that queen of spades too with the king of spades for a marriage. Or he may use it to help make 60 queens. It can also be used to help make a flush; but in that case the marriage is void.

The jack of diamonds may be used simultaneously to help form a flush and 40 jacks.

If a player melds a flush, he can use the king and queen involved to help meld a *roundhouse*, but if he does so he gets only 200 points for the *roundhouse*, making a total of 350 points for that meld and the flush together. (A *roundhouse* melded by itself is valued at 240 points.)

But if the player melds a flush in diamonds plus a *roundhouse*, he gets credit for 390 points—the extra 40 points being contributed by the Pinochle meld.

STANDARD BONUS MELD—AND TRIPLE AND QUADRUPLE MELDS

Often players like to incorporate bonus melds into their game. If you choose to do so, use the following standard table of bonus, triple, and quadruple melds. The table may be adopted *in toto* or in part, but it is to be stipulated and re-emphasized that this system of meld values is valid and binding only if it has been agreed upon by all players before the start of the game. Upon such prior agreement, the scorekeeper *must* make on the score sheet a record of the melds to be honored and their value in points.

THE STANDARD BONUS MELDS

1. Two flushes in one hand, usually called *double flush. Scoring value 1500 points.*

2. Eight aces in one hand (two in each suit), usually called *double aces. Scoring value 1000.*

3. Eight kings in one hand (two in each suit), usually called *double kings. Scoring value 800 points.*

4. Eight queens in one hand (two in each suit), usually called *double queens. Scoring value 600 points.*

5. Eight jacks in one hand (two in each suit), usually called *double jacks. Scoring value 400 points.*

6. Two jacks of diamonds plus two queens of spades in one hand, usually called *double Pinochle. Scoring value 300 points.*

7. Two kings and two queens of the same suit in trump, usually called *double marriage in trump. Scoring value 300 points.*

8. Two kings and two queens of the same suit (not trump)

in one hand, usually called *double marriage*. *Scoring value 150 points.*

When playing with two or three decks of Pinochle cards consolidated as one deck, players may, in conjunction with the above standard bonus melds, incorporate into their game and scoring the following triple bonus melds.

TRIPLE BONUS MELDS

1. Three flushes in one hand, called a *triple flush*. *Scoring value 3000 points.*
2. Twelve aces in one hand (three in each suit), called *triple aces*. *Scoring value 2000 points.*
3. Twelve kings in one hand (three in each suit), called *triple kings*. *Scoring value 1600 points.*
4. Twelve queens in one hand (three in each suit), called *triple queens*. *Scoring value 1200 points.*
5. Twelve jacks in one hand (three in each suit), called *triple jacks*. *Scoring value 800 points.*
6. Three jacks of diamonds plus three queens of spades in one hand, called *triple Pinochle*. *Scoring value 600 points.*
7. Three kings and three queens of the same suit in trump, usually called *triple marriage in trump*. *Scoring value 600 points.*
8. Three kings and three queens of the same suit (not in trump) in one hand, commonly called *triple marriage*. *Scoring value 300 points.*

QUADRUPLE BONUS MELDS

A quadruple bonus meld is what its name sounds like—a triple meld plus an additional, fourth, meld of the same kind. It scores double the value of the corresponding triple bonus meld.

VALUE OF CARDS WON IN TRICKS

There are three radically different methods of scoring cards won in tricks:

1. The old-timers' count, which gives the widest latitude for strategy in play and is generally favored by the Pinochle expert.
2. The simplified count.
3. The streamlined count.

Whatever count is used, it must be mutually agreed upon by all the players before the start of actual play.

Note: Although these are three different methods of scoring, the total count under each method adds up to the same figure, which is 240 in cards plus 10 for the last trick won, for an invariable total under any system of 250 points.

Old-timers' Count

Ace counts	11 points
10 counts	10 points
King counts	4 points
Queen counts	3 points
Jack counts	2 points
9 counts	0 (zero, nothing)

Simplified Count

Ace counts	10 points
10 counts	10 points
King counts	5 points
Queen counts	5 points
Jack and 9 count	0 (zero, nothing)

Streamlined Count

Ace counts	10 points
10 counts	10 points
King counts	10 points
Queen, jack, 9 count	0 (zero, nothing)

NUMBER OF PLAYERS

Although some variations involving the use of double and triple decks allow up to eight persons to play at a time, the most popular forms of Pinochle are played two- three- and four-handed. These include the partnership games.

SELECTING THE DEALER AND ESTABLISHING SEATING
POSITIONS AT THE TABLE

Two methods are feasible, as follows:

1. By mutual consent any player may shuffle the cards. Then he puts the pack on the table for any other player to cut. The player completing the cut squares the pack. Now each player, starting with the leader (the player to the left of the player who shuffled), and going clockwise around the table, cuts a group of cards. After each has cut, the players turn over their group, exposing their bottom card. The player cutting the highest-ranking Pinochle card becomes the first dealer. If two or more players tie for high card, the tied players cut again until the deal is determined. Under this method the player cutting the highest card (the dealer) has the first choice of seating position. The player cutting the next highest has second choice, and so on until all players are seated.

2. Any player by mutual consent shuffles the cards. Any other player cuts them. The acting dealer deals the cards face up one at a time to all the players, starting with the player at

his left and dealing clockwise, until a player is dealt an ace. That player becomes the first dealer. Now the acting dealer proceeds to deal until a second ace has been dealt. The dealer gets first choice of seating position. The player getting the second ace has second choice. The process goes on until all the players have been seated. Any player dealt an ace is dealt out on the succeeding rounds.

SELECTING PARTNERS AND SEATING POSITIONS

Generally, Pinochle players come to the table with a pretty clear idea of how they want to team off into partnerships, but if four players prefer to establish partnerships by impartial chance, the following two methods are recommended:

1. Each player cuts a group of cards, as described under Rule No. 1 for selecting the dealer. Players cutting the two highest-ranking Pinochle cards form one partnership. The partner cutting the highest of the four cards has the choice of seats. His partner must sit opposite him. The player cutting the lowest-ranking card has his choice between the other two seats, and his partner must of course sit opposite him. If three players tie for high or low, all players must cut again until no tie exists.

2. The acting dealer deals cards face up one at a time until two players have been dealt an ace (omitting from subsequent rounds of the deal any player who has been dealt an ace). These two players become partners. The first player dealt an ace has his choice of seats. Partners must always sit opposite each other.

CHANGING PARTNERSHIPS OR SEATING POSITIONS

Any player may on the completion of any hour of play ask for a new cut or deal to try changing partnerships, seating positions, or both. The cut or new deal becomes operative immediately on the conclusion of the hand or game being played. The dealer whose turn it is next to deal becomes the acting dealer, or shuffles for the cut, and the rules set forth immediately above apply to the new deal or cut. The same rules are to be observed if a player quits the game and another player wants to come into it.

DISCUSSION BEFORE THE PLAY

1. There must be clear and common agreement and understanding among all players as to what type of game is to be played.

2. When the play is for money, the amount involved must be amply discussed and must be agreeable to all players.

3. Penalties must be agreed on for infractions such as *holes* and *reneges*.

4. Extra bonuses for certain hands must be agreed on; for example, double on spades, triple on hearts, the kitty, etc. Bonuses for special extra-high hands must be agreed on, and players must in writing establish the specific point value of special hands.

5. Bonuses for special melds must be agreed on. The point or cash value of bonus melds must be expressly understood by all.

6. If it is a bidding game, players must agree on the minimum bid.

7. If a kitty is being played for, the amount of money to be put into the kitty and the amount of the minimum bid that can win the kitty must be mutually established.

THE SHUFFLE

The cards are shuffled by the dealer. Any player may call for a shuffle before the cards are cut. The dealer, however, retains inviolable his right to shuffle the cards last.

THE CUT

The suffle completed, the dealer places the cards before the player to his immediate right to be cut. If that player declines to cut, any other player may cut the deck. If no other player cuts, it becomes mandatory that the dealer himself cut the cards before starting to deal.

For the cut to be legal there must be at least five cards in each cut block of the deck.

CHAPTER THIRTY

Two-Handed Pinochle

Scarne's Rules for Two-Handed Pinochle
(Turn-up Trump)

Although not played so often as three- and four-handed versions of the game, two-handed Pinochle is in my opinion the one game of the family demanding of the player the most in skill. No, I'll go further than that: in this game there is more room and need for strategy than in any other two-handed game currently being played. In most two-handed games, including Gin Rummy, a lucky beginner can occasionally hold his own against an expert in a session lasting over several hours. In two-handed Pinochle the element of skill is decisive, over the short or the long run.

REQUIREMENTS

1. Two players.
2. A standard Pinochle deck.

(For description of Pinochle deck and rules on rank of the cards, value of melded cards, and value of cards won in tricks, see "Scarne's General Rules for Pinochle," page 311.)

OBJECT OF THE GAME

To score 1,000 or more points before one's opponent and thus to win the game. The value of melded cards and the value of cards taken by winning tricks in successive hands or deals are added until the winning score has been accumulated. (The average point total per player per hand is somewhere near 250.) But see "Other Ways to Win," page 325.

SELECTING THE DEALER AND ESTABLISHING SEATING
POSITIONS AT THE TABLE

The other consenting, one of the players shuffles the cards. The other player cuts, carries the cut, squares the deck, and puts it in the center of the table. The players cut for high card, that player cutting the higher card becoming first dealer—if he wants to deal; if he doesn't, he can specifically choose to be the nondealer. In case of tie, the cards are cut again. The player who gets high card may choose the seat he wants. His opponent must sit at the table opposite him.

THE SHUFFLE

The cards are shuffled by the dealer. His opponent may ask for and have the right to shuffle before the cut, but the dealer retains the privilege of shuffling last.

THE CUT

The dealer puts the cards in the center of the table to be cut by the nondealer. If he refuses to cut, the dealer must cut, and in any event five cards must be in each cut piece of the deck to render the cut legal.

SCOREKEEPER

Selection of the scorekeeper is by mutual consent. If there's a kibitzer, he usually keeps score. Better use a pencil and paper; memory is not entirely trustworthy in a fast-running game. The scorekeeper enters under each player's name on the sheet his scores *as* they are made. Player A wins a trick and melds 20 points. The 20 is entered immediately under his name on the sheet. Player B wins a trick and melds 40 points. His 40 is forthwith posted to his credit. Totals are computed at the completion of each game, and the play proceeds until one column or the other totals 1,000 points or more and a winner is declared.

Note: Some players in scoring drop the last digit from their running account; so that a 40 meld, for instance, is entered as 4, a 20 as 2, etc. Under this system, of course, the winning score is 100.

And here's a way to score, using poker chips. Each player gets the following stack:

Nine blue chips, each valued at 100 points.

'our red chips, each valued at 20 points.

Two white chips, each valued at 10 points.

Each player keeps his chips at his right side. When he makes a meld he switches to his left side chips equal in point value to that meld. Likewise, when he counts his points won in tricks he switches from right-hand stack to left-hand stack chips equal in value to the points won. When the chips on his right side are exhausted he has scored 1,000 points.

THE DEAL

The cards are dealt four at a time, alternately, first to the dealer's opponent and then to himself, until each has twelve cards. The next card dealt from the top of the deck, which is the twenty-fifth card, is placed on the table face up. The rest of the stock goes face down next to the upturned card, but the stock is fanned out to facilitate drawing from it.

Players alternate, hand by hand, in dealing.

HOW TRUMP IS DETERMINED

The trump in two-handed Pinochle is determined by the suit of the upcard, the twenty-fifth card; if this card, faced in the center of the table, is a club, the trump for this hand is clubs . . . and so on.

If the twenty-fifth card is a 9, it's called the *deece of trump*, and the dealer is immediately credited in the scoring with 10 points.

BEGINNING THE PLAY

1. The nondealer plays first. He may lead off (start the game) by taking any card he elects from his hand and playing it face up on the table.

2. The dealer plays next. He may play any card he elects on his opponent's faced-up lead-off card.

In this phase of the game, the player is not required to follow the same suit as his opponent; nor is he required to trump should he fail to have a card of the suit led by his opponent. But be it borne in mind that in order to gain points a player must win tricks—

A. Because he can meld only after winning a trick.
B. Because points won in tricks are also tallied at the end of the hand.

To win a trick means:

A. To play to a trick a higher-ranking card of the same suit as your opponent's card, be it a trump or a non-trump suit.
B. If your opponent has led a card of a nontrump suit, to play a card of higher rank in the same suit or to play a trump card.
C. If two cards of the same rank and suit are played, to win the trick by having played the first card.

3. The player who wins a trick gathers the cards won and puts them *face down* in front of himself. *In no circumstances during the play may a player look through the cards he has won in tricks.*

4. The winner of the first trick is thereafter entitled to meld —if he has a meld in his hand and chooses to meld; it is not compulsory that he meld if he doesn't elect to do so. He is allowed only one meld for each trick won. A meld is a combination of cards (see standard values under "Scarne's General Rules for Pinochle," page 311), having special scoring values, played face up on the table.

5. If the winner of the first trick has the *deece* in his hand, he may exchange it for the face-up trump card, and doing this counts as a meld. However, he may make any other meld simultaneous with this exchange. When he exchanges the *deece* for the upcard he is credited with 10 points on his score. A *deece* can be melded any time after a player wins a trick, with or without another meld.

Note: If the *deece* was not turned up by the dealer and was not used in exchange by the winner of the first trick, then the upcard may be taken at any time by the winner of any trick for a score of 10 points if he holds the *deece* in his hand.

6. After the first-trick winner has picked up the trick and laid a meld or not, he now picks a card from the stock.

The meld must be down before the card is picked; melds cannot be laid after picking from stock.

7. A card that has been melded may be put into play at any time. It is still considered part of the player's hand though exposed.

8. The first-trick winner's opponent now takes a card from the stock. Each has played one card to the trick. Each has drawn a fresh card. Each still holds twelve cards.

9. The winner of the first trick leads off for the next trick. Play continues as particularized above. To summarize: lead-off plays a card, opponent plays a card, winner takes trick and is entitled to meld, winner picks a card from stock, opponent takes a card from stock, winner leads off anew.

This goes on until the stock is exhausted.

10. The winner of the last trick takes the last card from the stock and exposes it. The loser takes the upcard—by this time the *deece* or 9 of trump, but no score is credited now for this *deece*—it has already been scored for one player or the other.

11. Now each player picks up his melds, and holds them in his hand. Once again each player has twelve cards.

SPECIAL RULES FOR MELDING

1. Only the winner of a trick may meld.

2. Only one meld may be made at a time, *except* that a *deece* may be melded alone or with any other meld.

3. No meld may be made after a card has been taken from the stock.

4. After the stock is exhausted and the last stock card and upcard have been taken, no melds may be made.

5. A card used in one marriage meld cannot be used in another marriage meld.

6. A player may meld a roundhouse in two-handed Pinochle *only* by melding it all at once. He may meld kings separately, three marriages separately and then queens (in any order) but that is not a roundhouse, totaling at most only 220 points.

7. If dealer turns up a 9 (*deece*) as the twenty-fifth card he gets score credit for 10 points.

8. The winner of any trick, holding the *deece,* may exchange it for the upturned trump card, and is credited with 10 points.

9. The holder of the second *deece* (9 of trump suit) is also credited with 10 points *if* he melds the *deece.*

10. Loser of the last trick, who automatically draws the *deece,* is credited with no points for it.

RULES ON DRAWING FROM THE STOCK

1. If a player fails in his turn to draw a card, the deal is void because that player now has one less than the legal number of cards in his hand.

2. If a player draws two cards instead of one, he may replace the second card on the stock—if he hasn't seen it. If he has seen it he must show his own card to his opponent.

3. If a player has drawn out of turn, the drawn card must be returned to the pack. If that card properly belongs to his opponent, the player must show his next drawn card to the opponent.

4. A player is permitted to count the number of cards left in stock—but in no circumstances may he alter their order.

SECOND TURN IN PLAYING THE HAND

The stock being exhausted and the players having picked up their melds, play is continued. But there is a change, as follows, in the play of the tricks.

1. Winner of the last trick before the stock ran out leads off with any card he elects.

2. His opponent is obliged, if he has it, to play a card of the same suit as the lead-off. If he does not have such a card, he *must* play a trump card. (A trump card wins the trick against any card of any other suit.) If a trump is led, the opponent must play a higher-ranking trump, if possible; if he cannot do so, he still must play a trump card if he has one. Only when he has no trump at all may he play a card of another suit.

When two trump cards are played, that one having the higher value wins the trick.

When two cards of the same suit and value are played, the first card played wins the trick.

3. If the opponent does not have a card of the same suit as the lead-off card or a trump card, he may play any other card in his hand.

Play continues in accordance with these rules until all the tricks are played and each player has exhausted the cards in his hand. Winner of the last trick is credited with 10 points added to his score.

RENEGE

If, after the stock has run out and play for the tricks is in progress—(a) a player fails to follow the suit of the card led when he can; or (b) fails to trump, when he has a trump and does not have any cards of the suit led; or (c) trump being led, he fails to play a higher trump when he can, then—his opponent can call attention to this failure and, at any time while or after the hand is played, can claim a *renege*.

In any case the *reneger*—the player who failed to follow the rules—loses his entire count of cards made in tricks, and his opponent gets credit for 250 points, the total count of cards won in tricks. But the player who *reneged* retains his melds and their scoring values.

I have arrived at this decision after exhaustive investigation of two common practices.

1. To deprive a player who reneges of both his melds and his tricks won in cards is entirely too severe a punishment for what may be a merely mechanical mistake; remember that in two-handed Pinochle no one is required to follow suit before the stock is exhausted.

2. Unsound, I hold, is the practice of many players in simply not permitting a *renege*. They merely call the opponent's attention to his renege and compel him to play his cards properly, even after several tricks have been played.

What's wrong with this practice is that it virtually invites players to *renege* on the assumption that their opponent will not notice the infraction. What can such players lose? If their adversary catches them at it, the player who purposely *reneged* for profit receives no penalty.

DECLARING THE WINNER

Successive hands are dealt until one or both players score 1,000 or more points. The player who reaches 1,000 or more points is the winner, and the game is over. If (as occasionally happens) both players reach 1,000 points, the one with the highest score wins. If (as more rarely happens) the players are tied at some score higher than 1,000 points, one or more extra hands are dealt until the tie is broken; then the player with the higher score wins.

As long as neither has 1,000 points, the game continues and a new hand is dealt; each time the deal changes, the player who dealt the last hand next becoming the nondealer.

VARIATION IN DECLARING THE WINNER: THE CALL-OUT

The call-out is legal only if it has been mutually agreed on before the game starts. If, at any time before all the cards have been played, a player thinks he has scored 1,000 points or more, he may *call*. When he calls, the game ends forthwith, immediately. Then, if that player can prove he was right in calling (i.e., that his score is 1,000 or up), he wins the game. But if he is wrong, if his score is less than 1,000, he loses the game, no matter what his opponent's score is. A player may call out at any time during the game.

OTHER WAYS TO WIN

Although a score of 1,000 points or more is the accepted criterion for winning at two-handed Pinochle, some players prefer one of these alternatives. (*Note:* For a variation in scoring to be used legally it must be agreed on before the start of the game.)

1. One hand is dealt. The player scoring most points on that hand wins. In case of a tie score, a new hand (or new hands) is dealt until the tie is broken.

Under this scoring system, players may either keep a running score with pencil and paper or tally the score mentally. Example: Player A melds 20 points. Player B melds 40 points. Player B doesn't announce his 40; he merely says, "I have 20, right?" Players add and subtract as the hand develops until the last card of the stock has been picked. The player who has the plus credit then adds the points to his count in cards.

2. Or it may be decided before play starts that the winning total shall be not 1,000 but 1,250 or 1,500, or 2,000 points.

When the winning total runs into such high numbers as these, it is common and wise to keep score with pencil and paper.

Additional Rules for Two-Handed Pinochle

MISDEALS

There must be a new shuffle and cut whenever a misdeal occurs. The same dealer deals again.

MISDEALS: YES OR NO?

1. If one or more cards are exposed in cutting or reuniting cut cards, there *is* a misdeal.

2. If the pack has not been offered to the nondealer to be cut and the nondealer has not yet picked a card from the stock, there *is* a misdeal.

But, if the nondealer has picked a card from the stock, there *is not* a misdeal. The deal stands.

3. If one or more cards are exposed face up in the pack and the nondealer has not yet picked a card from stock, there *is* a misdeal.

4. But if the nondealer has picked a card from the stock and one or more cards are observed face up in the pack, there *is not* a misdeal, and the player whose turn it is must take the faced-up card.

5. If the dealer exposes one or more of his own cards on the deal, there *is not* a misdeal. If the dealer exposes one or more of the nondealer's cards, there *is* a misdeal.

6. If the nondealer exposes one or more of his own cards on the deal, there *is not* a misdeal.

7. If either player exposes one or more of his own cards during the game, there *is not* a misdeal.

8. If it is found that an imperfect pack is being used, a pack containing insufficient or duplicate (extra) cards, in violation of the rules on the Pinochle deck, play must stop immediately on the discovery. That hand is a dead hand and does not count, although all the previous hands are legal.

9. If either dealer or nondealer has been dealt fewer or more than twelve cards *on the deal* or if the cards have been dealt in any manner other than stipulated under the rules of the game, there *is* a misdeal.

INCORRECT MELDS

If a player lays down an improper meld or credits himself when melding with more or less points than is proper, he may correct the error, and there is no penalty. An incorrect meld or a credit for more or less points than correct on a legal meld may be corrected at any time before the last card is drawn from stock. After that the error cannot be rectified.

If a player lays an improper meld, he is allowed to replace the cards involved in his hand.

A player cannot meld if he has too few or too many cards in his hand.

LEADING OUT OF TURN

If, before the trick has been completed, it is established that a player has led out of turn, players merely pick up their cards and correct the error.

If the trick is completed and stacked with the completed tricks, the play stands, and the player who won the trick makes the next lead.

DRAWING A CARD FROM THE STOCK: SLIPS OF THE HAND

1. If in his turn of play a player fails to draw a card and his opponent has already picked a card from stock and put it in his hands, then the former draws two cards in his next legal turn of play to give himself a legitimate hand of twelve cards.

2. If a player draws two or more cards instead of the legal one, he puts the extra cards back on the stock in their proper order.

If he has looked at the cards he picked by mistake, he must show them to his opponent, and in addition must show his legally drawn card to his opponent. After the cards have been shown, they go back on the stock in their original order.

3. If a player has too many cards in his hand, he draws no more until his hand is reduced by discarding to the legal number.

4. If a player has too few cards in his hand, he draws enough cards in his next turn of play to bring his hand up to the legal number.

5. If a player draws a card out of turn he may put it back on the stock—provided he has not looked at it. If he has looked at it, he gives the card to his opponent, but must then show the card he draws properly.

If both players draw the wrong card, the play stands; it is a legal play.

6. If on the last draw three cards are left instead of two—that is, two faced-down cards and the upturned trump card—the winner of the trick must draw the top card of the stock. The loser must take the upturned trump card. The extra card is taken by the player who has a hand with one card missing.

There is no penalty when this occurs, nor is a misdeal declared.

LOOKING THROUGH CARDS TAKEN IN TRICKS

If he has played his card for the following trick a player may look at the last trick gathered in; and this rule holds regardless of which player won the last trick.

In no other circumstances is looking through the cards permitted except when looking through tricks to determine whether a player has *reneged*.

There is no enforceable penalty for an infraction of this rule. Crooked players, when they want to look through the cards, will simply allege that their opponent has *reneged*.

It may be agreed preventively before the play begins that any one who violates this rule shall lose his count in cards and that examination of the tricks for a *renege* shall be allowed only on completion of the play of the hand.

Strategy at Two-Handed Pinochle

The well-trained memory plays a vital role in two-handed Pinochle. Accurate card memory is important in any game involving the play of cards to successive tricks, thus is important in any Pinochle game; but the two-handed version is especially demanding, because during any hand each player must handle twenty-four cards—many more than at any other variant. Playing accurately and intelligently to twenty-four tricks puts a high premium on the disciplined memory.

CARD MEMORY

There is no shortcut to the development of a vivid and dependable card memory. I happen, because I've practiced hours a day for many years, to be able to remember just about where every card in the deck is through successive shuffles and cuts; but they tell me this is regarded as unusual. Yet I know several players with no marked intellectual talents who can remember virtually all the cards played at Pinochle up to the time the stock is exhausted; whereupon, after due consideration of their own hand, they know exactly what twelve cards their opponent holds.

How do you do it? Well, how do you know, when riding in a bus or subway or railroad train and reading a paper or just dozing along, when you've reached your corner? What is the mental machinery that, quite independently of any conscious effort on your part, ticks off the corners and stations and jogs you when the total is your number? The human mind is a remarkable adding machine. All it requires is housebreaking.

Psychologists tell us a normal memory notices and marks down everything the senses perceive. You don't have to think you've a remarkable memory. All you have to do is start trying. Let me suggest ways to start:

1. At first, try only to concentrate on remembering trump and the play of the eight aces.

2. If you can't remember the number of trumps played up to the time the stock is exhausted, let me suggest you try practicing with a game I invented called *Teeko*. In this game the pieces played are out in the open, so that it is possible to check on your memory of what's happened.

3. Don't count the trump cards you hold; just the trumps played.

4. And don't count your aces; just the aces played to tricks.

5. After you've learned to run an accurate count on these cards you're over the hump; your memory knows what you expect of it. Now add another suit to the cards you're trying to remember.

6. Don't get discouraged if a card or so slips your memory in actual play. Some of the world's greatest Bridge players confess they've muffed hands because they simply couldn't count up to thirteen. The job you've assigned yourself is harder than that.

7. But don't take the easy out and say this is too hard for any mortal man. I know a little girl five years old who can remember every card played at Gin Rummy. She's no genius; she just taught herself that this is one of the things people do.

8. Keep trying. One of these days you'll find that, of course,

you remember the cards. "Doesn't everybody?" you'll add, surprised.

MELDING

One of the most important aspects of two-handed Pinochle is knowing when and how to meld. *Example:* If a player holds a flush in trump early in the game, it is obviously advisable to meld the marriage in trump first. Upon winning a later trick, the ace, jack, and 10 of trump are laid for a flush. Thus the player runs up credit for 190 points. *But,* let's assume a later stage of the game. Let's assume the stock has only about six cards left and that the player doesn't hold the extra ace and 10 of trump. Now it is advisable to lay the flush at once and get credit for the 150 points forthwith. Otherwise, the player may not be able to meld the flush, if his opponent prevents him from taking another trick.

Experience is the best guide as to when and what to meld.

A consistently profitable strategy which I cannot emphasize too strongly is sacrificing (as cheaply as possible) the first few tricks to one's opponent and then trying to win the last few tricks. The possibilities of melding are enhanced toward the end of a hand, because the player has had access to more cards. But the value of this line of play is variable too, and must be judged hand by hand after careful assessment of the possibilities in the particular holding.

Also, in the later stages of the hand, it becomes important that the player try to prevent his opponent from melding, particularly if his observation of the cards played indicates the possibility of the opponent's making a flush, 100 aces, or some other high-value meld.

COUNTING

Keep a count of the points made in tricks, as you go. This is very important in the later stages of the play of the hand. It is a crucial factor when you play the variety of two-handed Pinochle which scores each hand as a separate game.

WHAT TO SAVE

Nobody can state a rule on this point. The judgment in each case depends on the particular hand. But remember this: *you can't save everything.* You can't hold possibilities for aces, kings, a flush, and so on. Consider the chances and the relative advantages as the hand develops. If you have a lot to meld in your hand, you may be better off to break up your three aces and take tricks with them, rather than risk being unable to complete all the melds you already have. This is especially true when you take your opponent's 10's with your aces.

BUT WHAT DO YOU DO NOW?

The record as it has been set down in these pages will, I think, prove that I believe in the teaching power of the example. But I have a theory that sample hands—without which a chapter essaying to instruct a player what card to play next would be ridiculous—are a waste of printers' ink and of the reader's ability to concentrate. What's the use of cluttering up these pages with sample hands which exemplify nothing, which (at odds of millions to one) will never occur in the player's hand? Sure, I could give you a dozen screwball sample hands and tell you bright ways to play them; but this would approach in silliness the newspaper Bridge-column dissertations on the Vienna and the Deschapelles Coup—which happen to the ordinary citizen about as often as the Gallup Poll asks him a question or "Stop the Music" calls him on the telephone. Sound card play consists of handling intelligently the cards you're most apt to get. You learn that play not from erudite poseurs but from practice, from experience—from playing.

Having made this clear, here are a few tips that might help almost any one:

1. Try to hold back a few high trump cards to be used if necessary when the stock runs low.

2. If you hold duplicate cards and have melded one of them, always play to the trick the one which has been melded. *Example:* You have melded a marriage in hearts. You have the other queen of hearts in your hand. Now, if you must play a heart queen to a trick, play the one from the melded marriage on the board.

3. If you have 100 aces, meld them at your first opportunity. Melded, they are much more potent in the play than they would be in your hand. You'd hesitate to play an unmelded ace to a trick. This reluctance, with its inevitable effect on your timing, might be crucial in the development of the hand. Meld 'em and use 'em!

4. It is generally sound in leading to a trick to play a card from your long suit—provided that isn't your trump suit. Ordinarily the 10-spot of the long suit is the soundest lead, because rarely will your opponent play on it the ace of that suit if he has it. And even if he does play his ace (unless he holds the duplicate, paired, ace), he has sacrificed a chance of melding 100 aces. If he trumps your 10 with a trump card whose duplicate you hold, he has thrown away his chance of making a flush.

If your opponent does play an ace on your 10, you'd better

assume he has the other ace . . . unless it's in your own hand.

QUIZ TEST

Let's pose this problem. Let's assume that in a two-handed Pinochle game the last six cards held by each player are 160 in trump (a flush plus a deece); now, who scores most points, both contestants being understood to play their cards correctly?

Who scores highest: the player whose turn it is to lead No. 1 of the last six cards? Or his opponent?

Answer: The points scored in cards for each player would be the same. But the player who would lead the first trump card would take the last trick—and would defeat his opponent by 10 points.

Note: The nondealer at two-handed Pinochle, due to the fact that he leads the first card therefore has a greater opportunity to lay down melds.

Two-Handed Pinochle: Doubling and Re-Doubling

This is the same as regular two-handed Pinochle with this exception:

At any time a player may call "Double!" His opponent then has to decide whether to accept the double, in which case the stakes for that hand are doubled, or to concede the hand, in which case only the normal stakes are paid. If the double is accepted, the acceptor has the option to re-double at any time. When a hand is re-doubled, the original doubler must decide whether to play for re-doubled stakes or to concede the doubled stakes. The privilege of re-doubling passes to the original doubler if he accepts the re-double. And so on.

Almost invariably this variation is played on each-game-a-separate-game basis, not on the 1000-point game basis.

Two-Handed Pinochle Turn-up Trump with a Sixty-four-Card Deck

This is played exactly as is two-handed Pinochle (see page 320), with the following exceptions:

1. To the standard Pinochle deck are added eight 8's and eight 7's (two cards in these ranks of each suit), to constitute a sixty-four-card deck.

2. The 8 and the 7 are ranked below the 9, the 7 being the lowest-ranking card.

3. The deece is the 7 of trump instead of the 9 of trump.

4. Excepting only the deece, the 7's and 8's have no value in the count.

5. Instead of the usual twelve in standard two-handed Pinochle, sixteen cards are dealt each player, four at a time.

6. The thirty-third card is turned face up to identify the trump suit.

CHAPTER THIRTY-ONE

Three-Handed and Four-Handed Pinochle

Three- or Four-Handed Pinochle, Individual Play, Turn-up Trump

REQUIREMENTS

1. Three or four players.

2. The standard Pinochle deck. (For description of the deck, rank of suits and cards, value of melded cards, rules for melding, special bonus melds, and value of cards won in tricks, see "Scarne's General Rules for Pinochle," page 311.)

OBJECT OF THE GAME

To win the game by scoring 1,000 or more points before any one of one's opponents does so.

THE STAKES

X being what you think you can afford, the game is played for X cents to X dollars per 1,000 points, which is game, but most players let the stakes range from 25¢ to $1 a game.

THE SCOREKEEPER

He is selected by mutual consent. The score is recorded with pencil and paper. Melds are recorded as they are made, and are scored formally after a trick has been won. Valuable cards won in tricks are scored at the end of the game.

RULES OBTAINING BEFORE THE ACTUAL DEAL

Under "Scarne's General Rules for Pinochle" (page 316) are set forth the laws governing selection of the dealer and establishment of seating positions at the table, changing seats, the shuffle, and the cut.

THE DEAL

When the game is three-handed, the dealer deals to each player sixteen cards four at a time, starting with the leader (player to the dealer's left) and dealing clockwise until the dealer has four cards left in his deck stock. The top one of these four cards is turned face up in the middle of the table. (It's the forty-fifth card from the top of the original deck.) He takes the three remaining cards for himself.

When the game is four-handed, each player in the manner above described is dealt twelve cards. Again, the forty-fifth card is faced up on the table. Again the dealer takes into his own holding the last three cards.

HOW TRUMP IS DETERMINED

The suit of the upturned card in the center of the table, the forty-fifth card dealt from the deck, establishes the trump suit.

If the upturned card happens to be a 9-spot (deece), the dealer is immediately credited in the scoring with 10 points.

If the upturned card is not a deece, the privilege of exchanging the upturned card for a deece passes to the player to the dealer's left. If he lacks a deece or chooses not to exchange it for the upturned card, the privilege moves to *his* left, and rotates clockwise until the upturned card has been exchanged for a deece. The player exchanging the upcard for the deece gets credit for a 10-point meld. The holder of the other deece (9 of trumps) may meld it and get credit for 10 points.

If all players except the dealer fail or decline to exchange the upcard for a deece, the dealer may take the upcard as part of his hand.

If the upcard is previously exchanged for a deece, the dealer *must* take the deece to complete his hand, but he is not credited with 10 points for that deece; the exchanger gets the 10-point credit.

The players now meld. The card which had been the upcard may be used by the holder in his melding.

MELDING

All the players lay down their melds, and the scorekeeper enters each player's total under his name on the score sheet. After the scores have been recorded, the players pick up their melds and put them back into their hands, and they are now ready for the play of the hand.

THE PLAY

The leader leads off. He may play any card he elects. Turn of play then rotates to the left, clockwise. After the first card has been led, each player in his turn of play (which, remember, moves to the left) *must* observe the following rules:

1. Each player, if he has it, must play a card of the suit led. *Example:* A diamond is the first card led; therefore all players must follow with a diamond if they have one in their hands.

2. If the player does not have a card of the suit led, he must play a trump card.

3. If he does not have a card of the suit led or a trump card, he may play any other card in his hand.

4. When a trump card is led, is the first card played to the trick, each other player *must* play a higher trump card than any previously played, if he has one.

5. But if a nontrump card is led and a player trumps that card, succeeding players if compelled to trump are not obliged to play a trump card higher than the one already played.

6. The highest-ranking card played to it wins the trick. When two cards of the same value tie for the trick, the winner is the first one played.

7. The winner of the trick leads off again, and play rotates to the left under the rules above set forth.

8. Winner of the last trick is credited with 10 points more on his score.

This routine of play continues until all cards in the players' hands have run out and all cards have been played to tricks. Then the score for melds and points taken in tricks is totaled; and a new deal takes place and play continues until one of the players has scored 1,000 points and won the game.

Additional Rules

Whenever a misdeal occurs there must be a new shuffle and cut, and the same dealer deals again.

MISDEALS: YES OR NO?

1. If one or more cards are exposed in cutting or reuniting the pack, there *is* a misdeal.

2. If the pack has not been offered to the player at the dealer's right to be cut—

A. There *is* a misdeal if the trump card has not been turned up.
B. There *is not* a misdeal if the trump card has been turned up. The deal is legal.

3. If one or more cards are observed face up in the pack during the deal, there *is* a misdeal.

4. If on the deal the dealer exposes one or more of any other player's cards, there *is* a misdeal.

5. But if the dealer exposes one or more of his own cards on the deal, there *is not* a misdeal.

6. If a player exposes one or more of his own cards during the deal or the play, there *is not* a misdeal.

7. If any player including the dealer has been dealt fewer or more cards than constitute a legal hand, there *is* a misdeal.

8. If it is discovered that an imperfect deck is in use, i.e., a deck containing fewer or more cards than required under the rules for the game, play must stop immediately on the discovery. The hand in progress is a dead hand and *does not* count. All previous hands are legal and *do* count.

9. If when the last trick is played it is found that one or more players have an incorrect number of cards, there *is* a misdeal.

LOOKING THROUGH CARDS TAKEN IN TRICKS

If a player insists that a *renege* has been committed he may ask to examine any cards he or any other player has won in tricks. But he can look at another player's last trick or his own *only* after playing his card to the following trick. The rule provides that cards taken in tricks must not be looked through except on an allegation of *reneging*. But no penalty is provided for infraction of the rule, since any player determined to violate its spirit can still comply with its letter by charging a *renege* before examining the cards.

LEADING AND PLAYING OUT OF TURN

If a player leads or plays a card out of turn and this is discovered before the trick has been covered and a card has been played to the next trick, the card played in error must be taken back by the offending player and the error must be corrected. But if play to the trick has been completed and the player who won the trick has led a card to the next trick, the play is legalized *de facto*, and cannot be corrected.

NO ANGLING!

It is not feasible to define a penalty for any player's instructing any other player what card to play verbally, by grimace, by gesture, or by flashing a tip-off card. Angling is often indefinable. The player who consistently resorts to devices inimical to decent sportsmanship and fair play is a crook. The only enforceable penalty against him is refusing to play with him.

RENEGE RULES

Any of the following violations shall be construed as a *renege*, providing the offender's card has been covered by a card played by the next succeeding player or (if there is no further play to that trick) the trick has been taken and a card has been led to the following trick. A *renege* may be corrected if the error is noted before the next proper play in the game has been made. These are *reneges:*

1. If a player able to do so fails to follow the suit led when the laws of the game require him to do so.

2. If a player able to do so fails to trump when required.

3. If a player able to do so fails to play a higher trump card when the laws of the game he is playing require that he do so.

PENALTIES FOR RENEGES

1. If the bidder *reneges*, the amount of the penalty against him shall be the same as if he had played the hand and failed to make his bid.

2. If a player reneges, the amount of the penalty he must pay the bidder shall be the same as if the bidder played the hand and made his bid.

3. When any player defending against a bidder *reneges*, his *renege* is binding upon any other defending player. The amount of the penalty each other player must pay the bidder shall be exactly as if he himself committed the *renege*.

Partnership Pinochle, Turn-up Trump

This game is played exactly as is three- or four-handed Pinochle (individual play, turn-up trump), with the following exceptions:

1. Four players, two against two, play as partners.

2. Selection of partnerships is governed under "Scarne's General Rules for Pinochle." (See page 311.)

3. *Table talk is forbidden.* Partners are not permitted to cue their teammates as to what card it would be desirable to play, nor are they permitted to comment by word or sign on the play of the hand. For instance, to observe that the previous play, or any previous play, was good or bad is absolutely banned.

4. The scores of the two players forming a partnership are totaled as a single score.

Scarne's Rules for Auction Pinochle with Widow: Each Hand a Complete Game

Favored by money players because of its speed and its prompt and straightforward pay-off, this version of the game is probably the biggest gambling variant of the Pinochle family. You can play it for stakes ranging from a penny a hundred points to X dollars a hundred, and write your own ticket. The most popular scale of betting is five or ten cents a hundred; but not long ago I saw three beetle-browed citizens seeking a moment of carefree relaxation in a game whose stakes were $25 a hundred. In the kitty was $3,600 in cash.

REQUIREMENTS

1. Three or four players.

(When three are playing, each is dealt a Pinochle hand, and each is an active player. When there are four players, the dealer stays out of the play, only dealing a hand to each of the three others. Since in a four-handed game the deal rotates, each player takes his turn at dealing and staying out; hence in an extended session this feature will work mathematically to the disadvantage of no one. But I do recommend the three-handed version.)

2. A standard Pinochle deck.

(For rules on the deck, rank of cards and suits, value of melded cards, bonus melds, and value of cards won in tricks, see "Scarne's General Rules for Pinochle," page 311.)

OBJECT OF THE GAME

To make a winning bid and then score a number of points equal to or more than the number bid. In this competition, wherein every hand dealt is a game complete in itself, the objective of the opponents is to prevent the bidder from making his bid.

THE STAKES: HOW MUCH A HUNDRED?

The amount of cash bet, collected, and paid at this game depends on the number of points bid by the highest bidder. But, be it the minimum 250 or the maximum 700-plus, there is a standard ratio determining the cash worth of any hand.

Although players before the start of the game solemnly agree that they'll play for so much per hundred—a cent or 5¢ or 10¢ or 25¢ or 50¢, and on up to X dollars—it doesn't work out in that per-hundred ratio.

Suppose you're playing for a nickel a hundred. Very well; for the minimum bid of 250 and any bid on up to 290 points, the settlement is 10¢—which isn't anywhere near a nickel a hundred. Increase the bid 50 points, making it from 300 to 340 points, and the settlement becomes 15¢. An increase of 50 points over that, making the bid 350 to 390 points, calls for a settlement of 20¢ . . . and so on up in successive units of fifty and five.

The following chart has been set up to specify the pay-off in a game played for a nickel a hundred; but the last column will indicate the settlement at any stakes. To get the settlement on any bid in Column 1, multiply your stakes-per-hundred by the corresponding unit in Column 3.

Standard Table of Betting Limits and Units

Amount Bid in Points	Amount to be Paid at 5¢ a Hundred	Units by Which to Multiply Your Stakes per Hundred
250 to 290	10¢	2
300 to 340	15¢	3
350 to 390	20¢	4
400 to 440	25¢	5
450 to 490	30¢	6
500 to 540	35¢	7
550 to 590	40¢	8
600 to 640	45¢	9
650 to 690	50¢	10
700 and over	55¢	11

The maximum points a bidder can make at Auction Pinochle (holding a legal hand of fifteen cards plus the three cards buried, and disregarding such special circumstances as bonus melds, *reneges,* and bad play) is 720 points. This total is arrived at by making use of the simplified card count. Use of the so-called old-timers' count would reduce this maximum to 718 points, and use of the so-called streamlined count would reduce it further to 710 points. Since I've encountered some players who don't understand how to calculate this maximum, here's the way the cards can be distributed to pile up a 720-point total.

In the Bidder's Hand

1. Double flush in spades (ten cards).
2. Ace of clubs, ace of diamonds, and ace of hearts (three cards).
3. Two jacks of diamonds (two cards).
4. Bidder buries the ace and two 10's of diamonds (three cards).

Held by the Opponents

1. Opponent No. 1 holds a deece of trump and two 9's of diamonds. Distribution of other cards in his hand does not affect the score.
2. Opponent No. 2 holds a deece of trump and two queens

and two kings of diamonds. Distribution of other cards in his hand has no effect on the scoring.

Stipulating the above distribution, the bidder would meld 480 points (300 in trump, 100 aces, and 80 Pinochle), and the bidder's count in valuable cards won in tricks would total 240 points, for a grand total of 720 points.

It is possible for the bidder to make 730 points, providing the bidder's opponents played the hand incorrectly.

Next time a veteran Pinochle player or the self-styled card detective tells you the maximum possible is 690 points, point this out to him.

SPECIAL BONUS BETTING LIMITS

Many players like to pay off at certain special bonus rates for high bids. While any scale of bonuses is permissible, the most common rates are set forth below; it must, however, be observed that to be legal such special arrangements must be made before the start of the game and must be entered in writing on the score sheet.

Amount Bid in Points	Amount Paid Off in Units
250 to 290	2
300 to 340	3
350 to 390	5
400 to 440	7
450 to 490	10
500 to 540	13
550 to 590	17
600 to 640	21
650 to 690	25
700 and over	30

THE SETTLEMENT OR PAY-OFF

The terms of settlement in this game are customarily cash. Chips are often used, but since—except in most unusual circumstances—the chips are negotiable for cash in the house, it amounts to the same thing.

The amount of settlement on each hand is established by the betting-limit scale and the number of points a player *bids*. The extra points he may score above his bid are irrelevant to the pay-off.

I.

If the bidder plays the hand and makes his bid or his opponents concede the hand to him, and if hearts, clubs, or diamonds were trump, he collects a single unit amount from each

player. For example, if the betting limit is 5¢ a hundred and
the bid is 250 points, the winning bidder collects 10¢ from
each of the other two players.

II.

If, playing the hand, the bidder fails to make his bid or if
after playing one or more cards he concedes the hand, and if
hearts, clubs, or diamonds were trump, he must pay each other
player a double amount. For example, if the betting limit is
5¢ a hundred and the bid is 250 points, the losing bidder must
pay each other player 20¢.

III.

If the bidder concedes he cannot make his bid and throws
in his cards without playing a card, he pays a single amount to
each other player. For example, if the limit is 5¢ a hundred
and the bid is 250 points, the losing bidder must pay each other
player 10¢ as settlement.

IV.

If the bidder makes *spades* trump and makes his bid or his
opponents concede the hand, he collects double the amount
from each other player. With the betting limit 5¢ a hundred
and the bid 250 points, the winning bidder collects 20¢ from
each other player.

V.

If, making spades trump and playing the hand, the bidder
fails to make his bid or if he plays one or more cards and then
concedes the hand by throwing in his cards, he must pay each
other player double-double. For example, the betting limit is
the same 5¢ a hundred and the bid is 250 points; in this circumstance the losing bidder must pay each other player 40¢.

A player who makes spades trump and throws in his hand
without playing a card pays only a single amount to each other
player.

My ruling here is dictated by my respect for realism. If
opponents insist on their right to collect double on a spade-
trump hand, the losing bidder would coolly reply—and well
within his rights to do so—that in fact one of the other three
suits was trump.

Note: This rule, giving spades a special doubled value, is
incorporated into my rules for the game, but players may
agree that spades shall pay single value only. When this exception is played, however, it must, to be legal, be agreed on
before the start of the game.

VI.

In a four-handed game, even though the dealer stays out of the play of the hand, he is included in the cash settlement. When the bidder wins, the dealer must pay him as do the active players in the game. When the bidder loses, he must pay the dealer the same as he pays the active players.

HEARTS TRIPLE. YES OR NO?

The hearts-triple rule is optional, not incorporated into my standard rules. While choosing to play this rule is within the player's discretion, it must be agreed on by all the players before the start of the game.

I.

If the bidder makes hearts trump and makes his bid or his opponents concede the hand, the winning bidder collects a triple amount from each other player. The familiar example: betting limit is 5¢ a hundred and the bid is 250 points. Winning, the bidder collects 30¢ from each other player.

II.

If, making hearts trump, the bidder plays the hand and fails to make the bid or concedes the hand after playing one or more cards, he must pay each other player an amount called triple-triple (two times triple), six times the single amount. At 5¢ a hundred and 250 points, the losing bidder must pay each other player 60¢.

Note: For the realistic reasons cited above (referring to spades), a player who makes hearts trump and then throws in his cards without playing the hand is liable to pay each other player only the single amount. The triple-triple or any other special penalty here is unenforceable; the bidder would simply allege that trump was clubs or diamonds.

THE KITTY: TO HAVE OR NOT TO HAVE,
THAT IS THE QUESTION

The kitty is not a compulsory feature of Auction Pinochle. To be legal it must be agreed on by all players at the start of the game. It is simply a pot, additional to other routine settlements among the players, put aside to be collected by the player who bids and makes a 350-point hand. Since the kitty is optional, the rules for paying and collecting from it are also optional and subject to wide variation. However, here are the rules I suggest for the kitty.

1. Before the game starts each player antes into the kitty an amount equal to the stipulated settlement for a 250-point bid.

2. Whenever all contestants pass, or fail to bid, each player must ante into the kitty an amount equal to the first ante.

(By mutual consent, players may stop anteing whenever they choose.)

3. To collect the kitty a player must bid *and make* a minimum of 350 points.

4. If a player bids 350 or more irrespective of suits and then *concedes the hand* he must ante into the kitty an amount *equal to* the sum already in the kitty.

5. Moreover, if a player bids 350 or more irrespective of suit and *plays the hand and fails to make his bid* he must ante into the kitty an amount *double* the sum already in the kitty.

I do not recommend compelling the unsuccessful bidder to ante into the kitty an amount four times its value for failure to make a spade hand or six times its value for failure to make a heart hand. This arrangement is grossly inequitable. No matter what he bids, the player can *win* only the total amount in the kitty. That is, the kitty doesn't pay off any more if spades or hearts are trump; it proffers the player no advantage for the risk or responsibility he assumes; so why should his contract with kitty impose all the hardship on him?

That's a personal credo. But certain players will insist on a maximum of excitement and a minimum of logic. For them I append the following two rules, with this admonition: they cannot be binding unless they are mutually and unanimously understood and agreed upon before the start of the game.

1. If a player bids 350 or more points *in spades,* plays the hand, and fails to make the bid, he must ante into the kitty an amount triple the sum already in the kitty.

2. If it has been agreed that hearts are payable at triple value and a player bids 350 or more points *in hearts* and fails to make his bid, he must ante in the kitty an amount four times the sum already in the kitty.

These rules, as stated above, are optional. The following are compulsory.

1. If a player goes broke he is entitled to take out of the kitty an amount determined by the number of players in the game. If there are three players he may take out one-third of the kitty's total cash value. If there are four players he may take out one-fourth of the kitty's total cash value. *But* taking money from the kitty signifies the player has quit the game. He cannot resume play with the money he takes from the kitty.

2. If the kitty gets unusually big, the players may by mutual consent divide it among themselves in equal portions.

3. If the game ends and a kitty survives, it is split equally among the players.

4. If when a new player enters the game there is an existent

kitty, that player must put into the kitty an amount determined by the number of other players. If he is the fourth player, he must ante an amount equal to one-third of the sum in the kitty.

5. A bidder cannot play for the kitty unless he has on the table enough money to cover the kitty in the event he fails to make his bid. Lacking such a sufficiency of cash on the table, he may play for as much of the kitty as his means will cover—after deducting the amount he must pay the other players for an unsuccessful bid.

AGREEMENTS BEFORE THE GAME STARTS

To be marked on the score sheet by a scorekeeper, mutually chosen:

Amount of the stakes.

Rules governing the kitty, if any.

Special bonus pay-offs for high hands, if any.

BEFORE THE DEAL

(For selection of the dealer, establishment of positions at the table, and the shuffle and cut, see "Scarne's General Rules for Pinochle," page 311.)

THE DEAL

Starting with the leader, the dealer deals one round of cards three at a time clockwise until each player has three cards. Then he deals one card face down in the center of the table to start the *widow*. (The first *widow* card is the tenth card dealt from the pack.) He repeats this. (The second *widow* card is the twentieth card dealt from the pack.) The third round is dealt the same way. (Third *widow* card is thirtieth card off the deck.) Now, starting with the leader again and going clockwise, three cards at a time are dealt each player until the deck is exhausted and each player has fifteen cards in his hand.

Note: A method of dealing preferred by some players is to give each player in turn four cards and then to deal one into the *widow*. This method is continued for three rounds, after which each player is dealt three cards at a time until the whole deck has been dealt.

I have prohibited other current methods of dealing in order to minimize the likelihood of a cheater's dealing certain valuable cards to the *widow*—or to himself for that matter.

THE BIDDING

The bidding starts with the leader and rotates to the left, clockwise, until all or all but one player have passed.

A bidding turn:

1. *To pass.* When a player announces a pass, he indicates that he doesn't want to bid and no longer has any interest in bidding. Once having passed, a player cannot bid again on that hand.

2. *To bid.* When a player calls out a certain total of points, he commits himself to make those points with the hand he holds *and the widow,* if he wins the bid.

If the first bid is made by the leader or the player to the leader's immediate left, it must be 250 or more. But, should the leader and the man at his left pass, the last active player may bid—only he must bid at least 290 or 310 points. As 250 is the minimum for the first and second players, 290–310 is the minimum for the third. This last player cannot bid 300 flat; but he may bid any amount he likes over 310.

If all three active players pass, their hands are thrown in, and a new hand is dealt by the next dealer.

If a player opens the bidding by stating a legal bid and the other two players pass or have passed, the bidding player is the winner of that *bid.* If, the bidding being opened, one or both of the other active players want to enter the auction, the bids must be higher than the previous bidder's by at least 10 points. Bidding is permitted in multiples of 10 only.

Bidding rotates around the table to the left until at last two players have passed and only one bidder remains. That player has *won the bid.*

THE WIDOW, THE BLIND, THE BUY

In no circumstances may a player, be he active or inactive, look at the three cards in the *widow* while the bidding is still under way. The *widow,* the *blind,* or the *buy* is the name given the three cards faced down on the table during the deal. The bidder—the player who won the auction—takes these three cards and may use them in an attempt to improve his hand. But before putting them into his hand, he must turn them face up on the table to let the other players see them. Now, having incorporated them into his holding, he may do one of two things: He may concede the hand and throw in his cards; or he may decide to play the hand.

CONCEDING THE HAND

Having considered the potentials of his hand plus the widow and before leading a card to the first trick, the bidder may concede he cannot with his melds and prospective tricks make his bid. It is his right to throw in his cards and pay the other players a single amount—as well as the kitty, if there is one. (See "The Kitty," page 341.)

Or the concession may work the other way. The bidder, holding a good hand, may show a part of it plus his meld (equaling or nearly equaling the amount of his bid), and the opponents may concede and make their cash settlement with him. Or opponents may concede defeat at any time during the play by throwing in their cards.

But note: If only one of the opponents concedes the hand, the game must be played out to a formal decision.

Also, the bidder may concede defeat at any time during the play of the hand by throwing in his cards; but if he has led a card to start the play, he must pay each other player a double amount, just as if he had finished the hand and had failed to make the bid. This is unless the trump was spades, in which case he must pay each other player four times the single amount.

If neither bidder nor opponents concede the hand it must be played out. Before actual play begins, the bidder must discard and meld.

DISCARDING OR BURYING THREE CARDS

To reduce his hand to the legal fifteen cards for the play, the bidder must bury three cards after picking up the widow. These three cards are put face down in front of the bidder, and are counted as tricks taken or won by the bidder, although he must win a trick from his opponents to validate them.

DISCARDS

The following rules on discarding must be observed:

1. The bidder cannot bury (discard) any card used to form a meld—that is, a card melded for which he has already received credit in points. *If he should bury such a card* and his attention is called to the fact any time after the first card has been led in the play of the hand (but not after payment for the hand has been made), that bidder has *reneged,* and he loses the hand. His opponents collect on the same basis as if the bidder had failed to make his bid.

2. But the bidder may change his melds, exchange the buried cards, or change his trump suit at any time before he leads his first card in actual play.

3. A bidder may, if he elects, bury a trump card (that is, one not used in a meld), but he *must* announce the fact that it is a trump card he is burying. It is not mandatory that he reveal the denomination of that card. Failure to announce the burial of a trump card is to be construed as a *renege,* and loses the hand for the bidder; and the penalty is the same as if he failed to make his bid in play.

4. A bidder is not required to announce the burying of an ace or any other denomination of card.

5. If in starting the play of the hand the bidder leads a card and it is found he has buried too few or too many cards or has failed to bury any cards, his attention may be called to that fact, and it constitutes a *renege*. The penalty is the same as if the bidder played the hand and failed to make his bid.

MELDING

As he sees fit, a bidder may meld before of after discarding, providing he adheres to the rules for discarding or burying. The bidder, i.e., the player who won the auction, is the only player permitted to put down melds. For the rules governing the meld, see "Scarne's General Rules for Pinochle" (page 313).

THE PLAY OF THE HAND

After a bidder has (a) discarded and (b) picked up his melds, actual play for tricks begins under the following rules:

1. The bidder may lead any card he selects from among the fifteen in his hand, putting it face up on the table to start the trick.

After a card has been led, no changes in melds may be made.

2. Each other player must follow the suit of the card led, if he has a card of such a suit.

3. If another player does not have a card of the suit led, he *must* trump.

4. If he does not have a card of the suit led or a trump, the opposing player may play to the trick any card he chooses.

5. Only when a trump card is led must a player play a higher-ranking card if he has one.

6. If a nontrump card is led and the second player trumps it and the third player is then compelled to trump because he does not have a card of the suit led, this third player is not compelled to play a trump card of rank higher than the previous player's.

7. Winner of a trick leads off to the next trick.

To win a trick, a player must:

A. Play a higher-ranking card than the other players', in the suit led, be it trump or a nontrump suit, or

B. In trumping a trick, play a higher-ranking trump card than any other player.

When two cards of the same value are played and are tied to win the trick, the first card to have been played wins the trick.

Play continues thus until all the cards in the players' hands are exhausted, fifteen tricks in all.

COUNTING VALUABLE CARDS IN TRICKS

To the value of the three cards he has buried, the bidder adds the value of the cards he has won in tricks. This total he adds to the points he has scored in melds. If the resultant grand total equals or surpasses the amount of his bid, he has made his bid and wins the hand, collecting from each player the amount at stake. If the grand total is less than his bid, the bidder has lost the hand, and must pay each opponent the amount at stake.

The bidder's opponents count their valuable cards in tricks won to certify that the bidder's count is correct.

Additional Rules

MISDEALS

Whenever a misdeal occurs there must be a new shuffle and cut, and the same dealer deals again.

1. If one or more cards are exposed in cutting or reuniting the cut packets of the deck, there *is* a misdeal.

2. If the deck has not been offered to the player at the dealer's right to be cut and the bidding has not started, there *is* a misdeal. If the bidding has started, the deal is legal.

3. If one or more cards are observed face up in the pack during the deal, there *is* a misdeal.

4. If in the deal the dealer exposes one or more of any other players' cards, there *is* a misdeal.

5. If in the deal or during the play the *dealer* exposes one or more of his own cards, there *is not* a misdeal.

6. If a *player* exposes one or more of his own cards during the deal or the play, there *is not* a misdeal.

7. If during the deal the dealer exposes one or more cards of the widow, there *is* a misdeal. If the widow has been dealt more or fewer cards than the legal amount, there *is* a misdeal.

8. If the dealer or one or more players have been dealt fewer or more cards than constitute a legal hand, there *is* a misdeal.

9. If it is found that an imperfect deck is in play—having fewer or more (duplicate) cards than required in the standard Pinochle deck, play must stop immediately on discovery. That hand is a dead hand, and it does not count; although all previous hands shall stand as legal and binding.

10. If when the last trick is played, it is found that one or

more players have an incorrect number of cards, the hand *is* a misdeal.

LOOKING THROUGH CARDS TAKEN IN TRICKS

Except in determining whether a *renege* has been committed, no player is permitted to look through the cards taken in tricks. A player may ask to see any of the cards he or another player has won in tricks, if he is willing to insist that a *renege* has been committed. A player may ask to look at another player's or his own last captured trick *only* after he has played his card to the next succeeding trick.

There is no enforceable penalty for the infraction of looking through the cards, because a shrewd player determined to examine the cards can always legally allege that he is only checking on a suspected *renege.*

IMPROPER BIDDING

If a player bids or passes out of turn, or bids an incorrect amount, or bids after passing, *there is no penalty.* He may correct his error. If a player in his proper turn bids an amount equal to, or lower than, the previous player's bid, he *must* correct his bid; he must make a bid sufficiently higher to be legal.

LEADING AND PLAYING OUT OF TURN

If a player leads or plays a card out of turn and the error is detected before the trick has been covered *and* a card to the following trick has been p!ayed, the card played in error must be taken back by each offending player, and the mistake must be corrected.

But if the trick has been completed *and* the winner of that trick has led a card to the following trick, the play however in error shall stand as a legal and binding play.

ANGLING—IT'S BANNED

There is only one practicable remedy for angling. If a player or an inactive player tells the bidder or any other player what card to play next—whether orally, or by gesture, or by grimace, or by showing a card during the play of the hand—that player is simply and baldly crooked.

It is impossible to write a penalty for such flagrant infractions of the laws and spirit of a sportsman's game. I shall not attempt to phrase a rule governing coarse abuses.

My only opinion on the subject is that it is humiliating and unprofitable to play with a crook. Don't do it. If an angle player wants to know why you're withdrawing from the game, open this book to this page, and show him this paragraph.

RENEGES

Any of the following violations shall be construed as a *renege*, providing the offender's card has been covered by a card played by the next succeeding player or (if there is no further play to that trick) the trick has been taken and a card has been led to the following trick. A *renege* may be corrected if the error is noted before the next proper play in the game has been made. These are *reneges:*

1. If a player able to do so fails to follow the suit led when the laws of the game require him to do so.

2. If a player able to do so fails to trump when required.

3. If a player able to do so fails to play a higher trump card when the laws of the game he is playing require that he do so.

PENALTIES FOR RENEGES

1. If the bidder *reneges*, the amount of the penalty against him shall be the same as if he had played the hand and failed to make his bid.

2. If a nonbidder *reneges*, the amount of the penalty he must pay the bidder shall be the same as if the bidder played the hand and made his bid.

3. When any player defending against a bidder *reneges*, his *renege* is binding upon any other defending player. The amount of the penalty each other player must pay the bidder shall be exactly as if he himself committed the *renege*.

Strategy at Auction Pinochle with Widow

My assumption, based on my own observation of how people behave at the card table, is that when you play three- or four-handed Pinochle with a widow (each hand a complete game), you play for money. This is the most popular game in the Pinochle family. It is played oftener and for more cash than all the other variants combined.

One owes it to himself and other people, I hold, to play any game as well as one can. I can't abide the ham who, duly butchering the hand, explains in a wheedling way that he's just a social player—as if a reasonable skill at cards were antisocial. The game above just discussed is well worth playing for all it's worth; and it's worth a lot. In it is enough of the scientific to arrest the interest of the most serious student of cards. In it too is more than enough of the chance element to fascinate the most reckless of gamblers. Understand it; learn it; enjoy it.

Its scientific side may be divided into three big parts:

1. The evaluation of the hand; that is, deciding what it's worth for bidding purposes.

2. How, after the melding, to play the cards to their maximum advantage.

3. How to discard, or bury, properly and profitably.

Chance plays its dominant role in these two phases of the game:

1. Bidding in hope of finding in the widow one or more cards whose addition to your dealt holding will give you a cinch hand.

2. Doggedly playing out a borderline hand and hoping that certain crucial cards held by your opponents will fall on the tricks as you want them to.

Unquestionably the best way to improve your Pinochle game is to play and play and then play some more, but there are thousands of Pinochle addicts who've been playing for years, decades, all their lives and still play very bad games. If experience is the best teacher, why hasn't it taught them anything? Simply because they have stubbornly refused to learn. To play a good game of Pinochle requires native intelligence, a certain humility, and an awareness that one doesn't know all the answers by a long shot.

Some players evaluate their hands very accurately before the bidding starts, and then bid like fools. They're a little like the fishermen who can cast a fly like angels, who know all there is to know about tackle and water and trout, but never catch a fish. Once the bidding gets under way, the Pinochle professor loses his head or his nerve, gets angry or stubborn, lets a wily opponent needle him, and winds up by overbidding his cards to an impossible level. The gymnasium fighter is a commonplace in every kind of competition: the sound theoretician, the flawless stylist, the perfect critic. The only thing wrong with him is that he can't perform when the chips are down. That's one kind of Pinochle player.

There's another. There's the hard-headed realist who bids like an angel—never too much, never too little; he never loses his nerve; he never loses his temper; and he winds up broke. He has never noticed that the play of the cards at Pinochle is as much a test of a man's nerve and skill as is the bidding. He has never bothered to learn the subtleties in the play of the hand. All he has missed—if you don't count $300 or $400 a year in cash he's dropped to more observant comrades—is half the fun of the game. Learn, as a fine Bridge player learns, to enjoy the play of the hand. . . .

I have no formula, no short cut, to guarantee you'll win at your next Friday night Pinochle session. Successful Pinochle is, I guess, a little like successful writing: it's a matter of keying yourself up to a certain level and sweating to sustain that level. Every step of the game must be a new problem to be solved. That's what makes Pinochle—or gardening, or music, or living—the fun it is. Don't ask me for formulas. But you do have a right to ask me for tips. And it's a pleasure to share with you certain general truths I've learned.

First. Study the rules. The player who knows the Pinochle rules has a decided advantage over the player who's never quite sure what happens next. Knowing the rules enables you to defend yourself. It prevents your acceding to an unfair or inequitable decision against yourself. It saves you money.

Second. The Pinochle player must by all means be alert at all times. If you're tired or have had a bad day at the office or plant, don't sit in on that Pinochle game. Order a beer, get a sandwich, lean back and watch.

Third. Make it a matter of principle never to let another player exasperate you, whether on purpose or with unconscious mannerisms. Few players—those being the geniuses of the game—play a cool, sound game when they're angry. That's why professional gamblers try to get amateur opponents roiled up.

Remember the old gambler's saying: "Lose your head," it goes, "and lose your money."

Let's get down to business.

BIDDING

In Auction Pinochle there are three kinds of bidding available to the accomplished player. They are:

The Safe Bid. This bid never exceeds the total of visible points in melds plus the points certain to be won in tricks.

The Risk Bid. Depending on how far it exceeds the certainties, this may be either a brilliant gamble or sheer recklessness. It is the bid surpassing in total points the points in meld plus points certain to be won in tricks.

The Fake Bid. This corresponds approximately to the blind psychic at Bridge. It is an attempt to push an opponent's bid past the safe-bid level and thus to trap him in an unmakable contract.

It may be noted that the fake bid not uncommonly boomerangs on the fake bidder. I advise you to use it, if at all, at a very low level of bidding. And I further advise that, if you find you've gotten a reputation for fake bidding, you abandon it; wait until you have a rock-crushing hand, then make a bid that sounds like a fake, and let your opponents topple into that deadfall.

It is obvious that if a player sticks to the safe bid as defined above he will rarely if ever go into the hole. But it must also be clear that safe bidding is by no means the best bidding. The really fine player must use all three kinds of bid. How? When? This is to a degree a psychological problem, a matter of timing and card sense and the other almost telepathic conditions around the table. The player must judge for himself.

But you have to start somewhere. So I'd suggest using the risk bid. Overbid your visible hand with this in mind: that you do not expect with the widow to improve your holding more than 30 points with the improved meld and playing hand.

I'm not going to yield to the temptation to tell you when to throw in a fake bid. It depends. It depends on whom you're playing against, what time of night it is, what's happened so far, the looks on your opponents' faces, the distribution of your cards. Psychology, as it's called, is crucial in any game involving competitive bidding. Psychology is a very unstandardized variable. If I tell you to fake with such-and-such a hand on the assumption you're playing Caspar Milquetoast, you may fake against Josef Stalin next time you're out, and you may get your ears pinned back. People react differently.

I'm about to be reminded.

Not long ago I stood back and watched a Pinochle game in whose kitty was some $50. A friend of mine bid 350 on a hand that wasn't worth 250. The next player proceeded to bid 360, took the bid, and after looking at the widow tossed in his hand—and in addition to paying off his opponents had to ante $50 into the kitty.

"Very effective," I told my friend, "but on what theory did you make that fake 350 bid?"

This in effect was his reply:

He knew that $45 of the cash in the kitty had been put in by the second player, the one who raised and lost. He knew that this player would desperately raise any 350 bid simply to protect his $45 in the kitty. He knew too that this player was reasoning that, even if he didn't win the bid, he could hole my friend for a handsome contribution to the kitty.

He was right, my shrewd friend was.

By the time the kitty was won it totaled $200. An on-the-level bid of 450 won it for my friend after a series of raises from the second player.

HELP FROM THE WIDOW

Most of the grave errors made in the bidding are traceable to the fact that unreasoning players insist on bidding in the hope of finding in the widow enough valuable cards to justify their excesses. It is a queer fact that if there's one reckless player at the table the other players will bid badly. If that guy can expect so much from the widow, goes the reasoning (if any), then why can't I? But if a player understands the rudiments of sound bidding and can keep his skull screwed on, seldom need he have a losing session at Auction Pinochle.

But to bid well a player *must* have some acquaintanceship with probability and reasonable expectation, *must* have some general knowledge of the chances for finding a wanted card in the widow or at least a valuable card affording him an extra meld or a stronger playing hand.

Don't shy away from "probability" and "expectation." As any gambler in this country can tell you, I'm not long-hair. This is your business. If the average Pinochle player would acquaint himself with just the rough outline of probabilities, he'd stop being a bidding fool. Bear with me. It's your money.

I asked a Pinochle-playing friend of mine whether he'd lay me four to one that he'd toss a head on one toss of a coin.

"You crazy?" he snapped. "It's even money, and you know it."

"All right," I said; "are you crazy? The Pinochle hand you just threw in was just as bad a bet and a little worse, and, Buster, you were betting it."

Paying off his opponents, he asked me how I figured that.

Well, he'd been bidding in the hope of finding a 10 of diamonds in the widow to form a flush. If he found the 10, he'd make the bid; if he didn't, he'd lose and pay off, as he was now doing.

Now . . .

1. His chances of find that 10 of diamonds in the widow were 1 in 5.67.

2. If he had found the 10, he'd have been paid off at even money.

3. And that's a sucker bet.

In the breakdown and printed chart I'm about to set down you'll find the bidder's chances of buying one wanted card in the widow. I haven't calculated the chances of finding more than one wanted card. I'd like to insist that a bidder should never bid a hand in the hope of finding more than one needed card.

So that we shall understand each other, the reader will bear in mind that a Pinochle deck consists of twenty-four cards each duplicated once, making forty-eight cards in all. Thus each card twin (the two aces of clubs, the two kings of heart, etc.) must be considered as one chance, since it is not necessary for our purposes to find both in the widow; all we need do is find one of the twins. Right? If a player were holding one of the twin cards of a given rank and were seeking the other, he would have only half the tabulated chance, but the appended chart and analysis will not cover half-chances.

Also in the interest of better understanding, these presents:

To calculate the chance of finding one card or any one of several cards in the widow we must first establish the number of possible combinations of the three cards in the widow. To start, we subtract from the forty-eight cards in the deck the fifteen cards the bidder holds. Now, making use of the formula described in ascertaining the probabilities at Poker (page 273), we set up the following

$$\frac{33 \times 32 \times 31}{3 \times 2 \times 1}$$

and we find there are 5,456 ways of combining the deck's remaining cards in three-card combinations in the widow. The same formula is used to determine one's chance of finding any desired card or one of certain desired cards in the widow.

CHANCES THAT A WANTED CARD WILL BE FOUND
IN THE WIDOW

Wanted cards out of number in the widow	Chances of finding it in the widow	Odds on finding that card
1 of 1	961 in 5456	1 in 5.67
1 of 2	1802 in 5456	1 in 3.02
1 of 3	2531 in 5456	1 in 2.11
1 of 4	3156 in 5456	1 in 1.72
1 of 5	3685 in 5456	1 in 1.47
1 of 6	4125 in 5456	1 in 1.31

In a word, a player has a better than even chance of finding in the widow a valuable card that will help him *only* when he has four or more openings in the hand. I shall concede cheerfully that in every player's experience there has occurred the widow that gave him two or three cards he needed and a cinch hand; but the Pinochle player who consistently relies on this fantastic improbability is *not* a good player.

The sound bidder rarely expects to find an additional meld

in the widow. He anticipates improving his playing hand with the three widow cards, but that's all. A player who says the widow ruined his hand is not telling the truth. The widow can't, under the rules of the game, hurt your hand. You can always bury the three widow cards and still have the same (unruined) hand with which you started.

The best Pinochle players I know calculate the average value of the widow at 30 points. This means melds and additional points won in tricks by using the widow cards. I agree with them. If in your bidding you give a tentative value of 30 to the widow you'll have a soundly conservative bidding technique.

WHEN TO PLAY OR CONCEDE THE HAND

Having examined the widow and decided he can't meld enough points to make his bid a cinch hand, the bidder must make up his mind then whether to concede the hand or play it out. If he plays and wins, all very well! If he concedes and throws in the cards, he must pay his opponents but a single unit each. But if he elects to play the hand and then fails to make his bid he must pay each opponent at least two units. It is not uncommon (see page 318) that he is compelled to pay each four units if spades were trump and six units if hearts were trump.

Hence the hesitant bidder calculating the tricks he may lose (which is the right way to estimate a hand for the play; not tricks it may win!) is confronted with a situation not quite comparable to anything else in cards.

He must reckon the number of trump cards held by his opponents (and the cards in the other suits) and must decide under what distributional conditions he can make the bid. That is, how must the adverse cards be distributed to make it possible for him to make them break favorably?

It is quite a delicate calculation. If some crucial suit breaks unfavorably—that is, if the cards in one opponent's hand total grossly more than the cards in the other's—then he can't break the suit, and he can't possibly make the bid.

Master Contract players have been through some of this, but theirs is quite a different kettle of fish. Our Pinochle bidder, for example, holds six trump cards. Six trumps are out against him in the other hands. If those six are distributed between his opponents evenly, three and three, he can break the suit, control the other suits, and bring home his bid. If they're five to one or four to two or—horror of horrors!—six to zero he hasn't a chance.

It is impossible to decide on this problem by reliance on card sense. Card sense is too variable, if it is really anything at all. The player who depends on what he thinks is some abstruse instinct at cards is a player generally headed straight for the cleaners'. You need something more tangible, something based more on demonstrable reality, to estimate the probable distribution of cards between your opponents.

Again, since it's your bank account, I must petition you to stay with me. Let's say a player has to decide on the distribution of the missing ace and 10 of diamonds. If he's an average player, he concludes there are four ways in which these cards can fall:

1. Opponent A holds the ace of diamonds, opponent B holds the 10 of diamonds.

2. Opponent A holds the 10 of diamonds, opponent B holds the ace of diamonds.

3. Opponent A holds the ace and 10, opponent B holds neither.

4. Opponent A holds neither, opponent B holds both ace and 10.

Hence, our average player decides, the ace and the 10 can be divided two ways so as to fall on a single lead, and also they can be so divided that they won't fall on a single lead. There are two ways either can happen. Thus the chances that either will happen are exactly even.

But it doesn't work out that way. As you'll note below, the correct percentages are 48 in favor of the 2-0 distribution and 52 in favor of the 1-1 distribution. The mistake our average player made was to consider only the two crucial cards, whereas he should have taken also into consideration the twenty-eight other cards that made up the hands.

Maybe you'd rather work it out for yourself, since I think the principle is up to this time unexplored. First, find the number of ways one card can be arranged with fourteen other cards out of a total of thirty cards. (Remember, fifteen cards are held by each of the bidder's opponents.) Now, bear in mind that either opponent may hold either of the two cards in a 1-1 distribution. All right. The probability of any event is the number of *favorable ways* it can happen divided by the *total number of ways* it can happen. We must establish the total number of fifteen-card hands that can be formed from thirty-cards. Let's put down all our figures at the same time. They are:

$$\frac{2 \times 28 \times 27 \times 26 \times 25 \times 24 \times 23 \times 22 \times 21 \times 20 \times 19 \times 18 \times 17 \times 16 \times 15}{14 \times 13 \times 12 \times 11 \times 10 \times 9 \times 8 \times 7 \times 6 \times 5 \times 4 \times 3 \times 2 \times 1}$$

divided by

$$\frac{30 \times 29 \times 28 \times 27 \times 26 \times 25 \times 24 \times 23 \times 22 \times 21 \times 20 \times 19 \times 18 \times 17 \times 16}{15 \times 14 \times 13 \times 12 \times 11 \times 10 \times 9 \times 8 \times 7 \times 6 \times 5 \times 4 \times 3 \times 2 \times 1}$$

which equals 15/29 or approximately 52 per cent. Or maybe you'd rather take my word for it? I assure you I've worked it out. The chances of 1-1 distribution are approximately 4 percentage points better, in the circumstances specified, than the chances of 2-0. But note this, in all other circumstances, the chances of even distribution are not only less than even, the chances of 3-1 are greater than 2-2, of 4-2 greater than 3-3, etc.

Here's a percentage-wise table of suit distribution that will help any player:

POSSIBLE DISTRIBUTION IN SUITS

Bidder holds	Distribution of missing cards	Approximate probability
10 of one suit	1-1	.52
	2-0	.48
9 of one suit	2-1	.78
	3-0	.22
8 of one suit	3-1	.50
	2-2	.40
	4-0	.10
7 of one suit	3-2	.67
	4-1	.29
	5-0	.04
6 of one suit	4-2	.48
	3-3	.35
	5-1	.15
	6-0	.02
5 of one suit	4-3	.61
	5-2	.31
	6-1	.07
	7-0	.01
4 of one suit	5-3	.467
	4-4	.318
	6-2	.180
	7-1	.033
	8-0	.002

BE SURE YOU'RE RIGHT, THEN DON'T GO AHEAD

Conceding that the hand, unless it is a cinch, is in the long run a costly habit. How you manage yourself at this critical stage of the game is decisive as to whether you can win or must lose. Before deciding whether to play it out or throw it in, the bidder of any hand should refer mentally to the above table of suit distribution.

If the probability is 33.3 per cent or more that the suits will fall in the bidder's favor, he should play out the hand. Another way of saying it: he should not concede unless the probability is 66.7 per cent that the cards will fall adversely.

I select the 33.3 per cent figure because at that level the bidder has the same mathematical case whether he concedes or plays; in the act of deciding to play it out he neither gains nor loses; he is no worse off playing than he is conceding.

Let's break down three theoretical hands:

1. If the bidder concedes all three hands he must pay each opponent three units, one for each hand.

2. If he plays out the three hands and the probabilities turn out as predicted by the mathematics, he must lose two hands and pay each opponent four units, two for each hand; but meanwhile the bidder wins one hand and collects one unit from each opponent.

So far our man's even. He loses three units by conceding. He loses three by playing.

3. Thus, if the probabilities are any better than 33.3 per cent in the bidder's favor, he *must* play out the hand, and he *must* win in the long run.

Example: The bid is 470 points. You have melded 220 points. There are two trumps out against you: the ace and the 10. You need 250 points to make your bid. If the ace and 10 are divided between your opponents, you make all the tricks and win the hand. If one opponent holds both ace and 10, you lose a trick and fail to make the hand.

Question: Shall you elect to play the hand?

Answer: Absolutely yes; you must play it out. You have a 48 per cent chance to win, which is much higher than the 33.3 per cent chance which is our minimum.

But note this well: When spades are double or hearts are triple, this 33.3 per cent rule is out. I recommend that you do not play out a spade hand unless you have at least a 50 per cent chance to break your suit and that you do not play a heart hand without a 56 per cent chance.

CASH VALUE OF YOUR OPPONENT'S INCOMPETENCE

It is not generally sound to elect, on the theory that one of your opponents will make a feeble-minded mistake favorable to you, to play out a squeaker hand. You can't build a good game of any kind on the assumption that the adversary will drop the ball or consistently behave himself like a fool. Obviously better—so obviously that I hesitate to state it—is building up your game in the expectation that your opponent will play or defend his hand like a master. But . . .

There is always a "but." *If you know* your opponent's game, if you are sure he'll average to make a mistake, know what kind of mistake it's apt to be, and can maneuver the play so as to enhance the odds he'll make it, then you're entitled to take account of that consistent margin of error in your bidding and play.

Only don't forget that for every weakness in your opponent's game there's very likely to be one in yours. Maybe you have little consistent flaws of which other people are aware. Maybe you regularly overbid or underbid; maybe you play the hand like a butcher; maybe you lose track of trumps and make a practice of trying to break unbreakable suits. When you undertake to play mistakes for profit you're assuming risks.

The only sound advice I can give you is to be reckless most carefully. Know what you're doing.

AND COUNT TRICKS AS THEY ARE WON

The most common fault I find in the majority of Pinochle players is a peculiar hoggishness. The player isn't satisfied to make his bid and rack it up. He takes it for granted, at a certain stage of the game, that he'll of course make his bid, and he proceeds to concentrate on running up a count higher than his contract.

Don't do it. *Make your bid.* The player who does this is not a losing player. But the player who concentrates all his faculties on amassing a high count is almost invariably a loser. The play of the hand for a high count is radically different from the play for a low or modest count. It is necessary to take long chances, to risk adverse suit breaks, to neglect safety plays. It is even sometimes necessary to set up good tricks for the opponent in side suits. The risks are never commensurate with the potential gain. They are a bad bet. Play for your bid.

The player should always count, as they are made, the points taken in tricks so that he will have an accurate calculation on his hand as it goes along. Often a player neglects an opportunity to put on a trick a high-ranking card which would win the hand for him; not having counted his points, he thinks he needs more points than he in fact does need. Failing to play the high-ranking card at the right time, he never gets another chance to take a trick.

Count your valuable cards won in tricks, whether you're the bidder or his opponent. It pays off.

And—while I've said this before, it's worth repeating—by all means train yourself to count the trump cards as they're played. Once you've mastered that, you'll find it's not so hard to keep track of the cards played in the side suits too.

It's a great game. It's worth playing as greatly as you can.

Scarne's Rules for Auction Pinochle with a Widow: Game—1,000 Points

REQUIREMENTS

1. Three or four players. When three are in the game each is an active player and each is dealt a Pinochle hand. When four are playing, the dealer stays out, only dealing hands to the other three players. Since in a four-handed game the deal rotates, each player has a mathematically equal chance to win, other things being even, but I recommend the three-handed variety.

2. A standard Pinochle deck. (For description of the deck, rank cards and suits, standard value of melded cards, bonus melds, and value of cards won in tricks, see "Scarne's General Rules for Pinochle," page 311.)

OBJECT OF THE GAME

To score, before any other player does so, 1,000 points, totaling the value of melded cards and of cards taken in tricks during successive hands.

BEFORE THE DEAL BEGINS

Selection of the dealer and establishment of seating positions, changes in seating positions, the shuffle, and the cut are governed by "Scarne's General Rules for Pinochle," page 317.

THE DEAL

Starting with the leader and dealing clockwise, the dealer gives each player one round of cards three at a time face down, then deals a widow card face down in the center of the table. The first widow card is the tenth card off the pack. Another round is dealt the same way, and the second widow card is the twentieth off the pack. And another, a third, round is dealt the same way. The third widow card is the thirtieth off the pack. Now, starting with the leader, each player is dealt three cards at a time until the deck is exhausted and each player has fifteen cards in his hand. As in Auction Pinochle of the version just described, some players elect to deal each contestant four cards, then one into the widow; this goes on for three rounds, after which each player is dealt three final cards. I have barred other methods of dealing so as to minimize the possibility of a crooked deal.

THE BIDDING

The leader may do either of these two things:

A. *Pass,* which means he doesn't choose to bid; or
B. *Bid* at least the minimum of 250, which signifies he thinks he can make the number of points bid by the end of this Pinochle hand.

The player to the leader's left may pass or bid, but if the leader has bid, the next player's bid must be at least 10 points higher; bids may be raised only in multiples of 10. And the third player may pass or bid—*but* if the first two players have passed, the third is required to bid at least 290 to buy the widow.

If two or all players bid, the bidding continues in multiples of 10 until only one bidder remains, the others having passed.

Once having passed, no player may bid at a later stage in the same hand.

If all players pass, a new hand is dealt by the player to the previous dealer's left.

THE WIDOW

The three cards dealt face down in the center of the table are the *widow* or *blind* or *buy.* In no circumstances may a player, be he active or inactive, look at the cards in the widow while the bidding is still going on. The highest and last bidder, having won the auction, is entitled to take up the widow in an attempt to improve his hand. But before incorporating the widow in his hand he must turn up its three cards so that the other players can see them and judge their value. Now, having taken in hand the three widow cards, he examines the entire holding's potentialities, and chooses:

1. To announce that he is *taking a hole,* i.e., conceding that he cannot make his bid. However, he is required to play out the hand nevertheless, since the other players' scoring is involved.

In this case he is not permitted to meld cards, and must take a *hole,* or a deficit, for the number of points he bid.

A player electing to *take a hole* may bury any three cards. When burying a trump he must announce what he is doing, but failure to make this announcement involves no penalty, since the bidder is already on the minus side.

2. Or the bidder may choose to play the hand, under the following rules.

DISCARDING OR BURYING THREE CARDS

To lower his holding to the legal fifteen cards, the bidder must discard three cards after taking up the widow. These three go face down in front of him, and are counted as tricks won by the bidder—although he must win at least one trick to make these good. These rules govern discarding:

1. The bidder cannot bury or discard any card used to form a meld for which he gets credit in points. Should he bury such a card and should his attention be called to his misplay, he has reneged, and he loses the hand. A bidder who reneges is holed for the number of points he bid.

2. So long as it has not been used in a meld, a bidder may bury a trump card, but he must announce that it is a trump card when he does so. He need not reveal the denomination of the trump card or cards. Failure to declare the burial of a trump card is a renege, and loses the hand for the bidder. The penalty is as if the bidder failed to make his bid in play.

3. The bidder is not required to announce burying an ace or any other nontrump card.

4. If the bidder leads a card to start the play of the hand and his attention is drawn to the fact that he has neglected to bury three cards, or has buried too few or too many cards, this constitutes a renege, and the penalty is as if the bidder played the hand and failed to make his bid.

RULES GOVERNING THE PLAY

1. The bidder may lay down the cards he wants to meld, if any; and the cards he bought in the widow may be used in making up the melds.

2. He must announce which suit he is making trump. The winner of the bid may make trump any suit he chooses.

The bidder having announced trump, the other two players put down their melds, and each player's meld is entered on the score sheet under his name. (See rules for melding under "Scarne's General Rules for Pinochle," page 313.)

Next, the bidder must bury three cards to bring his total holding to the legal fifteen. These may be any three of the eighteen cards in his hand; but they must not be any cards used to form melds; and if a player discards one or more trump cards he must so declare. The discards go on the table face down in front of the bidder, care being taken not to reveal their identity to the other players.

The scorekeeper records the total points melded for each player. Each player plays for himself. After melding, the players pick up their melded cards and return them to their holding, and they are now ready for the play of the hand, as follows:

1. The bidder leads any card he elects, taking it from among the fifteen in his hand and putting it face up on the table to start the trick.

(After a card has been led no changes in melds may be made.)

2. Each player must follow the suit of the card led, if he has a card of that suit.

3. If he cannot follow suit, the opponent must trump.

4. If he does not have a card of the suit led or a trump card, he may play any card.

5. Only when a trump card is led must a player follow with a higher-ranking card—if he has one.

6. If a nontrump card is led and the second player trumps it and the third player is forced to trump, he need not play a trump card of higher value than the second player's.

7. Winner of the trick leads off to the next trick. To win a trick, a player must:

A. Play a higher-ranking card than his opponents' in the suit led, be it trump or nontrump suit.

B. When trumping a suit, play a higher-ranking trump card than his opponents'.

When two cards of the same value are played, the first card played to the trick wins it.

So play continues until the cards in the players' hands are exhausted, fifteen cards, fifteen tricks.

COUNTING TRICKS

1. The bidder counts his tricks. If he has scored enough points in his melds and tricks to equal or exceed his bid, he enters the total on his score. The other players' points in tricks and melds are scored for each, in his own respective column. A player must win at least one trick to score his melds.

2. If the bidder fails to make his bid he loses the melds previously credited to him on his hand, gets no credit for the number of points won in tricks, and he is holed for the amount of the bid. This amount is subtracted from his total score. If that (his total score) is less than the amount he is holed for, his deficit is entered on the score sheet with a minus sign. The other players get credit for their tricks scored.

This scoring goes on until one—or more—players scores 1,000 points or more.

If one player alone scores 1,000 points, he is the winner. If two players have 1,000 points or more *and neither is the bidder,* the player with the higher score wins. If two players, excepting the bidder, are tied with 1,000 or more points, they both are declared winners and share equally in the stakes. If the player who won the bidding is one of the two players to score 1,000 or more points, he wins the game, even if another player (or players) has a higher score.

OPTIONAL RULE FOR HOLED PAY-OFF

Often players collect an amount in addition to the penalty detailed above from a bidder who is *holed.* Generally, the additional penalty is one-fourth of the stakes for the game. If, for example, it is stipulated that each loser shall pay the winner $1 per game, a player going into the hole would have to pay each opponent one-fourth of $1, or 25¢. But this rule must be expressly agreed on before the start of the game.

ADDITIONAL RULES

Additional rules set forth under "Auction Pinochle with Widow, Each Hand a Complete Game" (see page 347), apply to 1,000-point Auction Pinochle.

CHAPTER THIRTY-TWO

Partnership Pinochle and Other Variations

Scarne's Rules for Partnership Auction Pinochle with a Widow

REQUIREMENTS

1. Two partnerships of two players each—four players in all.

2. The standard Pinochle deck.

(For description of the deck, rank of cards and suits, standard value of melded cards, standard bonus melds, and value of cards won in tricks, see "Scarne's General Rules for Pinochle," page 311.)

OBJECT OF THE GAME

For one partnership, by scoring 1,000 points or more before the other partnership does, to win the game.

DETAILS BEFORE THE ACTUAL DEAL

(Selecting partnerships, choosing the dealer, establishing seat positions, changing partnerships and seat positions, the shuffle, and the cut, are governed by "Scarne's General Rules for Pinochle," page 316.)

THE DEAL

Eleven cards for each player and four cards for the widow are dealt. For the first four rounds, starting with the leader and dealing clockwise, one card is dealt each player face down and the fifth card of the round is dealt fact down in the center of the table for the widow. Thus the fifth, tenth, fifteenth, and twentieth cards off the deck are dealt into the widow. After the last card is dealt the widow, the fifth and succeeding rounds are dealt the players only until the deck is exhausted and each player has eleven cards.

THE BIDDING

The leader may pass, i.e., indicate he doesn't want to bid; or, make a bid. *But* the player who makes the first bid is not required to bid any stipulated number of points; he may bid any amount he likes.

Each player in his turn, starting with the leader and rotating clockwise, passes or bids. But if one player bids, the following bidder's bid must be higher by at least 10 points; bids can be raised only in multiples of 10.

This bidding continues until only one bidder remains unchallenged. He has won the bid for his partnership.

Once a player has passed, he cannot bid later in the same hand. If all players pass, the cards are thrown in and a new hand is dealt by the player to the left of that hand's dealer.

THE WIDOW, BLIND, OR BUY

The four cards dealt face down on the table during the deal of the hand are called the *widow, blind,* or *buy.* It must be re-emphasized that in no circumstances, be he active or inactive, may a player look at the four cards in the widow while the bidding is going on. The bidder—the player who has won the bid—may take up these four cards in an attempt to improve his holding, *but* before placing them in his hand the bidder must expose the widow cards and let the other players see them. Now the bidder may either put the widow cards in his hand with his other eleven cards or leave them on the table and use them in a meld.

The bidder may announce his trump suit either before or after melding.

DISCARDING OR BURYING FOUR CARDS

Now, to give himself the legal eleven cards, the bidder must discard four cards. These four are placed down in front of him and are counted as tricks he has won—although his partnership must win a trick from the opponents to make his meld good. Any points among these four cards are counted in the bidder's favor as points won in tricks. These rules on the discard must be observed:

1. The bidder cannot bury (discard) any card used to form a meld for which he has received point credits. If he buries such a card and if his attention is called to the misplay, he has reneged, and he loses the hand. The partnership which reneges is holed for the number of points bid.

2. The bidder may bury a trump card (one not used in a meld), but he must announce the fact that it is a trump he's burying. He does not have to reveal its denomination. But failure to announce burying a trump card is considered a renege by the bidder, and loses the hand for him. The penalty is the same as if he failed in play to make his bid.

3. The bidder is not required to announce burying an ace or any other card not a trump card.

4. If the bidder leads a card in starting the play of the hand and his attention is drawn to the fact that he has neglected to bury four cards or has buried too few or too many cards, he has reneged and the penalty is as if the partnership had played the hand and failed to make the bid.

THE PLAY

This game is governed by the rules for "Auction Pinochle with Widow, Each Hand a Complete Game" (see page 336).

COUNTING VALUABLE CARDS WON IN TRICKS

Each partnership counts its tricks, adding up the total of valuable cards won in tricks. The partnership which won the bid also adds the four cards the bidder buried. If the bidding partnership makes the bid, its total points won in tricks are added to its credit on the score sheet. The other partnership adds to its credit its own total, whether the bidding partnership did or did not make its bid.

If the bidding partnership fails to make its bid, it loses the melds previously credited to it on that hand plus its points won in tricks, and the partnership is holed for the amount of the bid. This amount is subtracted from its running score.

If the total of this score is less than the amount of the holed bid, a minus sign is used to indicate the deficit, and the partnership must cancel this deficit before it can enter any score as a plus.

MELDING

After the bidder announces his trump all the other players may meld. Once the bidder has named trump and one or more other players' have melded, he cannot change his trump suit. The melds of each partnership are added into a single unit and entered on the score sheet.

After the melds have been entered in the score, each player picks up his melds, restores the cards to his hand, and goes on with the play.

(For standard value of melded cards and rules for melding, see "Scarne's General Rules for Pinochle," pages 311–313.)

DETERMINING THE WINNING PARTNERSHIP

Play continues until . . .

1. One partnership has scored 1,000 or more points and won the game.

2. If both partnerships score 1,000 or more points, the team which won the last bid wins the game, no matter whether the other has a higher score; because the bidder has first count of cards and is thus legally first over the finish line.

OPTIONAL PAY-OFF

To be legal, this rule must mutually be agreed on before the start of the game.

Often an additional sum in cash is collected from one partnership by the other for the former's failure to make its bid. The *holed* partnership's pay-off is usually one-fourth of the agreed stakes of the game.

STANDARD BONUS MELDS

Under mutual agreement reached before the start of the game, players may make use of the standard bonus melds. (See this table under "Scarne's General Rules for Pinochle," page 316.) It may be stipulated when using this table of melds that game shall be 1,000, 1,500, or 2,000 points.

ADDITIONAL RULES

This game is governed by the additional rules set forth under "Auction Pinochle with a Widow, Each Hand a Complete Game" (see page 347).

Scarne's Rules for Cutthroat Pinochle

This is played exactly as is Partnership Auction Pinochle
with a Widow—with the following single exception:

The game is played four-handed; there are no partnerships;
it is every man for himself.

Double Deck Auction Pinochle with a Widow: Individual Play

This is played exactly as is Auction Pinochle with a Widow:
Game 1,000 Points (see page 364), with the following additional values:

REQUIREMENTS

1. Two Pinochle decks—from which all the 9's have been
removed—shuffled together and used as one. Packs of contrasting color or design may be used. The consolidated deck
adds up to a total of eighty cards.

2. Four players, each playing for himself.

(Some play this game three-handed, but I don't recommend it.)

THE DEAL

3. As follows, nineteen cards are dealt each player and
four cards are dealt into the widow. The first round of cards,
starting with the leader and going clockwise, is dealt four at
a time. The next four cards are dealt into the widow. Thereafter each player is dealt five cards at a time until the deck is
exhausted.

THE SCORING

4. The winner of the last trick is credited with 20 points
instead of 10 points, as in Pinochle with a single deck.

5. For special bonus melds, often used in Double Deck
Auction Pinochle, see "Scarne's General Rules for Pinochle"
under standard bonus melds and triple and quadruple melds
(pages 316, 317).

6. When using standard bonus melds, game is 3,000 points.

7. When using triple or quadruple melds, game is 10,000
points.

Double Deck Partnership Pinochle with a Widow

This is played exactly as is Partnership Auction Pinochle,
with the following additional rules:

REQUIREMENTS

1. Two Pinochle decks—from which all the 9's have been removed—shuffled together and used as one. The consolidated deck totals eighty cards. Packs of contrasting color or design may be used.

THE DEAL

2. Nineteen cards are dealt to each player and four cards to the widow, in this order: the dealer deals the first round four at a time, starting with the leader and ending with himself, and deals the next four cards into the widow. Thereafter each player is dealt five cards at a time until the deck is exhausted.

THE SCORING

3. The partnership winning the last trick is credited with 20 points instead of 10, as at Pinochle with a single deck.

4. For special bonus melds, often used in Double Deck Auction Pinochle, see "Scarne's General Rules for Pinochle" under standard bonus melds and triple and quadruple melds (pages 316, 317).

5. When using standard bonus melds, game is 3,000 points.

6. When using triple or quadruple melds, game is 10,000 points.

Six- and Eight-Handed Auction Pinochle with Widow

Auction Pinochle, either six- or eight-handed, is played exactly as is the four-handed partnership game above described, with these exceptions:

IN THE SIX-HANDED GAME

1. Partnerships may be formed of . . .

A. three teams of two players each; or
B. two teams of three players each.

2. Two full decks of Pinochle cards are used as a single deck. There are ninety-six cards in all.

3. The partnership winning the last trick of the hand gets credit for 20 points.

THE DEAL

Each player is dealt fifteen cards and the widow is dealt six cards:

The cards are dealt clockwise, starting with the leader and including the dealer, three at a time to each player. Then three cards are dealt into the widow, these being the nineteenth, twentieth, and twenty-first cards off the deck. A second round of three cards is dealt each player, and the fortieth, forty-first, and forty-second cards off the deck are dealt into the widow, which now has a total of six cards. The remaining cards are dealt each player, but not the widow, in turn, three at a time, until the deck is exhausted.

IN THE EIGHT-HANDED GAME

1. Partnerships may be formed of . . .

A. four teams of two players each; or
B. two teams of four players each.

2. Three decks of Pinochle cards, 144 cards in all, are used as one deck.
3. The partnership winning the last trick of the hand gets 30 points.

THE DEAL

As follows, each player is dealt seventeen cards, and eight cards are dealt into the widow:

Starting with the player to his left, rotating clockwise, and including himself, the dealer gives each player five cards. Then he deals the next four cards into the widow.

On the second round, each player is dealt four cards, and the next four cards off the deck go into the widow, which now has eight cards.

No more cards are dealt into the widow. The remaining cards are dealt the players four at a time in rotation until the deck is exhausted.

Note: Very often, in these two variations of Auction Pinochle, players use standard bonus melds, triple melds, and quadruple melds. For the scoring of these see "Scarne's General rules for Pinochle" (pages 316, 317).

Scarne's Rules for Auction Pinochle Without a Widow Individual Play: Game—1,000 Points

REQUIREMENTS

1. Three or four players.
2. The standard Pinochle deck.

(See "Scarne's General Rules for Pinochle," page 311, for description of the deck, rank of cards and suits, value of melded cards, rules for melding, special bonus melds, and value of cards won in tricks.)

OBJECT OF THE GAME

Eventually to win the game by scoring 1,000 or more points before any one of your opponents; when you are the bidder, to score enough points, or more, to cover your bid and by the same token to avoid going into the *hole*.

SCOREKEEPER

He is selected by mutual consent. The score is kept with pencil and paper, each player's points in melds and valuable cards won in tricks being entered on the score *as* they are made.

THE STAKES

This game is usually played for 25¢ a game, but there is nothing arbitrary about that; X cents per 1,000 points is the formula, and you fill in the value of the X.

AGREEMENTS COMPULSORY BEFORE THE START
OF THE GAME

These details must be entered on the score sheet before the start of any game:

Amount of stakes to be collected or paid out by each player.

Special bonus melds.

Additional penalties (if any) for failure to make the bid or going in the hole.

RULES OBTAINING BEFORE THE ACTUAL DEAL

Under "Scarne's General Rules for Pinochle" will be found rules for selecting the dealer and establishing seating positions at the table, changing seats, the shuffle, and the cut.

THE DEAL

Whether there are three or four players in the game, the deal goes the same. If four, each is dealt twelve cards, four at a time, starting with the leader (player to the dealer's left) and rotating clockwise, the dealer including himself in the deal. If three, each in the same order is dealt sixteen cards, four at a time.

THE BIDDING

The leader may:

1. Pass.

2. Bid any amount he thinks he can make with the hand just dealt him.

In this version of Pinochle there is no stipulated minimum bid. The first actual bidder may make any bid he elects. Each successive bidder thereafter, the bid going to the left, clockwise, *must* bid at least 10 points higher than the previous bidder; bidding can be done only in multiples of 10.

A player once having passed cannot bid again during the same hand. A bidder cannot alter the amount of his uttered bid. If all players pass, the deal moves on to the player at the left of the one who dealt that hand.

NAMING TRUMP AND MELDING

The highest bidder, i.e., the player who won the auction, has the right to name as trump any suit he chooses.

After the bidder has named the trump suit, all players including him lay down their melds, and the scorekeeper after verifying the claims enters each player's melds on the sheet under each name. Also on the score sheet is noted the number of points bid.

THE PLAY

After the melds have been recorded, the cards are restored to the players' hands and the play begins.

1. The bidder leads the first card. It may be any card he likes.

2. Thereupon, the turn of play rotating to the left, each player in his turn must behave according to the following rules:

He must play a card of the suit led—if he has one.

If he does not have a card of the suit led, he must play a trump card.

If he has neither a card of that suit nor a trump card, he may play any other card in his hand.

If a trump is led, each player *must* play a higher trump card if he has it.

If he hasn't a higher trump card, he must still play some trump card if he can.

Only if he has no trump at all, does he play to a trump-card lead a card of another suit.

Once a card is led, it cannot be taken back into the player's hand.

If a nontrump card is led and the next player trumps it, and if one or both or all of the following players must trump (because they lack a card of the suit led), they do not have to play a trump card higher than the trump card of the previous player who trumped.

3. The highest-ranking card played to the trick wins it. If

two cards of the same value are played to the same trick, the first card played wins it.

4. The winner of the trick leads off again, and play rotates to the left according to the rules just set forth.

5. Winner of the last trick played wins an additional 10 points. Play continues in this order until all the cards in the hands have been played. The score for melds and points taken in tricks is totaled for each player; a new deal takes place; and play continues until one of the players has totaled 1,000 points or more and won the game.

FAILURE TO MAKE THE BID

If the bidder fails to score, in melds and points won in tricks, enough points to equal or exceed his bid, he loses: the hand, his melds for that hand already scored; and the amount he bid is subtracted from his score. He may find himself *in the hole* for the amount bid if he had no previous score or for the difference between his losing bid and his previous score if the former exceeds the latter. His deficit is indicated by a minus sign on his score.

IN-THE-HOLE PAY-OFFS: YES OR NO?

An additional sum may be assessed against the bidder for failure to make his bid, collectible by each other player—if the penalty is mutually agreed on before the start of the game. The penalty is usually one-quarter of the amount staked by the player on the game.

WINNING THE GAME

1. The player scoring 1,000 or more points wins the game.

2. If two or more players score 1,000 or more points each, the player with the highest total wins the game;

Except . . .

3. If the bidder of the last hand scores 1,000 or more points, that bidder wins the game regardless of whether any nonbidding player's score totals more than his.

ADDITIONAL RULES

Additional Rules, as set forth on page 347, apply here, with the exception of Rule No. 7.

Scarne's Rules for Partnership Auction Pinochle Without a Widow: Game—1,000 Points

REQUIREMENTS

1. Four players, two against two as partners.
2. The standard Pinochle deck.

(For description of the deck, ranks of cards and suits, value of melded cards, rules for melding, special bonus melds, and value of cards won in tricks, see "Scarne's General Rules for Pinochle," page 311.)

OBJECT OF THE GAME

For one partnership to win the game by scoring 1,000 or more points before the other partnership does.

If both partnerships score 1,000 or more points on the same hand, the partnership which won the game-going bid on the last hand is the winner.

THE STAKES: THE SCOREKEEPER

The scorekeeper is selected by mutual consent. Score is kept with pencil and paper. Each partnership's melds and valuable cards won in tricks are entered on the sheet as they are scored.

The game is popularly played at 25¢ per 1,000 points, but name your own X cents per game. Each member of a winning partnership collects from one member of the opposing partnership at this rate.

Such optional conditions as the amount to be paid for special bonus melds or for going into the hole—failing to make a bid—must be recorded on the score sheet before the start of of the game.

RULES OBTAINING BEFORE THE ACTUAL DEAL

"Scarne's General Rules for Pinochle" govern selection of partners, selecting the dealer, establishing and changing seating positions and partnerships, the shuffle and the cut. (See page 316.)

THE DEAL

To each player, including himself, the dealer deals twelve cards three at a time, starting with the leader and dealing clockwise until the entire pack has been distributed.

INFORMATORY BIDDING

It is permissible to make informatory bids in this game, although all bidding must be in multiples of 10. Thus a player cannot bid 105 to notify his partner he has five aces.

Sample informatory bids:

1. The first bidder says 120. He is notifying his partner he holds a 20 meld.

2. The bidder says 200. He means he has 100 points in meld.

In comparison with the delicate and ornate Contract Bridge conventions, this is, of course, fairly rudimentary.

The only informatory bid absolutely prohibited is one instructing one's partner (a) what suit to make trump if the team wins the bid or, along the same line (b) the number of cards one holds in a certain suit.

As in Bridge, the leader is in the best position to bid informatively, because at his stage of the first round the bidding has not yet reached a forbidding point total.

Partners may at the start of the game discuss what kind of informatory bids they propose to use; but it is not compulsory that they use such bids, nor, if such bids are used, is it compulsory that they mean what has been agreed. Such bids are to be liberally construed, and are used at the user's risk.

The leader is the first bidder. For the subsequent play— that is, as to bidding, naming trump, melding, the play, failure to make the bid, winning the game, in-the-hole pay-offs, additional rules, and all else—apply rules as set forth on pages 368 to 370.

Firehouse Pinochle

"Scarne's Rules for Partnership Auction Pinochle without a Widow, Game 1,000 Points" (see page 370) govern this game —with the following exceptions:

RULES FOR BIDDING

1. Starting with the leader and rotating clockwise, each player is allowed but one bid.
2. The highest bidder names the trump suit.

Partnership Aeroplane Pinochle

That "aeroplane" looks a little old-fashioned in this day of airplanes or mere planes; but this is what they call it.

Rules, as set forth on page 370, govern this game—with the following additional rules:

1. Each player is allowed to make only two bids.
2. The minimum permissible bid is 250 points.
3. The highest bidder names the trump suit.
4. After naming the trump suit, the bidder may pass any four cards from his hand face down to his partner, who in return
5. Must pass the bidder four cards in exchange, from his own hand, before looking at the cards passed him by the bidder.

Check Pinochle

This partnership variety of Pinochle has been ballyhooed lately as a new game. I remember having seen it played fifteen years ago in a half-dozen Midwestern States. Games do not move as rapidly across a country or a culture as some ex-post-facto historians would like to believe.

REQUIREMENTS

1. Four players—two against two in partnerships.
2. The standard Pinochle deck.

(For description of the deck, rank of cards and suits, value of melded cards, rules for melding, and value of cards won in tricks, see "Scarne's General Rules for Pinochle," page 311.)

OBJECT OF THE GAME

For a partnership on the completion of a 1,000-point game to have scored more *checks* (see below) than the opposing partnership. A *check* award is a unit of value given for a specified meld, for fulfilling a bid, for winning the game, etc.

THE STAKES AND THE SCOREKEEPER

The scorekeeper shall be selected by mutual consent. The score being kept with paper and pencil, the scorekeeper must in a separate column record the check awards won by each partnership.

The game may be played for any stakes, but 5¢ per check is a reasonable sum to play for.

RULES PREVAILING BEFORE THE ACTUAL DEAL

Under rules on page 316 are described selection of partners and dealer, establishment of seating positions, changing seats and partners, the shuffle, and the cut.

THE DEAL

Each player, including the dealer, is dealt twelve cards, three at a time, starting with the leader and going clockwise, until the entire pack has been exhausted.

On completion of each hand, the deal rotates to the player at the previous dealer's left.

THE BIDDING

The leader, who has the first opportunity to compete in the auction, may either bid or pass. The turn to bid rotates from player to player clockwise, to the left.

1. To qualify as a bidder the player must have in his hand

a marriage (king and queen in the same suit); regardless of the strength of his hand in melds, *he cannot bid unless he holds a marriage*. But see No. 4.

2. The minimum bid, no matter what the position of the player, is 200 points. Each succeeding bid must be at least 10 points higher than the current bid, the bids being raised in multiples of 10.

3. A player, having once passed, cannot bid again.

4. If the first three players pass, the dealer *must bid* whether he holds a marriage or not. If he holds no marriage he can bid only the minimum 200 points. If he holds a marriage he can put in whatever bid he likes.

5. The player bidding the highest amount becomes the bidder. (The highest bidder is the only bidder remaining in competition, the other players having finally passed.) Winning the bid, the bidder commits himself and his partner to win the hand by scoring the number of points stated in the bid.

NAMING TRUMP

The player who won the bid names the suit which is trump for the hand. The bidder must choose the trump himself: he cannot consult his partner.

INFORMATORY BIDDING

In this game, informatory bidding is permitted. In contrast to the rigid conventions of Bridge and even of some Pinochle games, the bidding may be whatever the players agree to make it. But it must be in multiples of 10, and the information must be conveyed by the amount of the bid and in no other manner.

A player cannot tell his partner the strength of any special suit he holds. Because his bid is put in first, before the auction has reached forbidding levels, the leader can best make an informatory bid.

Simple bid: The leader says 220. He means to tell his partner that he holds 80 meld. Their convention gives each 10 points bid above the minimum a meld value of 40. A bid of 210 would mean he has 40 meld, or 230 would mean 120 meld. Got it?

MELDING

The bidder having named trump, all the players put their melds face up on the table to be recorded by the scorekeeper. No melds may be put down by any player before the trump is named. Melds are entered on the score sheet under the partnership to which they belong.

A partnership's total melds are added together as a single score for that team.

Although melds are laid by individual players for the common benefit of the partnership, no player may use his partner's cards to help form a meld of his own.

THE PLAY

The melds having been recorded, the cards are taken back into the player's hands, and the play begins.

1. The bidder leads the first card. He may lead any card he likes.

2. After the first card has been led, each player in his turn must obey the following rules, the turn of play rotating around the table clockwise, to the left:

A. Each player must play a card of the suit led, if he has one.

B. If he does not have a card of the suit led, he must play a trump card.

C. If he lacks a card of the suit led and a trump card, he may play any other card in his hand.

D. If a trump is led, each player must play to the trick a higher trump if he has one. If he hasn't a higher trump, he must still play a trump card if there's one in his hand. Only if he has no trump at all may he play a card of another suit.

E. Once a card is led it cannot be taken back into the hand.

F. If a nontrump card is led and the next player trumps it and one or both of the following players are compelled to trump because they do not have a card of the suit led, it is not compulsory that they play a trump card higher than that of the previous player who trumped.

3. The trick is won by the highest-ranking card played. When two cards of equal value tie for the trick, first card played wins.

4. The winner of the trick leads off to the next trick, and play rotates to the left under the rules just described.

5. Winner of the last trick scores an additional 10 points.

This pattern of play is followed until all the cards in all hands have been played. Then the score for melds and points taken in tricks is totaled. After this a new deal starts, and play continues until one of the partnerships totals 1,000 points or more. (But note well the following passage.)

CHECK SCORING

Check Pinochle differs from other games in the family because of its distribution of check awards. There is some disagreement, generally based on a faulty conception of the mathematics among modern writers on the scoring of checks. I've decided to make official the following system, which is both sound and just now popular among experienced players throughout the Middle West. Players may, of course, increase the value of check awards as they see fit, but the increase should be in ratio to the scale here set forth.

Checks to which a partnership is entitled are entered on the score sheet under the check column. At the completion of the game, the partnership with the highest total in checks wins the game, and is paid off for the difference between its check total and the losing partnership's total. It is not uncommon for one partnership to score 1,000 or more points and still lose after the computation of checks which determines the final result.

Check Awards for Melding

Melds	Checks awarded
Flush (ace, 10, king, queen, jack of trump)	4
100 aces (four aces, one in each suit)	2
80 kings (four kings, one of each suit)	1
60 queens (four queens, one in each suit)	1
40 jacks (four jacks, one in each suit)	1
Double Pinochle (two jacks of diamonds, two queens of spades)	1
Roundhouse (four kings and four queens in different suits)	4

Check Awards for Bid

Number of points bid	For partnership making its bid	For defeating the opponents' bid
200 to 240	2 checks	4 checks
250 to 290	4	8
300 to 340	7	14
350 to 390	10	20
400 to 440	13	26
450 to 490	16	32
500 to 540	19	38
550 to 590	22	44

For each series of 50 points above 590 the bidding partnership is credited with three additional checks, and the partnership defeating such a bid gets six additional checks.

ADDITIONAL CHECK AWARDS

1. For winning the game in play—scoring 1,000 or more points before the opponents—the partnership gets seven checks.

2. For winning all twelve tricks in a hand the partnership gets five checks.

3. For winning all the valuable cards in one hand (scoring a count of 250 points in one hand, not necessarily all the tricks), a partnership gets four checks.

FAILURE TO MAKE THE BID

If the bidding partnership fails to make its bid, it loses its meld points and points won in valuable cards taken in tricks on that hand, and goes in the hole for the number of points bid. This deficit is subtracted from the partnership's total score; or, if the score is not sufficient to cover the deficiency, a minus sign is entered to indicate the amount for which the partnership is in the hole.

The bidding partnership can score nothing on a holed hand. Melds and checks already entered on the score sheet for that hand are canceled, and the opposing partnership scores *its* melds and cards won in tricks.

In addition the bidders' opponents score their own checks plus double the value in checks of the defeated bid.

WINNING THE GAME

1. If a partnership scores 1,000 or more points it is declared the winner of the game.

2. If both partnerships score 1,000 or more points, the winner is the partnership which won the bid on the hand, no matter if the other partnership's score is actually higher.

ADDITIONAL RULES

Additional Rules, as set forth on page 347, apply here, with the exception of Rule No. 7.

Contract Pinochle

This diverting variation uses several bids and rules adapted from Pinochle's cousin Bridge.

REQUIREMENTS

1. Four players, two against two as partners.
2. The standard Pinochle deck.
(For description of the deck, rank of cards and suits, value

of melded cards, rules for melding, and value of cards won in tricks, see "Scarne's General Rules for Pinochle," page 311.)

OBJECT OF THE GAME

For a partnership to win by scoring 3,000 or more points before the other partnership does.

RULES PREVAILING BEFORE THE ACTUAL DEAL

Beginning on page 316 rules are described for selecting partners, establishing seat positions, choosing the dealer, changing seats and partnerships, and the shuffle and the cut.

THE DEAL

Twelve cards, three at a time, dealt to each player, including the dealer, starting with the one at the dealer's immediate left and going clockwise. Four rounds of dealing exhaust the pack.

THE BIDDING

First turn to bid is the dealer's. He may either pass or bid at least 100. The turn to bid rotates clockwise around the table. One player having bid, the next bidder must bid at least 10 points more; that is, bids must be raised in multiples of 10. If all players pass there is a new deal. The player to the dealer left becomes the next dealer.

In the bidding, the trump suit must be declared along with the point total. That is, the bidder says, "Two hundred spades" or "Two hundred clubs."

The suits are equal in rank.

A player may bid a suit previously bid by another player, or he may bid any other suit. A player may re-enter the bidding after having passed. The bidding continues until three succes sive passes have occurred.

A player may double an opponent's bid, or he may redouble an opponent's double. As in Bridge . . .

1. Doubling multiplies by two the value of all points scored.
2. Redoubling, which doubles the doubled values, results in multiplying by four the value of all points scored.

The double and redouble may be used only against opponents' bids. Players cannot double and redouble their own partnership's bids.

MELDING

After three players in succession have passed, the partnership which won the auction and took the bid lays down its melds. The opposing partnership is not permitted to lay down melds.

(For value of melded cards and the rules for melding see rules on pages 312, 313.) The following are exceptions to the general rules:

Combination melds. By adding a card or cards to his partner's melds a player may make combination melds. If, for example, partner has melded the king and queen of spades, then the player may lay down a jack of diamonds which, in conjunction with partner's spade queen, makes a combination meld of Pinochle; or he may lay three queens of suits other than partner's spade queen to make a combination meld of 60 queens; or likewise he may lay kings or queens to combine for a roundhouse.

CALLING FOR MELDS

After these melds have been laid down, the bidder may call on his partner to produce a card to enable him to form another meld.

Example: The bidder holds the ace, 10, king, and jack of trump. Now he may call on his partner for the queen of trump to form a flush.

If the partner can produce the demanded card, the bidder lays down the new meld; and thereupon he is entitled to ask for still another card to help form another meld.

Only one card may be called for at one time. If the bidder calls for a card and the partner cannot produce it, the turn to call for a card passes to the partner. When the partner calls on the bidder for a card and the bidder fails to produce it, this phase of the game ends; neither of the partners may call for any more cards.

Combination melds may be laid down on melds developed in calling for cards, and this play does not affect the player's right of calling for cards.

If the partnership which won the bid melds points enough to equal or exceed the amount of its bid, it is not required that it play out the hand. In Contract Pinochle it is not necessary to win a trick to make the melds good.

The scorekeeper notes the bidding partnership's melds, but does not enter it on the score sheet.

If the bidding partnership fails to make its bid, then its melds are not entered on the score sheet.

CONCEDING THE HAND

Either the bidding partnership or the opposing partnership may concede the hand before the start of play or at any time during play.

1. If the bidding partnership concedes before a card is led in play, the opponents score one-half the value of the bid—but

the full value if the bid was doubled and twice the bid's value if it was redoubled.

2. If the bidding partnership concedes after a card has been played, the opponents score the full value of the bid—but double the value of the bid if it was doubled and four times its value if it was redoubled.

3. If the *opponents* concede the hand at any time before or during the play the bidding partnership scores the full value of its bid—with the relevant gains if it was doubled or redoubled.

In order for a concession to be legal and binding, both players of a partnership must agree to concede. If only one is willing to concede, the hand must be played out.

THE PLAY

The bidding partners pick up their melds, each player restoring his own melded cards to his playing hand.

1. The bidder leads any card he chooses, playing it face up on the table to start the trick. After a card has been led, no changes in melds may be made.

2. Succeeding players must follow the suit of the card led if they have a card of that suit.

3. If a player does not have a card of the suit led, he must trump.

4. If he does not have a card of the suit led or a trump, he may play any card.

5. Only when a trump is led must a player having a higher-ranking trump card play that card.

6. If a nontrump card is led and the second player trumps it and the third player is forced to trump because he does not have a card of the suit led, the third player doesn't have to play a trump card of higher rank than the previous player's.

7. Winner of the trick leads off to the next trick.

To win a trick a player must . . .

A. Play a higher-ranking card than his opponent's in the suit led, be it a trump or a nontrump suit;

B. When trumping, play a higher-ranking trump card than his opponents.

When two cards of the same value are played and are tied to win the trick, the card first played to the trick wins it.

This pattern of play is followed until all the cards in the players' hands are exhausted.

SCORING THE HAND

If the bidding partnership's total score in melds and valuable cards won in tricks totals an amount equal to or higher than its bid, then the value of the bid is entered to that partnership's credit on the score sheet. If the bid was doubled, the score-keeper doubles the value of the bid scored; if it was redoubled, the score entered is the bid multiplied by four.

If the bidding partnership fails to make its bid, the opposing partnership is credited in the scoring with the full amount of the bid, double its value if doubled, four times its value if redoubled.

WINNING THE GAME

The partnership first scoring 3,000 points wins the game.

ADDITIONAL RULES

Additional Rules, covering misdeals and other irregularities, are set forth on page 347, and apply here, with the exception of Rule No. 7.

Radio Partnership Pinochle

I've been holding this one back as a sort of dessert. Now, with some relish, I'd like to present to American players of Pinochle the newest and, in my own opinion, the most fascinating game of the whole Pinochle family. You call it Radio Partnership Pinochle.

I am—and you will be—indebted to my friend Peter Musto of North Bergen, N. J., in the heart of the eastern seaboard Pinochle belt, for calling my attention to the game. As far as I can establish—and I've put some leg work into it for the last year or so—Radio Pinochle originated in the North Hudson Men's Club in nearby Union City, N. J., where it has been played every evening since midwinter of 1933–34.

Basically it's Double Deck Partnership Pinochle. But its unique feature is an informatory exchange in certain arbitrary and authorized bidding terms, orally between partners before the bidding begins. This discussion, *which is not bidding,* is done with cues which must be explained to and understood by all the players. Secret conventions are barred.

A cue is not a binding contract. It need not even be an accurate description of what it purports to describe, namely, the card values in the player's hand. Players will often give their partners inaccurate cues—and thus lead their opponents, duly eavesdropping, to disaster.

This table talk is capable of being used with infinite subtlety, and it is of course fraught with risk. A misinformed opponent is a wonderful asset in any game. A misinformed partner, inspired by some harmless little cue of yours, can turn into a runaway and rush off into a beautiful accident.

REQUIREMENTS

1. Two standard Pinochle decks from which all the 9's have been removed, making one one deck of 80 cards. The decks may be of contrasting color or pattern.

(For description of the Pinochle deck, rank of cards and suits, value of melded cards, rules for melding, and value of cards won in tricks, see "Scarne's General Rules for Pinochle," page 311.)

2. Four players, two against two as partners.

OBJECT OF THE GAME

For a partnership to run up at the end of four hands a higher score than its opponents.

If at the completion of four hands the score is tied, a fifth tie-breaking hand is played.

There is no *bidder's choice.*

RULES PREVAILING BEFORE THE ACTUAL DEAL

"Scarne's General Rules for Pinochle," (page 316) govern selection of partnerships, choosing the dealer, establishing seat positions, changing seats and partners, the shuffle, and the cut.

THE SCOREKEEPER

Selected by mutual consent, he keeps a running score with pencil and paper, entering each partnership's points in melds and cards as they are made.

THE STAKES

At the North Hudson Men's Club, which is the only criterion available, the stakes are generally $1 a game, plus a 25¢ additional penalty for a partnership's going in the hole.

THE DEAL

Each player including the dealer is dealt twenty cards, five at a time face down, starting with the leader and rotating to the left, clockwise. The dealer gets the last five cards.

THE INFORMATORY DISCUSSION

Before the bidding starts the partners try, using terms familiar to all hands, to impart to each other an idea of each hand's strength.

In no circumstances may a player tell his partner in what suit his strength lies. *Example:* Holding a flush in diamonds— he *may* say, "I have a flush"; he is *absolutely forbidden* to say, "I've a diamond flush." Suits cannot be mentioned in the cueing.

Let's start.

A player looks at his partner and says, "Sing!"

Now the partner must respond—not necessarily telling the truth—in certain conventional terms, a sort of shorthand familiar to every one at the table.

Informatory Terms

The term	Its meaning
A ten	A flush
Twenty	A long suit—seven or more cards in the same suit, but not comprising a flush.
A five	100 aces
One	An ace
Two	Two aces
Three	Three aces
Four	Four aces, but not 100 aces

Any meld other than a flush or 100 aces is stated in precise terms. A player holding a 140 meld says, "A hundred forty." Holding 200 meld, he says, "Two hundred."

The player states his holding in a series of spoken numbers, which may seem complicated at first but which, as you'll see, break down into readily understandable units. What they're doing is putting informatory sentences together with numbers rather than words alone.

1. A player holds 100 in meld, 100 aces, and three other aces with the 100 aces.

"Sing," says his partner.

"One hundred three and a five," the player responds.

2. A player holds 160 in meld (not a flush), 100 aces, and an ace besides.

"Sing!"

And the player calls that hand thus:

"No ten, 161, and a five."

3. A player holds a double flush (300 points) and 40 meld, plus three aces (not a 100 aces)—"Sing." And the player calls the hand thus: "Double ten, and forty-three."

4. A player holds a roundhouse (240 points) and no aces. The player would call a weak 240.

After this informatory exchange has ended, the bidding proper begins.

THE BIDDING

The leader starts the bidding, and turn to bid rotates to the left around the table until three successive players have passed; the last bidder has won the auction for his partnership.

There is no minimum bid. A player may bid any amount he elects, but the amount bid must end with a zero—200, 300, 320, 400, and, so on up. The average bid winning the auction in this game is 600. Every bid after the first must be a raise in some multiple of 10, as in all other Pinochle games.

The final bid having been passed out by the other three players, the bid is entered on the score sheet.

NAMING TRUMP AND MELDING

The bidder has the privilege of naming the trump suit. Trump having been declared, players lay down their melds. After verifying each player's count, the scorekeeper enters the total meld score for each partnership as a unit to its credit on the sheet. Then players restore their melded cards to their holding in their hand, and are ready for the play.

THE PLAY

1. The bidder, playing any card he elects, leads off to the first trick. Turn to play rotates to the left, clockwise.

2. Each player must play a card of the suit led if he has one.

3. If the player does not have a card of the suit led, he must play a trump card.

4. If a player does not have a card of the suit led or a trump card, he may play any other card in his hand.

5. When a trump card is led to the trick each succeeding player *must* play a higher trump card than the lead-off card if he has one.

6. If a nontrump card is led and one player trumps that card, the succeeding player (or players) if compelled to trump need not play a card of higher rank than the trump already played.

7. The highest-ranking card played wins the trick. When two cards of the same value tie to win the trick, the trick is won by the first one played.

8. The winner of that trick leads off to the next, and play continues, rotating to the left, after the above pattern.

9. Play continues thus until the hands are exhausted and all cards have been played in tricks.

10. Partnership winning the last trick scores 20 points for it.

COUNTING VALUABLE CARDS WON IN TRICKS; THE HOLE

The value of cards won in tricks is totaled for each partnership and entered as a unit on the score sheet.

If a partnership fails to make its bid, it is *holed*, penalized, for the amount of the bid. It loses its melds previously scored, and the amount in which it is *holed* is subtracted from its recorded score—or a minus sign is used to indicate its deficit.

The bidding partnership scores nothing on a holed hand. The opposing partnership, however, scores *its* melds and valuable cards won in tricks.

CASH FOR GOING IN THE HOLE

A cash settlement must be paid by a partnership going in the hole. The amount is commonly reckoned as one-quarter of the total stakes for the game. The game being played for $1, the penalty for a hole is 25¢. This penalty must be agreed on before the start of the game.

Here is an optional way of paying off a hole penalty at the end of the game. If a partnership has gone into the hole but still goes ahead and wins the game, it is not penalized for having gone into the hole. But if the holed partnership loses the game it must pay a *doubled penalty* on the holed hand or hands.

COMPLETION OF THE GAME

After four hands have been dealt and played out, the partnership with the highest score at that point wins the game, which is thereupon completed. In case of tie, a new hand is dealt to break the tie and decide the winner.

ADDITIONAL RULES

Additional Rules, covering misdeals and other irregularities, are set forth on page 347, and apply here, with the exception of Rule No. 7.

CHAPTER THIRTY-THREE

Cheating at Pinochle

Cheating occurs much more rarely in Pinochle than in Poker. It is not a matter of virtue. As is true in Bridge, the first requisite for a career as a profit-showing crook is skill at the game. The combination of immense skill and microscopic conscience being relatively rare, the Pinochle cheat is uncommon. But by no means uncommon enough! Like all card games, Pinochle has its due quota of clip artists.

The methods detailed in Chapters Two and Three—stacking, crimping, shifting the cut, palming, marked cards, strippers, and so forth—can be used at Pinochle. Here's how.

MARKED CARDS

Particularly in Auction Pinochle with a Widow, the cheat is able to use cards marked both as to suit and as to numerical value. For means of identifying marked cards see page 22. For your first tip that something queer has been introduced into your sociable little game, keep your eye on the guy who keeps his eye on the widow with more fascination than she warrants.

Marked cards are not uncommonly used by cheaters at two-handed Pinochle. The crook can read the cards' backs as they come off the stock and gait his play accordingly. If the card on top of the stock is a valuable (point-producing) card, he tries to win the trick in play so that he'll get that next card. If it's a worthless card, he manages to lose the trick in play. That gives his opponent the useless card off the stock.

STRIPPERS: AT TWO-HANDED PINOCHLE

Cheaters use the stripper deck with deadly effect at two-handed Pinochle. Four aces are stripped (see page 24 for how they're made and how they're detected), so that they can be pulled out of the deck on the cut. These aces are in the four different suits. How are they used?

The cheater gets the sucker to agree that the first twelve cards dealt in each hand shall be dealt four at a time. When it's the sucker's turn to deal, the cheat gives the deck several running cuts, bringing the four aces (which are, of course, 100 aces) to the top of the deck. The sucker thereupon innocently deals the cheat the 100 aces as the cheat's first four cards.

STRIPPERS: AT PARTNERSHIP PINOCHLE

Something similar to this is sometimes played on green Pinochle fanciers by cheaters playing in partnership. First, they insist on dealing the cards four at a time. (And maybe now you'll understand better why I've been a little insistent about how the cards shall be dealt in the play of the various games.) Next, when it becomes one cheat's turn to cut the cards, he strips the four aces to the top of the deck. Third, the sucker proceeds to deal the first cheat's partner the four aces.

Cheating is done only on the sucker's deal. Cause for suspicion: any player's insisting that cards be dealt four at a clip. Three aces are good, but not good enough for the sure-thing element.

SIGNALING

Effective particularly at Partnership Pinochle is the use of signals, called by cheats, *offices* and *signs*. At a game as informal, not to say raucous, as Pinochle, the subtleties of a skilled cheat's signals are exceedingly hard to detect. Signals used by cheats are:

When to stop bidding.

When to raise a bid.

When to pass, regardless of strength.

When to throw in a suicide bid and go into the hole for a deliberate purpose. (I'll illustrate this delicate point later.)

What suit to lead, sometimes even what card.

The relative value of each other's hand.

Anything relevant can be signaled, and is. The methods are in general identical with the *offices* used at Draw Poker (see page 283), but here's an extra specimen I encountered not long ago.

Two players I'd never seen before were playing two earnest young chumps at a casino which had better be nameless. The strangers seemed to be winning pretty consistently. Moreover, they seemed to handle their cards with uncanny accuracy. Moreover and finally, they both had an unusual nervous mannerism.

They kept fiddling with the money on the table. Kept picking up coins and putting them down, picking them up and putting them down.

By this time you must know about how I work.

First, I observed that this uneasy fumbling with the money always seemed to happen during the players' examination of their cards before the actual bidding started.

Next, I slid over behind one of the strangers, glanced at his holding next time he reached for a coin to finger—and that was the end of the mystery.

These were cheats. If one held a 50 meld, he'd pick up and put down a 5¢ piece. If it was a 100 meld, he'd finger a dime. If it was 150, the coins would be a nickel and dime. And so on. That's all.

I don't think you can be expected to guard yourself against such techniques as this. But you *can* bear in mind that there's something fishy about it when one bidder consistently takes the bid with a weak hand and somehow his partner always has some important help for him. That's *prima facie* evidence that information has been exchanged. As for that evening, reach for your hat; as for the rest of your life, try to play Pinochle with people who lose once in a while.

Signals during the play of the hand, indicating what suit

one cheat wants the other to play, are generally some variants of this harmless-looking routine:

If the cheat wants his partner to play a spade to the trick in progress, he takes pains to put his own card neatly on the pile or in the exact center of the table.

If he wants hearts played, he slams his card down.

If he wants clubs, he leans back lazily and sails his card out onto the table.

If he wants diamonds, he hesitates momentarily before playing his card.

This is the pattern. Every crooked confederacy has its own variants, and most cheats take some professional pride in devising signals that will look natural to the unwary. If you, like me, are proud to count yourself among the unwary, learn at least to perk up and pay attention when you lose a little too consistently. Start watching your opponents. If (as you hadn't noticed before) they seem inordinately itchy, if they polish their glasses or scratch their nose or bite their lips or tap the ash off their cigarette more often than you do these things, see whether there isn't some diverting relationship between what they do and what they play.

And, by the way, don't misunderstand me because I've emphasized the partnership games. Crooks can work just as smoothly, only not quite so profitably, at every-man-for-himself games. See Sandbagging (page 231); and note that the use of signals between two opponents is almost certain to put any but the coolest and most self-disciplined bidder in the hole. Up, up, up you bid; and the next thing you know you're fattening a kitty for the killing. Which reminds me of a story. . . . ⌡

Card Mobs and the Cinch Hand

It's a story of the most prized secret of the ocean-liner card mobs. This is the first time it has ever been told in print. Only an elite inner circle of the transatlantic mob has ever heard of it. It's a story of the innocent chump who lost $20,000 in a 25¢ Pinochle game. It lasted only a couple of hours.

The game is Auction Pinochle with a Widow, Each Hand a Complete Game (to refresh your memory, see page 238), plus a kitty.

The sucker loses by 5 points on a cinch hand which any expert would swear is an absolutely rock-ribbed certainty to win.

The simplified count (page 316) is used. The stake is 25¢ per 100 points plus an ante into the kitty of $1 each. It is mutually agreed before the start of play that for going into the hole in spades the bidder must ante triple into the kitty.

All set? Ring the steward; get a round of drinks on the table; break out the cards. Nice trip, isn't it? Nice ship, nice company . . .

The sucker in this case was a Chicago department store head who, as everyone in the United States would know if I didn't think his name is immaterial, could have bought the ship if he'd wanted to. The crooks happened to know their man. But they don't always know their man. They don't have to. They are incredibly accurate judges of a prospective sucker's cash worth. They play the cinch hand on him for some calculated amount, say $10,000, say $50,000. He needn't pay them out of pocket then and there in United States currency. Not a bit of it! They'll trust him until the next day. They'll even go to the bank with him to get the cash. They'll cash his checks. They're mighty obliging.

So here's the Chicago merchant prince, anticipating a pleasant session at which with the worst imaginable luck he can lose no more than $100. And here are the two cheaters, behaving toward each other as they behave toward their sucker—like urbane, affable, handsome strangers. And here are the cards.

THE START OF THE PLAY

Each player antes $1 into the kitty. The cheaters do not bid even if their hand warrants a bid. Five hands are passed out. The kitty totals $15.

Then one of the cheats bids 300 or more on his next hand, no matter what it is, gets raised to 350 by his partner, buys the widow, and then concedes the hand. He pays off the sucker and his partner, and antes $15 into the kitty, running its total to $30.

(Even should the sucker catch a good hand and bid 350, one of the cheaters must bid him up until the sucker withdraws from the bidding. The sucker is not permitted to take a hand of 350 or more points at this stage of the game. What's necessary now is to fatten the kitty, build it up, set the stage.)

One of the cheaters now bids 350 in spades and proceeds to fail to make the hand. He must ante $90, three times the amount in the kitty, bringing its total to $120.

The next cheater's bid is 350. He fails to make it. His ante (double penalty) is $240. The kitty's total is $360.

Next bid is another 350 hole in spades. Kitty: $1,440.

In rapid succession, two more 350 played holes by the cheaters—and look! All of a sudden the kitty's total is $12,960!

The sucker is praying, even as you and I would, for a 350-point cinch hand, and you may be sure his prayers are promptly answered—by the cheaters.

They have switched in a cold deck (see page 15), and suddenly, his poor head is swimming, here's a sucker looking at a hand—a cinch hand—which holds 360 in meld, including a flush, the A-10-K-Q-J-9 of trump.

He bids a calm, conservative 350. One of the cheats drops out. The other cheat bids 390, and turns up the widow on the table.

"Hey," says the sucker.

"But you passed," the cheat replies, looking startled.

"I didn't say pass," the sucker protests. "I'm still in this."

The other cheat chimes in—on the sucker's side. By this time all three have observed that in the widow are two 10's and a nine of hearts.

"He most certainly did not pass," says Cheat No. 2; the error is corrected; the sucker gets his chance to bid. Now he realizes that the widow holds 20 points he can bury for a total cinch hand in melds and buried cards of 380 point value.

He bids 400. The cheat drops out, grinning ruefully. The sucker gleefully takes the bid. He buries the three cards he got in the widow. He names diamonds his trump suit. Here is his playing hand:

The Sucker's Hand

A-10-K-Q-J-9 of diamonds (trump)
K-Q-K-Q of spades
K-Q-K-Q of clubs
K of hearts

Here's a total meld of 360 points—160 in trump, 40 Pinochle, 40 in spade marriages, 40 in club marriages, and 80 kings. Counting the 20 points for the two heart 10's already buried, all the sucker needs for his diamond-crusted 400 is to make 20 more points in tricks. And you just simply can't fail to make 20 points with that six-card trump suit solid . . . or can't you?

The sucker plays out the hand.

He makes 15 points, 5 short of his required 20.

And he antes into the kitty for his failure to make his bid a cool $12,960.

I told you it was a cold deck. Naturally the cards were stacked. But, before you peek, can you conceive any lie of the cards which would prevent the sucker from winning any trick except the ace of trump, counting his pathetic 15 points?

Well, it'll be as famous in Pinochle as the Mississippi Heart hand is among Bridge scholars; so don't try to switch it into any private game. With that warning, here goes:

Cards Held by the Cheat at the Sucker's Left

> A-10-K-Q-J 9 of diamonds
> 9-9-J-J of spades
> 9-9-J-J of clubs
> A of hearts

Cards Held by the Cheat at the Sucker's Right

> A-A-10-10 of spades
> A-A-10-10 of clubs
> A-K-Q-Q-J-J-9 of hearts

The above hands, played correctly, will permit the sucker to make only 15 points at the very limit. The sucker only makes the ace of diamond trick (with a king and a 9) for a total of 15 points. Get out a pack of Pinochle cards, and try playing the hands.

That's all there is to the story. The cheats now have what they want, which is $13,000 of fresh new money in the kitty. The game goes on until one of the cheats does make a bid of 350 or more and does take the kitty.

After the sucker has failed to make his cinch 400 hand, the cheats revert to their original routine, outbidding him whenever he has a legitimate chance to win the kitty.

Just a friendly little 25¢ game!

Part Six

CHAPTER THIRTY-FOUR

Cribbage

Cribbage, known as "Noddy" in its original form, is one of the oldest card games in existence. Its invention has been popularly accredited to the English poet and soldier Sir John Suckling (1609–42).

About twenty years ago Cribbage enjoyed its greatest popularity in New England, where it was played more than in any other part of the country. But the present day popularity of Gin Rummy has caused the abandonment of most Cribbage clubs.

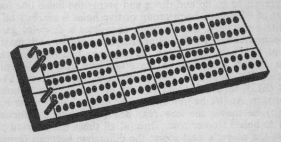

It is the oldest two-handed card game and was once the most consistently popular game in English-speaking countries throughout the world.

During World War II, our Navy boys took to this game quickly, and it proved very popular with sailors throughout the war. In fact, during my World War Navy Institution tour, I don't remember finding a sailor, however modest, who was not frank to admit that at Cribbage he was champion of his ship.

The game is simple to learn. The mechanics of Cribbage

can be thoroughly mastered after fifteen minutes' study. A few hours of play, and you believe you have mastered everything there is to know about the strategy of the game. Then, after becoming an inveterate Cribbage player, you learn that although memory counts for little in the strategy of the game, there are many real possibilities for skillful play and you begin to see its potential.

Cribbage is basically a two-handed game, but it can be played three-handed, and also four-handed—partnership style.

Rules for Playing Cribbage

REQUIREMENTS

1. Two players make the best game.
2. A standard fifty-two-card deck.
3. A Cribbage board.

As the scoring in Cribbage is practically one continuous operation, pencil and paper are seldom used. The Cribbage board keeps track of the score unerringly. The illustration shows what it looks like. The board is usually made of wood and is about 12 inches by three inches. Holes are recessed into the board, and two pegs are provided for each player.

There are thirty holes in each long row, and these allow the players to go up and down and across the finish line for a count of 61 points. Each group of five holes is marked off to facilitate the tally. Once around completes a 61-point game, twice around a 121-point game. Players score by each making use of two pegs, advancing the rear peg one hole for each point scored, beginning in the outer row and then coming back on the inner row. For example, a player scores (a) 2, then (b) 3, then (c) 6. At (a), he moves one peg to hole 2 outer row. At (b) he moves the rear peg to hole 5 outer row. At (c) he moves the new rear peg (originally the forward peg) to hole 11 outer row. Thus, at all times the forward peg shows the player's total score; the difference between forward and rear pegs shows the player's last score.

THE OBJECT OF THE GAME

To be the first to reach game, which may be either 61 or 121 points (as agreed upon before the start of the game), which sum total is made by combined play and meld.

THE RANK OF CARDS

The cards from king (high), queen, jack, ten, nine, eight, seven, down to ace (low). The ace counts 1, the two 2, the three 3, and so on up to the 10-spot. The king, queen and jack also count 10. For purpose of scoring a sequence, the cards rank in their natural order—king, queen, jack, ten, down to the ace.

THE SHUFFLE, CUT, AND DEAL

The players cut cards to determine who deals first; the player cutting low becomes first dealer. The dealer shuffles the cards, the non-dealer cuts, and dealer then deals six cards alternately to non-dealer and himself, the first card being dealt to the non-dealer.

THE CRIB

When each player has been dealt six cards, the remainder of the cards are put aside for the time being. Each player selects two of his six cards and discards them face down to the dealer's right. These four cards are known as the *crib*, which is actually an extra hand and is credited to the dealer's score upon completion of play.

THE STARTER

After the crib has been formed and laid away, the non-dealer cuts the undealt cards. The dealer places the top card of the bottom section of the cut packet face up on this bottom section. The cut is then completed, the turned-up card remaining on top of the undealt packet. This face-up card is known as the *starter*. If the starter is a jack, the dealer scores 2 points immediately, the non-dealer getting nothing. The dealer announces, "Two for his heels," and pegs 2 points. That is, on his side of the Cribbage board he advances a peg 2 holes.

THE PLAY

1. After the starter has been determined, the non-dealer places (plays) face up on the table on his side any one of the four cards he is holding, announcing its pip value. For example, if the card is a 5-spot, he announces, "Five," if it is a four, he announces, "Four," and so on.

2. The dealer plays next on his side of the Cribbage board, adding the pips on his card to that of the card played by his opponent and calling the sum total of the two cards.

3. The non-dealer then plays his second card on his side of the board and calls the sum total of the three cards played so far. For example, the non-dealer begins by playing a 4, announcing, "Four"; the dealer plays an 8, calling, "Twelve"; the non-dealer plays a 6, calling "Eighteen," and so on, until one of the players finds that each of his cards will, if played, carry the score beyond 31.

(During this procedure of alternate play, each player keeps

his exposed cards on his side of the table, separate from those of his opponent, and each one already played must be visible. Cards played are not stacked together as in other games.)

THE GO

If a player at his turn cannot play a card within the limit of 31, he calls, "Go." If the opponent also is unable to lay a card within the 31-count, he too calls, "Go," and a bonus of 1 point is pegged by the first player. But if the second player holds a card or cards that will keep the score under 31, they must be played, and that player pegs one point if the sum total is less than 31 and two points when it is exactly 31.

The final go may occur at any point between 22 and 31. To avoid confusion, when a final go or 31 has been reached, each player turns his previously played cards face down and continues to play the cards remaining in his hand. The player whose turn it is to play starts a new count toward 31.

The player who last called go must deal the next hand and now he has the advantage of the crib.

SCORING DURING THE PLAY

In addition to the points scored for go and 31, there are numerous other scoring factors in the play of Cribbage and they are as follows:

1. Each sum total of cards played that brings the score to 15 earns 2 points. For example, the non-dealer plays a 4, calling, "Four." Dealer plays a jack, calling, "Fourteen." Non-dealer plays an ace, and calls, "Fifteen—Two," and scores 2 points immediately.

2. Pairs. Two successively played cards of the same denomination score 2 points. For example, dealer plays a 6, calling, "Six." Non-dealer also plays a 6 and calls "Twelve and a pair," scoring 2 points.

3. Triplets—three of a kind. Scores 6 points. For example, if a player plays a card that is of the same denomination as the previously played pair and the pair is still exposed, he scores 6 points.

4. Four—four of a kind. Scores 12 points. For example, if a player extends a previously played three of a kind into four of a kind on his play, he immediately pegs 12 points.

5. Three-card run or sequence. Scores 3 points. For example, if a player plays a card that forms a run of three cards with the two previously played cards, he says, "Run of three," and pegs 3 points. The cards do not necessarily have to be played in numerical order, but they must form an unbroken run, such as 2-ace-3, ace-3-2, 3-2-ace, ace-2-3, and so on. The

ace cannot be used to form a run with the king and queen. It can be used only to form a 1, 2, 3 run or an extended run.

6. Four-card run or sequence. Scores 4 points.

7. Five-, six-, or seven-card run or sequence. Scores 5, 6, or 7 points.

8. Double runs. For example, 10-10-9-8, a double three-card run, using the 9 and 8 with each 10. Scores 8 points. 10-10-9-8-7 is a double four-card run. Scores 10 points. 10-10-10-9-8 is a triple run. Scores 15 points. 10-10-9-9-8 is a quadruple run. Scores 16 points.

9. Flush. Four cards of the same suit in the hand (but not in the crib) without the starter scores 4 points. Five cards of the same suit in the hand or the crib with the starter scores 5 points.

10. The limit of play. 31 scores 2 points. The final card played is considered a go and scores 1 point.

THE MELD

In Auction Pinochle and other games, the meld occurs before the hand is played, but in Cribbage, the meld is scored after the play of the hand. The non-dealer scores his melds first. This is important (and is known as *showing*) because if he counts out enough points to peg the game (61 or 121 points or more), he wins, even though the dealer may have scored an equal or higher total score.

If the non-dealer fails to score enough points to win the game, the dealer first scores his melds and then the crib. The melded cards must always consist of five cards—the four cards held by each player plus the starter, the turned-up card. When showing, the scoring is the same as in the actual play of the game. Each combination of 15 scores 2 points.

SCORED POINTS WHEN SHOWING

	Points
One pair	2
Three of a kind	6
Four of a kind	12
Runs of three cards or more	1 for each card
Double three-card run	8
Double four-card run	10
Triple run	15
Quadruple run	16
Flush, four cards of a suit	4
Flush, five cards of a suit	5
Jack of the same suit as the starter (called His Nobs)	1

In scoring 2 points for a 15 combination, it should be noted that each time an additional card is used to total 15, an additional 2 points is scored. Thus, K-K-5-5 invokes four 15's and is scored as 8 points. In short, four combinations of 15 can be formed with four such cards. By adding 2 points for the pair of kings and 2 for the pair of 5's, the total sum is 12 points. If the starter happens to be a third king, your count jumps to 22 points, 6 points for the three kings and 4 more for the extra two 15's.

MUGGINS OPTIONAL

Some Cribbage players still abide by the old rule of *Muggins*, which simply states that if a player overlooks a meld, his opponent may announce, "Muggins," point out the overlooked meld, and credit to his own score the total number of points overlooked by the other player.

DEALING NEW HANDS AND GAMES

At the completion of the hand, after the meld is counted, the next deal takes place. All the cards are shuffled together as at the start. If two decks are used, the second hand is dealt from the second deck, the third from the first, and so on. After the first hand has been dealt, the deal alternates between player and player. The loser of each game deals first in the next game.

THREE-HANDED CRIBBAGE

The game is played the same as Two-Handed Cribbage with the following additional rules.

Players cut for deal, high card dealing the first hand. Thereafter each new deal passes to the left. Each player is dealt five cards. The next card is put aside for the crib. Each player puts one card in the crib.

The player to the left plays first, the player to his left plays next, and the dealer last.

When one player scores game, the game ends; however, in some sections of the country, the two remaining players finish their game to determine the loser.

Cribbage boards with three series of holes to tally the points are available.

FOUR-HANDED CRIBBAGE

The game is played the same as Two-Handed Cribbage with the following exceptons.

Four-Handed Cribbage is played in partnership style. It affords many opportunities for skillful partnership play. Play-

to lead an odd card, if possible lead one that will let you score a run if your opponent makes a 15.

The lead of a 10-count card is not as bad as it is proclaimed to be. The argument against it has been that the opponent makes a 15 by playing a 5. Since there are sixteen cards with a 10-count value and only four 5's, the argument isn't too sound.

It is not always sound to pair the opponent's card. The type of hand and the scores must be taken into consideration. You might score 2 points and then possibly lose 6 points on three of a kind.

When the opponent leads a high card, extra care must be taken to avoid playing cards in sequence, or even irregular sequence. If the opening lead is a 10, a queen, jack, 8, or 9 may open the way for a run of three. With low cards there is the possibility of a comeback with a run of four, but with high cards there is no further chance of scoring but a possible go or 31.

TABULATIONS, OR THE SHOWING

Because the melding combinations that are possible at Cribbage are varied and some of them well hidden, a beginner is excused for missing a few points now and then.

The highest scoring that can be made with any five cards is 29 points. This 29-point score can only be attained by holding J-5-5-5 with the starter a five of the same suit as the held jack. The four 5's total 12 points, and the eight ways of forming 15 are worth 16 points, with 1 point for His Nobs.

It would be quite a task to list all the different possible scoring combinations, but selecting one combination in each category running from 12 to 29 points should prove helpful to the reader. The scoring totals of 19, 25, 26, and 27 do not appear in the following chart, and for a very good reason. They cannot be made. Whenever a player claims one of those four scores, something is wrong with his count. Some of the tabulated scores listed in the following chart include 1 point for His Nobs. Flushes seldom achieve a high score. The 5, 6, 7, 8, and 9 of a suit score only 14 points.

TOTAL SCORES WITH FIVE CARDS INCLUDING STARTER

Five cards	Total points	Five cards	Total points
1-1-6-7-7	12	6-9-9-9-9	20
1-1-7-7-8	12	7-8-8-8-8	20
1-4-4-4-10	12	7-8-8-9-9	20
2-2-4-9-9	12	3-3-6-6-6	20

Five cards	Total points	Five cards	Total points
2-6-6-7-7	12	4-4-4-7-7	20
1-1-6-7-8	13	3-3-4-5-5	20
1-4-4-4-*J*	13	1-1-7-7-7	20
3-3-6-6-9	14	3-4-4-4-4	20
4-4-7-7-7	14	4-5-6-6-6	21
1-2-2-2-3	15	7-7-7-8-9	21
J-Q-Q-Q-K	15	5-5-J-J-*J*	21
1-1-2-3-3	16	3-3-3-4-5	21
2-2-3-3-4	16	5-5-5-K-K	22
2-6-7-7-8	16	5-5-5-J-*J*	23
6-7-8-9-9	16	4-5-5-5-6	23
2-3-4-4-4	17	3-6-6-6-6	24
2-3-3-3-4	17	4-4-5-6-6	24
3-4-4-4-5	17	4-5-5-6-6	24
3-3-3-6-6	18	7-7-8-8-9	24
5-5-J-Q-K	18	3-3-3-3-9	24
6-6-9-9-9	20	4-4-4-4-7	24
6-6-7-7-8	20	6-7-7-8-8	24
3-3-4-4-5	20	5-5-5-5-10	28
7-7-7-8-8	20	5-5-5-5-*J*	29

The italicized jack designates it as the same suit as the starter, and 1 point allowed for His Nobs.

Fifteen may be formed with as many as five cards and as few as two: 1-2-3-4-5 totals fifteen as does 10 and 5. The high scores are usually made when holding triple and quadruple runs. This is especially true when a series of fifteen is included.

In counting melds, it will help matters to remember that all three-card double runs score 8 points, triple runs 15 points, and quadruple runs 16 points. A four-card double run scores 10 points. These total counts include the pair or three of a kind, but not the 15's. They must be added. The ace can be used in a low run only, it cannot join the king and queen. All other cards may extend at both ends.

CHAPTER THIRTY-FIVE

Pitch or Setback

Pitch or Setback is a variation of the Old Fours, a game played in England for the past couple of centuries. There are many variations of Pitch played in America. I have selected the most popular present day variation to include in this text.

REQUIREMENTS

1. Two to seven players. Four make the best game. Each player plays for himself.
2. A standard fifty-two-card deck is used. The card values rank as follows: ace (high), king, queen, jack, ten, nine, eight, seven, six, five, four, three, deuce (two low) in descending order. Suits have no rank. (Some players add a joker to the deck and rank it either above the ace or below the deuce. However, this ruling must be agreed on beforehand.)

SELECTING THE DEALER

Players cut for deal. The player cutting the high card deals first; thereafter, the deal rotates to the left, clockwise.

THE SHUFFLE AND CUT

Any player may shuffle the deck, the dealer last. The player to the dealer's right cuts.

THE DEAL

Each player, beginning with the player to the dealer's left and going clockwise, is dealt three cards at a time until each has been dealt six cards. The remainder of the deck is not used.

THE OBJECT OF THE GAME

To become the first player to score 11 points (or 7, 9, or 21, as agreed upon). The points are counted after the hand has been played and are as follows.

1. High. One point for the original player holding the highest trump showing during the play of the hand.
2. Low. One point for the original player holding the lowest trump showing during the play of the hand.

405

3. Jack. One point to the player who wins the jack of trumps during play. Naturally, if it is not in play, no one scores it.

4. Joker. If used, the joker counts 1 point for the player who wins it.

5. Game. One point to the player scoring the most number of points. Cards are valued as follows: each 10 counts 10 points, each ace 4, each king 3, each queen 2, and each jack 1.

THE BIDDING

The player to the dealer's left bids first. Each player, rotating clockwise, has one chance to bid or pass. He may bid one, two, three, or four. Suits have no value, hence are not named. Each bid must be higher in numerical value than the preceding bid, and the highest possible bid is four, which is known as a *slam, smudge,* or *shoot the moon.* If all players pass, the hand is declared dead and the same dealer deals again.

THE PLAY OF THE GAME

The highest bidder, known as the *pitcher,* leads to the first trick and the suit that card happens to be establishes the trump suit for the deal. On a trump lead, each player must follow suit when able; when any other suit (but trump) is played, a player may either follow suit or play a trump card, as he prefers. If unable to follow suit, a player may play a trump or throw off any card he pleases. The highest card of a suit wins the trick if no trumps are played to the trick. When only one trump card is played to a trick, the trump wins. But if more than one trump is played, to a trick, the trump wins. But if more than one trump is played, highest trump takes the trick.

The winner of a trick leads a card to the next trick.

The play of each trick continues as described above until all six cards have been played.

SCORING

When the six cards have been played, each player receives credit for the points he scores, except that if the player who took the bid fails to score as many points as he bid for, he is *set back* the same number of points as he bid. The full total of his bid is deducted from his previous score. If his set back is greater than his previous or plus score, a minus score is recorded for the difference. A circle is usually drawn around a minus score and the holder is said to be *in the hole.*

END OF GAME

The first player to reach 11 points (or 7, 10, or 21, as agreed on), wins the game. In the event the bidder of the last hand and any other player or players have scored 11 or more points (or 7, 9, or 21 points as agreed on) the bidder is declared the winner of the game. If two players other than the last bidder could reach 11 points with the last hand, the points are counted in the following order: High, low, Jack and Game.

The winner receives from each player the difference in points between his score and each player's score.

Additional Rules

MISDEALS

1. If the dealer does not offer the deck to be cut.

2. If an ace, deuce, or jack is exposed during the deal by the dealer. Because the deal carries an advantage, a misdeal by dealer loses him the right to deal, and it passes to the player on his left.

IRREGULARITIES IN BIDDING

1. A bid out of turn, or a bid lower or equal to the previous bid, loses the bidding privilege for the offender. He must pass. A card once played cannot be taken back.

2. If a player plays out of turn, the bidder reserves the right to force the offender at his proper turn of play to play his highest or lowest card of the suit led, or to trump or not to trump.

3. If the bidder has played to an incorrect lead, he cannot take back his played card. However, he is permitted to name the proper trump and must then lead it at his first opportunity, that is, immediately after winning his first trick.

REVOKES

When a player fails to follow suit when able to do so, a revoke is committed. If the bidder revokes, he is set back the amount of his bid. Each of the other players scores the points he makes. If a player other than the bidder revokes, an amount equal to the bid is deducted from his score and the same amount is added to the score of all other players, including the bidder, even though the latter scores fewer points than he bid.

CHAPTER THIRTY-SIX

Casino

Casino is a hardy perennial two-handed game which was greatest in popularity prior to the advent of Gin Rummy. Casino is a game that can be played very scientifically, and the best Casino players are very expert, at least as expert as the best Gin Rummy players are at their game. For this very reason the average player when pitted against an expert is bound to lose unless he knows some of the scientific aspects of the game. If you lose constantly against a certain player, it is because you are not as good as the other fellow, not because of the "bad cards" you are dealt. Although Casino is sometimes played three- or four-handed, I do not recommend either method since they considerably reduce the strategical possibilities of the game. For that reason the rules for Three- and Four-Handed Casino are omitted from these pages.

REQUIREMENTS

1. A standard deck of fifty-two cards.
2. Two players.

NUMBER VALUES OF THE CARDS

The play of the game requires that the cards be given number values: ace counts 1, two, 2; three, 3; four, 4; five, 5; six, 6; seven, 7; eight, 8; nine, 9; and ten, 10. The jack, queen, and king have no given point values. Rank of cards does not enter into the game.

OBJECT OF THE GAME

To win the hand or game by scoring more points than your opponent. Six or more points win a hand.

POINT-SCORING VALUES

1. Each ace taken in counts 1 point.
2. Two of spades (known as *Little Casino*) taken in counts 1 point.
3. Ten of diamonds (known as *Big Casino*) taken in counts 2 points.

4. Seven or more spades (known as *spades*) taken in counts 1 point.

5. Twenty-seven or more cards of any suits (known as *cards*) taken in counts 3 points. If both players take in twenty-six cards there is no score for cards.

All told there are 11 points to be scored in each hand.

THE SHUFFLE, CUT, AND DEAL

1. Players cut for deal, and low card deals the first hand. Thereafter, the deal alternates between player and player.

2. The dealer shuffles the cards and offers them to his opponent to cut.

3. The dealer deals his opponent two cards face down, then turns two cards face up on the center of the table. He then deals two cards to himself face down. Two more face-down cards are dealt to his opponent, two more face up on the table, and next two more face down cards to himself. In brief, each player now holds four cards, and four face-up cards are resting on the table.

THE PLAY OF THE HAND

Beginning with the non-dealer, each player alternately may play any card he wishes from his hand. A player may make any of the following possible plays at each turn of play:

A player possessing a card of the same number value as any on the table removes the card from his hand and places it face down on the matched card, picks up the matched pair and places them face down in a pile in front of him. One card or several can be paired in this way.

In addition, a player may take in any group of cards resting on the table whose total numerical value adds up to the number value of the card he plays.

Example 1. Suppose that a player at his turn of play has a 10-spot card in his hand, and exposed on the table are three 10-spot cards and an ace, a 6, and a 3. The player can take in the three 10's and also the ace, 6, and 3, which total 10. All seven cards (which include the player's 10-spot) are taken on the play and placed face down in a pile in front of him.

Example 2. Suppose that there are three deuces on the table and a player holds both a deuce and a 6-spot. He can play either the deuce or the 6 from his hand to take in the three deuces. He can play his deuce since it is a card of the same number value as the cards on the table, or he can play his 6-spot since the three deuces add up to 6. Or if there were three deuces and a 6 on the table the player could play the 6 from his hand, call, "Six," and take in the three deuces and the 6-spot with his lone 6, thereby cleaning the board.

A player may take in only one picture card (jack, queen, or king) on the table with a matching picture card from his hand, unless he holds the fourth to a set of three on the table.

Example. If a player holds a king in his hand and two kings are exposed on the table, he may take in only one of the exposed kings at his proper turn of play. But if there are three kings, or three queens, or three jacks on the table and a player holds the matching fourth card, he is permitted to take in all three picture cards exposed on the table, plus the one card in his hand, making a total of four picture cards.

A player may play a card from his hand onto a card on the table, leave it there, and announce he is *building*, simply by naming the number value (from 1 to 10) he is building. There are a number of ways of making builds.

Suppose there are a 6 and a deuce on the table, and the player possesses an ace and 9 in his hand. He places the ace with the 6 and deuce in the group and announces, "Building nine," which statement indicates that the player holds a 9-spot in his hand with which he can take the 9 build. This type of build is known as a *single build*. Either player may change any single build resting on the table to a higher number value at his proper turn of play by adding a card from his hand to the existing single build.

Example. Suppose a player has made a single build of 5. His opponent at his proper turn of play adds an ace to it and calls a new build of 6. Only a six can take this build. Naturally the player who increases the 5 build to a 6 build holds a 6 in his hand. This 6 build can be increased to a 7, 8, 9, or 10 build providing player abides by the above single-build rules.

A player may not make use of a card on the table to change the number value of a single build. He must play a fresh card from his hand.

A player may take in an opponent's build when it is his proper turn of play only if he holds a card of the same number value as the build.

Once a player has made a build he must, on his next play, either take in a trick, make another build, increase a single build to a higher number, make a single build into a multiple build, or add to a multiple build.

A *multiple build* is a build in which more than one unit of the number is built. For example, a build of 9 made of 6 plus 3 and a duplicate made of 8 plus 1. A player may add to a single build and make it a multiple build at his next turn of play by adding a card from his hand, with or without another card, or cards, from the table.

Example 1. A player has built 9 at his previous turn of play. He has two 9's in his hand. He puts one of them on his single build of 9, making it a multiple 9 ready to be taken with the second 9 in his hand.

Example 2. A player has a single build of 9. In addition to holding a 9 he holds a 4- and a 6-spot. If there is a 5 on the table he can add his 4-spot to it, call, "Nine," and place both cards on his build pile of 9's, making a multiple build which he must take on his next turn of play, unless he can add another 9 build or his opponent takes the build with a 9-spot.

A player may not change the number value of a multiple build.

Example 1. A multiple build of 7's has been made consisting of a 7 and a 4 and 3. No player may add a card to this build and call a higher build.

Example 2. A player has played a 4 from his hand, placed it atop another 4 on the table, and called, "Fours" (a multiple build). No player is permitted to take this build with an 8.

When a player does not take a trick or make or contribute to a build he must discard a card from his hand face up onto the table. This is known as *trailing*. A player may discard at any time he pleases providing he does not have a build of his own on the board.

CONTINUED DEALS

After both players have played their first four cards one at a time, the dealer picks up the stock (the undealt cards) and deals four more cards to the non-dealer and himself in the same manner as in the original deal. However, he does not deal any cards face up on the table at any time for the rest of the deal.

Play then continues until all the cards in the deck have been exhausted (dealt).

When each player is dealt his last four cards, the dealer must announce the fact by saying, "Last" or "Deal's up."

TAKING IN THE LAST TRICK

The player who takes in the last trick also takes in any other cards that may be left on the table.

END OF GAME

When the hand is over, the players look through their pile of cards (the tricks they have taken) and score as described under "Point-Scoring Values." The player scoring the greatest number of points is declared the winner of the game. The lower score is deducted from the higher score, and the difference is the winning margin.

CASINO MATCH-STYLE

Instead of considering each deal a separate game, the players may decide to make the goal of the game a point total, in which case the deals continue until the goal is reached. For example, the player first to reach 11 or 21 points wins the match. If both players score 11 or 21 points or more in the same hand, the player with the higher score is declared the winner. The reward for the winner is usually stipulated before play starts.

Strategy at Casino

The important thing is to keep a mental count of the cards, spades, and points you have taken in. This count can make all the difference between winning and losing by indicating which is the best play. For example, on the board there is an ace, a 3, a 5, and an 8. You have already taken in twenty-three cards and 3 points. You have in your hand an ace, a 7, an 8, and a queen. If you take the 3, 5, and 8 with your 8 you will have 27 cards, and the 3 points this wins will, with the 3 points already in, give you 6 points on the game. If you take the aces you will have a total of only 5 points and will lose if, as is possible, you don't take another card.

Additional Rules for Casino

MISDEALS: YES OR NO

1. If a player accidentally turns up a card or cards belonging to his opponent and this occurs with the first twelve dealt cards, that deal is void, a misdeal is declared, and the same dealer deals again.

2. If a player accidentally turns up a card or cards belonging to his opponent and this occurs after the first twelve cards have been dealt, the previous dealt hands stand. However, the current dealt hand is retrieved and shuffled back into the stock and a new hand is dealt.

3. If a player turns up a card or cards belonging to himself, he must play that hand. No new deal or shuffle takes place.

4. If a card, or cards, is found face up in the deck during a deal, the play stands. However, the player receiving the face-up card or cards has the privilege of removing the same number of cards from his opponent's hand, looking at them, and returning them to the opponent.

5. If a player has too few or too many cards and this is discovered before the first trick is completed, a misdeal is declared and the same dealer deals again.

6. If a player has too few or too many cards after the first trick, and this is discovered after one or more cards of the hand have been played, he loses the deal and his opponent is credited with 11 points.

ANNOUNCING THE LAST DEAL

If the dealer fails to announce, "Last deal" when the last eight cards of the deck are dealt and a trick is played from the last eight cards of the deck, he loses the game and his opponent is credited with 11 points.

FAULTY BUILDS

If a player makes a build and does not have a proper card to take it in, he loses the game and his opponent is credited with 11 points.

If a player trails (plays a card without taking in a trick) and he has a build, already lying on the table, he loses the game and his opponent scores 11 points.

LOOKING THROUGH CARDS TAKEN IN

If a player takes in a trick, his opponent may ask to see the trick even though the cards have been gathered and placed in the taker's pile. This is the case only if the opponent has not played after the taker of the trick under consideration. If a player makes a play after the opponent has committed an error, the incorrect play is considered condoned.

In no other instance is it permitted to look through gathered cards. The penalty for such infraction is loss of game and a score to the opponent of 11 points.

Cheating at Casino

Cheating at Casino is as common as cheating at Gin Rummy, and the same methods are used, such as marked cards, stacking, shifting the cut, and belly strippers. When the cheat uses strippers, he usually has all the point-scoring cards gaffed.

CHAPTER THIRTY-SEVEN

Kalabrias, Klobiosh, Klabberjass, or Klob

Kalabrias (pronounced "ko-lob-ree-yosh"), known also as Klobiosh or Klabberjass and by its abbreviation Klob, is one of the best of all two-handed games. Prior to the advent of Gin Rummy, Kalabrias was the most popular two-handed money game among the gentry who liked to put their money up to prove their skill at the game.

Its origin has been variously claimed by the Dutch, Swiss, French, and Hungarians, but the fact that the game first became popular in Jewish goulash joints (card rooms) causes me to lean toward the Hungarian claim.

Rules for Playing Kalabrias

REQUIREMENTS

1. Two players.
2. A thirty-two-card deck is used, made up by removing all cards ranked below a 7 (6's, 5's, 4's, 3's, and 2's). In other words, the thirty-two-card deck is comprised of aces, kings, queens, jacks, 10's, 9's, 8's, and 7's.

RANK OF CARDS

In a trump suit they rank as follows: jack (high), 9, ace, 10, king, queen, 8, 7 (low). The jack of trumps is known as the *boss* or *jazz* (pronounced "yass"). The 9 of trumps is known as *menel*. The 7 of trumps is known as *dix* (pronounced "deece").

In a non-trump suit they rank as follows: ace (high), 10, king, queen, jack, 9, 8, 7 (low).

THE SHUFFLE, CUT, AND DEAL

1. Players cut for the deal and low card deals the first hand. Thereafter, the deal alternates between player and player.
2. The dealer shuffles the cards and offers them to his opponent to cut.

3. The dealer deals three cards at a time to his opponent, then three cards to himself. Then three more cards to his opponent and three more cards to himself. Each player now holds six cards.

4. The next card (thirteenth) is placed face up on the table and the remaining stock (undealt cards) is placed partially over this face-up card. But the stock must be placed over the face-up card in such a manner that the face-up can be seen and identified at all times.

OBJECT OF THE GAME

To try to score 300 or 500 points, as may be agreed, before your opponent, which takes into consideration the following factors:

1. To try to establish one's best suit as trump.

2. To meld certain combinations which have the highest-counting values.

3. To score points by taking tricks which contain certain cards possessing point value.

MAKING THE TRUMP

1. The non-dealer has the first say in naming trump. He may accept the suit of the turned-up card as trump by merely calling the name of the suit of the turned-up card and saying that specific suit is trump, or he may pass. If he accepts the suit of the turned-up card, it becomes trump and the deal continues.

2. If the non-dealer refuses the suit of the upturned card as trump, he says, *"Pass."* Then it is the dealer's turn to accept the suit of the turned-up card as trump, and the deal continues. If he also passes, the hands are considered void and thrown in, and the cards are shuffled and cut and two new hands are dealt.

3. Instead of committing himself on the suit of the up-turned card or passing, a player may say, *"Schmeiss"* (pronounced "shmice") or, *"Throw them in."*

This is an offer to throw in the hands and have a new shuffle, cut, and deal. If the player's opponent agrees, both hands are thrown in and a new deal is effected. But if the opponent says, "No," which means he has refused the offer, the player who called "Schmeiss" or "Throw them in" must name the trump suit.

If schmeiss was called in the first round (see 1. above), the suit of the turned-up card is trump. If it was called in the second round (see 2. above), the caller of schmeiss may name any suit he desires as trump.

THE CONTINUED DEAL

After trump has been named, the dealer deals to each player three additional cards from the top of the stock (the undealt cards) beginning with three to the non-dealer and then giving three to himself. He then indicates the end of the deal by taking the bottom card of the remaining stock and placing it face up on the stock. However, this card does not enter into play, nor do any of the cards in the remaining stock. Before play begins, the holder of the dix (7 of trumps) may exchange it for the card originally turned up for trump. The exchange must be made before players declare their melds prior to the play of the hand.

MELDS OR LAYS

Players compare matched sets called *melds* or *lays* for the right to score them. The melds may be a sequence of three, four, or more cards in the same suit. For example, the 7, 8, and 9 of hearts; or the ace, king, queen, and jack of spades. It is possible to meld eight cards in a single sequence. A three-card meld or lay is valued at 20 points. A meld or lay of four cards or more is valued at 50 points.

HOW TO SCORE MELDS OR LAYS

Only one player may score a meld or melds. The method of establishing which player scores his meld or melds is as follows:

The non-dealer has the first say. If the non-dealer possesses a meld he announces its point value. For example, if he holds a three-card meld, he calls, "Twenty"; if he holds a meld of four or more cards he calls, "Fifty." A player holding a meld of five or more cards may show only four cards of the meld. The extra cards carry no additional value or significance with reference to scoring or deciding the highest meld.

If the dealer has a meld of a lower point value or no meld at all, he replies, "Good." If the dealer has a meld of a higher point value, he replies, "No good," shows his meld, and scores his meld. If the dealer has a meld of equal point value, he replies, "Same" or "How high?" In this instance the non-dealer names the highest ranking card of his meld. The dealer then replies, "Same," "Good," or "No good," depending on what the highest ranking card of his own meld happens to be.

Players holding melds that are equal in point value and highest ranking card, neither of which being in trump, the meld belonging to the non-dealer is considered the best and is scored. The dealer's meld is considered void. As between melds of the same point value and the same highest ranking card, a trump meld is considered the best.

If non-dealer has no melds, he says, "No melds," and the dealer then calls out the point value of any meld or melds he wishes to score points for.

The player who claims the best meld receives credit for its point value after showing the meld to his opponent, and the player holding the best meld may also receive credit for other melds he shows. The opponent who held the inferior meld scores nothing, but he does not have to show his meld; nor is a player required to show a meld he does not wish to receive point credits for.

Following is an example of meld comparing and the conversation involved.

Non-dealer holds a meld comprised of A-K-Q-J in one suit and Q-J-10 in another suit. The dealer holds K-Q-J-10 in a third suit.

The non-dealer calls, "Fifty" (the point value of his ranking four-card meld).

The dealer replies, "How high?" (since he has a meld of equal point value).

Non-dealer responds, "Ace high."

Dealer acknowledges, "Good" (since his highest ranking card is a king).

Non-dealer shows his 50-point meld and his 20-point meld, and scores 70 points.

Dealer does not show his meld because it is valueless and cannot be scored.

There is another meld which carries a value of 20 points. It is the king and queen of trump and is known as *bella*. It scores automatically and does not have to be announced until the game is completed and the cards taken in by each player are being counted for scoring.

THE PLAY OF THE HAND

Regardless of who made the trump, the non-dealer plays first. He may play any card he chooses. The dealer then plays a card. If the lead card is of a non-trump suit and the dealer has no cards of the led suit, he must play a trump if he is able to. Otherwise, he may play any card he desires. If the lead card is a trump, the dealer must play a higher trump if he is able to do so, but he must follow suit in any case.

A trick is comprised of two cards and is won by the highest ranking card of the suit led. But if a trick involves one trump card, that trump card wins. If a trick involves two trumps, the highest ranking trump wins. The winner of the trick takes the two cards and places them face down in front of himself. The winner of a trick leads the first card of the next trick, and so it goes until all nine tricks have been played and the hand is ended.

When all the nine tricks have been played, each player takes point credit for the valuable cards amongst his gathered cards. The point values of the valuable cards are as follows: jack of trump, 20 points; 9 of trump (menel), 14 points; ace of any suit, 11 points; 10 of any suit, 10 points; king of any suit, 4 points; queen of any suit, 3 points; jack of any suit except trump, 2 points.

Winner of the last trick is credited with 10 points more on his score. There is a total of 162 points in the game. This includes the 10 points for the last trick. However, because only eighteen of the thirty-two cards are in play, the greatest possible total of points scored in any single hand is 156.

SCORING THE HAND

If the total score of the bidder (the player who made trump), which includes melds and points scored in tricks won, is greater than the non-bidder's (opponent's), each player receives credit for his own score. But if the non-bidder's total score is equal to or greater than the bidder's score, the non-bidder receives credit for his own scored points plus the total points the bidder scored. These are comprised of points scored in tricks and melds, including bella, be it announced or unannounced.

The bidder in this instance scores zero and is said to have *gone bate.*

END OF GAME OR MATCH

The first player to reach 300 (or 500) points wins the game. If both players score 300 points or more in the same deal, the player with the highest score is declared the winner.

Additional Rules

MISDEALS BEFORE START OF PLAY, YES OR NO?

1. If the dealer or the non-dealer turns up a card belonging to his opponent, that deal is void, a misdeal is declared, and the same dealer deals again. If the dealer or non-dealer turns up a card or cards belonging to himself, the opponent may let the deal stand or call for a new deal.

2. If either player is dealt too many cards and this is discovered before a trick is played, opponent removes the excess

cards from player's hand and has the right to look at them
before they are placed at the bottom of the undealt cards. If a
player is dealt too few cards and this is discovered before a
trick is played, the deficiency is made up from the top of the
deck.

RENEGES

If, when play for tricks is in progress, (a) a player fails to
follow the suit of the card led when he can, (b) fails to trump
when he has a trump and does not have any cards of suit led,
(c) trump being led, he fails to play a higher trump when he
can, then his opponent can call attention to this failure and, at
any time during play or after the hand is completed, can claim
a renege.

In each case the reneger (the player who failed to follow
the rules) loses all his scored points and the opponent receives
credit for the reneger's total points plus his own scored points.

IMPROPERLY CALLED MELDS

If a player is found to have made a call that has under-
valued or overvalued a meld, his opponent can call attention
to this irregularity at any time during play or after the hand is
completed and claim a renege. The offender loses all his scored
points and his opponent receives credit for the offender's total
points plus his own scored points.

IRREGULAR HANDS

If a player possesses fewer or more than the allotted nine
cards and one or more tricks have been played, the player
possessing the irregular hand is declared to have reneged and
loses all his scored points. His opponent receives credit for the
offender's total points plus his own scored points.

LEADING OUT OF TURN

If, before a trick has been picked up by a player, it is established that a player has led out of turn, players merely pick up
their cards and correct the error.

If the trick has been completed and stacked with the completed tricks, the play stands and the player who won the trick
makes the next lead.

LOOKING THROUGH CARDS TAKEN IN TRICKS

If he has played his card for the following trick, a player
may look at the last trick gathered in, and this rule holds regardless of which player won the last trick.

In no other instance is it permitted to look through the gathered cards, except when looking through tricks to determine whether a player has reneged.

There is no enforceable penalty for an infraction of this rule.

Cheating at Kalabrias

Cheating at Kalabrias is as common as cheating at Gin Rummy, and it is just as easy.

Watch out for marked cards, second dealing, palming, stacking, shifting the cut, cold decks, and belly strippers, which are often used at Kalabrias to clip the sucker on his own deal. Usually all the spade cards are gaffed to strip out.

CHAPTER THIRTY-EIGHT

Hearts According to Scarne and Regular Hearts

Hearts According to Scarne

Hearts According to Scarne retains a secure hold on the affections of its numerous devotees. Hearts is a real cutthroat game when played "according to Scarne," a deceptively simple game that never fails to provide much amusement, arguments, and conversation after the play of each hand or game. Hearts According to Scarne is almost unsurpassed for opportunities to apply skill and deduction in analyzing the meanings of your opponents' play and in planning your own strategy so as to make the most of what you deduce about the other players' hands when compared with the strength of your own hand. Hearts is one of the most popular games in the country, but is played in many different forms in various sections of the country. The only variations I will discuss in this book are Hearts According to Scarne and Regular Hearts, for the obvious reason that neither of these games has any weak spots whereas each of the other variations possesses at least one weak spot.

Rules for Hearts According to Scarne

REQUIREMENTS

1. A standard deck of fifty-two cards.
2. Four players.
3. Each player plays for himself.

RANK OF CARDS

The cards rank as follows: ace (high), king, queen, jack, 10, 9, 8, 7, 6, 5, 4, 3, 2 (low). The suits have no relative values.

VALUE OF CARDS

The play of the game revolves about the thirteen hearts and the queen of spades, which is referred to as the *Black Queen*, *Black Lady*, the *Bitch*, *Black Maria*, and the *Slippery Bitch*. Each heart card counts 1 point. The queen of spades counts 5 points, making a total of 18 points per hand or game.

OBJECT OF THE GAME

Each to score the least number of points and at the same time to try to load each opponent with 1 or more points, or to score all 18 points.

SELECTING DEALER AND SEATING POSITIONS

1. The four players seat themselves at any places around the table; where they sit at the beginning is not important.
2. Any player may shuffle the pack and offer the pack to any other player to cut.
3. Each of the four players is dealt a card face up. The player drawing the highest card selects his seating position, then the drawer of the second highest, and so forth. In case of ties, the tied players each receive another card until the tie is broken. On the first draw, should two players receive high card, they each receive another card to decide the order of seat selection.
4. The player who was dealt low card starts the game by dealing the first hand. From then on the deal moves to the dealer's left, clockwise.

THE SHUFFLE, THE CUT, AND THE DEAL

1. The first dealer shuffles the cards and offers the pack to the player to his right to cut.
2. Dealer serves each player one card at a time until all the cards have been equally distributed—thirteen to each player.

THE PLAY

The leader (the player at the dealer's left) makes the opening lead. He may play any card he desires. Each player in turn must play a card in the same suit, if he is able to do so. If he is unable to follow suit, he may play a card of any other suit. A trick is constituted when each player has played a card to the lead, and it is taken by the highest card of the suit led by the first player.

The winner of the trick leads the next play of the hand. This manner of play continues until thirteen tricks or all cards have been played out.

SETTLEMENT OF HAND OR GAME

After thirteen tricks have been played, each player looks through his cards (won tricks) to determine how many points he has scored. These include 1 point for each heart and 5 points for the queen of spades. The player who has taken the fewest points wins the hand and collects from each player the difference in points between his own total and the other player's total. For example, A has 2 points, B has 4 points, C has 4 points, D has 8 points. A wins 2 from B, 2 from C, 6 from D. However, if a player has scored all 18 points he is said to have made a *step* and he collects 18 units (points) from each of the three losing players. If two or more players tie for the fewest points taken, they divide the winnings, and if there are odd units left over, they cut or draw high card to determine who shall receive the odd units.

Hearts Match-Style According to Scarne

For the players who prefer their games to run longer and their scores higher, this match game variation is highly recommended. The rules of play are the same as in Hearts According to Scarne described in the foregoing text, with the following exceptions.

END OF MATCH

The match ends when five hands or games have been played.

DECIDING THE WINNER

The player who scores the fewest number of points is declared the winner of the match and receives the difference in' units between his points and those of each of his three opponents.

THE SCORING

As each hand or game is completed, each player's score is recorded on the score sheet.

If a player steps and collects 18 points, he receives a zero (0) on his score sheet. Each losing player is penalized with 18 points.

Losers of the match each receive a penalty bonus of 50 points, which is added to their five-game total.

Below is an example of Hearts match scoring:

POINTS SCORED BY EACH PLAYER

Games	John	Joe	Pete	Mary
First game	18	0	18	18
Second game	2	2	6	8
Third game	1	5	3	9
Fourth game	9	1	4	4
Fifth game	8	5	2	3
Total five-game score	28	13	33	42
Penalty point bonuses	50	—	50	50
Total match scores	78	13	83	92
Minus winner's (Joe's) score	−13	—	−13	−13
Joe wins by	65 points		70 points	79 points

At a penny a point, Joe receives 65¢ from John, 70¢ from Pete, and 79¢ from Mary, for a total of $2.14.

Hearts for Three, Five, or Six Players According to Scarne

Hearts for Three, Five, or Six players lacks the opportunities to use strategy found in Hearts According to Scarne.

The game is played exactly as Hearts According to Scarne, with the following exceptions.

After each player has been dealt an equal number of cards, the remaining cards (odd cards) are dealt face down into the center of the table as a *widow* or *blind*. These cards go to the winner of the first trick.

Some players prefer to remove the odd cards from the deck before the start of the play. This may be done as follows:

If three play, remove the deuce of diamonds.

If five play, remove the deuces of diamonds and hearts. If six play, remove the deuces of diamonds, hearts and clubs and the three of diamonds.

Additional Rules of Play for Hearts According to Scarne

MISDEALS: YES OR NO

1. If a dealer or player turns up a card or cards belonging to another player during the deal, that deal is void, a misdeal is declared, and the same dealer deals again.

2. If a dealer or player turns up a card or cards belonging to himself, that deal stands.

3. If a card is found face up in the deck during the deal, a misdeal is declared and the same dealer deals again.

4. If one or more players have too few or too many cards and this is discovered before the first trick is completed, a misdeal is declared and the same dealer deals again.

5. If a player has too few cards and this is discovered after the final trick is completed, he must take the last trick. If he is more than one card short, he must take in every trick to which he cannot play.

PLAY OUT OF TURN

A lead or play out of turn must be retracted if demand is made by a player before all have played to the trick; however, if all have played, the play out of turn stands as a regular turn of play without penalty.

RENEGES

Failure to follow suit when able constitutes a renege. If two or more players renege they divide the penalty. A renege may be corrected before the trick is turned face down and picked up from the table. If not discovered until later, play immediately ceases when the renege is established, and the reneger must pay each player 18 units if played as a single hand. In match-style play the 18 points are multiplied by the number of opponents, and this total is entered in the offender's column on the score sheet. For example, in a four-handed game the points penalty is computed as follows: $18 \times 3 = 54$ points. Other players jot down a zero for each of the scores.

Regular Hearts

A variation of Hearts played for years throughout the country. This variation of Hearts is not played as a money game nearly as often as Hearts According to Scarne. The stategy of the game does not equal that of Hearts According to Scarne.

Scarne's Rules for Regular Hearts

THE OBJECT OF THE GAME

To win the game by scoring fewer points than any of your opponents. In short, to try to avoid as many hearts as possible and also the queen of spades.

REQUIREMENTS

1. A standard pack of fifty-two playing cards.
2. Three to seven players. Four is the best number. Each player plays for himself.

RANK OF CARDS

Ace (high), king, queen, jack, 10, 9, 8, 7, 6, 5, 4, 3, 2 (low). The suits have no relative rank although the play revolves about the hearts.

SELECTING THE DEALER

Players cut cards to determine the first dealer, and the player cutting lowest rank card deals the first hand. Thereafter, the deal passes to the left.

SHUFFLE AND CUT

Any player may shuffle, the dealer last. The player at the dealer's right cuts the cards.

THE DEAL

The cards are dealt one at a time as far as they can be dealt equally. The remaining cards are placed on the table face down, forming a widow or blind. The player who wins the first trick takes the blind; no one may look at these cards during play.

THE PASS

Right after each deal and before the start of play, after looking at his hand, each player selects any three cards in his hand and passes them face down to the player at his left without exposing them to the others. Each player must pass these three cards before looking at the three cards he receives from his right. In six- and seven-handed play, only two cards are passed to the left.

THE PLAY

The leader (the player to the dealer's left) makes the opening lead. Each player must follow suit to a lead if able; if unable, a player may discard any card he wishes. However, the player holding the queen of spades must discard it at his first opportunity. Highest ranking card of the suit led wins the trick.

When mutually agreed upon before the start of the game, the rule that the queen of spades be discarded at the first opportunity is set aside and the queen of spades may be discarded any time during play, the agreed rules permitting.

SCORING

Each heart counts 1 point, the queen of spades 13 points. When Hearts is being played as a match, five hands constitute a match. At the end of each hand the points taken in tricks by each player are totaled and entered under his name on the score sheet. When a single hand is played as a game, the player who scored the fewest points is declared the winner and he collects the difference in points between his score and that of each of the other players. In brief, he collects 1 point for each heart held by the losing players and 13 units for the queen of spades. If two or more players tie for the fewest points taken, they divide the winnings, and if there are odd units left over, they cut or draw high card to determine who shall receive the odd units.

The player who scores the fewest total points for the five games is declared the winner and gets credit for the difference between his score and that of each of the losers, as in Hearts According to Scarne (see page 420).

Additional Rules of Play for Regular Hearts

The additional rules of play for Hearts According to Scarne as shown on page 424 under "Misdeals: Yes or No" and the "Play out of Turn" apply to Regular Hearts, together with the following rule.

RENEGES

Failure to follow suit when able, constitutes a renege. A renege may be corrected before the trick is turned face down and picked up from the table. If this is not discovered until later, the renege is established, play immediately ceases, and the reneger must pay each player 10 units. In match-style play, 10 points for each of the other participants is added to the offender's score sheet. For example, in a four-handed game the offender adds 30 points on his score sheet. The other players jot down a zero for their scores.

Cheating at All Forms of Hearts

Cheating occurs more rarely in Hearts than in other card games. It is not a matter of virtue. As is true in Bridge, the first requisite for a career as a profit-showing crook is skill at the game. The Heart cheat is uncommon, but by no means uncommon enough. Like all card games, Hearts has its due quota of cheats. The most common are players teamed up to clip one or both of the other participants, and this is usually done by signaling and shuffling point cards to an opponent who is trying for a step. The methods detailed in Chapters Two and Three—stacking, crimping, palming, strippers, shifting the cut, and so forth—can also be used in Hearts. So beware!

INDEX

429